Slim Dusty and Joy McKean married in 1951 and travelled and performed together across the country for over fifty years.

Joy McKean first appeared on radio in 1939 at the age of nine and was performing professionally with her sister Heather by 1946. They were the first women to host their own radio program in Australia, called 'Melody Trail Show', which was on air for eleven years. Joy was awarded the Order of Australia and received the inaugural Golden Guitar for her song 'Lights on the Hill'. Today she is a bestselling author and is involved in the Slim Dusty Foundation and the completion of the Slim Dusty Centre and Museum in Kempsey, NSW.

Slim Dusty was one of Australia's most prolific recording artists. He made his first commercial recording in 1946 and went on to release more than a hundred albums, selling more than seven million records and earning over seventy gold and platinum album certifications. Including the early process records, his sixty years of recording for the one company, EMI, is a world record. Slim was awarded an Order of Australia and the MBE. He was the first Australian to receive a gold record, the first Australian to have an international hit record and the first singer in the world to have his voice beamed to earth from space. Slim Dusty died in Sydney in 2003, but his music lives on and is enjoyed by a multitude of fans and new generations of listeners.

www.slimdusty.com.au

T0301118

Also by Joy McKean

I've Been There . . . and Back Again
Riding this Road

SLIM

ANOTHER DAY, ANOTHER TOWN

SLIM DUSTY
& JOY McKEAN

This book is dedicated to the memory of Lorna Cormack,
whose cheerful patience never failed her—or us.

First published by Pan Macmillan Australia Pty Limited in 1996, updated in 2003

 hachette
AUSTRALIA

This edition published in Australia and New Zealand in 2014
by Hachette Australia
(an imprint of Hachette Australia Pty Limited)
Level 17, 207 Kent Street, Sydney NSW 2000
www.hachette.com.au

10 9 8 7 6 5 4 3

Copyright © Slim Dusty and Joy McKean 1996, 2003, 2014
Foreword © Anne Kirkpatrick 2003

National Library of Australia
Cataloguing-in-Publication data:

Dusty, Slim, author.
Slim: another day another town / Slim Dusty; Joy McKean.

978 0 7336 3342 3 (paperback)

Dusty, Slim, 1927–2003.
McKean, Joy.
Country musicians – Australia – Biography.

Other Authors/Contributors:
McKean, Joy, author.

781.642092

Cover design by Luke Causby
Cover photographs courtesy of John Elliott
Typeset in New Aster by Post Pre-Press Group and Bookhouse, Sydney
Printed and bound in Australia by Griffin Press, Adelaide, an accredited ISO AS/NZS 14001:2009
Environmental Management System printer

AUTHOR'S NOTE

On 19 September 2003, Slim lost his long and private battle with cancer. We three – Anne, David and I – were with him when he began his last journey; it was the one road I could not travel beside him and this time he could not wait for me. Until about a month before his death, he worked on what was to be his last album. When he could no longer play his guitar or sing his songs, it was time to move on.

Slim was given a State funeral at St Andrew's Cathedral in Sydney. It was televised nationwide, and, with the cathedral filled to capacity, crowds stood outside to watch the service on huge TV screens set up in Sydney Square. Singers, musicians, entertainers and government ministers, including the Prime Minister, attended the service alongside people who came from all over Australia to pay their respects. The NSW Mounted Police volunteered to escort his hearse out of the city, fitting companions for a country man's final road.

Eleven years on, and where are we? Slim's name and his music still echo everywhere. In September 2014, one of his albums achieved a remarkable 800 weeks in the ARIA country charts, the longest ever for any country music album. Throughout the decades of his sixty years of recording and nearly fifty years touring Australia, he became the voice for myriads of Australians whose everyday lives were the stories of the nation. Whilst others were admired, Slim was respected and loved as a mate who understood their battles and their triumphs, who knew what it was like for them, and told it 'like it was'.

In Kempsey on the mid north coast of New South Wales, the Slim Dusty Centre now stands. This coming year will see the installation of the first stage of a museum dedicated to the story of Slim's life and his music. It is an ambitious project for the Macleay Valley, but the community is encouraged by the support nationwide to raise funds to complete and run the Slim Dusty Centre. Truckies, farmers, factory workers, fishermen, small business owners – men, women, teenagers and even children – keep tabs on the progress and look forward to the Centre's official opening.

Every day of the week, people visit the modest farmhouse and paddocks in Nulla Nulla Creek where Slim spent his boyhood and worked the farm until his early twenties. We keep Homewood, the original house of Homewood Farm as it is now known, in good repair and visitors treat it with the respect it deserves. It is listed on the State Heritage Register as part of our culture and heritage of the land. I was at the farm gate one day when a four-wheel drive vehicle arrived bearing a group from Denmark who were bent on seeing for themselves just where Slim Dusty came from. The quiet Nulla Nulla Valley is often host to international visitors these days.

On the highways of Australia amid the thousands of trucks, road trains and semis, a traveller may happen to see a prime mover adorned with paintings of Slim; or the plaque in honour of their patron at the Australian Truck Drivers' Memorial in Tarcutta. Or maybe they will see truck trailers painted with pictures of Slim and Queensland's Truck and Coach Drivers' Memorial, or a ute going past with Slim's picture on the bonnet. All these are part of an ongoing tribute that is gathering momentum.

I receive so many letters and emails . . . from young and old, they relate to Slim. I hear from the thirteen-year-old girl who is determined to learn every single thing she can of Slim's life. She sends photos of herself visiting Slim's old home in Nulla Nulla Creek. I meet the young balladeer who busks to raise funds he donates to the Slim Dusty Centre. I hear of the bush pilot who says Slim keeps him company on long, lonely days of checking water tanks and pumps, and mustering cattle in the Gulf Country. I have long known of the Australian surgeon in the USA who played Slim Dusty in the operating theatre as he worked.

So Slim has not left us. He is still very much a part of the lives of Australians. His voice still sounds in the cabs of working tractors; in the trucks criss-crossing the highways; in the utes heading off for a night out or carting feed out to the paddocks; and in the homes and at the barbecues of people everywhere. And wherever there are fishermen in their boats or on a riverbank . . . you'll very likely find Slim too.

He'd be happy, I think.

Joy McKean

FOREWORD

I was two years old when Mum and Dad set off on their great adventure – an adventure that became a way of life for our family. It was 1954, and not the 'norm' to throw in your day job and hit the road with your own country music show, but with me in tow, they hooked up old 'Betsy' to the caravan and started travelling . . .

As I read through the story of their journey, which my brother David and I have been part of, I can only feel thankful that Dad decided to follow his heart all those years ago, when he made the tough decision to tell his mother he was finally leaving the farm to take up the recording contract he'd always wanted.

Growing up on the road, I remember happy times as part of this big extended family; for a while on the showgrounds, as well as many years of night showing. Being the daughter of a travelling showman was an exciting life, and I remember two parents who were full of life, always looking forward. I'd listen to them brainstorming in the car as we travelled, making plans, clearly loving the life they were leading. I remember Christmas with the showies under the big top, caravan days camping out under the stars in western Queensland, eating mud crab and duck at beautiful Keela Valley at Bowen with the Williams family, always with the wonderful panorama of the outback as a backdrop.

During the 1960s, Mum and Dad were night showing around Australia for the best part of ten months each year, so at various times, David and I attended boarding school. This meant many sad partings but as many happy reunions. We would fly to join the show for school holidays only to have to leave for the next school term. It was hard on all of us at times, but somehow it made the four of us even closer. Usually we'd have the big Christmas break together at the family home in the Gippsland and then in February, the show headed off around Australia and we'd be off to school until the first holidays at Easter. Once, I remember David and I saying goodbye to Mum and Dad as they headed off with the show, while we were to return to school the following day. However, Mum had to return a few hours later to pick up some forgotten gear. She only recently told me that having to say a second goodbye, she cried all the way back to join the show.

David and I must have seen more country airports than most kids at that time, and the connections usually worked well. However, I do remember a rather peeved fourteen-year-old arriving at this little bush airport outside Wandoan in Queensland, and finding no-one there to meet me. As the airport was rapidly becoming deserted as everyone headed into town, I said I was looking for the Slim Dusty Show and a lady gave me a lift. Mum and Dad were sitting up in the caravan having a cup of tea filling in time before they came to collect me, thinking the plane wasn't due for another hour, when I flounced in all hot and bothered! They were mortified!

But David and I wouldn't have had it any other way. We are immensely proud of their pioneering spirit and what they have achieved together. The list of awards and accolades is astonishing enough, but as importantly, in the overall picture of this travelling life they have led, I have seen first-hand how Dad's music has touched so many lives and made a real difference. He connects at a very real level to a great cross-section of people. I see the letters that arrive at the office and the replies that go out. The stories of children soothed to sleep with Slim Dusty tapes, a truckie buried with his favourite Slim Dusty recording, Dad's music requested for all manner of family occasions such as weddings, a message of encouragement recorded and sent to a desperately ill fan in hospital, and so on. I've seen the people that come to his concerts year in, year out, and how Slim Dusty and his music have been woven into the fabric of their lives. I am indebted to Dad for imbuing in me his great passion for Australia. And through it all, the strength of a relationship that has endured, and certainly another story waiting to be told – my Mum's!

I think this is an amazing story, but then I'm just an adoring, biased daughter! I thought it might be appropriate to end with a verse and chorus of a song I wrote about Mum and Dad and recorded on an album of the same name and released as a duet album with Dad:

Well he left the farm and the family home
To follow his boyhood dream
She loved her plays and poetry
Who'd have thought they'd make a team
Her sister said he's wild at heart
With his hat turned down in front
But 'twas a passionate turn of the heart
That led them down that country mile

Together their star would shine so bright
Travellin' through the darkest night
Together they'd climb the highest high
Travellin' still, always will

. . . Travellin' still, always will . . .

(from the song 'Travellin' Still . . . Always Will'
by Anne Kirkpatrick, 2002)

Anne Kirkpatrick
Written for the 2003 edition

CONTENTS

ACKNOWLEDGMENTS

To all the wonderful people who came to our shows in those early, struggling days—thank you. If you hadn't taken us into your lives, we couldn't have made it past the first three months.

To the Aboriginal people of Australia—you made us welcome in your home lands and we appreciate it.

To the showies—you're a great bunch, and you gave me a lot of memories.

To the radio announcers in all the country stations of Australia—thanks for playing my songs and inviting me on to your programmes.

To the performers who were part of the years of touring—it was hard sometimes, but we had a lot of fun, too.

To the musicians who made touring hilarious and arduous at the same time—you brought our songs to life.

To the writers who put their lives into the words they sent me—you have been part of the recording of our bush history. Thanks to every one of you.

There are some special people who have helped so much with this project. Aunty Una and her husband, Tony Ray, laughed with us as Una recalled memories of her days on the road with the Slim Dusty Show. Thank you both for the memories and the photos, and for those little daily road diaries.

Ev Swanson—thanks for trusting us with Allan's book with its lists of towns and dates. It was a great help, and it must have been hard for you to let it out of your hands.

My sisters, Lorna and Kathleen, and my sister-in-law Grace told tales of the Nulla and my childhood days, and my old mate

Shorty Ranger reminded me of so many incidents and stories from our adventures together as young blokes. Thanks, old mate!

So many people have taken an interest in the writing of this book, and willingly helped in some way. Kent Chadwick, producer of the *Slim Dusty Movie*, sent movie photos and encouragement; John Elliott—who initiated the idea of writing this book—provided great photos as well. Ron Wills, my old friend and early record producer, checked recording facts for us; and interviewers offered transcripts of the interviews for research purposes. My niece, Dr Noeline Kyle, provided details of my grandparents' early life from her research. EMI Music Publishing Australia kindly allowed the reproduction of lines from 'The Showman's Song', 'The Biggest Disappointment', 'A Pub with No Beer', 'The Saddle is his Home', 'Gumtrees by the Roadway', 'My Final Song' and 'To a Mate'. Eric Bogle kindly granted permission to reproduce an excerpt from 'No Man's Land'. Eric and Hilary Scott of Hadley Records and BAL Marketing's editorial team made available archive copies of *Country Express* and *Capital News* to help jog our memories. We appreciate every bit of help.

My sister-in-law Heather—who still doesn't approve of me at times—has become a very good mate. Thanks for all you have done over the years.

Anne and our daughter-in-law Jane sifted through hundreds of photos and papers to make the final selection easier. Judging by the exclamations and laughter coming from the photo area, they found some funny ones and we are sure that some unflattering shots of the girls have been well hidden. Thanks just the same!

To all the people of Australia from all walks of life who have listened to my songs, come to my shows, written to me, and let me know that they consider me a personal friend—your friendship is my most treasured memento.

INTRO & TURNAROUND

Belfast, August 1994

I was walking the streets of Belfast in clear sun and cool wind. I thought I'd be out of place here, but instead I felt quite at home.

It was a long way from Nulla Nulla Creek in Australia, and I couldn't help wondering what Mary and Hugh Kirkpatrick would have thought about a grandson thumping along Albert Bridge Road in his R.M. Williams boots and Akubra hat turned down in front. What the blazes was I doing here in the first place?

I had driven into Belfast to find why I keep thinking of Ireland, and to find where my grandparents had actually come from. What I did find first of all, with a BBC camera crew in tow, was the Mt Pottinger Methodist Church. Towering red brick and respectable beyond all doubt, it told me in no uncertain terms that here was the beginning of the family and its adventures. This was where Hugh and Mary married in 1880.

102 Albert Bridge Road is now a row of modern terraces, but it was the site of my great-grandfather's home where Hugh lived till his marriage. 13 Howard Street South, where my father was born, is now covered by the city's main fire station.

So Belfast, where my origins lay, had not a lot to show me after all.

What it did show me was the way to go home. To Australia.

Why me?

I keep asking myself that question, and I shake my head. Why did my dream come true when so many other people worked and tried just as hard and it didn't happen for them?

What's he really like?

My musicians and colleagues are always being asked this and I hate to think of some of the replies! In self-defence, I think I'd better tell you. I read one interview where a muso friend described me as a bodgie lair who likes driving camper-vans at 120 kilometres an hour. Not quite correct, but I still talk to him.

Is his name really Slim Dusty?

This is the curly one . . . and to answer even a part of this, I'll have to explain quite a bit about my background. Maybe the story will answer all the other questions everyone's been dying to ask but aren't quite game enough.

ANOTHER DAY, ANOTHER TOWN

May there always be an endless road
That I can ramble down
May there always be another day
That leads to another town.
It's satisfaction still to me
To be just moving round
So I can say, 'It's another day,
another town'.

Chapter One

THE THREE MILE LIMIT

Oh, I come from the Nulla Nulla, and I'm the son of
Noisy Dan . . .
'THE SON OF NOISY DAN' SLIM DUSTY

'Sure as the Lord made little green apples, I'll break your *bloody* neck!'

Dad was in full flight again and so was I. This time it was because of the Tom Thumb firecrackers someone had given me.

I tagged along after Dad as he went down to the cream stand to meet the cream lorry and pass the time of day with the driver as well as any passengers who were getting a lift to Kempsey. This particular day the passenger was Darrell Holden, who later became famous as Dally Holden the rodeo rider. Dally still laughs at the way my father leapt as I threw down a string of crackers behind him, and then took off with Dad's familiar threats ringing in my ears. 'Little bastard's always up to something,' Dad grumbled to Dally.

My father was David Kirkpatrick, born in Belfast, Northern Ireland, in 1883. He was brought to Australia at the age of eleven months by his mother Mary (née Magee) and father

1

Hugh Kirkpatrick. Their first born, a little girl called Janet, died in Belfast of meningitis. In Glebe, Sydney, they lost their new baby, Mary Anne. A second son, George, was born in Armidale, NSW, in 1889, but he died in France in the First World War after winning the Military Medal and being recommended for a posthumous VC that was never awarded.

Nurse Mary Kirkpatrick: 'My husband put his
last penny on a dog.'

My grandparents didn't get on for all that long, as Granny soon got sick and tired of Hugh's constant gambling and lack of steadiness. She obviously decided that she was a lot better off without Hugh and by 1891 Mary Kirkpatrick was listed in the census as head of the household in Armidale. Family oral history always said that Granny kicked him out after he gambled the money she had put aside for the baby's clothes. From what I remember of my Granny Kirkpatrick, I'd say the family history is accurate.

She was a strong woman, especially in those times when divorce was not to be considered and was so hard to get anyway. Apparently, she decided to go it alone as the sole support of her two sons so it's quite possible that, young as she was, she was working as an unqualified midwife in Armidale before she moved to Kempsey.

In the meantime, Dad was growing up. By the time he was fourteen or so, he was working for the milkman in Aberdeen, NSW, delivering milk and generally practising to become the endearing larrikin he always was. Mind you, he watched his Ps and Qs when he was around Granny, but he must have spent all his formative years working well out of Granny's reach because I can't see how she'd have let him get away with his shenanigans if he'd been inside her household.

Anyway, back to Granny. On her own, she raised the two boys and when they were able to work for themselves she moved across the Dividing Range and down to the Macleay Valley and the town of Kempsey. Mary Kirkpatrick was a midwife and for years she walked to her patients in the district. She took her big black dog and carried a stout stick and a lantern when she walked. She must have been good at her profession, because the local doctor persuaded her to train at Sydney Hospital for her Certificate in Midwifery. After completing her formal training, she opened the Macleay district's first maternity hospital in 1905.

Nurse Kirk, as she was generally known, was a tall, well-built woman with wavy, fair hair that she kept tied back under her navy pillbox cap. Her uniform was cream, with a navy cloak over it. She was strict in her outlook and her expectations of family and staff, but kind and generous. My sister Lorna remembers how Nurse Kirk used the kitchen oven as a make-do incubator for the weaker of twins. Although no one expected the tiny baby to live, the weakling left her hospital in good health.

She was popular in the town, and everyone knew her. She'd nod and say 'That's another of my babies' and even when some of the 'babies' were having kids of their own they'd still expect Nurse Kirk to remember them.

'Who's that, Granny?' I'd ask.

'Lord knows, boy. I certainly don't,' she'd reply quite cheerfully.

Nurse Kirk ran two or three successful hospitals, one after the other, and did well enough to help her boys select and then pay for two farm blocks of virgin bush in Nulla Nulla Creek.

She sent for Dad and George who were working up-country when Nulla Nulla Creek was thrown open for selection. Previously, there had been a couple of stations there and the small village of Bellbrook grew up at the entrance to the valley, but the main activity was cedar cutting. Nulla Nulla Creek was forty miles upriver from Kempsey towards Armidale, and some of the biggest cedar trees in the world were taken from there. One, in 1882, was forty-eight feet in girth ten feet up from the base and they had to weld two pitsaws together to saw it through.

Dad, true to form, celebrated in Sydney where he went to catch the steamer up the coast to Kempsey. He cruised down George Street to Circular Quay, singing at the top of his voice and carrying his saddle on his shoulder. A great zest for life, had my dad.

He and George must have worked very hard out on those bush blocks. Dad cleared most of the land, kept 300 acres as bush, and built a house on the property. He began dairying and built up a good solid mixed farm, but it must have been lonely for the two bachelors. It was an isolated valley and stayed that way even when it was more settled. Nurse Kirk sent regular supplies up by wagon, including big tins of jam that Dad referred to as 'the boghole'.

Whenever Dad was in town, he had dinner with Granny who was more than pleased to see him or George. Dinner, of course, was the hot midday meal served at noon in our family routine. Dad met Mary Partridge, who worked for Granny Kirkpatrick in the Maternity Hospital in Kempsey. Mary Louisa Florence Partridge was born at Summer Island, now called Kinchela, near Kempsey. She had lovely creamy skin and bright hazel eyes. A good cook and housekeeper, she was very quick on the uptake with first aid and home nursing. Her training was with Nurse Kirkpatrick and Dad began coming into Kempsey more often than was necessary.

It's more than likely that Dad had a good opportunity to see Mary's cooking ability in Granny's hospital kitchen and he also had a good chance to make himself agreeable to young Mary. In the long run they married and, with her young son Victor, they set up married life on the Nulla farm.

A couple of months later, in December 1914, George decided he'd rather be a policeman than a dairy farmer and took off for a posting in Broken Hill. It was from the Hill that George joined the AIF in March 1915, having been given an ultimatum (we believe) that it was the Army or a king-sized row within the police force. Those were the days when police walked in twos in

Broken Hill—it was a wild, wild town. Of course, I've no idea just what George got up to, but his Army record was a distinguished one for a boy from the bush, so I reckon any nonsense in Broken Hill couldn't have been too bad.

Dave and Mary's eldest child, George, was a great kid apparently. He was always around the farm with Dave, and when the girls Lorna, Jean and then Kathleen came along, the family was complete—so Mary thought. However, at the age of nine Georgie became desperately ill and paralysis set in.

'It's a tick!' Dave reckoned.

But no tick was found. They took him in the sulky eight miles to Bellbrook where the mail car met them and carried him the forty miles to Kempsey to the local doctor. After some time, the doctor diagnosed meningitis and Nurse Kirk took Georgie by train to Sydney, 400-odd miles away. Dad followed soon after, and when they told him George was dead, he walked the streets all night as he struggled to accept the fact. Then he had to go back to Nulla Creek and tell his wife that she had lost her boy. Mary railed against fate and the isolation that had cost the life of their son. She found it hard to forgive the farm and the forty miles between George and medical skill. A kind of bitterness set in.

Lorna was eight when Georgie died and she used to ride to the school that was over three miles away. She sometimes said that she didn't learn anything at the Nulla school because the teacher didn't explain what he wrote on the blackboard. At age nine, watering her pony in the creek below the school, she slipped over its head and fell to the hard ground, breaking her arm. That was enough for Mary. The combination of being so far away from medical help and now having no satisfactory schooling for the girls was the last straw. She prevailed on Dave to lease the farm, move the family to Kempsey and take a job on the local council.

I was born in Kempsey on 13 June 1927 and for a superstitious man like my father, the date wasn't a good omen. It's always been my lucky day and although I have my superstitions and foibles like anyone else, I'm always glad to greet the thirteenth of anything.

I believe he was very happy about my arrival at Nurse Kirkpatrick's hospital in Marsh Street, even if it was on the thirteenth. It was something to celebrate after all. Dad didn't have much going for him at the time. He hated working for a boss, and fretted for his farm up the Nulla. The job on the council paid a living wage and the family was comfortable in the little house that Nurse Kirkpatrick had lent them for the five years they spent in Kempsey, but 'there's nothing like your own place', he'd declare.

Council work didn't impress Dad, especially when a falling limb knocked him out and left a permanent indent on his skull.

'Here, have a look at this,' he'd say. 'There's a good map of Australia for you.' Sure enough, the edges of the hollow did resemble a rough map of the continent.

After five years, Dad had had enough of town life. Workers were being put off, the Depression was rearing its ugly head and the farm offered a more secure way of life and the prospect of being able to live reasonably well, if not lavishly. The girls had a bit of education behind them; Lorna was about fourteen, Jean was twelve and Kathleen ten. I would have been about three when we went back, so all I remember is arriving at the back of the house in some sort of horse-drawn sulky or wagonette. It was a solid house, and is still standing today with a plaque on a rock outside explaining that this was the original 'Melody Ranch' where Slim Dusty spent his childhood.

The Nulla Nulla valley provided living for about twenty families up and down the Creek. Our place was about ten miles above Bellbrook, more than three miles from the school and about five miles from the church. There were no really close neighbours and it was a solitary life for a small boy. For Mum and the girls too, come to that. Lorna left for Kempsey after twelve months.

My parents' marriage was not a successful one. They were too different altogether. I've been told that Dave was the life of the party away from Mary and that she didn't like him to have a drink or mix with anybody, or do anything much apart from the farm. If Dad went to Kempsey, he'd get on the tear sometimes and then as he sang his way home in someone's old car he'd end up saying, 'Well, better calm down, boys. Got to face up to Mary soon.' They had some flaming rows, and the old saucepans got a good workout now and then.

Dad had an Irish temper, a loud voice, an awe-inspiring command of swear words delivered at top volume, a lack of finesse or refinement, and a knack of annoying my mother whether he meant it or not. He also played the fiddle—laid down his arm in the old-time style—as he sang his old Irish and music hall songs and his parodies (some of which don't bear repeating here). He recited Lawson and Paterson, also at the top of his voice, and it's no wonder, I suppose, that he was known locally as 'Noisy Dan'. I don't think the neighbours were exaggerating when they said they could hear him yelling for five miles in either direction of our farm. He was very popular, nevertheless. What they call a rough diamond, or maybe Dad was a real diamond in the rough.

I was painfully, agonisingly shy. There was such a protective cocoon woven around me that I just didn't know how to get on with other kids when I did see them. The Kyles were the closest young family to our place, but I didn't see much of them until I started school and sometimes went over to play with them in their old orchard.

I soon knew all about Georgie, my dead brother. I was given to understand that I was his replacement, and that if he hadn't died I wouldn't even be here. 'Georgie was such a farm boy; Georgie was such a good rider; Georgie was going to take over the farm from Dad later on if he hadn't died.' I got such a

7

teasing that I once flew for my tormenter with Dad's claw hammer.

Mum would not allow me out of her sight. She became paranoid with fright if I got a cold, let alone cut myself.

'Gordon can't do that.'

'Don't let Gordon go there.'

'Gordon mustn't.' 'Gordon shouldn't' . . . the restrictions were endless. I became more and more isolated, shy, and alienated from my casual, rowdy father.

Even though she was a capable home nurse with a good knowledge of first aid, Mum dreaded something beyond her skills happening to me as it had done to George. There was the time one of the cedar cutters was brought to Mum with a horrifying cut leg, the result of a misplaced swing of a broadaxe. She doctored and bandaged him with care and thoroughness, and the leg mended as good as new, but that didn't stop her constant worrying about me. I probably began to think I was the centre of the universe, and I certainly seemed to be the centre of Mum's.

Life on the farm was hard, but comfortably routine. You rose early and went to bed early. The kerosene lamps gave adequate light at night, but they didn't encourage sitting up late and Mum certainly didn't believe in late nights either. Dad was always reading detective novels and magazines, or some non-fiction book. The Dunbars were the first in the Creek to get a wireless (or radio, they're called now). At times some of us would go down to listen to the cricket and cooee and shout when Don Bradman scored and scored.

Alf Smith used to help Dad milk and would also give him the benefit of his singing. Dad could be a bit of a crank at times, and after a few mornings of hearing Alf roaring out 'Lo-o-ones-o-ome V-a-alley S-a-ally' over the hissing of the milk into the bucket he flew into a rage. 'If you don't shut up that howling you can take yourself and your Sally to damnation.' When Alf subsided for the time being, Dad got his own back by loudly singing some of his own favourites, which didn't include 'Lonesome Valley Sally'. I don't know what Alf thought about it.

My feet would hit the floor before my eyes opened when Dad called me in the early morning.

'Time to get the cows in, boy.'

All these years later, when the alarm goes off or I wake in the night, my feet hit the floor and I start walking. The results are disastrous when I'm in a big hotel and sleepwalk out of my room. The doors in those places won't open from the outside, and I'm generally not dressed for a public appearance.

Meals on the farm were predictable, if not downright monotonous at times. We got fresh meat once a week and the rest of the time it was corned beef, boiled up for midday dinner and towards the end of the week minced up into fritters or hash so it wouldn't taste quite so dry. Mum worked wonders with corned beef. In the early days bread was baked at home, but when the mailman began his rounds up the Nulla three times a week we were able to get bought bread more often. That was one job less in the kitchen.

Breakfast was porridge with sugar and milk, hot toast with homemade jam or local honey and cup after cup of strong tea. On most of the dairy farms, no one took milk in their tea and very seldom used cream on their puddings. (Could have been a mouse drowned in the cream can so no one took the risk.) They seemed to prefer custard, or we did anyway. If the chooks were laying well, we might have eggs and a bit of bacon or 'bubble and squeak' which was yesterday's leftover vegetables fried up crisp and served hot with buttered toast.

Dinner at midday was always a hot meal, even with the temperature '100 degrees in the waterbag' as the saying goes. It might be corned beef with potatoes, pumpkin and cabbage or any other vegetable from the garden. Mum and the girls did the gardening and although there were no flowers we usually had some sort of vegetable to eat. We had to eat whatever was available, while it was available.

Like I said, we had fresh meat only once a week and didn't Dad lay into it. In winter, there was mostly a bowl of hot soup to start with but the highlight was The Pudding. No 'sweets' or 'desserts' for us, it was a good old pudding.

'What's for pudding, Mary?' Dad would enquire with anticipation.

Bread and butter custard, steamed golden syrup pudding, roly poly or lemon tart; whatever it was, Mum served it up with a good helping of custard on top.

Dad enjoyed his food and his dinner break, and didn't appreciate a grizzling small boy spoiling his enjoyment. It was usually Mum who chastised me, but on one occasion Dad got fed up and grabbed me by the scruff of the neck and the seat of my pants. Both Mum and I thought I was in for it, but Dad strode out the kitchen door to the paddock and dumped me down in the middle of the open space.

'Yell your head off then, mate,' he snapped, and fumed back to his dinner.

'You're seven now, Gordon. Time you started school.' Mum was making the beds, and I was making a nuisance of myself.

School was over three miles away, and attendance was not compulsory over the three-mile limit, but Mum was intent on my getting an education. It didn't worry Dad too much which was surprising as he was pretty well educated for those days.

I was thunderstruck. I had never been away from the farm and to be tossed into a heap of strange companions was a terrifying prospect. Mum did her best, but I was a little bastard. The mailman took me down, so I arrived at the school after school was 'in' and I had to run the gauntlet of all the kids eyeing me curiously. Then the mailman picked me up at a quarter to three while all the others stayed until half past three. This happened three days a week, so I wasn't getting very much learning pumped into me in those short three days. Added to this was the fact that I hated school and wagged it as often as possible.

When the cream lorry was running, I was supposed to go on that, but I could get down behind the fowlhouse where Mum couldn't see me and then spend the rest of the day down by the creek. That worked until Kathleen found me and 'told' on me. Jean was sent to catch and saddle the creamy pony and drag me back to school, and she went hell for leather down the road in a paddy. I beat her home though, because I ran over the paddocks while she stopped to talk to the boys on one of the farms down the road and got into trouble with Mum.

School was an absolute ordeal for me, and I couldn't cope with it. On my first day, Una Kyle took me under her wing. She could see that I was shy and knew how solitary a life I led. Una wouldn't let the others torment me while I was new and strange. I met Bobby Haberfield for the first time and we began a long friendship while sharing a coconut biscuit. The only thing I ever enjoyed at school was the singing, and I especially enjoyed any chance I had to sing by myself. Even then I was singing at home; songs I heard Dad sing and songs I heard on the new wireless.

Mum tried and tried, but between my truanting and a very laid back teacher, I learned very little. My school years ended when I turned twelve, because once again the 'three-mile limit' allowed me to leave at that age instead of fourteen, and I began work in earnest on the farm.

Chapter Two

THE KID FROM UP
THE NULLA

They had my future wrapped up in a parcel . . .
'THE BIGGEST DISAPPOINTMENT' JOY McKEAN

They did, too.

By this time, Victor had married Grace Kyle and moved down to Kempsey to live and work. Jean married Kelly Tyne, and Kathleen married Laurie Kyle leaving Dad, Mum and me on the farm.

It was a foregone conclusion that I would work on the farm, marry one of the girls in the Nulla (if one would have me) and take over the farm to live happily ever after. This was the plan from day one, but like the song says, no one thought of asking me.

I always had my small jobs to do around the place from the time I was little, and I learned to milk and bring in the cows when I was seven or eight. But as I grew older, I was still kept from working with my father, and looking back, I can see how I became my mother's property exclusively. I think Dad gave up for the time being, and just went his own way, not taking too much notice of what I was up to.

My love of singing and of showbusiness came out early. At

school I was mates with Bobby Haberfield, and we talked end-lessly of the songs we'd heard and tried to learn, and of our plans to become singing stars as soon as we could get to Kempsey and the wide world awaiting us. At home, I found the cream stand was a good stage when and if I could get a few visiting kids from the farms next door, mostly the Kyles.

The cream stand was down by the road and once a week in winter and three times a week in summer the cream (or milk) lorry came by and collected the cans full of cream. I would climb to the top of the stand and direct the others to sit in a semi-circle at its foot while I sang every song I knew and mimed some fancy guitar playing on a piece of board. It's a funny thing—I was never shy when I was singing, and although my nervousness and shyness sometimes made my speech hesi-tant, I never stammered when I was singing. These days, the hesitation is much less and is still non-existent in my singing.

By this time everyone possessed wind-up gramophones and I was in seventh heaven when Nurse Kirk gave me her old portable. Keeping up the supply of needles was a problem sometimes, but I found that they could be used more than once and when they got to the stage of ploughing furrows in the records I would use the long thorns from the old lemon trees. Some of the other kids used rose thorns if they could get them.

Dad bought a wireless, and I became a knob-twister as I fol-lowed all the 'hillbilly' programmes all around the dial. The old valve wirelesses were driven by dry batteries and they picked up stations from all over the place. I listened regularly to 2TM Tamworth, 2KM Kempsey, 2GF Grafton, 2XL Cooma, 2WG Wagga and any others I could manage. Tex Morton was the local idol, and many were the heated arguments about who was the better yodeller out of Tex Morton and Wilf Carter, the Canadian. The Kyles had Jimmie Rodgers and Tex Morton records and Kelly Tyne brought down Wilf Carter records. Gene Autry was the top singing cowboy in the pictures and

Harry Torrani the 'Swiss' yodeller was coming into popularity. The Hillbillies from England, the Rocky Mountaineers, and Carson Robison were just some of the artists on record. I lapped it up, beginning to write my own songs and plan my own career as a cowboy singing star.

Bobby Haberfield was greatly enthused by the idea that we were going to go out into the world and impress it with our singing and songwriting gifts. So I wrote, and he wrote, I sang and he sang and together we made ever grander plans for our futures as singing stars. My first song was 'The Way the Cowboy Dies', and was a plaintive song full of sentiment and sorrow. I thought it was great, and carefully wrote it out in an exercise book that I had earmarked for writing in all my future masterpieces.

By the time I was eleven, I was darn sure that I wasn't going to be Gordon Kirkpatrick in my glittering future, no way. Gordon couldn't do this, Gordon couldn't do that, and Gordon wasn't allowed to do or say this or that. But, by hell, someone like a Slim Dusty, for instance, could and would do all the wonderful things I had in mind. That's how Slim Dusty was born, and I was so sure of it that I wrote the name in pencil across a photo of myself as a serious small boy in short pants and striped blazer. That photo showed me as the family expected me to be, not as I wanted to be. Bobby decided that he was going to have a show name too, as all the stars of the day did. There was quite a choice of names that were in cowboy fashion and tradition and he eventually settled on Shorty Ranger. So there we were, Slim and Shorty, about to set the world on fire at ages eleven and twelve.

At this time, around 1937–38, there were travelling rodeos, circuses and variety shows on the road and Tex Morton came to town at show time with the Skuthorpes. The newly christened Slim Dusty and Shorty Ranger begged rides to town and also begged and borrowed the necessary spending money to get to the Kempsey Showgrounds.

I was thrilled to the back teeth when we shot off from Mum and Dad, and Shorty and I headed for Sideshow Alley. There were clown joints, shooting alleys, ghost rides, music shows, haunted houses and everything a small boy's heart could desire in the way of a good time, but we posted ourselves outside the Skuthorpe tent. Old Lance Skuthorpe was a legendary name throughout the country. Not only was he one of the, if not *the*, greatest buckjump riders of all time, but he was also a footrunner, storyteller and writer, sketch artist, fighter and a showman to beat all showmen. His son and daughter, Lance Jnr and Violet, went on to become Australia's top riders heading an Australian contingent of riders, whip crackers and rope spinners to the USA to star in the Tom Mix show, among their other many achievements.

The Skuthorpes were on the road with their tent show, and often played the agricultural shows in country towns as part of their itinerary. As well as the riding, whip cracking and rope-spinning displays and so on, they would usually star a country singer and this year it was Tex Morton. Tex Morton always said that he was in the right place at the right time, but whatever the reason, he was the period's equivalent of today's top rock stars. His records sold like hot cakes, and his appearances drew crowds like magnets.

We hung around the entrance to the tent, hoping for a glimpse of our idol. The ground was getting dusty and we were getting thirsty, when this great long car came crawling along Sideshow Alley heading for the Skuthorpe tent. Normally, no vehicles were allowed on the showgrounds in among the tent shows, but Tex made his own rules and broke everyone else's if he wanted.

He was a star, and we wanted to reach out and touch the glamour. The car crawled along through the milling crowd, with Tex seated in the front. Big cowboy hat, tailored gaberdine suit, people singing out 'How ya going, Tex?', attention centred on the star. The car moved so slowly that we were right alongside Tex, and I said to Shorty in a sling-off way, 'She's a bit stuck-up, isn't she?'

I thought I said it softly, but Tex's head swivelled around.

'You think so, son?' he said with amusement.

I tried to back into the crowd and hide myself, but the mass was too thick. Shorty and I dodged along out of Tex's sight, and prepared to spend our bit of money on getting the best spots possible on the old 'stringer and jack' seats in the tent. These tiers of wooden seats were quickly erected. No wonder they were used by all the travelling circuses and rodeos.

We jiggled and wriggled with impatience waiting for Tex Morton to make his appearance in the sawdust ring. Mouths open, we admired the whip-cracking display and the buck-jumpers, and just about wet ourselves with excitement when Tex was announced and he strode into the ring and onto a small dais. I couldn't tell you what songs he sang except for one: 'I'm Gonna Yodel My Way to Heaven'. He announced the title and then said, 'Lance Skuthorpe says it's the only bloody way I'll ever get there!'

Tex was very popular with the showmen; after the show he went walking along the Alley, showing off his shooting prowess in the joints, throwing balls at the clowns and generally bringing the crowd with him. The crowd this day included two boys absolutely agog at being able to study at close quarters an example of their planned future.

Grace (my sister-in-law): 'It was the charging a penny to get in that tickled me.'

I sometimes got to Kempsey on visits to Victor and Grace when Mum or Mum and Dad went down for the day on business, or Mum came down to visit. Grace's eldest son, Philip, was six years younger than I was but we were good friends. Victor had built a good house in Kempsey with a long verandah in front and around the side.

With Philip as my backstop, I borrowed a grey blanket

16

from Grace and hung it along the verandah rails. This was the stage area. I prepared my repertoire, and instructed Philip in the handling of the ticket box that was just his hand. Then we recruited the Bakers and the Cook boys from across the street, and Philip collected one penny from each kid as they filed up the steps and sat down on the floor of the verandah. I'm not quite clear what part Philip played in the stage performance, but I know I sang and strummed my make-believe guitar to my heart's content and felt that the kids were getting their money's worth. Philip and I split the pennies in righteous satisfaction.

There was no hall in Nulla Nulla Creek and many of the dances were held in George Fuller's barn. Old Billy Kyle played the fiddle and someone else had an accordion that they sometimes brought. Dad was always in demand either to play his fiddle as he sang the old songs he knew, or to recite Lawson or Paterson poems. Being a great reader, he knew a lot of poems and I'd like to be able to say that he was the one who opened my eyes and ears to the words of these two bards. But the truth of the matter is that it was an old chap living in a hut up the Creek. He had heard me singing around the place and he shoved an old book at me: 'Here. This is what you should be writing like, and singing like it too.'

'This' was a book of Henry Lawson's poems; I was fascinated and filled with admiration. I read it from front to back, and then started all over. I would dip into it whenever I wanted inspiration or encouragement, and I still do today.

I was writing songs long before I had a guitar, and Dad began listening and letting me know he enjoyed it. It was probably better than Alf's version of 'Lonesome Valley Sally' anyway. I had taken Alf's place in the bails, and although my daydreaming and mental songwriting caused a few mishaps I learned farming the best way: hands on. Ploughing, milking, planting, everything ran to routine and to the seasons. Dry times we had and floods as well. In flood time, I can remember being a little bloke sailing boats on a fast-running Nulla Creek, down behind the house.

That was a favourite fishing spot for Dad, and one day he was fishing down there with Laurie Kyle and catching nothing but turtles, one after the other. Across the creek, Alec Kyle was ploughing. Round and round the horses pulled the plough as Dad caught yet another turtle. Dad swung the turtle round his head, hoisted it into the furrow alongside Alec and roaring with laughter he sang out, 'Here, Alec. Plant that and see how many you can raise.'

Dad and the neighbours were talking about some place called Abyssinia and some bloke called Mussolini, which didn't interest me much. Next thing, in September 1939, war broke out in Europe. Milking and washing up had to finish in plenty of time each morning to hear the news on the wireless, and Dad had to be back in the house at midday to listen to the midday news. In a matter of months, young men began leaving the Creek to enlist in the AIF and the older men began thinking about the home front.

Shorty and I held earnest conferences. This war could possibly interfere with our careers and that made it a matter of great concern. We had been making great strides, because I now had a guitar. Jack Kyle (later calling himself Clem Rodgers) bought a little white guitar by mail order and when he got a better one, said he'd sell me the old one. I coveted it, I wanted it more than anything I'd ever wanted, but I didn't have the £2 Jack was asking. After a lot of haggling, and a lot of hassling my parents, I got 30 shillings and broke Jack down to that. It might have been as much as he expected to get, but I thought I'd done a good deal. Especially as he threw in an E–Z tutor with it. This little book had all the illustrations of the chords and where to put your fingers. By using that and then playing the Tex Morton and Buddy Williams records over and over I knew when I'd got the chord right because it sounded like the one on the record.

By this time, Buddy Williams was on record as well. Buddy was from the north coast, near Dorrigo, and often broadcast from 2GF Grafton. His first release was in September 1939, and I liked his style right from the first. Also, his guitar playing was so clear, that when I finally got my guitar, I could practise chords and tell if I had them right just by listening to Buddy's sound.

Once I began playing and singing, I was still writing my own songs and Dad began to take an interest in what I was doing. He enjoyed the music, and I sometimes heard him say to one of the neighbours, 'The boy's got talent, you know. He might go somewhere.' The only one to take Dad seriously at the time was me. I was fixing my eyes upon a career as a singing star, and nothing less would do. Farming was just a necessary evil, a means to an end. I liked the steady routine of the farm; in those days there were so many small farms affording a living to families that the Nulla was a thriving community. The war changed all that.

Shorty and I spent even more time together once we left school. He was twelve months older than I was, and we used to ride to each other's place and spend hours just singing and playing our latest compositions and planning how to further our music careers. First of all, we decided we should get onto the radio and get known. So 2KM Kempsey was the right place to start. All we had to do was get the manager to hear us and see what talent he had right on his doorstep. Perhaps we could get our own radio programme, and after that we'd make records.

The only recording company in Australia at that time was the Columbia Graphophone Company, based in Homebush, Sydney. The height of our ambition was to record for its Regal Zonophone label which featured Tex Morton, Buddy Williams and Wilf Carter among others. It became almost an obsession with me. Young as I was, I knew that if I was to have any sort of music career I had to get on record and Regal Zonophone was the one I had to be on.

Shorty and I determined that we should dress the part if the world was to receive us in suitable style, and I got hold of a Tex Morton shirt from Dooley Waters. It had plenty of trimming on it, and I managed to put silver studs on my belt and to turn up my old farm hat. Dooley came from up the Nulla, and used to sing all the Tex Morton songs. Tex had a sort of mail order system going at the time, and Dooley had sent away for this shirt. I don't quite know how I managed to get it off his back, but I wasn't too backward in coming forward at times.

Radio station 2KM at Kempsey was a sort of shopfront onto the street up West Kempsey. I reckon Shorty and I must have worn a track into the footpath outside its front door as we strolled up and down nervously trying to work out how to make the approach. I said Shorty should front up, because he was the elder. Shorty said I should front up because it was my idea in the first place. In the end neither of us fronted up, but went home to my sister Lorna's place a bit cranky and disappointed.

Next day, we marched up and down again until the manager, sick and tired of seeing these two cowboys traipsing back and forth, erupted from the door.

'Do you two boys want to sing on the air? Is that what you're hanging around for? If it is, for heaven's sake come in and get it over and done with. I'll have a listen and if you're any good at all you can have a go.'

Rex Morrisby was a bit of a showman himself. He scared the tripe out of me and Shorty but he did listen, and as he promised, we were given a go. He told us to come back and sing on the kids' session, and from there we progressed to a Sunday morning request session whenever we could get into town.

Then the Japs bombed Pearl Harbor. Australia was on a war footing and things were changing even in Nulla Creek. Dad and the other older men held meetings and elected rangers to take charge of evacuation in the event of invasion. The 'burnt earth' policy was to be put into action. We were to have plenty of supplies of flour, sugar and salt laid in at all times; we would burn everything we couldn't take with us, and would drive the cattle up through the ranges to the New England district. Shorty and I checked out Yellow Gully for a few safe spots and secret caves . . . just in case, we said.

Life on the farm went on, but my inner life took over for me. I was thinking ahead. I'd go into Kempsey and sing on 2KM, and I was getting lots of requests from listeners for songs—including many of my own compositions. A young announcer, Tom Crozier, would write scripts and we'd put on our fifteen to thirty minute show.

I still have one of the scripts: 'Slim Dusty and Cousin Tom'.

TOM: Straight from Melody Ranch comes your Yodelling Stockman, Slim Dusty.
[Enter Slim.]
TOM: Hullo there, Slim.
SLIM: Howdy, Tom, and hello customers!
[Shades of Bob Dyer.]
TOM: You look well, Slim. Have a good trip down from Melody Ranch?
SLIM: Very good, Tom. But I was so hungry when I got here that I eight o'clock!
TOM: You don't say so! That's rather strange, Slim, because something happened to me just a while ago. I went into a cafe and asked for some fish. When I got it, I said to the waitress, 'Smell this fish.'
She smelt it and said, 'It does appear to be on the turn.'
'On the turn?' I said. 'Why, it's halfway down the straight.'
Well, Mr Dusty, they tell me you sing songs?
SLIM: That's right, Mr Crozier. Do you sing, too?
TOM: Well, I very often sing to myself.
SLIM: How do you sing?
TOM: Very badly . . . er . . . I sing through my teeth.

SLIM: Oh, falsetto!

TOM: After that, I think we'll hear from you, Slim. What's the first number to be?

SLIM: 'Be Honest with Me.'

TOM: And who are you singing that to, Slim?

SLIM: That's rather personal, don't you think, Tom? However, I really want everybody to . . . 'Be Honest with Me' . . .

[Song.]

There's more, but I think that'll do us for now!

This was the era of the big radio shows with Bob Dyer and Jack Davey, and Tom and I certainly weren't any opposition to them. But we did try to put on a bit of a show, and if the mail was any indication, the listeners liked what they were hearing. By the age of fourteen, I was answering a swag of fan mail and I even had a letter from Buddy Williams which I treasured. I got cocky enough to send a cheerio to my hero who apparently used to hear me on 2KM, while I picked up his broadcasts on 2GF Grafton. I was having a great time. Down to Kempsey on the cream lorry every chance I got, swaggering down the street in my finery and Shorty doing the same.

We came to a full stop one day when the army recruiting officer pulled us up in the street. 'Alright, you two. How old are you fellers?'

Shorty and I were as big at fifteen as we are today, and we must have looked like a couple of draft dodgers. With visions of what Mum would say if I were hauled off into the army at the ripe old age of fifteen, we started both talking at once. It was obvious then that we were a couple of youngsters acting big and he went off, probably grinning to himself.

We sang at interval in the Mayfair Theatre and I appeared on numerous amateur musical group concerts all around the district. My shyness as Gordon Kirkpatrick disappeared the minute I put on my stage clothes and picked up my guitar.

When I hit the stage, Slim Dusty took over and he was the person I wanted to be, not 'that Kirkpatrick kid from up the Nulla'. It's a funny thing. Slim Dusty was doing what he wanted to do; Gordon Kirkpatrick was tied to a farm, and felt a nobody. The farm wasn't so bad—it was a good life—it just wasn't the life *I* wanted. As my sister Kathleen said, 'You can't be what someone else wants you to be'.

I was normally so shy and self-conscious that I had little to say, even to girls from up the Nulla that I'd known all my life. I was therefore tickled pink to find that Slim Dusty was attracting attention from girls that I hadn't even met! This was a bonus I hadn't counted on and I loved it. I had fan mail from all over the place, I had girls asking for my autograph and paying me attention. This really was the life, and I reckoned I wasn't about to let it go without a good fight.

I knew very little about business, and my education was sketchy. Nevertheless, I did know that most businesses had to be registered and that it was a good idea to have your songs copyrighted. So, at age fifteen, I sent away to register 'Slim Dusty' as my name and wrote with a flourish on an envelope, 'Started business on 15 November 1942'. I also copyrighted songs as I wrote them.

My aim was to become Slim Dusty and become known on radio as a singer, then to record on Regal Zonophone and sell records and song books. From there, the sky was the limit, I thought. I'd probably star in my own rodeo and travel Australia and, well, who knows what might happen!

Shorty and I used to go to town for the weekend, and sometimes we ventured further. One time we went as far as Grafton because a Lieutenant Dick Ryan from the US Army was co-ordinating an Inter Services Rodeo there, and Buddy Williams was to appear. We held earnest conferences on what we would wear, and what songs we'd sing. At that time (about 1942 or '43) we used to sing a lot of duets as well as our solos; songs like 'Pistol Packin' Mama' or 'Hand Me Down My Walking Cane'. There was no doubt in our minds that once we put our request forward we would be allowed to sing on the programme.

First hurdle was getting through the gate to the rodeo grounds, and as usual, Shorty was the spokesman. Right throughout our ventures, Shorty mostly did all the pushing for appearances, whereas I provided the push and stickability for radio and recording. Between the two of us, we kept ourselves bolstered up with assurances to each other that we were on our way.

'Tickets, please.' The gatekeeper was busy.

'We're with the show,' said Shorty. One look at the pair of us in our cowboy hats and boots, with braid and studs all over our shirts and belts, and he let us in.

'Right,' said Shorty. 'Now we better find this bloke Ryan.'

We barged in and sure enough, Lt Ryan was an approachable man who was sympathetic to two youngsters of fourteen and fifteen who had the guts to say what they wanted.

'Okay, guys. What do you do?'

He put us on the programme and we got a good reception. He was kind enough to say how much he enjoyed our spot and that after the war, he'd like to hear from us in case there was anything he could do for us and our careers. 'After the war.' That was a phrase that haunted me. Everything was on hold until after the war.

Our meeting with Buddy was a bit disappointing. He was probably preoccupied with his stage appearance, and two hero-worshipping boys who had just appeared on the show were about the last thing he needed at the time. Just the same, we caught a taxi back to the town centre full of excitement. We were hitting the big time at last. The taxi driver heard our enthusiastic talk, and decided to join in.

'What makes you boys think you're gonna get anywhere in showbusiness? Forget it. You're just kids from the bush and that's it. Why don't you get back to where you came from, and do something sensible.'

We were crushed. He might have been right, but he needn't have enjoyed the crushing as much as he obviously did. I just hope he remembered my name about ten to fifteen years later.

Country music was big in the forties. It had begun in the late thirties to make inroads into the popular and Hawaiian music that was being played everywhere. On the north coast of NSW there were plenty of radio programmes featuring country, or hillbilly music as it was called then. The old wirelesses on the farms were driven by dry batteries, and their range was amazing. I used to pick up programmes from Cooma, Wagga, Gunnedah, Tamworth, Newcastle, Grafton and Lismore. At night I'd pick up hillbilly sessions from stations further afield, even down in Victoria and up in Queensland.

Travelling shows on the road were either big variety shows such as Barton's or Sorlie's, who showed in huge tents the same size as the circuses used, or rodeos with buckjumping, rope-spinning, whip cracking, clowns and challenges to locals to ride the champion buckjumper of the outfit. The rodeo tent shows usually featured a country singer as well. Many of these shows also set up on the showgrounds at show time, or down in the main street of the country town during the Agricultural Show Days. As well as these travelling tent shows, there were small night showing outfits. They generally came to town after an advance man had booked a hall, and put up posters in all the shop windows.

On the showgrounds, the showmen provided a variety of shows as well as the usual game joints. There was usually a music show of some kind, and perhaps a circus type of show such as the one run by Johnny Foster and his family. Johnny and Eily Foster had a family of one girl, Frances, and four boys—Johnny Jnr, Billy, Frankie and Pikey. In true show tradition, every one of them was a performer and Frances in particular was a top spruiker. Frankie came a close second, but even he said Frances could leave him for dead in that area. Frank's act was tumbling and acrobatics, Billy was the India Rubber Man, old Johnny did magic and lion taming, Frances provided the glamour, young Johnny the general acts and young Pikey was learning a knife-throwing act. Mrs Foster (Eily) worked the ticket box.

Frank was always on the lookout for a good 'gee' and he spotted me a mile off one Show Day in Kempsey. By the time he'd finished, he had me up on the line-up board pretending to be hypnotised into proposing marriage to one of the dancing girls. My sisters couldn't wait to get home and tell Mum that I was going to marry a showgirl and go away with the show-grounds people.

Dad had decided that I had possibilities, and he was taking a strong interest in me. I still had all my normal work to do, and as we were milking quite a few cows by hand he had some-one to help us. First of all it was Alf, who got the spear early in the piece, and then it was Ted. Ted liked to sing too, but Dad told him his crooning was turning the cream sour and to cut it out. So Ted thought he'd get even by teasing Dad and playing practical jokes—till Dad lost his temper. One day, Ted and I had to get out the horse and slide and get a load of wood for the household use. Dad decided he'd come too and see where we were getting this wood.

The slide was a kind of wooden raft mounted on two smooth wooden runners, with shafts out in front so that we could harness old Model, the mare, to it. We stood up on the front or walked alongside, and after we'd loaded the wood to Dad's satisfaction he seated himself on top for the ride home. We were heading for the last hill up to the house, when Ted whispered to me, 'On your guard, now.' He steered Model up to and around a good hump in the ground, put on a bit of speed and the slide flew over the hump with Dad and bits of wood going everywhere. Dad picked himself up, turned the air blue as he looked for his pipe and told us 'bloody buggers' what he thought of us. When we got to the back door with the load, he had Ted's cheque ready and told him to 'get'. Ted packed his bags and got another job two miles up the road and Dad decided he'd get milking machines that couldn't sing, yodel or answer back.

My taste of showbusiness made me eager for more, but I still had my heart set on recording. Dad went into town and talked to Rex Morrisby. They decided I should be given a chance, and I wrote to the Columbia Graphophone Company at Homebush asking for an audition, which was granted. When in Sydney, we always stayed at the People's Palace in Pitt Street, within walking distance of Central Station and the old Tivoli. On one trip, a few years previously, Dad had got out at one station to get some refreshments, and ended up just managing to catch the very last compartment as the train took off again. Mum and I, in a front dogbox compartment, had been in a state of panic because Dad had the tickets.

On this trip Dad and I went to the Tivoli to see Roy Rene in his character of 'Mo' McCackey. The old Tivoli shows were fantastic, and if you hadn't seen a Tivoli show you just hadn't lived. The next morning we went out to Homebush by train and walked down to Parramatta Road looking for Columbia Lane and the office of Mr Arch Kerr. I was sweating from a combination of heat, nervousness and sheer fright so Dad decided that at the outset of my career I needed a beer to bolster my courage. I suspect he could have done with one himself.

Dad, bless him, always managed to rush in where angels fear to tread and he *was* proud of me and our big venture. We stood up to the bar, and he informed the barman where we were going and what we were doing. In a rush of pride he exclaimed, 'The boy's only fifteen, you know.'

'Well, he shouldn't bloody well be in here, then,' the barman replied sourly.

Arch Kerr was an ex-musician who was in charge of artists' recording at Columbia. His word was gospel, and he let you know it. I had expected an audition in a studio or something like that, but he curtly told me to start singing in his office while he went on with his work, even taking a telephone call in the middle of one song. If I'd had visions of impressing Columbia Records with my performance, I came a cropper right there and then. He dashed any hopes I had of recording on Regal Zonophone, telling Dad and me that I should go away and do a bit of travelling and build up a name while I got better at singing and songwriting. Then he told us that I could make a process record of course, but at our own expense. It would cost £25 for twenty-five copies, but we needn't take all twenty-five at first. Dad decided to do it.

I was so disappointed and downhearted on the train journey back to Central that Dad decided we'd go to the rodeo in town. Where Mick Simmons' sports store is now, used to be a vacant block of ground, and being wartime, a rodeo had set up. There were US servicemen as well as AIF and RAN men on leave, and any sort of live entertainment did well. Once again, we fronted up and Dad asked if a 'bit of a lad from the bush' could sing a few songs in the ring. Sounds incredible, but that's the way we did it and there I was doing what I wanted to do—singing.

A couple of days later, we went back to Columbia. I went into Arch Kerr's office while Dad waited outside, and Kerr called in a young lady. 'Take this chap down to Mr Southey.'

That was all the introduction I had before I walked with her through the big office, under the curious eyes of all the office staff, along a narrow passage that led to the stockroom. Then we went down a long flight of wooden steps, past some of the factory, through the yard and into the studio where we found Reg Southey. She said, 'Mr Kerr said to bring this chap down to you.' She didn't know my name so I had to introduce myself and Dad.

There were no tape recorders in those days, and the recording was done directly onto a wax disc on a machine. Jack

Ashford did the actual cutting of the finished disc, but Mr Southey, who was a patient and courteous gentleman, supervised the recording. The idea of a process recording was that it was a finished vinyl record, identical in quality to the commercially available records, and lasting just as long. Not like the acetate records that were cheaper, but would not stand up to very much playing.

I stood up and sang 'Song for the Aussies' and 'My Final Song'. The young lady came back and forth to collect Dad's hard-won money and to bring his change. We certainly didn't have the £25 on the spot for the full twenty-five discs we were allowed to buy, so Dad paid what he could afford at the time. Back we went to town and the People's Palace before catching the mail train home the next day.

I already knew what I was going to do with this process recording.

Chapter Three

NO HIDE, NO CHRISTMAS BOX

*If you're goin' to get there, lad, you got to get up
and let 'em hear you.*
DAVE KIRK

I waited impatiently for the mailman to bring my precious records. By the time they did arrive, I had already written to radio stations such as 2WG Wagga, 2GF Grafton, 2XL Cooma and 2HD Newcastle asking if they would like a copy and if they would play it. They all replied saying that they would be glad to receive a copy and would give it airplay.

The reason I had my heart set on recording, and on Regal Zonophone, was because I had worked out by the age of fourteen that being on record was the major step to a career in singing. Nearly every radio station in Australia at that time had regular country programmes as well as request programmes. With the old valve wirelesses running on dry batteries, people like myself could pick up these programmes from every state. Radio announcers usually chose their own records to play, and were personalities in their own right with keen listener followings. The more information they had about artists, and the more new and unusual records they were able to play, the better for the announcer and his sponsors.

There were not the thousands of new releases in a year that there are now, and as records were released through the only record company in Australia—Columbia—they were received by every record store in the nation. So you could be sure that your recordings would be distributed very widely to start with. I reasoned that if I wasn't on Regal Zonophone with the record company distributing my records, I could send my process records to the stations myself. That way, I could build up the name and following that Arch Kerr seemed to demand from me before he would record me commercially.

When I think about it, maybe I pioneered this method of promoting an artist's record and name—at least in the country field—because I have never heard of anyone before me who did this. I wrote to every radio station that played country and asked them to take my record and play it (and incidentally, to 'please return the packing'). One letter of acceptance I received was from Ted Higginbotham, the founder of 2TM Tamworth, whose family carried on his tradition by inaugurating the now famous Country Music Awards of Australia and promoting country music to the hilt.

As I had only a few records to send around, I sometimes asked stations such as 3SH in Victoria to play a record for a time and then to forward it to another specified radio station. They were mostly very helpful in doing this.

This idea was so successful that a few months later I went to Sydney again, and recorded another four sides. Now I had three records spinning around the country and requests and fan mail were building up. Funnily enough, even though I was paying for all this recording myself, Arch Kerr insisted that he heard every-thing I was going to record and he even wanted changes made. Even funnier still, I suppose, is the fact that I accepted it. He did this with all the artists who recorded there. Shorty and I would hear Buddy Williams, for instance, broadcast on 2GF a song he was going to record and when the recording was released it would be different from the original that we had heard.

I was persistent in my efforts to make it onto Regal Zonophone, and I sent Arch Kerr copies of any write-ups I got and kept asking about making a commercial recording. The answer was always the same: 'Just at the present we're recording no one, especially new artists. Absolutely no one. Get out and build up a name, and after the war we'll see.' In actual fact, Regal Zonophone was releasing records by Buddy Williams and Shirley Thoms. Tex Morton and Arch Kerr had had a falling out over paying Tex's band, and neither would give in. Arch would say, 'Tex knows where we are. Trouble with him, he doesn't know if he wants to be an Australian or an American.' In fact, Tex was from New Zealand.

However, there it was again, 'after the war'. Another good reason for me to look forward to the end of hostilities. I had plenty of reasons to hope for the end of the war. Rationing extended to butter, tea, sugar, petrol and clothing. I didn't mind the sugar or petrol because it didn't affect me so much, but tea and butter were a different matter. Fortunately we were able to make our own butter on the farm, but the way we and most farm people drank tea we had to do the old thing of using the tea leaves twice when it looked like running out.

I was building up a name and fan mail began to take up more and more of my spare time to answer. I had changed the name of the farm to 'Melody Ranch'. Radio stations broadcast my address when fans requested it and mail flooded in. Some time earlier, I had printed a songbook with the words of my songs. This sold for two shillings and I did a deal with some stations to sell these for me on commission. This helped pay for the recording, and the postage on all the mail I was receiving. I even had to have a form letter printed to cope with the replies, so that I could just add a personal handwritten note to the bottom.

I used to have photos taken to sell at concerts and through

my radio appearances. The early ones showed me with the traditional turned up brim like all the film cowboys, and it didn't suit me at all. When I saw a Brownie snap of myself on the plough wearing my old farm hat, I saw at once that the turned down front that kept the sun out of my eyes as I worked was much more my style, and that's when the Slim Dusty trademark hat was born. People are so used to seeing me with my old Akubra stuck on the back of my head, that they don't really know me bareheaded. Some get a bit indignant and ask, 'Where's your hat?'

At the age of eighteen or so, I began wearing my hat with the brim turned down in front and today there's a queue waiting for one of my old ones. They can be sure it's well worn and worn well, too.

Selling songbooks and photos through my 2KM radio appearances and local concerts, and through the fan mail generated by the playing of the process records, now paid for a fourth process recording, 'The Soldier's Wife' and 'Baby of My Dreams'. Still no luck with Regal Zonophone, but I plugged on regardless.

I followed the routine of the farm. Early mornings out into the frost or the dew to bring in the cows, doing the milking with Dad and the dreaded 'Dangar G's' (milking machine). Feeding the calves, feeding the pigs, maybe ploughing and then planting. Fencing, branding, all the general work that came to hand. You were married to the farm and to those routine jobs that had to be done, day in and day out, year in and year out. Maybe that's why I'm a routine person when I'm out on the road today. Every day I pack my bags, get to the next town, get ready for the show, tune the guitar, check the stage clothes, get dressed for the show—it's all one thing after another, the same routine. I once said, 'I'm no gambler.' The reply was, 'But you gamble every night, on whether the show will be good or not.' I suppose that's right, too.

More and more, I was becoming Slim Dusty and more and

more, Gordon Kirkpatrick was moving into the background. 'Come on, Dusty, sing us a song', my mates would say. I was always happy to oblige. Mum did everything she could to discourage me, but Dad was on my side now and she was outnumbered two to one. Dad began teaching me some of the old songs he knew and even writing out the words for me. He began talking about what we might do together after the war. There it was again. 'After the war', when I was finally on record, he would back me as much as he could, even to the extent of selling the farm and helping me get started. My confidence grew along with my determination.

Dad fuelled this confidence and the determination. He had just missed out on being a redhead and had the fiery nature that went with it. He was about 5 feet 7 inches tall, of stocky build, with reddish hair on his arms, large bright blue eyes and he was outgoing, outspoken and loud. We were total opposites and yet we had begun to know and understand each other at long last, so it's a wonder I didn't wake up to it when Dad began to fail. I was about fifteen or so when he took some sort of turn out in the paddock one day and had to drag himself home. He got over it but I realise now that he probably had a minor stroke. After that, although he still encouraged and pushed me to go ahead with my ambitions and dreams, he worried aloud that the farm was slipping back on him. He may have guessed that I would be left to run the farm while I was still a bit too young, and I believe he knew my heart would never be in it. Perhaps Dad worried that I'd never have my chance if he wasn't around as a backstop. I'll never know now.

Mum was often in Kempsey: she was having a lot of nervous trouble. Dad and I would batch for ourselves, and it was in May 1945 that he said to me, 'I think you'd better go down and ring up the ambulance. I don't feel 100 per cent. I'll be alright in a day or two, but I'd better get a lift to Kempsey. I don't think I could drive myself.'

I couldn't drive his old car, so I did as he asked and I was there at the house when the ambulance drove up to the back door. Dad was quite jovial about it all, putting on a brave front as I now realise.

'Oh, I'm not crook enough to go in the back, boy. In the front'll do me.' He climbed in alongside the driver and waved a cheery goodbye as he left me to look after the farm.

I did that with the help of Jim Rose and Ron Kyle, and while we did all the work around the farm we got in a good bit of skylarking as well. With Mum and Dad both out of the way for the time being, we put up some rough yards on the edge of the bush and mustered a bit of young stock. It was a good chance to get some practise at steer riding and buckjumping. Nothing flash, but a lot of fun and a few bruises. Living was rough and ready, but we didn't starve by a long shot. All in all, I was desperately unprepared when I received a message that Dad was in Kempsey Hospital in a coma, and that I should come immediately—I'd had no idea at all that he was so bad. He was paralysed, and the only movement he could give me was a brave and defiant slight wink of one eye. He died two days later on 9 May 1945, just before peace was declared in Europe on the thirteenth.

I didn't break down until after the funeral when Horace Rose, Dad's old mate, came up and spoke to me. I think I was in shock until then. Dad's approval and pride had taken a long while to gain, and it was an empty world without it. It was expected that I would return to the farm with my mother, and at the age of seventeen would take it over and run it for the rest of my life. I thought, 'I can't, I just can't', and in the next second, 'I've got to, I've just got to'.

The neighbours were kind. They helped out wherever they could, but eventually my half-brother Victor came back to the Nulla to take over the farm with me. Victor liked music and played the fiddle. It was Victor who showed me how to write a basic melody line for each of my songs, and although he was inclined to be a stern man, much older than I was, he secretly sympathised with my longing for another life. He helped me get away from the Creek for days at a time, such as the time my cousin Billy Partridge invited me to visit him in Macksville, just up the coast a short way.

I went to Macksville to stay with Bill, who called himself Billy Williams. Billy was an amateur poet rather than composer and singer, and we spent a couple of days swapping lines and reading or singing to each other. Then on 6 August, the atomic bomb was dropped on Hiroshima in Japan. It was on the front page of all the papers, and even young blokes like us who were so preoccupied with our own concerns were stunned.

I went back to the farm and worked with Victor. I'd made a fourth process record earlier in the year, and continued my pattern of sending it out to any radio station who would play it. Tom Crozier had moved to 2LM Lismore by this time, but I still sang on 2KM Kempsey at every opportunity and dreamed of the day I would be on the Regal Zonophone label. It wouldn't be long now, surely, because the war in the Pacific was as good as over and recording would swing into action again.

Shorty and I planned to leave home. Not on the sly, of course, but against the wishes of our respective families. Mum was vocal, but I think Victor had a sneaking sympathy for me and reckoned he'd manage the farm without me for a while. Shorty was in disgrace for a time, but off we went to Taylors Arm where my sister Jean and her husband Kelly Tyne were farming. Kelly put us on the old mailcar to Macksville with our guitars, our old suitcases and our very low funds. Arriving late that evening with nowhere to stay and nowhere to eat except the local cafe we were a bit shy of spending our money.

'Have something to eat, fellers,' said the mailman. 'I'll take around the hat when you sing and you ought to get enough to pay for your dinner, anyway.'

We collected 35 shillings ($3.50, but worth a lot more at the time), a fortune to us and more than enough to get us by train to Coffs Harbour where a cousin of mine lived. My relatives up the coast and down in Sydney eventually became hardened or resigned to having me and Shorty landing in and expecting to be housed for anything from a day to a week or more. Forward planning was never our strong point.

Our aim on this trip was to catch up with the show run and start our trip to fame and glory via the showgrounds first, then perhaps a rodeo or a travelling show such as Dante's. To catch up with the run of agricultural shows, we planned to busk or get jobs singing in theatres at interval time to survive until the shows arrived. In Coffs Harbour we sang outside the Jetty Theatre at interval and got ourselves abused by the owner who didn't approve. At least the hat looked healthy when we passed it round! In Grafton we wanted to sing in the bar of Wylie's pub and had to get permission from the publican.

'You can come in from four to six and take the hat around.'

Wylie's was known as a good pub for buskers over the years and being allowed to work right up to six o'clock closing time was profitable for us.

'Got a room we could have?' Shorty again.

'There's a small one up on the verandah. Five bob a night, alright?'

Shorty and I had made a sort of pact that while we were out travelling, there was to be no drinking. So at the end of each day we'd have a lemonade and raspberry and leave the beer drinking to the future.

We had no luck getting work on the showgrounds, so it was back to the busking for a while. In Maclean, the picture theatre was showing a matinee so we sang outside the theatre and the owner blew a gasket.

'I'll have yers run in,' he snapped, and rang the police.

A large policeman arrived and warned us. 'If you want to sing in public, you'll have to have a licence,' he said.

'What's that? And where do we get it anyway? We've got to be able to sing to get our fares home,' we exaggerated.

We went to the Council as directed, and a lass wrote out our first and only permit to perform in a public place. So back to the theatre we went, and began singing as soon as the patrons came outside at interval.

The owner brought the police down again, telling us that he would have us run in. 'You can't,' we said nervously. 'We've got a licence.'

I reckon the owner just about blew another gasket. We carried that licence everywhere—even when it was out of date we would wave it around when needed.

We rode on top of show trucks, we slept in a police cell one cold night courtesy of a fatherly country cop and his wife, and we shared a hay bed in the stables of a local milkman and his huge draughthorse—who nearly walked over the top of us. We sang in and out of hotels, theatres and cafes, we put on our solo show in a local hall, but we didn't get a permanent job.

Then we met up with John Dante, the magician.

Over the years of our working together, John told me his real name was John Fleetwood Angus. He was born in Salt Lake City, Utah, USA, but of English parents. When his father died and his mother remarried, his stepfather brought the family to Australia where he set up a tobacconist shop in Sydney. When John was fourteen, he began training with the mechanist who was the partner of the original Dante the magician. This Dante died in a gun accident, and the mechanist was left with all the stage gear for the show. A mechanist in magic shows is the man who makes it all happen, and this man took over a small local hall, set up all the illusions and began training young John Angus. It took nearly nine months before he was satisfied, and so started the career of Dante the magician (even if he was Dante the second).

We went to Dante's hall show, and begged an audition with the star afterwards. Dante was kind and courteous, the perfect English gentleman in immaculate tie and tails.

'I don't have a position for you boys just now,' he said.

'However, I am putting together another show and will be starting from Lismore. I'd like to have you with me then.'

We worked and busked our way back to the coast, perfectly happy in the knowledge that we would be in a real travelling show and what's more, we were to be paid. Money, real money.

It didn't turn out quite that way. Dante was the star of the show, but he preferred to leave the mundane things like organising the show and putting up the money to start it with other people. The result was that De Silva's All Star Variety Show had some rather dicey people running it. Dave Stirling was Escapologist Extraordinaire, or was it Leo Cracknell? The worry was a nasty ex-army provost who was over-handy with his fists and even with a knife. After witnessing one episode where he took after a young worker who gave cheek with his knife, I thought it was time to get out. We weren't being paid, we lived off our photo sales, we often had to sleep in the hall or the tent, and the atmosphere was getting more and more risky.

I organised a telegram from home to say Mum was very ill, and I took off. That sort of telegram is the oldest lurk in the world, of course, but I believed I was the first who ever thought of it. I felt guilty when Dante saw that I had the night's small takings to pay for my way home but I took off with relief. Shorty decided to stay on for a while, and ended up shooting through about Bundaberg in Queensland. As he was in disgrace at home, he worked picking tomatoes around Gympie for a few months until he had £50 or £60 in his pocket and was able to come home in better shape than I did.

I got an earful from Mum, and silent sympathy from Victor.

I did a lot of solitary thinking back on the farm. I had never been a regular churchgoer, mostly because church was eight miles from the farm and transport had always been a problem until Dad got a car. When I rode down to Shorty's on the weekends I would go to church with the Haberfields. Other than that, Mum taught me the Ten Commandments, read regularly from the Bible and drilled morals and ethics into me. Nurse Kirk reinforced the 'honesty is the best policy' bit to me and to my sisters before me.

I wondered about life just like any other teenager. There wasn't a very cheerful or hopeful atmosphere in my home, and I began to wonder why we are born at all if we only endure being alive so that we can die at the end of it. It worried me, and made me pretty despondent for a long, long time. There was no one I could talk to about this sort of thing, and the general impression I was given was that life was like that and I should just put up with it.

By the time I was eighteen or so, I decided that if that was all there was to it, I might as well get on with the living and to hell with whatever happened afterwards. I would do as much singing as I could, and I'd be in touch with the world outside through all the letters I received and through my request programme on the radio.

I was sitting by the wireless, alone one evening, listening to the hillbilly programme from one of the country stations. My heart sank when I heard the announcer say, '. . . and here's a brand new record from Regal Zonophone's new star, The Yodelling Bushman, Gordon Parsons.' Well, that was it, then. I'd tried for years and had always been told that after the war when supplies of vinyl were more plentiful, I had the chance of recording commercially. Yet here was someone I'd never heard of released on record before me. That was a low point, if ever I had one.

I went to Sydney one last time in the hope that Kerr would record me. No way—but I could make another process record. This, despite the letters he was getting from record stores. Ron Wills, who later produced my recordings for EMI, said to him one day, 'Who's this Slim Dusty we're getting all the letters about?'

Kerr replied, 'Oh, he's just a young whippersnapper trying to force his way onto Regal Zonophone.'

Yes, I was trying to force my way on and by this stage I was just about ready to give up. I decided to make my last process record, seeing that I was already in Sydney. Kerr demanded to hear what I was going to record and I sang him 'When the Rain Tumbles Down in July'.

'We-ell,' he said, 'I wouldn't do that one today. Do something else and save that one for a bit.'

His word being law, Billy and I went away and manufactured a dreadful stopgap called 'The Happy Drover' which made a second side for the recording of 'Lover's Lament'. I went home heavy-hearted, and tried to resign myself to life on the farm for ever after.

Life in the Nulla Nulla valley altered after the war. The returning soldiers were changed men and they changed the valley. There were fights on the bus that ran down to Bellbrook for the dances or pictures, a thing unheard of before the war. There were social and economic changes that meant dairy farms were being phased out as a viable living for families. The small farms were being sold to make up larger grazing properties, and people began moving out of Nulla Nulla Creek. Community life as we had known it, with many young families, stagnated and eventually died.

There was not enough profit from our farm to support Victor and his young family as well as Mum and me, so Victor made plans to return to Kempsey where he could get work as a carpenter or on the shire council. I settled down to life on the farm with my mother. My old guitar broke and I didn't get it mended; there was nowhere to get it mended up there anyway. The despised self that was Gordon Kirkpatrick went through the motions of farming and living. The other self that was Slim Dusty still wrote songs and sang them to himself and to Shorty while sending out the old process records and songbooks and wishing that Slim Dusty's life could be reality.

On 21 October 1946, I picked up the mail from the cream stand, and wondered what the envelope with the Columbia Graphophone logo had in store for me. Probably the bill for the last lot of process records, I thought.

It was a letter from Arch Kerr offering me a recording session on Regal Zonophone. After five years of trying and getting kicked in the backside for my trouble, here it was. And here I was, with no guitar, no prospect of ever leaving the farm, and the total responsibility of a farm and my mother to think about. Mum was horrified. She had believed that at long last I was done with this showbusiness and singing rubbish, and she could look forward to seeing me settled on the farm where she could alternate between the Nulla and Kempsey.

'You've wasted five years or more on this nonsense and you've got nowhere. Now that your dad's died you've got to settle down on the farm. You don't want to be dropping everything just to go down there again.' I figured that she was probably right, so I wrote back to Kerr saying that I couldn't leave the farm and couldn't make the recording. I was in turmoil. I had turned down the opportunity I had struggled for, Mum was happy, and I—well, I was swinging backwards and forwards between acceptance and rebellion. I saddled my horse and rode around the paddocks and into the bush. I went up old Yellow Gully and did a bit of shooting, I wanted to be alone just then and alone I was. In the end, I rang Victor. He was downright in his reply.

'Don't let Mum stop you like she stopped me. She wouldn't let me study motor mechanics when I wanted to, so don't let her do that to you too. If you want to record, go ahead and do it.'

I broke the news to my mother, and sent a telegram to Columbia.

19th November 1946

For the sixth time in my life, I stood in the recording studios at the end of Columbia Lane. Victor and Philip had come to Sydney with me so that Victor could sign the contract. I was under age at nineteen years, and we were too unaware of business practice to know that the contract could have been sent to Kempsey for Victor to sign on my behalf.

I had a new guitar which cost me £35 at J. Stanley Johnston's music and record store in George Street, Sydney. If you'd told me that the guitar would be a showpiece in a museum display nearly fifty years later, I'd have told you to get off the turps. I didn't know how to check the concert pitch for tuning the guitar, so I had the shop assistant play a Wilf Carter record for me. I knew the song was in the key of D, and once I wound up my guitar strings to match Wilf's I should have been in concert pitch or near to it. I slunk off in embarrassment without buying the record. I had achieved my purpose, and headed for the studio with the unfamiliar instrument.

I began singing. My first song was 'When the Rain Tumbles Down in July'. I wrote it one day in 1945 as I worked in the bails and watched the rain pouring down outside. The creek was coming down in flood, and I just wrote what I saw happening in front of me and around me on all the properties.

'You'll have to do that again.' Kerr strode into the studio. I was confused. I knew I'd given a good version of the song.

'It hasn't got a yodel. Every song needs a yodel, so put it in.'

I didn't say it but I thought, 'What bulldust. It's a good ballad, and it doesn't need a yodel.'

So on the spot, I invented a sort of yodel which I have hated ever since and refuse to use when I sing the song. 'Hey, hey, hey; hey, hey, hey-ee!' A later version added 'Wheat, wheat, whee-at'— that's how much I thought of that so-called yodel.

I couldn't wait for the record to be released to see my name on the red and green label I respected so much. I didn't receive a copy from Columbia, and had to buy any copies I wanted.

43

Later, I tried to buy copies from them, but no—I had to get them from retail stores the same as everyone else.

I had an old desk in my room, made from Nulla cedar and it was from this desk that I made my contact with the singing world. I treasured a letter from June Holms, who did a lot of stage work but only made one recording session. I wrote to Gordon Parsons, and received cheery letters and sketches in response. Gordon had got onto record before me because he did well in the top-ranking radio show, 'Australia's Amateur Hour'. After that, he was in demand by rodeos and when I first met him two or three years later, he was a polished stage performer by my standards. Local concerts billed me as 'famous North Coast yodeller and recording star', but as a stage performer I was still an amateur. Although I recorded again in 1948, I was not a professional singer. I lived and worked on the farm, but Shorty was again pushing me to have another go at travelling—not that I needed too much of a shove.

I'd been receiving enthusiastic letters from Bob Fricker of 5AD Adelaide. Bob used to run shows as an extension of his hugely popular radio programme, and always said that we'd do well over in Adelaide.

'Let's go to Adelaide, Joe,' suggested Shorty. 'After we go there, we could come back through Sydney, and maybe get on Bob Dyer's show or even Jack Davey's.' (These were two of the top-rating radio shows in the nation—nothing but the best for us.)

'Well, I don't know about that, Joe,' I replied. 'What about the place here, and what about Mum?'

The seed had been planted, and it flourished in my restless mind. I had tried hard to settle down, and I'd even had a couple of mild flirtations with girls in the Nulla valley but nothing had come of them. There was nothing there to tie me to Nulla Creek so I decided to sell the herd and lease the farm to the Ryans. I remembered Victor's advice: 'If you want to go, go. It's your life. Don't let Mum stop you.'

The folk up the Nulla decided that they'd give us a send-off in George Fuller's barn with Bill O'Neill as MC. George made a great speech.

'Well, the boys are going off to further their careers. We all know they're going to do real well, and we wish 'em all the best.' A lot more was said in the same vein. We went off in a blaze of glory.

I had Mum settled in Kempsey, the farm was in good hands, and I had a bit of money for my fares this time. Shorty and I headed for Adelaide full of excitement and high hopes for the future. Bob Fricker looked at us in amazement when we turned up on the station doorstep.

'Why on earth didn't you tell me you were coming?' he demanded. 'I can't organise any shows for you just like that, and with the polio scare that's on, no one will go to any shows anyway.'

Like I said, we didn't plan ahead much.

Bob had been playing my records for some time, and as far back as 1947 was corresponding with me after having received a bogus letter from some idiot claiming to be me and giving him a lot of false information. We appeared on his programme, sold a lot of photos to pay for our keep and made our first visit to R.M. Williams, the Bush Outfitters.

We went out to Prospect to the factory and showroom, and asked to be measured for gaberdine shirts and trousers. I had mine in a blue-grey, Shorty's was in a two-tone brown. We thought it was R.M. himself attending to us, but I have my doubts today! When all the details were fixed, we broke the news that we didn't have the money to pay for them but if he would send them to us, we would be able to pay up then. He looked a bit disbelieving, but the outfits turned up and we paid on the knocker. At last we had professional-looking gear, just like the professional rodeo and stage performers.

We went back to Sydney by rail, and by singing in the carriages we made a bit of money to help tide us over. In Sydney we got nowhere with the Bob Dyer and Jack Davey shows. As a matter of fact, we got nowhere with anyone. Square dancing was all the rage and as we didn't have a clue about square dance calling, we weren't in the race to get jobs. There was nothing else to do but to go back to Kempsey. I had no farm to go to this time, and I think the good folk up the Nulla were a bit disgusted with us. There was no alternative other than to get a job on the shire with Victor. Shorty was in disgrace again, so he reckoned he'd be better off in Sydney with a day job to put some distance between him and the family.

I was working on the shire when the big flood of 1950 hit Kempsey. I had seen floods before—this wasn't my first experience by a long shot, but I'd usually been up the Nulla looking after stock and fences at home. This time I was in the middle of it. I'd been working on a road gang putting in culverts on the road leading from Kempsey to Bellbrook and the Nulla, when we were all brought back to town to help clean up. One of the jobs we had to do was take boats across the flooded creeks and tributaries to isolated dairy farms and ferry the cans of milk and cream to the factory. Not being any sort of a swimmer, it was the most unsettling part of the whole job for me. I could see myself floating down the Macleay among all the debris.

The floodwaters swept through the centre of Kempsey, smashing and taking away homes, shops and vehicles. My sister Jean and her husband Kelly lost their home and everything in it. The rest of us were up on the heights in West Kempsey and were safe. The gangs of council workers didn't have to take their lunch to work with them—all they took was some bread and a tin opener. At twelve, they checked the gutters and footpaths and opened one of the tins that were lying there by the thousand. We never knew what we were having for lunch each day but we were sure of variety.

After I'd spent about nine months on the shire, Shorty's letters became urgent.

'You should come down, Joe,' he claimed. 'It's all happening down here. Tim McNamara's got a big radio show on 2SM and he's holding talent quests and shows, the McKean Sisters are on 2KY, and there's plenty of work around. Come on down!'

This time, I knew that if I went there would be no return. I'd gone and come back with my tail between my legs, so to speak, and it was never going to happen again. If I went this time, that would be it. And so it was.

Chapter Four

BETSY AND B'S

*I laid down the foundations of my freedom
and the way I'd like to live . . .*
'YOU KNOW WHAT I MEAN' JOY McKEAN

The reason I listened to Shorty was that I'd had an offer from a travelling rodeo run by Captain 'Broken Nose' McFarlane. Show people called him 'Broken Nose' McFarlane so he would not be confused with Captain McFarland and the monkey show on the showgrounds. McFarlane was out at Finley, near Deniliquin on the Riverina plains of New South Wales, with his outfit and had sent a sample poster of the 'Slim Dusty Travelling Rodeo' and a contract. Dad and I had always talked about something like this, and I was tempted very strongly. Shorty's letter tipped the scales, and I accepted Captain McFarlane's offer to start in a month's time and caught the mail train to Sydney next day.

I went to stay with my cousins at Thornleigh in Sydney and Shorty also came over from his room in Glebe to stay. Over the next couple of years my big-hearted cousins put up with us off and on. We would blow in, expect a bed, and we always got one. We tried to repay as best we could, but in their quiet lives we must have been a bit of a worry.

Shorty took me down to meet Tim. Tim McNamara was tall, dark-haired and charming. He had a deep, crooning voice and one of the most persuasive personalities I have ever come across in my life. He could talk the leg off an iron pot, and if he'd really set out to sell refrigerators to Eskimos I swear he would have done it and had to send for more supplies. He was a generous man, had a wicked sense of humour and he fascinated us with his ability to down a schooner of beer without a swallow. I haven't seen many men do that, but it was a bit of a party trick with Tim.

Tim and his brother Tommy used to perform as a duo, but as they branched out Tim moved more into country music, and Tom into country comedy and compering. Tim eventually managed to get the job as announcer on 2SM's country music programme, and he built it into a live programme where he played records, sang songs and introduced guest artists. He welcomed visiting artists who dropped into the studio to yarn and swap songs, and before long his records were selling like hot cakes. Tim then enlarged his programme by getting 2SM and Rodeo Records to back him in putting on a huge talent quest with two recording contracts as prizes for the winner and the runner-up. This meant he could promote live concerts in suburban town halls as well as organising the radio programme, and country music boomed in Sydney.

There was another successful country programme on 2CH, and the McKean Sisters had the popular 'Melody Trail' show on 2KY every Saturday night. Stage shows were regular events in all the suburbs with Dick Sawyer and Bill Ferrier being the earliest entrepreneurs in the country music shows. Bill Ferrier was an American who arrived here with his young daughter, and began running talent quests and putting on successful shows in Sydney. By the time Tim McNamara dominated the country scene, there were scores of competent stage artists in Sydney. They had been attracted by the country music radio programmes which advertised the flourishing stage shows. Many visited Sydney regularly while others such as Gordon Parsons and the McKean Sisters were settled there.

Tim welcomed me with enthusiasm and before long I was one of the team. 'The team' consisted of Tim and his brother Tom, Gordon Parsons, Shorty and me. There were many others who came and went, but we five were the core. We'd go to the studio at 2SM and take part in the programme or just hang around and watch. Afterwards we'd all charge off to a party or to do a show.

All too soon, it was time to join McFarlane, and although I was having regrets I knew that I was committed. The team poured me on to the train at Central with Tim making loud and rude remarks about the amount of brains I didn't have, and they all went back to the Criterion to drink some more and speculate on how long I'd last before I was back. They seemed to know more about it than I did, especially Gordon Parsons who had been around rodeos and circuses a lot more than anyone else in the team.

I arrived at Finley and went looking for Captain McFarlane. I found him and one girl rider, an ancient caravan, no tent, no truck, no sidewalls, no riders. My heart sank into my boots. Here we go again, I thought. Another fiasco. Why did I have to learn everything the hard way? Why couldn't I just do something right for a change? I got some legal advice, and caught a train back to Sydney, knowing that while the 'rodeo' might have got under way eventually, it was going nowhere financially or career wise. Maybe I did do something right that time in getting out from under before I was stranded again.

Back in Sydney, Tim was putting on occasional shows as he geared up for the talent quest which was to finalise in a show in Sydney Town Hall the next January. Shorty and I were enjoying ourselves, but we needed more money to keep the enjoyment going. We looked in the local papers, and found lots of advertisements for gardeners.

'Right, Joe,' we told each other.

'We're farmers, so we're gardeners or the next thing to it, aren't we?'

'Of course we are. We're experienced, too.'

We were quite a success at this job, and as we didn't mind physical work we impressed a lot of our customers. One lady asked us if we could decorate the garden and make it look nice for a big party she and her husband were holding the next weekend. Of course we could. We hung coloured lights, we planted extra flowering shrubs, we helped with tables and chairs and were generally the white-haired boys.

We thought we'd make a bit extra so explained that 'We're singers, too. Any chance of doing a bit of entertaining on the night? Reasonable prices, of course.' We landed that one and made a few extra bob. Next on the list was the cleaning up.

'Ah, who's going to help with cleaning up all this mess?' we enquired.

We landed that job as well, and turned up bright and early next day to begin. It was a bit hard to know where to start when we looked around. Flowerbeds were trampled, our coloured lights were fused and drooped everywhere, chairs and tables scattered all through the extensive grounds, cigarette butts and empties all over the lawns.

'Right, Joe,' I said. 'I'll start with stacking the tables and chairs, you clear a space in the garage to put them and then we'll get on with the rest.'

Shorty headed for the garage and then gave me a hoy. 'Hey, Joe, just look here.'

I looked, and there in the melting ice in the tubs were a number of large bottles of Richmond Tiger (a particularly strong beer available then).

'Pretty hot outside already, don't you reckon, Joe? No harm in taking a break and a cool drink, eh?'

That was it, of course. By the time we finished the supply of Richmond Tiger, Shorty and I were in the flowerbeds along with all the rest of the empties. The cleaning up is still waiting to be done, so far as I know.

There were odd shows we could do, but we were counting on some shows down the south coast with Rex Morrisby, who had moved from 2KM Kempsey. A few days before we were due to go down to Moruya, Shorty fell asleep on the train home and someone rolled him, taking every penny we had. I say 'we' because Shorty, as the responsible one of our duo, always handled our money. He then stumbled home in the early morning, where I had arrived only a couple of hours earlier. We'd been with Gordon and Tim down in Redfern at a sly grog shop, and then at a party. With six o'clock closing it was always hard to get supplies to take home or to rage on with at a party, and sly grog shops flourished.

Shorty told his tale of woe, and I could have killed him except that I was no better than he was and it was a wonder it hadn't happened to both of us before this. Our cousins, once again, came to the rescue along with the drinkers at the Pennant Hills pub. They had a whip around which financed our train tickets to Moruya. The minute we spotted Rex, we put the bite in.

'Rex, what about a sub? We're in a bit of a spot.'

Rex was disgusted. 'Doesn't take you pair long to bite a man, does it!'

Tim was preparing to run a series of big shows culminating in the talent quest final, and then he planned a tour of some of the towns in the mid west and south. He was to do a show one night on Flockhardt's Showboat on the harbour, and said to us, 'Come on over to my place this afternoon, and we'll all go down to the Showboat together. I want you to meet some of the others because you'll be doing a lot of work together soon.'

The 'others' he wanted us to meet were the McKean Sisters, Joy and Heather. The girls were well-known stage performers in Sydney and recorded for the Rodeo record label.

We all had a good time that evening, but Shorty and I

concentrated on chasing two girls from Queensland. The McKean girls weren't particularly impressed with us, but couldn't see any great objection to working on the same shows with us. Joy and I ignored each other most of the time that night, and when she held her twenty-first birthday party the next January she didn't invite Shorty or me.

The Tim McNamara Shows in all the suburbs of Sydney were huge successes. They were always booked out, and still crowds turned up for cancellations. One memorable night at Parramatta Town Hall we did two shows—one for the audience seated inside and one for the crowd of 200 or so who stood outside and refused to move.

Tim McNamara to Shorty Ranger:
'What'd you bring him down here for? It'll be the Slim Dusty
Show soon.'

I didn't hear that joking remark, and Shorty didn't repeat it for years after. I was getting the stage experience I lacked, and the company of other artists was stimulating. There was always talk about songs, writing and performing them, recording, shows and get-togethers. Among many other girls, I met a lass with big brown eyes who came to every show I appeared in. She was very interested in me, and I enjoyed the admiration. I had lost some of my shyness by that time, and although I was no Casanova I thought I was doing alright for myself one night. After a rather intimate moment, she looked at me with those same big brown eyes and said, 'Can I have your autograph, too?' It rather took the wind out of my sails.

Tim decided to take the show on tour. It was probably a good idea for me because Brown Eyes had become a bit keen and was turning up at my cousins' place as well as at the shows. The cousins weren't impressed, and I was getting nervous.

In Sydney the shows often featured comedians and comperes of the calibre of Freddie Meredith, George Foster, Gordon White, Frank Strain, Buster Noble and the like, but on tour it was to be the old team again—Tim, his wife Daphne, Gordon Parsons, the McKeans, Shorty and me. So we had to do some of the comedy sketches as well as the singing, and a pretty hilarious stage show it turned out to be. Tim treated the tour as one big party, onstage and off, and the McKean girls sometimes wondered what they'd got themselves into.

They tried confiscating the bottles of rum whenever they saw them, and that worked until we got better at planting them. They stiffened their backs and lifted their noses when we'd got a bit too bright and they had to sit for miles between us in the back seat of the car. Joy had one of the very first portable radios which weighed a ton, and she travelled it on the dash in front of the back window. I was fast asleep one day when it bounced off and landed on my head. Joy swears I didn't even flinch, and she decided I was beyond redemption. For the time being, anyway.

I wasn't all that keen on Joy at first, and she wasn't over-excited about having me around all the time either. I thought she was stuck-up, and she thought I was conceited. We were both wrong and Timmy's tour gave us the chance to find that out. First up, I began to wonder how a stuck-up city piece could write the songs she was writing and that's when I found out that she and Heather were country-born and bred.

Their father, Silas McKean, was a schoolteacher born and raised in the country. Their mother, Millie, was the daughter of a dairy farmer in the Hunter Valley, and together Silas and Millie had been posted to quite a few small country districts. Joy was born in Singleton, and Heather in Gresford up in the Hunter River area. However, it was when Silas (more often called Mac) was teaching at Birchgrove in Sydney that Joy contracted polio. There was an epidemic of 'infantile paralysis' as it was called then, and the health authorities made the mistake of keeping it quiet for fear of public panic instead of giving out information about the symptoms to be aware of. So by the time Joy was diagnosed, her left leg was completely paralysed and did not respond to the treatment she had to undergo.

Luckily for her, Mac and Millie were sensible parents who did not encourage any mollycoddling or any attempts by well-meaning outsiders to make Joy feel that her disability entitled her to any special treatment in or out of the family. Apparently they concentrated on teaching her to be independent and to have a go at everything. I suppose that's why she took hurdles in her stride, and if she could not participate in team sports to any extent, she became a good debating team member. She took up swimming and concentrated on becoming a good long-distance swimmer in school and club events, winning quite a number of trophies. All of these things I found out a lot later. Joy did not discuss much of this; she was too busy talking about music, singing and songwriting, books, parties and enjoying life.

As the tour progressed and the girls took the good and the bad along with all the rest of us, I decided that she wasn't as stuck-up as I had thought and in fact, she wasn't a bad sort after all. I liked the way she hurtled along the street and had a go at everything and again, I liked her songs and I liked talking to her about songwriting and travelling. She was the first girl I'd ever met who didn't have marriage and settling down on her mind and I couldn't believe it.

She had wavy, chestnut brown hair and bright blue eyes that looked straight at me. Those eyes either laughed or shot sparks, depending on what caper Shorty, Gordon and I were getting up to at the time. I thought she had a nice figure, too, and I'm sure she won't mind my saying so. She also had a boyfriend in Sydney who had told me to keep an eye on her for him. Most of the time, I ended up keeping both eyes on her. I suppose I should apologise to the bloke for cutting him out, but I can't say I'm sorry!

In the meantime, apparently Joy was having second thoughts about me. She had spotted the real person behind all the bravado and realised that I was not as confident and brash as I worked so hard at appearing. The polio, at the age of four, left her stuck with wearing a metal brace on her leg. The caliper was heavy and awkward at times, but she didn't worry over it and after a first meeting, no one else did either. One day on tour, the heel of her shoe gave way and the caliper broke through. She couldn't walk in shoes without the caliper, and it gave me great pleasure to take the shoe to be mended and to do the final adjustments when she put it on. I was thankful that I was useful with my hands, and Joy privately decided that I was a lot gentler and more thoughtful than I made out I was. More, I hadn't embarrassed her independence when I helped her and that made her study me a little more closely.

Heather didn't like all this at all. Joy had a nice, dependable boyfriend back in Sydney and Heather wasn't too sure that her sister should be getting tangled up with some fly-by-night bloke like me. For one thing, so far as she was concerned, her sister was far too good to be wasted on Slim Dusty. She set out to let me know that Joy was this, Joy was that and she ended up intimidating me quite a bit. Just the same, I was Slim Dusty now and not Gordon Kirkpatrick and if I was going to go on with my life as Slim Dusty I was going to do what I wanted to do, and what I thought I was capable of doing. Gordon Kirkpatrick would have given up, but not Slim Dusty.

I waited till we got back to Sydney, and took the train from Thornleigh to Parramatta. Joy worked for Gerry Ormsby at Alert Radio in the Arcade at Parramatta, and I walked in the door and asked her if she would go out with me. I was sure she liked me, but I was relieved when I didn't get a knock-back. She said she would love to come out next Saturday.

I had done it—I had made the big step. Now what?

To take a girl out, you had to have transport. If there was plenty of public transport, there wasn't a problem. But I lived at Thornleigh, over the north near Hornsby, and Joy lived at

Granville in the western suburbs. By the time I took trains, changed trains, took another train, walked a mile to her place and then we walked back again, caught a train, changed trains and so on and so on, the romance of the evening was suffering a bit. My feet were hurting too in my high-heeled riding boots.

Shorty and I were old hands at train travel, having often slept our way home after a night out with Tim or Gordon. Many a time we woke up in the railway yards when the train we were on had finished its last trip for the night. But none of this was suitable for courting, and I took one of the cousins with me on a car hunting mission. We found a 1938 'humpy back' Ford which seemed ideal and in good order. Only problem, of course, was the price of £350 which my cousin assured me was a fair one. Fair or not, it was more than I had or could see myself having in the near future. I walked all around the car, and walked back again. The salesman could see I was hooked, and happily took my small deposit. I'd already mentally christened the car 'Betsy'. She just looked like 'Betsy' to me.

'Right,' I thought. 'Who is likely to fork up the rest of it?' (Besides good old Mum.) I remembered Gordon Parsons telling me that he used to go down to APRA (Australasian Performing Rights Association) or Nicholson's when he was a bit short, and get any royalties that might have been owing to him. I hadn't ever come at that but this was a different spot I was in. So off I went down George Street to Nicholson's and asked to see Mr Ken Jones, the manager of the publishing arm of Nicholson's.

It was an established custom with Columbia Graphophone that when you recorded with Regal Zonophone, you were supposed to go to Nicholson's Publishing and sign over your copyrights. Nicholson's would then publish the songs in song albums which were available in all the record stores. The catch was, of course, that in those days the books would not hit the shops until Nicholson's share of your performing and mechanical rights had just about paid for the expense of publishing the books. It was a long time before I had the knowledge and plucked up the courage to change this set-up.

Ken Jones was a small man with a misshapen shoulder and a quietly authoritative air. He was probably an accountant, I don't know. He looked disapproving when I asked for any royalties owing plus an advance, and my heart was in my boots. Before I knew it, I told him why I wanted the money and I walked out of Nicholson's with a cheque for £200.

'I don't mind seeing the money go out when I know it's being put to good use,' he said gently.

It must have fretted his thrifty soul to see from his window Gordon Parsons heading for the Criterion with the latest cheque in his pocket, but who's to say it wasn't being put to good use so far as Gordon was concerned!

Now I had wheels, and I headed straight to Granville to show off Betsy. Joy's young brothers piled in with us and we went for a spin while I told Joy what a wonderful car Betsy was and enthused about her non-stop. My first car, and I still think she was an absolute beauty.

About this time, the Fosters from the showgrounds contacted Shorty and me and offered us a tour up the coast, and then onto the north run which went up the Queensland coast as far as Cairns. It sounded good, and the work in Sydney was slowing a bit, so off we went. Betsy stayed in Sydney with the cousins, and Shorty and I took the train to Coffs Harbour to meet up with the Fosters. They used to follow the agricultural show runs, and fill in the time between dates by 'still towning'—putting on a full show at night in the nearby towns that weren't on the show run.

Before I go any further, perhaps I'd better explain some of the showground expressions. When I say 'gee', I mean someone from the crowd who has been teed up to be a part of the show. For instance, take the boxing troupe. They usually needed a gee in the crowd to trade insults with the boxers, and stir up the locals until at last they got the necessary challengers. When I geed for Frankie in Kempsey, I had to stand in the crowd and volunteer to come up on the board with him and do the hypnosis bit. No harm in it, just part of the show.

When a showman refers to a mug, and tells another showman to 'stop acting like a mug', he usually means anyone who is not a true showman. He doesn't mean they're idiots or anything like that; he simply means that they are not members of the elite showbiz community and therefore don't understand a showman's view of life. Furthermore, they don't have a clue about how a showman or entertainer runs his or her life and business. 'Ah, he's just a mug; he wouldn't know' is a tolerant aside from one showman to another about a local. I have to admit that another common saying is: 'Never give a mug a chance'. That stems from the attitude over the decades of the settled community against the traveller. By tradition, the travelling showman has been in the position of having to rely on his wits and his ability to survive in a world where the traveller is generally regarded with suspicion. On the other hand, if you think a showman might be a 'con' you should hear what he's thinking about *you*. If you want a fair deal, best be one of the showmen's community. They stick together.

Showmen resent the way the local paper writes up 'showman convicted of . . .' etc, whatever petty crime it may be. In almost every case, the 'showman' is only one of the 'warbs'—a casual worker picked up along the way. In the showie's colourful language, to describe someone as 'a bigheaded warb' is an expression of contempt. To be a showman, you have to get into the Guild, either by coming from one of the old show families, or by having them stand for you. You have to work for many years on the grounds renting space from showmen, and prove your ability and worthiness to become a member of the Showmen's Guild. I'm proud to say that I'm still a member.

A spruiker is the man or woman up on the line-up board 'telling the tale', which means performing some sort of trick or antic to get a crowd around the front of the tent. Frank used to wave a big sword around and go through the actions of cutting a threepenny bit off the tongue of some kid from the crowd. His wife, Merlene, would whisper to the kid to pull his tongue in as the sword descended, and Frank would go through it all again. When all the exciting drama was over he would introduce the performers of the show and finally end up with 'Get your tickets now. Starting now, don't miss out, get your tickets now.' The girl in the ticket box would then usually have to handle the rush for tickets. In between houses (performances), someone else would take over up on the board with the microphone as the 'dragger'. He would just keep talking to encourage the stragglers to come in, and if the show were in progress, to buy their tickets for the next show.

The 'illywhackers', pronounced as heelywhackers or eelywackers on the showground, were the blow-ins who sometimes followed the shows doing old lurks such as the pea and thimble and other confidence tricks. 'Got to be a heely to it' was usually the remark made when something sounded too good to be true.

Old Johnny Foster was a showground character. Poke your head in the caravan door and he'd bark 'Cuppa tea, Eily!' to Mrs Foster who was as quiet as Johnny was raucous. Eily Foster lived her life and raised her family on the showgrounds and in the small towns of the east coast, worked the ticket box, made endless cups of tea and put up with Johnny's cheerful neglect. When she died, however, old Johnny followed her a bare three weeks later.

At Brisbane Exhibition each August, Johnny would parade around in a brand new white or cream suit, new panama hat, and a dark red tie neatly knotted. By the end of the Ecca, the white would be looking decidedly dusty but Johnny wore his suit with flair. Johnny preferred the show runs to still towning because there was plenty of time for fishing in between the weekend agricultural shows. He taught me to enjoy seafood, whether it was freshly caught fish grilled on the coals of the fire he'd light outside the caravan, or prawns from a local trawler.

We'd sit around the fire and out would come the old banjo and our guitars, and when we tired of the music Johnny and his mates would tell yarns. Plenty of leg-pulling went on, of course, and plenty of exaggeration. A favourite trick of Johnny's was to seat a visitor on a solid-looking cane basket. This basket would be very comfortable until a gentle bumping began, unnerving the visitor enough to enquire what was going on?

'Lift the lid and see what's wrong, then,' Johnny would say with concern.

The visitor would either swear or scream when half a dozen snakes lifted their heads towards the opened lid, and Johnny would just about collapse with laughter.

Up north one time, Johnny had managed to collect a small crocodile and was bringing it down south as an attraction in the show. Being Johnny, the conditions for keeping the croc safely caged up were about non-existent and at Cardwell it escaped and took off into the dark. Small or not, the crocodile had a very serviceable set of teeth and everyone in the team spent a nervous night cooped up in their caravans, not game to walk outside.

'Can't understand the silly mugs,' Johnny grumbled. 'Should have had that croc properly tied up. Here, give me a hand to find it.'

He had no takers, and that crocodile is probably a fair size by now and living in the mangrove channels around Cardwell.

Granny Foster: 'Don't ever marry a mug.'

His old mother travelled with the family, and when I met her she was almost bedridden. They took me into the caravan to introduce me and to let Granny give me the once-over. She gave me the best piece of advice I ever had: 'Don't ever marry a mug. Make sure you marry into the business.' It was just what I needed to make up my mind that I had found the one girl who would understand what I was on about, and who knew as much and maybe more than I did about songs, singing and show life.

I didn't know show life really, I just thought I did. But I decided then to take up Tim McNamara's offer to work exclusively for him in Sydney because I would be working with the McKeans and I knew by then that I loved Joy and wanted to do something about spending my life with her. It meant breaking my partnership with Shorty who wanted to go on with the Fosters, but I was determined to go back to Sydney. I was saving up for an engagement ring.

I had been writing regularly to Joy while I was away, and if anyone needed proof that I was in love, this should have been enough. I am no letter writer, and never was. Years later, I discovered that she had kept my letters, and just as well, because once I got her married I didn't write any more. We were seldom apart for long at any time in the next fifty years. Good old Betsy helped me get up the courage to ask Joy to be my wife, but I believe that we both knew it was going to happen whether I made a formal proposal or not. We just fitted together. Mac and Millie accepted the inevitable with very good grace, and actually made me feel welcomed into the McKean clan.

Getting engaged was one thing, but supporting a wife was another and I gave much thought to it. I was working exclusively for Tim, but I needed a full-time job as well. I tried bread delivering for a while, but I wasn't fussy about what sort of bread I ate and couldn't see why anyone else should be. So I didn't last long at that, and as luck would have it, I landed a job offsiding on a plasterer's truck at Pennant Hills. There used to be a plaster factory there, and George Prentice (everyone called him Uncle George) not only gave me the offsider's job, but when I married and when he saw that I was keen to work, offered me the chance to get my ticket as a plaster fixer.

Millie McKean: 'But, dear, what's his real name?'

Joy and I were engaged to be married after I had gone through the ordeal of asking her parents' permission, and we planned a December wedding. The factory closed for three weeks and we were going to have a travelling honeymoon. First of all, though, Joy had a question to ask of me. Her mother had said to her, 'What is Slim's proper name? It couldn't possibly be Slim Dusty, er . . . could it?'

Apparently, Joy had looked blankly at her mother as she realised that she had promised to become Mrs Someone or Other, but didn't know who. She was embarrassed at what she thought was her stupidity, but I was jubilant. Joy had fallen in love with me, just me, not Gordon Kirkpatrick but Slim Dusty. Just the same, I think I saw a look of relief when I told her 'My real name is Kirkpatrick.'

She probably thought she'd had a narrow escape from spending the rest of her life with a name she couldn't stand.

In the meantime, Tim had us both working on his shows and the girls were still running their 2KY radio show. Then Tim had a brilliant idea, not that all Tim's ideas weren't brilliant according to Tim. He would run two shows in the one night in different suburbs. The artists in the first half in Penrith would drive over and do the second half in Hornsby, while the artists in the first half at Hornsby would do the second half in Penrith. There was a catch so far as I was concerned. The McKeans were a big drawcard and I wasn't too bad either, so Tim didn't want us both in the same half of the show. That meant that Tim would drive the girls from one show to the other, instead of me and Betsy doing the job.

I jacked up. Now, you might think I was being a bit over the top, but you forget that I had spent a fair amount of time in a car with Tim and as a driver he was an accident waiting to happen. We were all in his car coming back from 2SM one night along Parramatta Road in the heavily built-up area around Leichhardt. Tim was laughing like a maniac as he drove about sixty miles an hour along the tram lines, through a set of red lights bringing a taxi in the side street to a screeching halt and reducing Joy and Heather close to tears of fright. On one of our tours, Tim changed his mind about travelling out to Jenolan Caves on the gravel road and his method of turning was to wrench the wheel around and skid in full circles through scrub and loose gravel till he was facing the opposite direction.

Then there was the time he headed for Newcastle to do a show with Gordon Parsons and some others in his car. He managed to hurtle off the highway, ending up over an embankment and in a sort of ditch. No one was hurt and Tim was still laughing.

'Alright, then,' he said in his best growling voice. 'Hop in, better get going, got a show to do, you buggers.'

'Well,' drawled Gordon. 'You might have a bit of a job, Tim. There's no front wheel left, and the back one's looking a bit sick as well.'

That's why I jacked up on Tim driving the girls from show to show. Getting all protective and that, I suppose. I was sorry to fall out with Tim, because he'd been good to me and heaps of other people on the country music scene. Tim McNamara and his shows on stage and radio were the starting point for so many people and a stimulus for country music. His recording output was amazing for the time and he always had a joke to make or a story to tell. We came across each other later on the showgrounds, and Timmy was still the same old devil.

In December 1951, we were married at St Mark's Church of England in Granville by the Reverend Oliver. I remembered important jobs such as getting the keg of beer collected in the morning, getting my new wedding suit brushed again and again, and keeping old Ned in a fit and sober state to be my best man. Just the same, I think someone (probably Ned) helped my nerves with a bit of 'something' before I entered the church. I was standing in front of the altar feeling my collar was going to choke me when the minister very softly said, 'Turn around, lad, and look at her.'

When I turned, I should have seen all the pews filled with our friends and relations but I focused on Joy on Mac's arm, all white lace and tulle. She looked so different from my travelling and singing mate that I got quite a jolt. She looked a lovely lady from somewhere else, but when she stood beside me and smiled up at me, everything came back to normal. I had been disappointed that none of my immediate family had been able to make the journey to Sydney, although all of my cousins turned up in force, bless them, but right then it seemed that I had the most important part of my family beside me, after all. She's still beside me.

Our wedding reception was held in one of the local halls in Granville, with plenty of oldtime dances, including the barn-dance. I got excited and trampled all over Joy's lace train as I swung her around; Gordon got up to make his best man's speech with some of his fluent witticisms and was so sober he just 'dried up' and couldn't say a word; my cousins and Joy's aunty who worked together and had told each other they were going to a wedding were flabbergasted to find they were at one and the same wedding. It was a good night, and a good time was had by all.

I had converted Betsy's interior to a camping body, and with an old tent fly to extend out from her door at night, we headed off on our honeymoon. We went south as far as Cann River in East Gippsland before heading north again through Bombala into New South Wales. Cann River is only a couple of hours away from our 'second home' today at Metung where our friend Mack Cormack used to live. It was at Bombala that my new wife got her first taste of my paddy and my swearing ability. The road was white dust in the summer heat and Betsy got a flat tyre. The jack kept slipping out of place, Joy sat on the white dusted grass by the edge of the road with my black hat on her head and listened in awe and with great interest to my efforts. Apparently the bit that had her intrigued was the fact that I could swear at length with rhythm and expression, and with a string of words all beginning with 'b'. Over the years since, she has done her best to curb my swearing and I do try but it just slips out somehow.

Our married life began at Granville, living with Joy's family. Mac and Millie were tolerant people, and used to having lots of people around. Millie read me the riot act occasionally, Mac and I had a few beers occasionally, and I worked solidly at the plaster fixing. I had my ticket in eighteen months instead of the three years it usually took, again thanks to Uncle George, and we were confident enough to begin looking for a home of our own. We were saving well because we were both working shows, while I also kept on with the plaster fixing. We even began putting on shows ourselves, advertising them on the 'Melody Trail' radio show.

We were still living at Granville when our daughter, Anne, was born in 1952. She did the time-honoured thing of announcing her arrival in the early hours of the morning. This meant that Betsy had to get us to the hospital in a hurry, where I ushered Joy into the foyer. To my horror, we were greeted with a trolley bearing two layers of swaddled babies all howling for their 2 am feed. I was paler than my wife. When I left the hospital, I was halfway home before I realised that I hadn't turned Betsy's headlights on.

Becoming a father made me all the more keen to buy or build a home of our own, but for the time being Anne became the centre of attention in the McKean household. She was surrounded with music and company. Every Friday evening, other country performers arrived to swap songs and stories, handing the guitar from one to the other. Many of these friends appeared on the programme when we started promoting concerts ourselves and advertising them on the 'Melody Trail' Show.

The forties and fifties were exciting times in music and showbusiness. The Tivoli was the top variety theatre and its presentations were legendary. Bob Dyer came to Australia to appear at the Tivoli with his Hillbilly act, and stayed to become one of our top radio quiz show presenters. Roy Rene with Hal Lashwood and his team were the 'Mo McCackey' stars, there were stage shows and concerts in every suburb at regular intervals, and country music was one of the biggest draws at these concerts.

Radio stars appeared at movie theatres during interval, and radio announcers ran programmes of community singing, live theatre and live artists. It wasn't long before 'Bonnington's Bunkhouse Show' was a top favourite on Radio 2GB and featured comedians George Foster and Keith Walsh as well as many of the country artists such as Lily Conners and later, Reg Lindsay. Reg came from South Australia to win Tim McNamara's talent quest final in January 1951, and to start his long career in country music and television.

Gordon Parsons had married Zelda Wislang, daughter of Ruby Ashton of the Ashton Circus family and they were on tour a lot with Skuthorpe's Wild West Stampede run by Noel George. Gordon and Zelda were good mates with Vi Skuthorpe and John Brady, who were working in the show too. Vi was the daughter of the great Lance Skuthorpe, the showman and rider, and her husband John was a rider, whip cracker and rope spinner. Vi Skuthorpe was the nation's champion lady buckjump rider, a top act with whips and ropes and a showwoman through and through.

Zelda's mum, Ruby, lived in Kippax Street near Central Station in Sydney and all the show people seemed to end up there, visiting or dossing down for the night when they were passing through the city. It was a fascinating place to visit because you never knew who would be there or who would drop in. Ruby, with her thick, wavy, white hair and her rich, cigarette smoke voice, would wave a hand around the room and say 'You know So-and-so, don't you?' If you didn't, you weren't game to let on anyway, or you'd be classed as a mug who shouldn't be there among the real people. We met acrobats, tumblers, spruikers, riders, singers; we met old showmen and women, we met international class acts back in town between jobs from all around the world.

Ruby believed in a bit of elegance, even in the terrace house with a dunny down the backyard. She believed in calling a spade a spade, too. A few beers down the track and she'd liven up the party by hauling out the old tuba from under the bed in the corner.

'Right, then,' Ruby would declare. 'Here, you sing lead, and you over there, you can sing seconds. I'll sing thirds, not everyone can sing thirds. Seconds are easy, anyone can do that, but thirds, now that takes doing.'

Whoever had been stuck with singing seconds felt useless, but had to sing up. Ruby would give a few kapok laden blasts on the tuba to give us all the right key, and away we'd go. She was a dominant figure, a handsome woman and an awe-inspiring hostess.

Vi and John were living with the Skuthorpe family at the home they used as a base when they weren't on the road. Old Lance was there with some of the stock from the rodeo, and his life was a constant source of stories for Vi and John to tell. Lance had always been a good boxer, and in the days of travelling with his show he certainly had to fight at times. When he was in his old age, he still travelled and bossed the show and told Lance Jnr and Vi how it should be done.

He was poking around the ring one night and suggesting to one of the local hoons that he better put up or shut up—in other words cut down the heckling or do better himself. The loudmouth declined, and Lance further suggested he leave the show quietly. Once again the hoon declined, so Lance flattened him and shoved him outside. Not satisfied, the bloke brought back the local constable, and pointed to Lance as the brute who had knocked him out. Lance at once seemed to shrink into a tall, frail old man and the policeman turned on the hoon in scorn. 'What! You mean that poor old man knocked down a great lump like you? Get on out with your bloody lies. Any more rubbish out of you and you'll be the one I run in.'

Lance shuffled off around the back of the tent, where he straightened up to his usual seventy-odd years hale and hearty self, and bragged to his family about his quick think-ing as well as his good right punch which was still as effective as ever.

Gordon and I were good mates from the start, and often did a bit of singing and writing together on the quiet. Our mateship got me into bother sometimes, especially if Gordon and Zelda had had a row and Gordon would get on the tear. The pair of them were supposed to come out to William Street to have tea with us one weeknight, and I was surprised to see Gordon roll up to the plaster factory in Pennant Hills just before knock-off time.

'Thought we'd have a couple, eh?'

We strolled down to the pub, where he told his tale of woe. The couple stretched to four, and so it went. In the long run, we decided that Gordon should go home and apologise for his mis-behaviour and that I should come along and assure Zelda that her husband was truly sorry for upsetting her and it would never happen again. Famous last words. Neither of us thought of the specially cooked tea waiting and spoiling at William Street. Mateship had to come first, and a man had to stick to his mate, didn't he?

About nine o'clock that night, standing at the back door of the Kippax Street house, I heard the back gate click open and through the light rain I also heard a familiar step. Joy had woken up to where I was and had decided to join the party if there was one and to tick me off if there wasn't. Gordon might have got out of his trouble, but he certainly didn't get me out of mine.

Gordon and I were having a great time with this song, and reckoned we had a good one. Trouble was, how did we work out who was going to own it and record it? We were both recording at this stage, and always looking for suitable songs.

'Let's toss for it, Ned.' Where Shorty and I called each other 'Joe', Gordon and I called each other 'Ned'. Don't ask me how these things come about, they just happen.

'Right. Heads I take it, tails you do,' I agreed.

Gordon produced a penny, threw it up and we both inspected the result.

'You bastard!' said Gordon.

That is how 'Losin' My Blues' has the name Slim Dusty as composer, and that is why I recorded it. Some time later the same thing took place with 'Ellensborough Falls', where I wrote most of the lyrics and part of the melody, but Gordon won the toss, and it was my turn to say, 'You bastard!'

I was still writing when I could, and also remembering some of the old songs Dad had taught me not long before he died. I recorded as regularly as possible, and when Joy and I moved from William Street to share a house in Merrylands with Rick and Thel Carey, we kept on with our stage and radio work as well. Thel Carey had the words of 'Rusty, It's Goodbye' and after I set them to music I recorded them in the same session as 'Losin' My Blues' with Joy singing harmony with me for the first time on record. It was the same year that Rick and Thel first recorded, and one of the songs was 'I'll Never Be Fooled Again' which I had written in 1951 on the train to Kempsey to visit the family. I remember Rick and Thel coming home after their session of two sides, and Rick finally telling me that when they were asked if it were their song, he had nervously blurted out that it was! I looked a bit blank at first,

I guess, but said, 'That's alright, Rick.' I didn't mind, really, as there was a lot of give-and-take in those years, and after all, we were planning to do shows and maybe a tour together. Besides, the look on Rick's face was worth it!

Joy and I bought a block of land in West Epping and arranged for a house to be built. I worked weekends as a labourer for the builder to cut down the price a bit, and what with the plaster factory and weekend night concerts to do I had my time cut out for me. Still, it was worthwhile when we moved in with Anne early in 1954. You'd think we were set for life, but we ended up living in the new home for only eight months.

Chapter Five
LIVING THE DREAM

The time is here to pack your gear,
and do the best you can . . .
'THE SHOWMAN'S SONG' SLIM DUSTY

Country music was big all along the north coast of New South Wales in particular, and my old friend Tom Crozier was still at 2LM Lismore where he and a couple of other announcers ran 'Radio Ranch', a very popular country music programme. Branching out from this, Tom and co-announcer Geoff Ryan began mounting stage shows in all the surrounding towns. Joy and I had gone by train for a couple of these shows, one of them with our daughter Anne in a carry basket. These short trips out of the city—performing to packed houses of really keen audiences—made me discontented with life in Sydney, where I would never realise my original dream of travelling and singing my way through life. Also, I was separated from my country roots and writing became harder.

Joy and I talked and talked about how we could realise my dream. The farm had finally been sold, Mum was living in Kempsey in her own home, and I now had a few pounds put aside from my share of the farm sale. We reckoned we would have a go. We would rent out the house in Epping at a rental which would cover the mortgage payments each month. We had enough cash to pay for a caravan of sorts, some stage gear and some deposits on the hire of halls, and we decided to give it a trial for three months. That trial run is still going forty-nine years later.

No sooner said than done. Originally, we planned for Rick and Thel Carey to be part of the venture but when they couldn't make it we looked around for someone to fill out the programme. Joy and I could sing, Joy could play guitar and piano accordion, I could compere and act straight man in skits, but there it ended. So we talked Malcolm Mason into coming as rope spinner-cum-straight man-cum-advance man, and looked around for someone else. Someone else turned out to be Barry Thornton, who we met when he appeared in some talent quests around town, and who turned up at the Epping pub when Mac and I were having a beer there one time. That's how he came to mind. Barry sang and yodelled and we reckoned that with us, Malcolm and Barry—and if we ran a talent quest on our shows—we'd be able to keep an audience happy.

We had decided that even with all this talent, we needed a comedian. Every show had a comic, and a star portion of the programme was always devoted to comedy sketches or skits as they were known. We certainly couldn't afford another act so we cast thoughtful eyes upon Malcolm and Barry, though we didn't tell them anything about it at the time. Malcolm had done some work on the showgrounds and with Buddy Williams, and was the sensible choice to send ahead publicising the show by putting up posters and placing radio advertisements. That left Barry. All we had to do was convince him.

It wasn't all that hard, as it turned out. The money we offered was better than he was getting as an apprentice, and he liked the idea of getting into showbusiness and being on stage performing as a living. The down sides to the proposition came to light only gradually.

I tried to be diplomatic. Not my strong point, but I think I did alright this time.

'Barry,' I started, 'I was wondering if you've ever thought about how important it is to have comedy in the show? You know, someone like Freddie Meredith is really a star in all the shows around town.'

'Yeah, Freddie's terrific, isn't he? I mean, he just lays them in the aisles.' Barry's praise was generous.

'Well, you know we haven't got anyone to do that on this tour, and you know, we reckon you've got the talent to take up comedy, Baz.' I was still being diplomatic.

Barry struck a pose. 'You mean like this?'

'Ah, not quite but you could get it, I'm sure you could.'

Next thing Bazza knew, he was being outfitted for comedy sketches and Freddie Meredith was coaching him in the serious business of being a comedian. We tried him out at a couple of shows around Sydney; Barry nearly died of fright and we nearly died with him but it was 'like it or lump it, Baz, you're it'.

Such was the beginning of Mulga Dan, one of the most successful bush comedians in the history of the travelling shows.

I had to be a bit more diplomatic when it came to accommodation. We would not have the money to stay in hotels, so I had to get some sort of a caravan to house Joy, Anne and me. I had only one vehicle, Betsy, so another caravan was out of the question. I bought a tent and explained to Barry and Malcolm that sometimes they could sleep backstage in the halls, and how healthy and comfortable it would be the rest of the time in the tent. Then I bought one microphone, a Ronette, and a very small amplifying system; I also bought one of the very first tape recorders, a Ferrograph. The idea was that the prize for the talent quest would be a recording on the Ferrograph which would be played on 'Melody Trail' and entered for the finals of the talent quest. Heather was running the radio programme while we went on the road.

Joy sent telegrams and letters and booked a run up the coast as far as Toowoomba and back to Sydney via the New England Highway. She paid deposits on all the halls, and while she was doing this I was looking for a caravan. There weren't all that many around and we didn't know where to start looking for a good one, but I found one we could afford in a yard at Parramatta. The walls were of masonite, it was shaped like an egg, it took all of us to lift the front and it wasn't wired for electricity. The water tank didn't work, either, but it was all we could afford and we thought it was fine.

The other assault on our funds was a vehicle for the advance man. This was the bloke who went ahead of the show, pasting posters on any available wall or telegraph post before the coppers caught up with him, getting shopkeepers to display the advertising poster or handbill in their window in return for a complimentary ticket, and perhaps putting in the radio and newspaper ads. There was no way we could afford a car, so Malcolm headed out from Sydney astride a motorbike and that left us with £19 in kitty.

That £19 had to get us to our first town—Maitland—pay petrol, feed the troops and pay other expenses like the balance of the hall rent and hope like blazes we got a good enough house to get us to the next town. It was all the cash we had left from our savings and from the sale of the farm; we had gambled everything except the house, which wasn't paid for but was at least paying its way.

We started packing Betsy and the caravan, and I started tearing my hair out. Joy wanted to take every household good she possessed, all of Anne's toys and clothes, and even an iron for heaven's sake. I began pelting things out of the van, and things got a bit tense. I reckoned that if I wore the new shirt made of the newfangled nylon that had just come on the market, it could be washed out overnight and wouldn't need ironing so why the hell did she want an iron? Joy told me I was a selfish, inconsiderate idiot who expected her and Anne to look like tramps on the road, and she wouldn't put up with it. Just the same, the iron didn't go, but a petrol iron quietly appeared in the van about a week later. Joy had discovered that she couldn't get electricity in most of the places we camped, and the shellite-driven iron was the best thing to have anyway. How she didn't blow herself up with it I'll never know.

Betsy's springs were flat instead of curved, and I went on the rampage again. 'We won't get as far as Hornsby with them.'

I would have cried if I hadn't been so wild. By this time, Joy's brother Bob had been recruited as advance man, after Malcolm got things started, and he and Barry stayed well out of the way while I did my bellowing and roaring act with the car and van. I unloaded, and I loaded. I went through everything again and again. I was in despair. I had to fit into Betsy and one small caravan all the gear for the show which meant the Ferrograph (which weighed a ton, it seemed), the PA system and microphone, the tent for the boys, my guitar, Joy's piano accordion, Barry's guitar, all the luggage for Baz and Malcolm (and at times, Bob as well) plus our stage clothes and all the sundries you need on the road. No wonder Betsy sagged when we tried hooking on the van.

I decided that we would start early next morning, and to me 'early' meant about 4 am. I wanted to hook on the caravan the night before to make it easy to get away in the early morning dark, so I lined Betsy up with the towbar of the caravan.

'You stand beside the towbar, and tell me when I'm close,' I instructed my wife. 'When I get close tell me, and see if I'm to straighten up or if I'm in line.'

Joy had never even seen a caravan before, and was quite intrigued with the whole thing and wanting to help.

I began backing. 'Wait a bit,' she sang out.

I thought she said 'Back a bit' and I backed, jamming her hand between the towball on Betsy's towbar and the coupling of the van. By the time I realised what was going on, Joy's hand was pretty well squashed. I dragged her inside and when she passed out on me, I nearly did the same. We were very lucky. The metal missed the knuckle of her hand and bit into the flesh between two knuckles, otherwise her hand would have been mashed and I would have been without a band. She was the only instrumentalist I had.

Sunday, 18 September 1954
It was dark when we left next morning at 3.30. I have a bad habit of always being not just on time, but before it. It drives some people mad, but not being on time drives me mad too. It was pouring rain to add to the misery, but once we got going with the boys in the back bouncing with excitement, Anne wondering what on earth was going on and the sense of the big adventure beginning at last, we looked at each other with a sort of excitement and contentment. However it was going to turn out, at least we were giving it a go.

We reached Maitland and pulled up in front of Aunty Eily's place. Aunty Eily was Joy's aunty, and she got a bit of a surprise when we turned up but gave us a great welcome. It was still pouring cats and dogs, and Joy was putting a blight on our great adventure by having an abscessed tooth as well as a squashed hand. By the time the dentist had finished with her on Monday morning, he was upset and so was she. She didn't like facing an audience looking as if she'd been in a punch-up but she had no alternative; we couldn't spare anyone from our little line-up.

The town hall was big and cavernous, especially with a small crowd in it. Freddie Meredith had come up to give us a hand on our first night on tour, and he kept telling us 'Bad start, good finish'. We kept telling ourselves that the next day through what seemed like mountains of mud and hillsides of boulders as Betsy pulled four feet forward and slipped two back. To finish it off, the hatch blew off the roof of the caravan and the rain poured in. Betsy was so overloaded that we'd had to put lots of luggage on the floor of the caravan and it was soaked when we got to Bulahdelah, our next town.

In 1954 there were very few caravan parks and we had to park wherever we could manage to get permission. Most times we could park at the hall, as we did at Bulahdelah. There were puddles of water and mud all around, and we pulled the van in front of the hall. Every time anyone came into the van, tons of sticky mud came too. The seats were wet, the luggage on the floor was wet and muddy, the kerosene primus wouldn't work for ages, and as the water pump wouldn't pump, every drop of water for cooking and drinking had to be carried from the kitchen at the back of the hall. The caravan was small and crowded, and it was hard to be cheerful.

Luckily, the crowd that night was a good one and they were happy and ready to be entertained. It was our first show without Freddie's expertise and encouragement, and we were feeling raw and a bit lost, but Anne livened up the proceedings by walking onstage to watch me perform one of my most heart-rending songs. I didn't realise that she was onstage with me and I wondered why a sad song should make the audience smile and point.

Talk about the rain tumbling down in July! It was September and the rain not only tumbled, it burst from the clouds and kept on bursting. The roads were a mess, and we nearly came to grief as we turned a sharp corner and found ourselves heading into a flooded creek crossing. I jammed on the brakes, and nearly jack-knifed the caravan which would have pushed us straight into the creek—not to mention smashing the front of the van. We crawled through to the locals' amazement, as the road had been officially closed all morning.

We were gaining confidence in our show by now, and Barry was getting quite a kick out of being Mulga Dan as well as 'Barry Thornton, the Southern Swiss Yodeller'. He used to have a bit of fun with the kids who used to always get down to the front of the hall, and would sometimes try to get on stage with us. One of his acts was to fall off the stage, scatter the kids, and run back onto the stage. At one place, the kids were too quick for him and latched onto Mulga's baggy pants. We pulled, and the kids pulled harder, hysterical with excitement. They began to pull the pants off him, and as we weren't too sure what was underneath or rather what wasn't underneath, we were alarmed. Baz was always a bit touchy about doing the 'off the stage' act after that.

Freddie Meredith had turned up again to add some expertise to the show. I particularly wanted the show to go well in Kempsey, my home town. I had been back quietly to see Mum and the family, but I had never been there professionally since the day I caught the mail train to Sydney, knowing that I wouldn't go back until I had proven myself. Mum was ensconced in her little home in Cameron Street, and loved seeing Anne in particular, but she was adamant that she wasn't going to the show.

It took some coaxing and eventually she agreed to come. It wasn't in her nature to praise my singing efforts, but I could tell that she was at last proud of me. There was a good crowd with lots of folk from the Nulla, and the show went extra well. I was so nervous that I sang my heart out and had no voice left by the end of the night. But it was worth it. I wasn't just 'that Kirkpatrick kid from up the Nulla', I was Slim Dusty, recording artist on Regal Zonophone and on tour with his own show. I reckoned I could make a go of this travelling life; mud, dust, or whatever it took, I still thought it was worth having a crack at it. Maybe I wouldn't be quite the disappointment that I always believed I was.

We were a happy little band most of the time, bitching to each other about crook caretakers and high hall rents, our spirits up one minute and down the next, finding new friends in little towns, and always, always talking to the ordinary bloke and his ordinary wife and asking them how it was going for them. Wrapped up in our own concerns we might have been, but we were learning invaluable lessons about how the other half lives.

One thing that has always fascinated me about country towns is the way adjoining districts and townships can be so different in the character of the people. A showman will tell you, 'Stay out of that one, mate. It's a graveyard.'

They were nearly always right. Where one town would be show-going people, another only thirty miles away would be hopeless and you needn't waste your time going there. Not just once would this be right, but every time and right through the years. I don't know what the explanation is, but the reputations of the various towns have stuck to them and I'd say there's only one instance where I have found things to change. Barry used to say, 'This'll be a good one. Kids all over me all day.' By the same token, if Baz looked mournful and advised that the town was like a morgue you could be sure we'd die a death that night.

We had to camp wherever we could. Sometimes it was behind or beside the hall, which was a good camp because we could get electricity and water easily and if it rained we weren't cooped up in a small caravan with a toddler and three young men plus us. Sometimes it was down in the local showground, hopefully near a shelter of some sort, and hopefully with the use of a toilet block. Sometimes, when we got to know some people on the way we could put the van in the backyard or beside a farmhouse. Sometimes, the caravan was on the street outside the hall. Caravan parks were few and far between and were heaven compared to some of our camps.

Showers were a 'line-up at the local pub' deal. For a couple of bob you were allowed to use their bathroom, but in the caravan we used a big tin washtub that doubled as Joy's laundry. Nappies were boiled up in a kerosene tin on an open fire in the backyard of the hall or wherever we were. Meals were cooked over a kerosene primus that blew up on us one time, and the water container sitting up on a bench was an enormous white enamel jug that must have held a couple of gallons at a time. Lighting was provided by a pump-up Tilley lantern and we had to keep a constant supply of mantles for it because the fragile mantles broke every day as the caravan shook and shuddered its way over the corrugated gravel roads.

Travelling and showing while bringing up a young child had its good times and bad, but Anne was a good show kid most of the time. Each night, we took out the seat cushions from the caravan and put them on the floor of the dressing room backstage. Joy made a bed up for Anne there, and while Joy went into the ticket box at 7 pm, I kept an eye on Anne, and Barry and Malcolm kept her entertained as well. Of course, there was the time she disappeared and 'went for a walk, Mummy'. Frantic searching found her strolling down the street in search of a milkshake.

Our technical equipment onstage consisted of one microphone and two small speakers; all instruments were acoustic, not amplified, so the noise backstage did not stop Anne from sleeping through most of the show. She managed to make it on to the stage a couple of times, much to the audience's delight, but on the whole, she would just come home to the van after the show with us and have a snack as we had our cup of tea and then go back to sleep for the rest of the night. Ideal show baby!

There was hardly one hall the same as the next, and there was hardly one caretaker ditto. An old Irish woman was caretaker at Gatton, and she looked so frail that we all did her cleaning and stacking for her; then there was the beaut who snarled his way around, picking fault with everything we did in his filthy domain.

I coaxed old Betsy to greater efforts, and patched and mended our equipment. The hatch that had blown off the caravan in our first two days had to be replaced with a bit of an old tea chest for the time being, and then I had to make a new one. There were constant mechanical and electrical repairs to do, apart from booking halls and working out the billing of the towns ahead.

There were a lot of ups and downs, and I found myself getting pretty irritable at times through lack of sleep and worry over whether we were going to get a decent house at the next town or not. But we were living the life I wanted, and my dream was on its way to coming true. It wasn't quite star material as yet, but I was going to get there by hook or by crook.

Joy and I decided that we could make a go of it if we watched what we were doing and watched our finances carefully. We enjoyed the life and the constant change of scenery and people and towns, and every hall in every town had an incident for us to remember, be it good or bad. We spent three months on this first tour, finally coming back down south from Queensland to spend Christmas at home.

I knew recording and songwriting were the key to being able to tour successfully, and I kept recording every time I came back to Sydney. The other avenue I thought might be handy was *Spurs* magazine, and as it was the first of its kind in Australia, I didn't want it to go down the drain. My old 2KM mate, Tom Crozier, had started the magazine but said he couldn't keep it going any longer. Joy and I paid a small amount of goodwill to take it over and from February 1955 *Spurs* was issued from Sydney.

Joy did a lot of the writing and contributing for it under various pen names, and her mother Millie edited and published it. It began as a subscribers only magazine, but we managed to have it distributed through Gordon & Gotch to newsagents and we were able to keep it going for some years. Eventually, Millie's ill health meant she was unable to continue with it and as we were full-time on the road there was no alternative that we could see to closing it. With much regret, I must say.

Chapter Six

FOOLS RUSH IN . . .

When the shine wore off and I began to
feel the heavy weight we bore . . .
'YOU KNOW WHAT I MEAN' JOY McKEAN

I had learned, through *Spurs*, that there was a thriving country music scene in Melbourne. I decided that we would tour Victoria and then Queensland. We were flushed with our success in New South Wales, but I didn't want to wear out our welcome so we headed south via the mid west in the middle of a hot January in 1955.

Barry Thornton was still with us, we still had the talent quest going in the programme and I had booked Johnny Ashcroft for the year's touring. Johnny recorded for Rodeo and not only was a good singer, but he was also a compere and straight man who would fit in with our little show and didn't mind turning his hand to anything that needed doing. He needed a vehicle so we sold him Betsy while we plunged into the cold waters of hire purchase and bought a Fargo Suburban van that we christened Bertha and later called Bumbling Bertha.

Betsy was still in good order but was getting a bit cramped for all the gear we had to carry. We sold her complete with all sorts of instructions such as 'she doesn't like to be rushed in the mornings. Take her easy till she's ready and then she'll take you anywhere.' Johnny thought we were touched in the head until he had driven Betsy for a month or two, and then he knew what we were on about.

The Merediths came with us for the first two weeks, until the Ashcrofts could join us. Freddie Meredith was one of the finest comedians on the Sydney circuit, and I can never thank him enough for the help and encouragement he gave me when we were setting out. He gave me comedy scripts, he gave me props, he coached Barry as Mulga Dan, and twice he came out on the road to get us started and help out. Over the years he continued to give me comedy material which was, after all, his bread and butter. Freddie Meredith has my undying thanks; he was one in a million.

Although the talent quest idea filled out our programme and roused a lot of local interest, it also aroused a lot of other things. The local drunk, or two, always seemed to harbour an ambition to appear on stage . . . our stage. His mates would barrack for him and perhaps want to join him. In the cramped backstage area there would sometimes be up to a dozen hopefuls milling around getting in the road while we dashed on and off stage in skits and performances. There would be much heartburning when the win was not a popular one and sometimes a loser would cause disputes backstage and appeal to us. However, the vote was by the audience, not by us, and therein lay another problem. If one performer were more personally popular than another, talent got lost in the audience's judgment. In those casual days, there were often visitors backstage. I remember one bloke turning up to announce that he was 'the world's greatest illusionist'.

I am not an electrician, nor am I a sound engineer. I am simply a man from the land, a singer-songwriter and guitar strummer, but when you're on the road and doing it tough at times you soon learn to have a go at anything once. We carried our little PA system and microphone for onstage sound, but we had no lighting. We depended on what there was overhead in each hall. I remember one place where we groped our way through the whole show under one miserable light globe to be told by the caretaker afterwards that he had a set of footlights in the cupboard which we could use 'next time'!

I decided to make a set of footlights myself, and while they weren't a professional job by any means they looked alright with a coat of silver paint. I got a bit careless and accidentally touched a live socket. The electricity grabbed my hand and in panic I frantically thrashed my arm around until the fitting fell to the floor. Going into Victoria, we were told that the law said we had to have exit lights above each door and that it was our responsibility and not the hall's. So once again I set to work with tin and tin snips, sockets, bulbs and silver paint. That's the way it was in those days. In between times, I fixed cupboards in the caravan. There's nothing like being the star of a show our size—it keeps your ego under control, that's for sure.

I am reasonably, or unreasonably, superstitious about some things. My father was Irish and he would never put thirteen cows in the yard nor would he start a job like ploughing on a Friday. He'd either take a beast out or put one in, and if necessary he'd harness up the horses and turn a few furrows on Thursday so he could say he didn't start the ploughing on the Friday. I can never understand why modern theatres have a Green Room, which is the lounge where artists can rest and wait to go on stage. Green is an unlucky show colour and I won't have it on stage in my show. Ruby Ashton had once warned us, 'You're not going to take a broom with you! And a cat! They're bad luck, you'll see!' After Ruby's warning, we didn't have a cat or a long-handled broom with us.

The Merediths headed home when the Ashcrofts arrived two weeks later, and naturally Shirley had a broom in her caravan. Neither Joy nor I could see ourselves going up to her and saying, 'Shirley, your broom is bad luck so will you please throw it out?' So the broom stayed.

We headed down through Cooma and Nimmitabel to Adaminaby. The huge Snowy Mountains Hydro-Electric Scheme was well under way at the time, and Adaminaby was marked for extinction in about three years' time when it would be covered by the immense dam. We tried to picture the streets and buildings still and silent under the waters. A whole town vanished forever.

The road to Tumut led over the Monaro Range, through wild and splendid country. At times there were drops on both sides, and I glanced down quickly to see paddocks like patchwork quilts and twin ponds gleaming in the sun. We passed through Kiandra and into the mountains again till we were on top of the Talbingo Mountain. I barely noticed the sign 'steep descent', figuring that I could see that for myself. The mountain road was about four miles from the top to the valley floor, and I travelled very slowly in low gear with the heavy caravan pushing hard behind. We were about three-quarters of the way down when my foot on the brake went straight to the floor. I pumped madly as Bertha began to pick up speed.

'No brakes!' I yelled. 'No brakes! Hang on!'

Joy clutched my knee with one hand, and held Anne with the other. The handbrake on the new Fargo had never been any good, and now did exactly nothing to slow us down. There was a sheer drop on one side and the mountain cliff face on the other. I had no choice but to turn into the cliff and up the embankment. There was a horrible rocking and jerking, and the crunching sound of metal and wood caving in. The truck kept going and swung out to the road again towards a hairpin bend. I knew we'd never make it round the bend at this speed, and there was a long drop to the river in the valley below awaiting us. Another hard swing of the wheel threw the caravan over onto its side, and that stopped us.

We sat stunned for a full minute. Then Barry in the back seat resumed rolling his cigarette and said, 'Gee, isn't that a cow!'

The truck was scratched and dented and one tyre was cut about. Joy shed a few tears at the thought of our wrecked caravan, and couldn't bear to look at first. The old van lay on its side, tyres crushed and terrible holes smashed through its wall by the rocks on the mountain side. But it wasn't wrecked, and I reckoned we'd get it going again.

We didn't try to get inside or rescue anything, we just wanted to get down that mountain in one piece. I held Bertha in low gear, and without the caravan we crawled down the rest of the way without brakes to find Johnny and Shirley getting ready to come looking for us. Shirley had seen us start the descent and they knew we should have arrived by this time. Betsy brought the caravan down the mountain after we got it back on its 'feet', and although John, Barry and I were filthy, dirty and exhausted we were on the move again.

We held a ceremony where we cut Shirley's broom to bits and threw it away. Like I said, I am just a bit superstitious, but even the rest of the team admitted that since that broom arrived we'd had a lot of bad luck and breakdowns, and even Betsy had been playing up. The old girl did seem to be almost human at times.

Joy's young brother, Bob, was now doing all of the advance work. The advance man has a lonely job unless he has been at it for years and has built up a network of contacts and friends in all the towns. But Bob seemed to enjoy it alright. Off he'd go on the motorbike, loaded up with posters, pens, complimentaries, all the advertising gear plus a small tent and sleeping bag. He'd go and order a milkshake at the local cafe and settle himself at a back table. By making the milkshake last an hour or so, he'd write out all his posters before going out to attack the shopkeepers.

Bob felt that he wasn't getting enough posters up and decided to do some pasting, which involved getting his brush and paste tin and keeping ahead of the local constable as he sloshed some gunk onto prominent telegraph poles and fences and slapped up Slim Dusty Show posters. We rolled into some Riverina towns to a procession of bright posters and a delegation consisting of the local police, the council health inspector and various community figures all bent on suing us. As I couldn't afford the £50 fine threatening me, I had to enlist the help of Barry and Johnny and scrape down every blasted poster in each one of those towns. The worst of it was that until Bob contacted me by telegram or by his sudden arrival, I had no way of telling him to cut it out.

Things were going from bad to worse. As soon as we crossed the border to Victoria the complaints about our ticket price began. Victoria still had entertainment tax in place, and we had to buy tax tickets from the post office and sell them in conjunction with our own. It made hard work of the box office when you had to charge 6s 7d. In the end we began charging 7 shillings flat, but after a week of abuse we dropped our price to 6 shillings and paid the tax ourselves. They still complained, and we could ill afford the tax. I suppose that the only satisfaction we could take was in the fact that even the grizzlers were clapping happily by the end of the show. That is, except for one place which shall remain unnamed.

This audience just sat there, and refused to laugh or applaud. We got not one clap when we finished the show, and played 'God Save the Queen' as the law decreed at that time. Then as they left the show by the side doors we heard them telling each other how much they enjoyed themselves and what a good show it had been. I just don't understand some people, and I guess they don't understand just what a bit of appreciation means to an artist. We thrive on it, and it carries us from one town to the next.

In Melbourne we found that we needed the radio advertising

that we couldn't afford at city prices, and for the first time we simply could not open the show one night. Twenty-four people turned up, so we sang them some songs and gave their money back. Not all of them would take their money back, bless them. Most of them turned up the next week at a neighbouring suburb when we were able to show, one of the girls bringing flowers for Joy.

We got a great welcome in Melbourne from Tex Banes and all the members of the Trailblazers, the Australian Hillbilly Club, and the Banjo Club. There were three popular country music programmes on city stations every weekend and we were invited to perform on all of them and all their artists simply lined up to record for the 'Melody Trail' radio show on our Ferrograph tape recorder. This recorder was one of the first to be available to the general public, was built like a tank and weighed as much (I used to think). Still, it survived the years of touring and only hiccupped a bit when we accidentally tried to use it on DC instead of AC.

This was another trap for young players. For instance, when we eventually toured the Gippsland district we showed in Orbost over in East Gippsland. It was a timber and dairying town and we had a good crowd, but we just couldn't get our equipment to work. When the PA gave out a few whiffs of smell and smoke, we woke up. The power was DC, and our amplifiers, microphones and tape recorder couldn't be used. Luckily for us, we could haul out the battery set that we used when spruiking from the truck, and although it wasn't very strong it got us out of trouble. Not like a place in NSW where we had to sing and do the comedy skits with no mike at all. None of us could even croak the next day after that.

When we met Jack Gill from Gill Bros Rodeo in the Riverina, he told us to go out to Gippsland—so long as we got there before the rain.

'Good towns, and good people. You want to get there before the winter rains, and you'll do alright, I reckon.'

We knew we had to 'do alright' and do it soon or we wouldn't have the money to get back home. The responsibility of other people's livelihood upon our shoulders began to feel heavier by the minute as I sat with Joy and put together a Gippsland tour. Our hopes were pinned on it, but with our usual optimism we went to the first drive-in theatre in Australia to have a bit of a night out. Might as well be hung for a sheep as for a lamb seemed to be our philosophy in those days.

The Gippsland area of Victoria is beautiful, there's no two ways about it. We had never seen such rich dairying country except maybe on the south coast of New South Wales, and the further east we went the better the business became. Our spirits lifted along with our kitty, and even when the cold winds began blowing we lit fires in the dressing rooms of the old halls and convinced ourselves that it wasn't going to get any colder . . . it couldn't, could it? It did, though.

By this time we were quite a streamlined little show, even if I do say so myself. Mulga Dan was a hit, and so long as his moustache was in place and his baggy pants held up by the braces, Barry enjoyed the comedy work. Baz had also been doing some guitar picking ever since we had a bit of a jam session up on the north coast of New South Wales. Barry had plugged his guitar into the tape recorder to use as a rough guitar amplifier, and together we had begun singing and playing in a style that Barry perfected and we called 'bush ballad guitar'. While we were in Melbourne, Tex Banes showed Barry a certain picking trick which Baz used so effectively in the recording of 'Winter Winds' that it has become a classic in Australian-style guitar picking.

We camped at Lakes Entrance, and showed one night at Bruthen. The ticket box was in a large room, and when Mulga Dan first came on and the laughter was loud, an elderly gentleman asked Joy if he could bring his granddaughter into the room. He explained that Allison was retarded, it was her first visit to an event like this, and the noise, even if it was happy laughter, was so loud that it distressed her. Allison was happy enough away from the noise and Mr Gilsenan took her back into the hall as soon as the music began. Each time he had to bring her out while Joy was there, he explained a little more about her. After the show, I sat on the steps to the stage and sang 'Bimbo' for Allison. She loved it, as she loved all music.

Her father, 'Mack' Cormack, her grandfather Gordon Gilsenan, and her aunt Cora Gilsenan-Waters had brought Allison to the show because hearing my songs on the radio appealed to Allison and she made an effort to sing the words. As she couldn't speak clearly, her family thought that seeing me in real life and seeing the songs performed would perhaps encourage her to make the effort to speak and sing more. Allison had a good time, and through her, I made one of the most wonderful friendships of my life.

Mack and Lorna Cormack lived with Lorna's parents, Gordon and Janey Gilsenan, at Metung on the shores of Bancroft Bay. Their old home sat on a headland, and the tourist boats from Lakes Entrance used to tie up at their jetty so that tourists could climb the steep hill to their house, where they were served afternoon tea on the verandah. Gordon, or the Boss as he was called, used to sing out to Janey and Lorna when he saw the boat come around Bells Point: 'Here she comes. Put the scones in, now.'

Into the big double oven in the kitchen went the scones. Out onto the tables went the jam and cream dishes, and the big teapots and milk jugs were readied. When the tourists came panting up to the verandah, the piping hot scones fresh from the oven were being put on the tables.

Once a week, the boats brought tourists up for the Aboriginal concert which was held around a huge campfire outside the house. The men sang and played gumleaves, they danced, they gave demonstrations of firemaking and with a singsong it was always a good night. We were invited to come to the very next one, and we jumped at the chance. Cora came to guide us to 'Bancroft', and as we wound further into the bush which was dripping with rain on a black night, we began to wonder if we had been quite wise to just follow a perfect stranger, who was accompanied by a one-eyed Aboriginal man, into the unknown.

'Of course, you would want to come no matter what,' was my opening remark to my wife.

'Where's the willy [cash takings]?' I asked.

'Under the seat, where do you think it is?' she snapped back.

'Well, keep it out of sight. I don't like the look of this. Where the hell are we?'

We stopped. There was blackness all around, only the lights of Cora's car ahead of us and still the rain dripped down. If it had poured, I think I'd have been more comfortable, but it just dripped. It seemed sinister somehow. Lance, Cora's companion, got out of the car and opened a gate. Cora stuck her head out of the car, and called cheerfully, 'Alright back there? Not far now, not far now.' Next thing, we turned a bend and there were the lights of a big old white house and everything returned to normal.

The campfire concert was cancelled because the boats couldn't risk being on the lakes in such bad weather, but we had a wonderful time.

Allison's father, Mack, was a tall, skinny character with a long serious face that belied his sense of humour. I had been singing one of my songs called 'Bushland Boogie' and also 'When the Sun Goes Down Outback'. In those days I was still a bit touchy about my singing and songwriting, probably because I felt I was still proving myself, and I didn't take kindly to Mack's criticism.

'I reckon those words could be a bit better,' he said. 'Not strong enough, I reckon.'

'Why don't you do better yourself, then?' I flared.

'Well, I wouldn't mind having a go, I suppose,' muttered Mack.

When I read the words of 'Since the Bushland Boogie Came This Way' that he sent a few weeks later, I knew that he had done better and that he would continue to do better if I had anything to do with it. Mack had a way with words, and whether it was a light-hearted story such as 'How Will I Go With It, Mate?' or the wistful softness of 'Camooweal' I always found his verses warming and inspiring. I have recorded many of Mack's lyrics, but I think 'Camooweal' is his classic.

We treasured the memory of the evening as we went back to our procession of filthy halls that had to be cleaned before we could work in them, and the sling-offs by the smart alecs outside the ticket box. I got used to being told, when there was a poor house, that 'you should have been here last week' or 'next week' or 'last night', and so when we turned up at one little place and were greeted with 'Hello, Slim! You should have been here last night', I yawned with boredom. To my horror, he was right. The wrong date was on the bills, and a big crowd had turned up . . . but *last night*. About thirty still turned up on the right night along with us, but I've never spent a more uncomfortable night.

It was during this run that Joy was told she was married to an imposter, that the real Slim Dusty's name was Stan McCartney or McCarty and he came from Melbourne. When Rusty Shannon and the Melody Twins (a Melbourne act) called in to see us, Rusty told us that he had actually worked in a show for this bogus Slim Dusty. He also told us where he used to work, and remarked that he sang in my style and copied my voice very well, besides looking enough like me to be, say, my cousin. I wasn't impressed and Joy was even less impressed. If she had gone through all this flak, mud and cold for the sake of an imposter, she was going home to her mother!

We had one more trip to the Gilsenans' place at Metung when we went back to show in Bairnsdale, before we headed back north. The Boss and Mack taught us how to throw the boomerangs they had given us (Mack had made some more from wattle root for us too), and we all had boomerang fever.

When we got to Ballarat, we learned that we had stayed far too long in Victoria. The cold came up from the ground, and in the old caravan we huddled around the primus stove which we put on the floor to warm the air. Boomerang practice went on in a paddock near the railway line with train passengers hanging out the windows, not believing their eyes.

By the time we crossed the border to New South Wales, we had quite forgotten what it was like to work to a red-blooded audience after the quiet, restrained Victorian crowds and we loved the warmth and enthusiasm. I lapped up the applause, and we all regained some of our confidence that had been sadly bent down south.

Anne had her third birthday out around Forbes, and we headed for Sydney for a break before tackling Queensland.

Chapter Seven
... WHERE ANGELS FEAR TO TREAD

... that was when I paid my dues and seemed to
go on paying more and more ...
'YOU KNOW WHAT I MEAN' JOY McKEAN

Queensland, here we come!

That's how we felt after five weeks back in Sydney booking towns and burying Bob's old bike. We sent him off this time in an old black Chev, and hoped for a reasonably trouble-free run—if there is such a thing in an advance man's life. We planned to head for Queensland through the north-west of New South Wales but first of all we would show some of the north coast to help us pick up our sorry state of finance.

Showman's saying: 'It's the back-up that beats you.'

The welcome we got in all the towns was absolutely great and I was feeling that all of our efforts to give a good value show were paying off. People came back to see us and by the time we arrived in Kempsey I was feeling that I could show my mother how well I was doing at long last. I had written as persuasive a letter as I could, asking her to travel with us for a week or two.

She would be able to spend time with Anne and see for herself that our life was working out for us.

At first, she said she'd do nothing of the sort, but when we left Kempsey Mum was sitting up in the back seat with Barry and Anne, two of her favourite people. It didn't last too long, of course, as Mum was like a fish out of water moving every day and not having all her little bits and pieces around her. She had a great time talking to the caretakers at halls and parks, but the minute Bob arrived back at the show she demanded to be driven home to Kempsey. I was content, because she could see now that I was set on my life's course, that there was no way I was going to return to Kempsey to work on the shire, and that at last, I had my little family and I was happy. From that time on, Mum faced the facts and was more contented too.

We had stayed in Victoria too long, and as we headed for Queensland we soon realised that we were late enough to strike an early summer storm weather pattern. From Kempsey we had travelled across the New England Range and headed out through Gunnedah and up through the north-west to Walgett and the border towns. We landed in Moree just after the council had placed a colour ban on the town's Aborigines, refusing them access to the local baths and so on. We had always got on well with our Aboriginal friends, and I found it hard to work out what the problem was. There's good and bad in all kinds of people, I guess, and I just want to take them as I find them. I found the people in the west and north-west to be nothing but friendly and helpful to our little show, no matter what colour skin they happened to have.

We began doing longer distances as we headed west and north, and the roads grew worse. When you are pulling a caravan and you hit badly corrugated gravel roads, you can't get up speed to get over the ruts. If you try it, you're likely to have the caravan start dancing sideways until it pulls you and your truck into the gutter, most likely in a crumpled heap. As a result, we had the combination of bad roads and long distances making the day's travel hours longer in an early summer heatwave.

At the town of Baradine, Joy's great-uncle, Billy Schumack, was waiting to greet us. Uncle Billy was in his seventies, I'd guess, and the little old bloke was tickled pink to see Joy again after many years.

'Slim,' he said, 'I want you to meet some of my mates down at the pub if you've got a few minutes. Come on down and we'll have a yarn and catch up on what you and Joy are doing.'

Normally, I'd have said 'No, not before I work' but Uncle Billy seemed so frail and eager that I thought, well, a couple will knock the old bloke over and I'll be okay to bring him home and get on with the work. I couldn't have been more wrong. Uncle Billy drank me under the table, the bar, and everywhere else, and I came home to the caravan plaiting my legs with Uncle toddling along beside me chatting away.

That night, when Barry came around from the front of the hall to tell Joy we had a great house and couldn't fit any more in so we might as well start the show, no one could find me. Joy was at panic stations as she checked everywhere she could think of, and I was finally found sleeping it off in the front of the truck. They hauled me out, dowsed me with cold water and pushed me into my stage clothes and I got through the night with the beginnings of a whacking great hangover. Joy always waited till I had the hammers of hell in my head before she went crook on me. I suppose it had more effect then, but gee, I wished she'd shut up till the little men stopped banging in the old scone.

Even in the heat next day, the frost in the Fargo was noticeable. It didn't thaw until we got to Coonamble, where we learnt that rain was forecast for the next day when we had to get to Walgett. We couldn't buy chains to fit the Fargo, and after seventeen weeks of rain off and on, it would only take a light rainfall to make the Walgett road impassable. Johnny checked with the local policeman.

'If it's such a bad road, and it does rain tonight, can we get there by train for the show tomorrow night?'

The policeman grinned and shook his head. 'The railway ends here, mate.'

'Well, how about plane?' Johnny was determined.

'Nope. Did you see that plane land? Well, did you see it take off? No? Well, he stayed here about five minutes and took off again before he could bog down, and if the rain keeps on, there'll be no plane at all tomorrow.' This last bit said with relish.

All of Coonamble was convinced that we weren't going to get to Walgett, but we were as lucky as tin hares and the rain stopped after a couple of hours. There was a bit of sun and breeze in the morning—surely we'd get through. After a good season in the west, the plains were covered with flowers of yellow, blue and pink. The road was unformed, and in many places the wheel tracks running through the high grass and flowers were the only indication of the way to go. We got there after a bit of weaving and ducking across ruts and greasy spots, and then after a successful show we headed up through Brewarrina to Goodooga and the border towns. Some of the kids at Goodooga had never seen a show before, and thought it was all over at interval time. They were hysterical with delight when they realised that there was another hour!

We went through Collarenebri, Mungindi, St George and Dirranbandi and we were showing Queensland towns. Barry wanted to go to the Thallon Rodeo as there was a show family lass he had his eye on, but with storms forecast for the next two days we had to head for Goondiwindi, 218 miles away, without any mucking around. The most direct route was through Thallon, and we were warned about a bad bore drain crossing.

This was the worst road yet. Without a caravan, it still would not have been good, but it wouldn't have been any real problem. With a van on, I was dodging trees and turning off the wheel tracks into the paddocks to get around the branches and the ditches in the so-called road. Where there weren't ditches, there were big rocks; where there weren't rocks there were patches of bulldust like red talcum powder, six to seven inches deep. It took us one hour to cover fourteen miles, and then we reached the bore drain.

Right across the track and across the paddock was a channel about four feet wide and one to two feet deep. The crossing was already partly filled with sticks, branches and old pieces of iron by earlier travellers who were lucky enough not to be towing caravans. Barry and I carried pieces of sleeper from the railway line nearby and packed it up pretty well. We were nearly across and the truck was starting to pull out of the drain, when the ground just dissolved into greyish-black greasy mud and Bertha went down to the axles in the sticky slime. She was so far down that the towbar of the caravan was resting on the mud.

We unhooked the caravan from the truck, and finally got Bertha out. I looked for my jack and discovered that it hadn't been returned by the last borrower. Barry and I nearly busted ourselves lifting that rotten old van's towbar inch by inch, until we could hook on the Fargo at a different angle and with Bertha's engine roaring, out we came. It took us three hours of struggling in the heat, and we couldn't even be bothered giving the traditional cheer. We just flopped, and stewed in the heat.

We reached Goondiwindi about seven that night, and I'd had to really drive that truck and caravan every inch of the way. The corrugations almost shook the vehicle to pieces and in fact the jolting loosened the bolts holding the carburettor so that they were only finger tight. A gasket in the carbie had also split and was letting in air but it wasn't affecting the old truck and I was so dead beat that I left it. We didn't need any rocking when we got to bed that night.

A couple of days later, we left Texas (Australia, mate, not USA) and headed for the town of Inglewood. I felt as though the flesh was leaving my bones with the hammering I was getting from the rough road and corrugations that were deep enough to bury a cow. Next thing, Bertha's engine was blazing. It was so sudden. Barry and I leapt out and for the first few seconds we couldn't think what to do, as we didn't have such a thing as a fire extinguisher. Then we threw handful after handful of sand and gravel from the road all over the engine. Joy had to make up her mind whether to get Anne out first or throw us some blankets and ended up doing both at once to Anne's bewilderment. Barry's new singlet went west followed by pillowcases and blankets before we could safely say the fire was out. Luckily it didn't get back into the petrol. It turned out that the oil filter had jumped off its seating and the oil mixed with some petrol (which must have been leaking)—a good recipe for a fire in an engine.

When we got to the next garage we stayed put till that oil filter got fixed, but good.

We were getting our first taste of Queensland summer heat, and with the storms around every day, it was like a weight on our shoulders. We found snakes in plenty around the old halls and were lectured regularly to watch out for the 'plains tigers', a big black-brown snake with a sort of flat, V-shaped head. They can be aggressive at times, we were told. We headed west to Roma over roads and creek crossings so steep that we had to crawl into the gully and roar out of it; take it at a run and you'd snap a towbar like a carrot.

In Roma, we met Wave and Elaine Jackson from Injune. Waverley had a property north of Injune which in turn is north of Roma. He was writing songs, although he couldn't play an instrument at all. He recorded some of his songs for me on the old tape recorder, and over the years I have recorded a number of them. This was the beginning of my actively collecting lyrics and songs from people who were living out there in the bush, and writing it all down. You'd almost think they were just waiting for someone like me to come along and take the songs out to the rest of Australia.

Nick Erby, CM broadcaster: 'The bush ballad songs have become important historical documents.'

For the past forty-odd years I have collected, edited, set to music and recorded songs that have been written by blokes like Wave Jackson. Joy and I kept writing our own songs based on what we saw and who we met and the stories we heard on our long travels. We found that the fascination of the outback eventually grabbed us and we have become addicted to it now. In the beginning, though, we felt insignificant and lonely out on the plains where you could see the horizon all around you, no matter where you looked. I don't understand it when people say the outback or the west of Australia is all the same . . . deadly flat and boring. They can't have their eyes open to the changing colours, or to the changes in the surrounds when the plains give way to low hills, and then the hills to ranges in the distance.

I was seeing the west for the first time, and I grew to love it.

When Joy woke me at four in the morning hissing, 'It's raining! Get up!', I wasn't in love with western Queensland and its roads at all. If we didn't get moving right then to beat the rain we wouldn't make it to the next town. We'd already missed one because of the weather—first time it had ever happened, too. After the first sprinkle it held off and we held high hopes of getting to Blackall for breakfast, but ten miles out of town we stopped to help a family who had been broken down all night with their car and caravan. After towing them back to the nearest road workers' camp, the rain caught up with us. We slipped and slid, the road was as greasy as a pork chop, and though Barry and Joy did their best to push I gave it up when the van jackknifed and nearly turned over. We sat there for three hours till, luckily, the road dried up.

Supplies out there were not always easy to get. We carried some tank water with us for the children (Anne and young Mac

Ashcroft), as they weren't used to the bore water and it made them sick for a while. All of us had the equivalent of Delhi belly or Montezuma's Revenge while we acclimatised to the bore water. There was no fresh milk either, though in Blackall there was plenty of goat's milk supplied by the herds of goats that wandered all around the streets, camping under the hall and going home to be milked when they were ready.

By the time we got to Longreach, a sizeable town, the springs on the heavy old caravan were smashed and the van was riding on the chassis. We had to leave it in Longreach and book into the pub at Muttaburra while we did the show. The bar was good and lively with a buzz of voices one end, a mouth organ going at the other and some old songs being belted out. There were plenty of people in town for the show and they were having such a good time they didn't want to go home.

'Hey, mate, any chance of a bit of a dance? Bit early to be knocking off and going home, and the pub's shut now so how about it, eh?'

Well, it was about eight years since Joy had played the accordion for a dance but I persuaded her, and with plenty of wrong notes but lots of swing the crowd stamped gaily around the floor.

Barry and I went back the seventy-odd miles next day to pick up the caravan, got caught in another storm on the way back and busted the springs again. When we opened the door in the middle of the hot day, there were about a hundred of my new photos in the middle of the floor dripping with melted butter, garnished with the insides of a packet of tea. It's moments like these you need Minties, I always say.

While I was away in Longreach, Joy was making the acquaintance of just about every woman in Muttaburra as she walked down the street. By the time I got back, she was good mates with the only other woman staying at the old rambling hotel. This lady was tall and thin, and freckled with reddish hair. She was awaiting the arrival of her fourth child in Muttaburra

102

where there was a Bush Nursing Hospital, and she was then going back to the out-station on a property that was about a hundred miles from the nearest small town. She had tried to grow her own vegetables because those that came from the coast by train were mostly mouldy or rotten by the time she got them, but the creek flooded each time. She made her own bread, taught the children by correspondence, and got sick on the bore water until her husband nagged the boss into giving them a tank.

The out-station was fourteen miles from the main homestead. Until they saved enough for a utility they had no transport, and much of the time the single telephone line wouldn't work. 'Why stay there?' Joy wanted to know. 'Surely there's work elsewhere for you?'

'Oh, my husband loves it up here. We come from Victoria, but there wasn't room for two brothers on the one farm and the hubby likes Queensland so I'll stick it out for his sake, I guess.'

By the time we reached the coast we felt sure we'd 'seen it all'. We'd played in a railway siding that had a small hotel boasting a pet pig that squealed blue murder when the children picked it up. Then there was the even smaller hall that held everyone who turned up—and that was everyone in the district. They were thrilled that we'd come and didn't even charge us for the use of the hall. We had also been abused by a neurotic theatre owner in a larger town, who seemed under the impression that we were working for him and he didn't like our general efficiency or attitude. Anne was attacked and bitten by a cattle dog in the caravan park at Charters Towers. Joy met a lady from her childhood days who told her a story about Joy's mother, Millie, and Millie's moral courage. Joy later wrote the story into a song that she called 'The Local Mary Magdalene'.

We were at the beginning of almost a lifetime of stories and experiences, some funny and some very sad.

Chapter Eight

FOLLOWING
UP THE SUN

When the wintertime comes on, we hit the northern run,
Travelling round like millionaires, following up the sun . . .
'THE SHOWMAN'S SONG' SLIM DUSTY

We drove straight through the main street of Townsville and parked where we could gaze across the blue water to Magnetic Island. Our first stab into the outback with our little show was complete, we reckoned we could back up alright, the kitty was looking healthy again, and we were going to have a good time on the Queensland coast.

Sugarcane fields fascinated us: with the feathery, arrow-pointed tops of the stalks of cane, the little cane train lines weaving alongside the canefields, and the awesome sight of the cane blazing at night. The men cutting the cane were black with soot, but burning it was better then dodging the snakes and rats and struggling through the undergrowth to cut it. In past years, the cane-beetle had cost farmers a lot of money in lost crops and Australian scientists imported and freed a number of cane toads from South America. In the previous two years, the toads had fixed the cane-beetle problem but were on the way to becoming a problem themselves.

We had camped at Rowes Bay under the spreading banyan trees, grateful for the shade they afforded, and enjoying the fallen leaves underfoot around the step of the caravan. At night, it was quite a walk to the toilet and shower blocks and we noticed the rustling and scurrying around our feet. A torch revealed an unpleasant sight to our southern eyes . . . there wasn't one square foot of ground unpopulated by at least four or five brown, horny-skinned toads staring balefully up at us. They went in all directions when we approached, but 'froze' in the torchlight, and they gave off a distastefully musty smell. We saw none larger than about five inches in body length, but were told they do grow larger. Snakes were no threat to the toads, because the toads shoot out a kind of poisonous froth which swells the glands in the snake's throat and suffocates them. Dogs soon learn to leave them alone. They have no natural enemies that I know of, and it's no wonder then that they eventually spread as far as they did.

I remember our first show in the old Theatre Royal at Townsville. Joy seemed to be a bit laid back during our duets in the second half, and I was working harder to make up for it. As soon as the show ended, she told me that at interval she had taken a mouthful of cold soft drink straight from the bottle and a piece of glass had lodged in the side of her throat. She'd been trying to sing without taking any full deep breaths, and by the end of the show was mentally writing her will after thinking of all the drastic things glass can do to your insides. She'd also been trying to swallow bits of cotton-wool from her makeup kit, and she was hanging out for the show to end. She knew, of course, that I'd have stopped the show and carted her off to the hospital if she had told me earlier. As it was, I threw her into Bertha and raced down to Emergency where a tired, red-headed young doctor couldn't find the glass. He told her to go home, and if she was still alright in the morning we could stop worrying. He didn't tell us, and probably didn't know, how to stop worrying overnight, but we were both so tired we collapsed into bed. Joy survived and so did I.

Our first tour of the Queensland coast, in November and December, was one of contrasts as we showed in every type of hall from the smallest to the biggest of theatres, and it was a very happy time. We were happy in our travelling life; steak and ice-cream one day and fried up leftovers the next. Without actually saying so, we had decided that we would continue touring while ever we were making a go of it.

My records were selling well, and through doing appearances in record and music stores, live interviews and performances on the radio stations, as well as the live shows, the sales were consistent and steadily growing. All in all, we were feeling quite confident as we headed down the coast, Barry and the Ashcrofts to Sydney and us to Kempsey for Christmas.

Before we left for Kempsey, we couldn't resist going to Brisbane to have a look at some second-hand caravans similar to ones we had seen in northern caravan parks. We came across a beauty, the nicest we had ever seen, with a permanently made-up bed. In the old caravans you had to pull down the table to make a bed for yourself. At night, after travelling and then doing the show, that particular job became a real bugbear. This Arrow caravan sold itself to us because of that bed, plus all the other comforts we had only dreamed about. Things such as a permanently set-up table and seats, a sink and water pump (that worked), a pantry, and cupboards and drawers that I hadn't had to make. The last word in mod cons was a shower room. It didn't have the battery-operated shower of today, but with a tank of warm water attached to the roof, you could actually have a shower. No more tin tub!

The price was high but the van was worth it, and the bank replied that our account balance would stand the strain. Only just, mind you, but it would stand it. We would have to count on some fair to good houses for the rest of the run. We paid our cheque, hooked on the 'Silver Cloud' and drove off on our own particular cloud, cloud nine.

The cloud disintegrated three days later when we received a telegram to say our cheque had bounced. We scrounged every penny we had, rallied the tenants in the house to pay a month in advance, and rang Millie in desperation. Believe it or not, she had just won £100 in the lottery and after buying herself a washing machine, was able to lend us £50. With that, and a lot of promises, we made good our word with the caravan maker. It also taught us a lesson—never to skate on ice that thin again, and we never have. We breathed easier when we were able to wire the money to the maker, and no longer had visions of him appearing to evict us bodily from the travelling home we had very quickly settled into. Not much later, we changed the name to 'The Shiralee' after D'Arcy Niland's story. It was our burden, true, but a comfortable one.

We've had some characters travel with us over the years. When we began touring again in January the next year, we hired Chad Morgan, the 'Sheik from Scrubby Creek'. Chad had made a big hit on 'Australia's Amateur Hour' and his first taste of touring was for three weeks with the Slim Dusty Show up the good old north coast again. When we headed down to the south-west, Chad came with us and we met up with Gordon Parsons, who was staying with friends on a property down Caragabal way. Gordon came along too, just for a few shows, and camped in the boys' caravan.

Chad was a hit on stage with his crazy comedy act and his leering, howling carry-on. He was nineteen at the time, and had taken to entertainment full-time after a bad motorbike accident which damaged his leg badly and laid him up for quite a while. With his prominent teeth and his old army giggle hat, Chad was a sight to be seen and he had his standard reply to people's thoughtless 'Are they really your own teeth?' He'd come back with 'Is that really your own head?'. Sometimes people think they can say anything they like to an entertainer, and get quite upset if the entertainer has a shot back. Chad copped a lot of flak about his appearance, and that's a bit tough when you're only nineteen. Nevertheless, he had the last laugh. He has lasted as an entertainer.

This year, 1956, we headed for Queensland at the same time as the show run, which is the series of agricultural shows held in sequence up the coast as far as Cairns and finishing back in Brisbane for the Brisbane Exhibition in August. Chad was with us as far as his home town of Howard, but his eccentric view of life differed from the views held by his workmates, and it was better to part company.

We arrived in Townsville to find we were booked at the Theatre Royal during show week, one of the biggest on the run. The showgrounds were in full swing night and day, and we had a circus, two tent shows and another hall show in opposition— if you could call us opposition. I went looking for some local talent to fill out the programme, and came up with an island dance duo. The fair girl and the dark-skinned boy put on a ter- rific act, and Keith Enighi, who was houseboy to the bishop of Townsville, was asked if he would like to join our show. I'd say he barely hesitated except to say that he would have to have permission from the bishop.

Keith described himself as a 'coloured man'. He claimed that his father was Aboriginal or Islander, and his mother was part Chinese. Keith was a good-looking bloke who could do a soft-shoe shuffle, play piano and guitar, sing country songs like 'Don't Let the Stars Get in Your Eyes', and dance the hula. That hula! Keith rubbed oil all over himself till he glistened, put the traditional hibiscus in his black wavy hair, and used his hands to tell the story of the dance.

However, he was also very vague. When he first turned up to join the show, he 'forgot' his hula skirt; a hula without the trim- mings looks funny, not graceful. Keith called on his relations in the district to help him out until his own hula skirt arrived. He didn't have any good clothes for his singing spot, so we advanced money from his pay and he bought good trousers, shirt and swimming trunks for under the hula skirt. We were told that as Keith came from Yarrabah Mission outside Cairns we had to send his pay there, allowing him only 30 shillings a week pocket money. We got into trouble over letting him buy those clothes, but once he had them they couldn't take them off his back.

He had a laugh like a kookaburra and ended up with the nickname of 'Duncan', but Keith knew what was what and could act like Lord Muck when he wanted. We were unaware of the racial tensions in Queensland and Joy unwittingly caused a bit of a stir in Rockhampton. I had some radio work to do, and said I'd meet her and Anne in a local cafeteria-type restaurant for lunch. As Barry was with me, I told Keith to go with Joy and help her look after Anne. Joy walked into the restaurant with Keith Enighi as escort, Keith helping her to her chair, and sit-ting down with her. She couldn't understand the frosty stares she was getting, so she ignored them and enjoyed the chat with Keith and Anne. I realise now that Keith knew exactly what was going on, and his haughty air as he looked down his nose at the menu would have done credit to a movie star.

Gordon Parsons amused Keith mightily. Gordon was on the showgrounds with Tim McNamara, and as the houses hadn't been any good and we were short of an act after parting with Chad, Tim generously said 'Take him and be buggered to you!' when I asked if Gordon could join my show. I should add that he had a grin on his face when he said it. Gordon had been up to his usual antics, and although there hadn't been any decent houses there was always enough money for him and Tim to have a good old session at the bar. One evening Gordon was sleeping in the show tent, and in an alcoholic haze he put his hat along-side his bed and dropped his dental plate in it for safety. One of the dogs hanging round the grounds came sniffing about, and took off with Gordon's teeth. There was pandemonium next morning, and we hauled Gordon off to the dentist, trying to keep straight faces as he moaned about what he was going to do to the culprit when he caught him. Although the mangled dentures were eventually found, everyone had great fun singing a parody of an old Jimmie Rodgers' song the LeGarde Twins were featuring in their show. That's why I can never hear 'He's in the Jailhouse Now' without thinking of Gordon's teeth and 'They're in the Dog's Mouth Now'.

Barry had bought himself a utility, and was using it to pull the small caravan he shared first with Chad, and then with Keith. When Gordon arrived, the three of them would take off in the ute each morning to peals of laughter from Keith over some saying of Gordon's. Keith always had the teapot on the floor between his feet, his enamel mug in his hands being constantly refilled from the pot. If Gordon set Keith laughing backstage his kookaburra laugh would ring out across the stage and we'd be busy trying to shush him. It was a happy time.

Barry was my right-hand man, and good old Baz was always there. He'd developed into a good guitarist, and as well as singing his yodelling songs and doing the comedy he played backing guitar for some songs. With that and Joy's accordion we thought we were coming up in the world musically. From the word go, Baz had enjoyed himself touring and carrying on a bit like a sailor; he had a girl in every town or just about. Only once did he get himself into a spot of bother when he was taken more seriously than he meant, and before he knew what he was getting into, he was engaged to be married.

We began fixing up the small caravan for the soon to be honeymooning couple—painting everything Lotus Pink, making new curtains, and generally outfitting it to suit. But we could never find anything to suit so far as Barry was concerned. A more hangdog-looking bridegroom-to-be you never saw in your life. I held serious discussions with Gordon and Joy, and then approached Barry.

'I don't want to poke my nose in where it's not wanted, Baz, but there seems to be something wrong. Don't you like what we're doing to the van? Or is it something else? Maybe you'd better have a bit of a think about what you're doing 'cause you're a long time married, y'know.'

Barry thought a while. 'Think I'd like a couple of days off when we can manage it,' he replied, and he disappeared up country. He came back to continue being a bachelor for a few more years.

On the Queensland run, we ran into Frank Foster again. He had left the family show and set up on his own, running a show starring the LeGarde Twins country singers. Ted and Tom planned to move to America the next year, and Frankie was looking around to find another name act to headline his show. After seeing how well I went in Townsville, he asked me if I'd go into partnership with him. He'd supply the tent and gear plus his show know-how and I would supply the drawcard and the show. I didn't know about that—we were doing alright on our own and it's always dicey going in with someone else. Our show was getting known, and record stores kept telling me how well the records were doing.

There was one problem for record sales around this time. The record company was now known as EMI, and they were conducting a running battle with radio stations over the payment of a fee for the use of their records. EMI took the view that they invested a heck of a lot of money in the production of artists and records, and radio stations made a lot of money through using those records as entertainment on the air—to attract sponsors and revenue. Therefore they thought it only fair that the radio stations pay an annual fee to recompense them for their outlay. There were other principles involved as well, but it's all a bit too complicated for me to remember the details.

The radio stations in turn took the view that they helped

EMI's sales by playing and therefore publicising the artists and records, and although they had agreed to pay the original fee they viewed the annual increases with alarm. The radio stations decided that they wouldn't pay because they said they didn't know where the increases were going to end. There was a great stand-off, resulting in a ban on EMI's records being played on air. The ban was imposed on 1 December 1955 and we noticed the effect. It was frustrating for us. To begin with, if a radio station wouldn't play my records, my tour advertising lost quite a lot of impact. I had always been able to go into a radio station to do a live interview and maybe play a couple of tracks on air. So it was not only record sales that were affected, it meant that we had to buy extra advertising to publicise our tour dates.

During this time, new record labels came into being, and other recently established labels became much stronger as EMI was no longer the opposition in getting airplay. I had always felt that my records were the key to my having a successful touring career, and therefore I needed another way to let buyers know about a new release. It was because of this and another similar later dispute that we began to carry stocks of my records to sell at the shows. We figured that by selling even a few in each district, word of mouth would spread the word and maybe keep up sales by having people ask for the new record in the shops. As it turned out, we were right.

Nevertheless, we continued on our merry way trying to build up our funds to pay back what we owed on our travelling mansion, all sixteen feet of it. Gordon was a constant source of humour, and in turn he loved hearing about my escapades. Earlier that year we had Aunty Eily travelling with us for a while. I was in fine spirits as Aunty was having the time of her life and telling me how good the show was, how good I was, and all the rest of it. I got a bit carried away with myself, and I was dashing around the stage in the skits, impressing Eily, and making a great thing of chasing Mulga Dan offstage in the blackouts at the end of each sketch. After one such skit, I came tearing offstage into the darkened wings, forgetting that the stage was about four feet higher than the dressing room floor and that there were steps on the side of the stage. I missed the top of the steps, literally flew through the air, and made a three-point landing on my rump at the bottom. The whole hall shook to its foundations but the audience probably thought it was part of the show. The breath was knocked clean out of me, and when I got it back I couldn't even swear because Aunty Eily was there gazing in horror and I didn't want to blot my copybook with Aunty. I had a bruise like a dinnerplate where I couldn't show it off, and I slowed down from a gallop to a crawl for a while after that.

All the way down the Queensland coast, Gordon had been singing a song called 'A Pub with No Beer'. It had been going quite well in the show, but not bringing down any roofs that I noticed. I thought it was the funniest thing I'd ever heard, but no one else seemed to be over impressed. Gordon was not recording at that time, and because I was going to record again early in the next year and was short of one song, I asked him if I could use it. Gordon didn't mind, it was just another of his ditties to him. He had a knack of writing the most dreadful and screamingly funny lyrics and poems.

Apparently, when he was sleeper cutting on the NSW north coast, one of the cutters gave him a couple of verses from a poem about a pub having no beer, which tickled Gordon's fancy. He could just imagine the state of affairs at the local bush pub if such a catastrophe came to pass, so he pottered around with ideas for more verses whenever he happened to think of it. Actually, he finished it one night in the boys' caravan down south, over a bottle of whisky he was sharing with Chad Morgan. For once, Chad showed some sense of history by writing down the words as Gordon drawled them out. I heard them roaring with laughter over in the van until all hours of the night and thought to myself, 'I bet Bazza's not getting much sleep over there.' I took wicked pleasure in waking the two reprobates the next morning, bleary-eyed and hung over.

Chad was very quiet, and Gordon seemed to need sunglasses, but was still capable of having a shot at me.

'Ah, up and getting the fresh air before the mugs get any, Ned?'

'Come on, Ned, the day's half gone. Stay in bed any longer and you'll have bedsores,' I shot back.

Later in the day, when his head felt closer to normal, Gordon said, 'Hey, Ned. I finished that bit of a thing about the pub last night.'

'You finished what?' I replied.

'That pub with no beer thing. You know, the one I was mucking about with; here, I'll sing it for you.'

For the first time I heard 'A Pub with No Beer' right through, complete with a verse which I left out of my original recording of it. I recorded it on April Fool's Day 1957, just after Joy and I had joined Frank Foster on the showgrounds.

Frank turned up at Granville over Christmas and New Year with the news that he was to be married, and to persuade me to join him on the showgrounds. I mentally argued the pros and cons for days and finally said, yes, I'd join him at the Nowra Show in February. Then I spent the rest of the month wondering if I'd done the right thing and driving Joy mad with my endless worrying about it.

The night showing (or one night stands) is more constant work than the showgrounds. With the night show we moved nearly every day, and even if we didn't move the caravans, we still had to go out in the truck and bill the towns ahead. We would then come back to the vans ready to do any repairs, and move on again while doing the show each night. On the showgrounds you usually travelled one or two days a week and you showed either two or three days a week. Certainly, when you work you work hard, doing show after show during the day and most of the nights too.

There was a lot to be said for the showground work, and not the least was that Frank would be our partner and would take a lot of the load of organising and planning off our shoulders. That alone was tempting.

I wanted to record again before taking off on a long run with Frank, especially as I always reckoned that the records would stick to me if anything went wrong with the touring. Things were improving in the studios—artists were no longer required to complete six sides in a three-hour session. It had been broken down to four. I remember someone writing in to *Spurs* to say that Australian artists' product was not as smooth and finished as American artists', and I also remember the reply (written by Joy under another name) pointing out that Guy Mitchell, a top recording artist of the day, had made a big deal about actually completing one side in one full day, whereas Australians had to do six in three hours. It was a wonder that local artists could compete at all, but compete we did with one survey in 1954 stating that Australian country artists outsold Americans two to one.

No wonder I wanted to record again before I set out on another venture. Up north, I had taken the advice of Ron Wills, who was now producing my records, and contacted John Ashe in Townsville. John was an accountant who travelled a lot to properties in the Queensland country areas, and whose hobby was writing either the most beautiful island songs, historical songs, or rude comedy songs. I know it sounds a bit crazy, but John turned his hand to all these different kinds of writing, and as he said, 'When no one wanted to record my songs, I decided to record them myself.'

I first met John in a hotel after the bachelor had completed his shopping. This included a very large cabbage which was

115

parked on the bar along with all the other odds and ends. John was an exceedingly excitable character, and he got more and more worked up as we laid down the law to each other about too many songs about American heroes and none about our own Australian folk heroes.

'What about Harry Morant? What about him?' John thumped the bar. 'Harry the Breaker, he was called, and what do our kids know about him and his story? It should be written down, and it should be recorded! You're the one to do it!' Another thump, and the cabbage began rolling down the bar as John waved his arms and his handkerchief, ignoring the rumble of protests from the other drinkers. By this time, I couldn't get a word in edgeways, let alone tell him to capture the cabbage.

John and his old aunty lived in a little cottage on the side of Castle Hill in Townsville. The back room was a time capsule of family treasures and relics, plus records and sheet music. His piano was used regularly to compose his variety of songs, and John used to entertain at functions in Townsville whenever the spirit moved him. He was a cultured, educated man which made it all the more amazing to listen to his comedy songs, many of which were recorded eventually by Chad Morgan.

I left Townsville that time with a selection of John's songs, and in February I recorded three of them including 'Harry, the Breaker'. I also recorded 'Queensland, State So Fair' (which had started life as 'Victoria, etc.'), and another two of my songs—including 'Gumtrees by the Roadway' that I wrote sitting on a stump in the moonlight at a roadside camp outside Marlborough in Queensland.

I had more songs to record, but first of all I had to front up for the Nowra Show where Frank was setting up the tent and the brand new banners. At the Nowra showgrounds we parked our van near the tent and Frankie's camp beside a box-like trailer, which was surrounded by animals of different kinds. Anne discovered three half-grown kittens and decided she was in paradise, until one scratched her. An old rattletrap of a truck pulled in beside the trailer and we then found that Alan and Alice Hill owned the trailer, plus the various animals, and were the variety act in our new show.

They had three performing dogs; Dear, the ancient tortoise-shell cat who sat up on Alan's hand and begged; Artichoke the angora goat (known as Artie); as well as three ponies. Dixie, the black pony, could unseat just about anyone who tried to ride her, Tony was a cunning little devil, and Goldie was a creamy golden mare who looked a picture in the ring. I came to learn that while the act in the ring was professional and smooth, getting the act from one show to another was the opposite. Alan had Alice under the truck engine eighteen hours out of twenty-four because she was a much better mechanic than he was, and the truck with ponies and goat in the back, plus dogs and cats in the cab and the trailer, staggered from show to show, much to our amazement.

Barry and I helped put up the tent, and when the banners went up I felt a thrill of satisfaction. My first appearance on the showground was as a gee on Frankie's line-up board, and here I was now with fifty feet of colourful banners promoting the Slim Dusty Show. I looked around, and couldn't see any show front as bright and attention getting as ours, and when it came time to pull down at the end of the show, ours was the last tent to come down. To the showies, that meant that we had done the best of any show on the ground and had taken 'king money'. I felt good.

It was a show week full of accidents. Dixie tossed a drunk off and he landed on his nose. In old Johnny's show some seating collapsed and a girl fractured her knee. A big monkey bit an old cleaner's hand the next day and made a mess of it. One of Jack Gill's riders came off a buckjumper and fractured his ankle badly. The next day, the Brahma bull escaped and when Jack roped it, he dislocated his shoulder. I was wondering what would happen next, and was this going to continue? I sincerely hoped not.

We were worrying about Anne, as Joy was in the ticket box and on the stage, and Anne was having a ball. In and out of the ring, and back and forth to the caravan she went while we worked all day. We knew that this wasn't going to work, and Millie told us so when she came down with us the next week to Kangaroo Valley. Anne was four-and-a-half years old, and on show days we worked from ten in the morning till dark. On big show days we worked till ten at night as well.

At Bega Show, Tommy Castles with the 'Magical Variety Show' started up next door.

'Alright, alright, bring out the baby crocodile! Bring out the baby crocodile!' (I never saw any baby crocodile come out the whole time I was on the grounds.) As the crowd gathered, the spiel became hotter: 'When Candy starts to dance we invite you to clap. The more you clap, the more she takes off, the more she takes off, the more sensational the dance becomes. This is the dance that will make your father wish he'd never married your mother' and more of the same. We used to laugh to ourselves and say that father would wish he'd never married mother if mother caught him in there ogling pretty little Candy anyway! Then Anne went missing one day, Joy did a bit of quick thinking, flew into the tent next door and sure enough, there was Anne all eyes as Candy began her 'Dance of the Seven Veils'. Anne was dragged out protesting loudly, as she was a keen dancer and was bent on adding another routine to her repertoire.

Millie consented to come down to the next couple of shows to look after Anne for us. I think she was just as intrigued with life on the showground as we were, but she insisted that 'it was no place for a little girl'. I think she meant that Anne would not have enough supervision when we were working. When Millie finally went home, Anne went with her. While we were within travelling distance to Sydney, we drove back and forth between the show and Anne but eventually the miles became too great and we left Anne in Sydney with Millie and Mac while we went to Queensland with the show.

For the first years, Anne joined us whenever we came through Sydney and travelled with us to the Adelaide Royal Show and to the Melbourne Royal Show. She came to Tasmania with us and joined our square dancers in the show. Her first day at school was a big event in our lives—we flew from St George in western Queensland to be with her. It's hard to leave a little girl like that, especially when Anne had been with us on the road from the very first.

Before taking off on the show runs up north, I went back and forth to the studios to record. One of these sessions became a landmark in my life, and in recording history.

Chapter Nine

A PUB WITH
NO BEER

There's nothing so lonesome, morbid or drear
Than to stand in the bar of a pub with no beer . . .
'A PUB WITH NO BEER' GORDON PARSONS

I put down the 'Pub' in the EMI studios with Ron Wills, as producer, supervising. At this stage, I had Dick Carr and his Buckaroos as a studio backing band, but for the 'Pub' all I used was Reg Robinson on the slap (double) bass. Although I wanted to do another take, 'Mr Wills' was sure the first one was quite up to standard and should go through. I am still conscious of the slight roughness in one line, but who am I to complain when I think of the 'Pub's' success?

It was released on a Regal Zonophone 78 record in September 1957, and it began selling like hot cakes—despite it being the era of early rock'n'roll, when country was being pushed into the doldrums. This was the scene of Johnny O'Keefe, Col Joye and the Joy Boys, of Brian Henderson's *Bandstand* television show, and all the rest of the rockers who dominated the airwaves. Country music radio shows had all but disappeared from city radio stations, replaced by disc jockeys playing all the latest rock hits and refusing to play anything remotely connected with country.

I say they refused to play anything country, and I say, too, that the hit parades of the day were not legitimate—in that they were supposed to be based on sales. My recording of the 'Pub' had sold 30,000 copies compared with some rockers' sales of 500, and yet it was not even played on city stations while the same rocker headed the hit parade. When the sales hit 50,000, an unprecedented figure in Australia at that time, Ron Wills lost his patience at a record and radio function in Melbourne.

He stood up and said his piece. He asked them to explain how they had the hide to ignore the sales of the 'Pub', how they justified their hit parade listings when they were not playing the biggest selling record ever known in Australian recording history up to that time. The only people who did play the 'Pub' prior to his protest were Alan Lappan in Brisbane and Bob Rogers—who came to Sydney from Brisbane and wanted a gimmick to consolidate his position as 'new boy on the block'. His peers told him straight that he was committing commercial suicide to persist in playing Slim Dusty, but he stuck to his guns. He had better taste than I did, because I thought the 'Pub' was a B side for the single whereas it turned out to be the A side, and how!

City radio had been shown up by Ron Wills, and to save face they put the 'Pub' on their playlists. It soared to the top of the hit parades and stayed there for a total of six months. By the early 1960s, it had sold well over 50,000 copies in Australia and topped 270,000 in the UK. It was narrowly held out of top place on Britain's hit parades, but topped the Irish parades for ten weeks (the Irish must have recognised the Irish in the words as well as in the singer). It was released in Europe and played there, later being recorded by locals in Germany with the words translating as 'The Pub Where I Have No Money'. It raced up the charts in Montreal, Canada, where they'd had a brewery strike. It was pushed out of the American charts even after being predicted a hit in *Billboard*, the music industry magazine, because, as the disc jockeys pronounced, it was about an unsavoury subject. What a laugh! I had earlier recorded my version of an American song called 'Cocaine Blues' which I changed to 'Whisky Blues' to suit Australian conditions. Apparently it was alright for them to play something about cocaine, but not a song about beer or the lack of it. I can't help suspecting that the nationality of the singer may have had something to do with it.

At the time, I didn't know any of this was going on. I was out on the road and had my first inkling of the 'Pub's' roaring success when I drove back into Ipswich (near Brisbane in Queensland) and some showie mates began congratulating me on my hit record.

'What record?'

'The one on the hit parades, *you* know the one.'

'But I don't, come on, *what* hit record?'

'"A Pub with No Beer", of course. It's a beauty! Congratulations, mate.' I couldn't believe it until I actually heard it on the city hit parades and began seeing the increased reaction to the song when I performed it in the show. Whenever I switched on a radio, up and down the whole east coast and inland throughout the eastern states, I heard my voice singing the tragic story of 'A Pub with No Beer'.

Gordon called on Nicholson's and APRA quite regularly and bought himself a flash car. He was as astonished as I was, and when some recording executive cheerily referred to me as the 'white-haired boy' at EMI, I couldn't quite believe that, either. Country singers, or 'hillbillies' as we were mostly called then, were a bit low class for recording engineers who preferred to give the impression that they spent their time recording something worthwhile like classics. They didn't like to admit that the gently despised 'hillbillies' were paying the way for a lot of recordings of much 'higher class'.

For me, this marked the pinnacle of my success. As a kid, I had envied Tex Morton's star position in showbusiness—his tailored suits, the big car, the crowds clamouring for his songs and for his autograph—all these trappings of success now became available to me. Nulla Creek seemed a long way behind me; the years of struggling and making do had paid off. My dream of being a success on record had come true. All my records on Regal Zonophone had sold well, and the touring of the past three years had helped spread my name as a stage as well as a recording artist. On top of all this, the 'Pub' was a blockbuster of a record that took my name into every household in Australia, the UK, Europe, Canada and the United States.

When I wanted footlights on the stage, I bought them. No longer did I have to make them. Old Bumbling Bertha was a bit low key for the 'Pub with No Beer Man' (as Frankie advertised me), so I invested in a Ford Customline. It was one of the first automatic transmission cars released in Australia, and had a red, white and blue paint job that knocked your eyes out. I no longer had to get my stage clothes on a buy now, pay later system. I could pay cash on the spot. What's more, I had money in the bank and soon had enough to buy a big caravan to live in.

We were showing in Ingham, North Queensland, when Frank came around the back of the tent where I was preparing for the next house.

'Slim, I don't know what to make of this. There's a family out the front wanting to see you. They say their father wrote the "Pub", not Gordon.'

I stared at him in disbelief. 'They must be wrong. They have to be. I heard Gordon finishing the "Pub" in my caravan down at Wagga, you know that.'

Frank was looking worried. 'These people aren't idiots, mate. They're a nice family, not mugs. They seem to know what they're talking about alright.'

I'd never come up against anything like this in my life, and I didn't know what to think, so I went around the front and met the Sheahans. Frank was right, they were a nice family and they did know what they were talking about. It was an amazing story, and with Gordon's permission I have told the truth about the 'Pub' as I know it.

Shaun Sheahan's dad, old Dan Sheahan, was a cane farmer from Long Pocket near Ingham in far North Queensland. Dan was Irish born, and had the Irish knack of ironic humour as well as a built-in knack for putting that humour into story and into verse. The *North Queensland Register*, printed in Townsville, was a *Bulletin*-type weekly paper which published stories and reminiscences from old-timers and verse from contributors. In January 1944, the *North Queensland Register* published Dan Sheahan's poem 'A Pub Without Beer', written by Dan about the old Day Dawn Hotel in Ingham during the days of beer rationing in the Second World War. It was pure Irish humour translated into an Australian situation and put into verse.

The *North Queensland Register* was read widely throughout rural Queensland, and down as far as the border of New South Wales. Many country and bush blokes used to learn verse off by heart, and recite it at gatherings or by the fire at night, and some sleeper cutter from the north coast of New South Wales had apparently picked up Dan's poem. Gordon Parsons was timber cutting with Joe Cooper's team at the time, and he thought these couple of verses were the sort of thing you see on the walls of the local pub . . . just like all the sayings he incorporated into 'My Pal Alcohol'. Gordon was always messing around with ridiculous bits of funny sayings that he'd end up singing around the place. One sling-off piece was the maudlin 'The bride she died at the altar, the bridegroom died next day'. He'd screw up his face and hold forth while we laughed our heads off.

Dan's poem was published in 1944 and Gordon only wrote the song in early 1956, so he most certainly didn't see the original. Comparing the two versions, Gordon could have seen the first two verses only, or had them recited to him. There is little or no similarity after the first two verses of each version.

It makes me mad if anyone insinuates that Gordon pinched the 'Pub' from Dan Sheahan. It was nothing of the sort—it was a set of coincidences and circumstances where Gordon reworked two verses he thought were pub lore, and then he wrote the rest of the lyrics around the characters he knew at the Taylor's Arm Hotel out of Macksville on the north coast. He had no idea that he had written what was to become a worldwide hit, and there were times in later life when he said he wished he'd never heard of it—it had caused so much controversy.

I became mates with Dan Sheahan, and we had many good yarns in the caravan behind the tent when I came through with the show, still singing the 'Pub'. Dan said he was comfortably off and didn't particularly want the money from the 'Pub', but he would like some credit for it. I'd like to think that he now has that, and knew he had it, before he died at a ripe old age of ninety-odd. I've set to music and recorded other verses of Dan's such as 'When You're Short of a Smoke' and 'The Last of the Valley Mail' from a little booklet he gave me. He'd recite his poems to me in a rich Irish brogue that got richer and thicker with each rum, until I gave up understanding the words and just listened to his voice. He was an interesting bloke, old Dan.

Gordon Parsons wrote 'A Pub with No Beer' as it stands now. He made it into the song with all the extra, vivid characters, but he always acknowledged that he had seen or heard a couple of verses about a pub that had no beer. It is clear now that those verses had made their way by word of mouth down the coast from far North Queensland to the timber country of northern coastal New South Wales. That's the way that folklore works, I guess.

The travelling showmen of Australia have a unique history. When I first joined with Frank on the showgrounds there were all sorts of rides of course, but there were ghost houses, variety shows like old Johnny Foster's, music shows like ours, rock'n'roll music shows, girlie shows with dancers and strippers, boxing tents, magical illusion shows . . . you name it, the showground had it there for you. Many of the music and variety shows have disappeared now, to be replaced by bigger and better rides. Much of the magic of Sideshow Alley and its tent shows has disintegrated, to become the Midway of the dodgem cars and other rides.

The North Run, as it was called, was at one time the biggest exodus of show people in the world. The North Run was the run of shows up the Queensland coast, culminating in the Cairns Show where the Showmen's Ball was held. Then the mass of showpeople with their trucks, caravans and gear would head south to Brisbane for the famous Brisbane Exhibition, or Ekka.

In 1957, I did the North Run for the first time. The Queensland roads were famous or infamous, I should say. Much of the Redex trials were held over Queensland roads, and one horror stretch was between Rockhampton and Mackay, and another between Proserpine and Bowen. The showmen pulled their caravans, and crawled their semis with the Big Wheel or the Wheel of Death loaded on top, over these horrific roads from one show to the next. The alternative was the show train.

We travelled by road up to Cairns, but loaded the trucks and caravans onto the show train for the return trip to Brisbane. We had seats booked in the carriage, but as the caravan was loaded onto a flat top behind the carriage, we thought it was good fun to stay in the caravan and travel through the countryside, 'surveying the surrounding panorama' to quote another Gordon Parsons saying.

Old Digger McCarthy used to supply the ice for our caravans at every long stop, and would do any shopping you needed. Of course, you paid commission and you didn't expect any change either, so it was sensible to give him as close to the correct amount as you could. If you complained about the prices, as one showman did, you'd be charged twice as much

Nurse Kirkpatrick in full
uniform with 'one of her
babies'.

My uncle, Sgt George
Kirkpatrick, MM.

My father, Dave Kirkpatrick.
'Noisy Dan' on his best
behaviour.

My mother, Mary, with my
cousin, Philip.

My old home in Nulla Nulla Creek as it is today. You can see the plaque on the rock commemorating it as 'Melody Ranch'.

ABOVE: Shorty Ranger in his first outfit, about 1944.

RIGHT: SD and Shorty in civvies, in about 1942 or '43.

Aged about 15 years with my
first guitar and a fan letter in
my pocket.

This was how I looked when
Joy and I first met around
1950.

An unusual shot of Buddy Williams and Tim McNamara in
civvies—not a hat in sight! Slim Jim Pike is standing behind
them.

PARLOPHONE

FROM THE OFFICES OF:

The Gramophone Company Ltd. (Incorporated in England)

Columbia Graphophone (Aust.) Pty. Ltd.

The Parlophone Company Ltd. (Incorporated in England)

Telephone: UM 6671
Telegrams: "COLGRAF." Sydney

2 Parramatta Road.
HOMEBUSH, N.S.W.

IN YOUR REPLY
PLEASE REFER TO.....AK/VM

18th October, 1946.

Slim Dusty, Esq.,
"Melody Ranch,"
NULA NULA Via BELLBROOK.

Dear Sir:

Following on our conversation when last you
were in Sydney, I now have pleasure in advising
that I am in a position to offer you a recording session on the basis we discussed.

Would you kindly let me know when you will be
in Sydney next in order that a recording date
may be arranged in advance.

With compliments,

Yours truly,

Record Sales Manager.
(A.Kerr)

This letter changed my life. On 19 November 1946 I made my first
commercial recording for EMI.

Arch Kerr in later years.

That big trip to Sydney in 1946. *Left to right:* SD, Philip and Victor. Victor signed my first recording contract because I was under twenty-one years of age.

Taken in Kempsey on my way home from recording 'When the Rain Tumbles Down in July', in November 1946.

The McKean sisters, Joy and Heather, when I met them in 1950.

Joy and Heather with their parents, 'Mac' and Millie McKean.
This was the twenty-first birthday party I missed out on.

Leaving St Mark's, Granville, after the ceremony.

Gordon Parsons in his rodeo days in the 1950s.

'Betsy' – my first car. 'Betsy' was a 1938 Ford Deluxe.

'Betsy', loaded to the hilt crossing the flooded creek south of Nabiac, New South Wales, in 1954.

'Bumbling Bertha' and our first caravan, 1955.

Our full show onstage at Coffs Harbour Jetty Theatre in 1956.
ABOVE: *Left to right:* Barry Thornton, Slim, Joy, Keith Enighi,
Gordon Parsons. BELOW: *Left to right:* Keith Enighi, Slim, Joy, Barry
Thornton (as Mulga Dan) and Gordon Parsons.

Townsville at show time, in July 1956. *Left to right:* Barry Thornton (Mulga Dan), Gordon Parsons, Tom and Ted Legarde, Tim McNamara, Joy, Slim, Glen Davis.

'Mack' Cormack, my friend and mentor.

Our first flash caravan and car, on the showground in about 1960.

ABOVE: Camped at Collarenebri, New South Wales, in early 1955.

Keith Enighi dancing the hula.

ABOVE: Our show front at Maryborough, Victoria. The gold record on the banner was inlaid with real gold leaf.

Anne and David at the model of 'A Pub with no Beer' near Bothwell, Tasmania, 1961.

'Old Thunder' at an outback park. The door at the side opened to a loading area for chairs, sidewalls and gear. The rest of the body consisted of two berth living quarters fitted out like a caravan.

'Princess Firecloud' (Merle Foster) in full regalia.

Finale of the touring show in the mid-1960s.
Left to right: Gordon Parsons, Mulga Dan, Slim, Joy, Margaret Mile, Michael Cooke.

Same period and same cast. Note our updated sound equipment.

In the Solomon
Islands, 1969.

On the showgrounds. 'Old Thunder's' original
painted body in the background, in 1962.

Aunty Una—laughing
as usual.

next time. But Digger's services were invaluable when you were showing the capitals, because everyone was working flat out every day and night in the tent and the staff had to be fed.

My first Brisbane Exhibition was quite an experience. We set up on ground adjoining old Johnny Foster, and many were the squabbles between Frank and Pikey, his youngest brother. It was showground etiquette to wait till your neighbour had finished his line-up before you started yours, and it was expected that you would keep your dragging volume down to a minimum while next door's line-up was going on. Just for the hell of it, either Frank or Pikey would butt in now and then and it would be on for young and old round the back of the tent. I used to be concerned at first when I heard the rows going on, but after a while I realised that the brothers were having the time of their lives even if there was a strong rivalry underlying the argument. It wasn't just the brothers who could make the air thick with accusations and roars—you should have heard Frank and his bride first thing in the morning!

We sat bolt upright in bed on our first morning camped on the showground, next door to Frank's caravan. Merle was never too happy first thing in the morning, but the shrieks blasting out the caravan window taught us a lesson. If we wanted to sleep in, or even have a peaceful morning, we camped as far away from them as possible. It seemed to be part of life, and we got so used to it that we'd give each other reports.

'Wow, there goes that new jar of face cream. She got him, too. No, she just missed. Bet she has another go.'

Frank would needle Merle to shrieking point, then tear out of the caravan chuckling to himself. Merle took after him one day. Dressed ready to start work, she was in her Princess Firecloud costume of Indian fringes and beading, complete with a really spectacular feather headdress we'd had specially made. A sharp little tomahawk was the finishing touch, and it nearly finished Frank. He was dressed in his cowboy jacket and hat and high-heeled boots, and when Merle took after him screaming and yelling that she was going to 'kill him', he pounded down Sideshow Alley flat to the boards with Merle after him. The customers thought they were seeing a real Cowboys and Indians production. Before long, Frank and Merle were laughing so much they couldn't keep running, and that was the end of another of their rows.

We were beginning six years of showground life, years that were an education in themselves. They were years when my wife and I had to weather some tough times in our marriage and partnership. We were different from many of the old-time showpeople in our attitude to marriage and family, in that we were a working partnership from the word go, rather than a married couple where the wife stayed in the caravan with her girlfriends when she wasn't working in the ticket box or on the line-up board. Showmen and women had strong marriages and families, but there was also the underlying acceptance of 'anything goes'. Blind eyes were usually turned to any bloke having a bit of a run around when the circumstances were right, and you might hear someone remark: 'Looks like he's got a bit of brush on the side.' Actually, to squire one of the girls working in the show to the pictures or the races was seen to be alright if you could legitimately say that your wife or fiancée was otherwise occupied, or even working.

This was where I just about came undone.

In 1958, about Easter time, EMI presented me with Australia's first, and only, gold 78 rpm record to mark the phenomenal sales of the 'Pub'. It was Australia's first blockbuster record, Australia's first international hit, and I was so proud of the achievement when I finally realised what it all meant that I was in a state of shock. Our show banners now featured a huge gold record painted with real gold leaf, and the crowds simply flocked to the show. We worked the Royal Easter Show in Sydney, and on the main show day we hardly lined-up at all, as the crowds just waited outside for the previous show to finish before they filed in and took their places around the ring.

I was in demand for radio and television appearances, newspaper and magazine interviews, and parties. For the first time in my life, I went to nightclubs. All in all, I was a bit relieved to leave Sydney and get back to the show routine and follow the shows until it was time once again to head north on the Queensland North Run.

In Sydney, where we hired several usherettes to work through the Royal Easter Show, we recruited three to work and travel with us for the coming North Run. Merle was pregnant with her first child, and would not be able to continue dancing in the show so a lass called Kerry took her place as Princess Firecloud. Then two blondes took the jobs as permanent usherettes and moved into the girls' caravan with Kerry.

Joy was also pregnant with our second child, but as it was not due till June, she kept working in the ticket box and hid her rounded figure behind her piano accordion onstage. As we headed north for Queensland, it became more and more usual for Frank and me to spend time over at the girls' caravan talking about all the good spots they'd see up north and how much they'd enjoy the Showmen's Ball in Cairns.

I had decided to give up smoking, and carried bottles of olives everywhere to try and stem the craving for nicotine. Joy loved olives too, and as there was a constant supply on hand, ate plenty. She didn't know that the salt content was sending her blood pressure sky high, and by the time she saw a doctor at Bundaberg she was ordered to hospital. There was no way she was going to stay in Bundaberg on her own, because her mother and Anne were coming to Rockhampton to meet us and be with us until after the baby was born. So she had to go to bed, and stay there all day and every day that we weren't travelling until we reached Rockhampton, where she would remain while I went on with the show.

She could see no reason why I should have to stay in the

caravan with her all the time, and when I went out with Frank we usually took two girls with us. That was the start of it, and by the time we got a bit further north, Frank and I took separate cars to escort the blondes. I don't think my wife realised this or she certainly would have had something to say about it! Joy was preoccupied with the coming birth and her health situation, and while we'd both had plenty of propositions in the past four years, we'd laughed them off and refused to take them seriously. Joy had thrown things at me in fun, though one did hit me and I took offence; in turn, I'd kept an eye on any man taking too much notice of my wife, but we'd usually end up swapping notes on events and hugging each other.

Joy didn't want to be a spoilsport. She wasn't well enough to go out too much at the time. The baby was due within the next couple of weeks, and she didn't know exactly how much time I was spending over at the girls' caravan. Millie and Anne arrived at Rockhampton, and our son David was born on the main show day, 19 June 1958. I remember taking her to hospital in the morning, working all day at the show, and tearing up to the hospital during the tea break to be told that I had a son. I also remember telling Joy she was wonderful, and then racing back to the showground where I kept singing out 'It's a boy!' as the showies called enquiries during my dash along Sideshow Alley back to the tent. I was very, very excited and happy.

I left Rockhampton with the show, and moved on to Mackay and then to Proserpine, still living the life of Riley. I was young, famous, successful in my career and had a good-looking blonde on my arm when I went out on the town. The family was pushed well into the background.

Joy, with Millie, Anne and David, travelled by train to join me. They travelled in a carriage full of Italian canecutters going north for the sugarcane harvest, who were all interested in the new baby. Joy huddled in a corner to feed the baby, and was glad to see me and her caravan home.

I was pleased to see my family again, but was easily convinced that as Merle and Joy had their hands full with new babies, they were not able to join in the social life of the grounds and so the indiscretion with the blondes continued. It wasn't long before Joy was able to take a breath and look around her, and ask why she wasn't being invited out instead of the usherette.

'Well, how can you leave David when you're breastfeeding him?' I was righteous, but still a bit uneasy.

'I can do something about that with a bottle,' was her rejoinder.

'I don't think you should. Anyway, we're only going to the pictures and there's nothing that much on.' I always had an excuse.

By the time we reached Cairns, Joy had decided that it was time she got back to the show and kept more of an eye on things. I, too, had decided that I would come to my senses. I realised that this had to stop. Joy didn't deserve this treatment, she'd done nothing to me.

I was in the car with the blonde lass, and I looked at her with new eyes. She wasn't a bad type of girl, but she wasn't averse to a bit of a fling with a married man either.

I told her that I was finished, I was doing the wrong thing by my wife and I was ashamed of myself. I told her that I was doing the wrong thing by her too, and I hoped she'd understand what I was saying.

'I always knew it would end up like this, anyhow,' she said. 'You're not the sort for this kind of thing.'

For what it was worth, I took comfort in her words.

Since then, I've looked but I haven't touched (well, hardly), and Joy has been a lot quicker off the mark if she has sensed any nonsense going on. There have been times when there has been some very straight talking, but the ongoing commitment between us is strong and never ending. We understand each other, and no matter how we argue or disagree, at the end of the day we stick together.

Chapter Ten
A TRAVELLING SHOWMAN

*I joined a tent show as a kid, with a dream
and an old guitar ...*
'OLD-TIME COUNTRY HALLS' SLIM DUSTY

Once Joy and I had straightened out our differences, we set out to enjoy ourselves on the showgrounds. I swear Frank and the other showmen knew every fishing spot, hole, lake or river on the east coast and once they moved into Western Australia and the Territory they soon had them mapped out as well. The showgrounds were a big, travelling community which moved on each week. When we got within reach of another show circuit, different shows would join ours and some of our team would leave to go off on a different run. There was always news of how the shows were doing, what the fishing and/or shooting was like this year, and who was going on what run.

The showgrounds were like a big tent city, with the caravans parked behind the tent shows, rides and joints. With so much canvas, it is no wonder that showies are paranoid about the risk of fire. On a Victorian run one year, on a cool spring night, flames flared from a canvas knock 'em joint along Sideshow Alley. It was like kicking an ants' nest! We raced out

132

of our caravans, ran along Sideshow Alley and pulled down the canvas, threw buckets of water and smothered it with blankets while others organised hoses. There were never enough taps on the showgrounds to cope with the demands of so many house-holds, let alone an emergency like this.

In the midst of the smoke and the puzzlement over the cause of the fire, some women began screaming and calling out, 'Over there! Look, over there!' There was another flare, this time bigger, faster and angrier. We couldn't save that one, and the owner was in furious tears. By now, we knew we had an arsonist on the grounds and if he started a big one that we couldn't stop, it would leap from one canvas building to another and it would be almost impossible for the caravans behind to get out in time.

All night, we sat in or in front of our tents and caravans with shotguns and rifles at the ready. It was a sad time when the arsonist was finally caught, as he turned out to be the young son of a respected show family who were devastated by the discovery. Being one of our own there was no legal action taken, but despite the boy's shame and unhappiness, his father gave him a terrific hiding with his fists and the youth left the next day.

In the midst of all this, I was still writing and so was Joy. One day, I was reading an article about Aboriginal stockmen and it inspired me to write 'The Saddle is His Home' which is mostly referred to as 'Tall, Dark Man in the Saddle'. My Aboriginal friends tell me that this was the first song to acknowledge the part they and their forebears have played in the development of the cattle industry in this country. We'd have been up against it if Aboriginal men and women hadn't taken to stock-work with such a will.

I used to record at the beginning of the year, and again at the end, to fit in with the touring. On the road, I'd write and collect songs from people like John Ashe and Mack Cormack. One of the first songwriters whose song I recorded was Wave Jackson. Wave couldn't play guitar, was not the world's best singer and his sense of timing was a bit here and there, but his words in particular were spot on. Waverley wrote about what he saw and what he did in his everyday life. One of his later songs, 'Arcadia Valley', documented the end of an era of big holdings as the valley was being cut up into small blocks.

The first writer I met, although he didn't know he was one, was Mack Cormack. I'm proud to think that I was the one to bring out his hidden talent, and to put his words to music. I've mentioned John Ashe from Townsville earlier, and over the years I've recorded several of his songs. After the 'Pub', I recorded two more of Gordon Parsons' songs with the Country Rockers who were, in fact, Col Joye's Joy Boys. At the time, I was beginning to think I was a bit of a rocker but the ballads kept coming between me and rock'n'roll!

My old mate, Shorty, sent me a song which I recorded. It was 'Winter Winds', Shorty's best. By now, Barry was playing good guitar and he backed me onstage and on record. 'Winter Winds' has become a classic Barry Thornton guitar example. By the time we recorded this, Dick Carr had formed a studio band consisting of himself on Spanish guitar and electric steel, Herbie Marks on keyboards and piano accordion, Reg Robinson on double bass and someone like Tommy Spencer on drums. At times, Gordon Scott played fiddle. Barry played lead electric guitar on nearly every track I recorded throughout these years.

I recorded songs that Dad had taught me, songs from Joy, Shorty, John Ashe, Dan Sheahan, Wave Jackson and Gordon Parsons. Then in 1958, I recorded my first Henry Lawson poem that I had set to music. It was 'Sweeney', and I felt such satisfaction in singing the Lawson words that I worked out a setting for another of my dad's favourites, 'Middleton's Rouseabout', and later recorded that, too.

Things were changing in the record industry. The old Regal Zonophone label was being phased out, to be replaced by the new 45 rpm discs. Although I was sad to see it go, I was mollified by seeing our Australian country tracks being released on the same labels as pop tracks. Another paling in the fence between country and mainstream was knocked down. But the big thing was the introduction of the 33⅓ rpm long-playing record which held twelve tracks, and in 1960 I made my first long-play album. I had to come up with twelve tracks for this, on top of the sixteen I had recorded earlier that year for singles. I was short of songs, so I used six American songs, some Jack O'Hagan, some of Shorty's, and some of my own.

This was a big deal for me—a whole new ball game, as they say. Eric Dunn was Ron Wills' assistant, and he had to organise a cover photo for the album. Taking the song 'Roving Gambler' as a theme, Eric set up the cover shot at the photographer's. There I was, sitting at the card table with a handful of cards and a gorgeous redhead alongside who was looking at the gambler opposite. The big gambler was Eric Dunn, all kitted out in black hat, cigar and riverboat gambler-style coat, while keeping his face well out of camera reach. The redhead was his secretary, Beverley, who had been pegged into her too big saloon girl costume by a row of plastic pegs all down her back. She wasn't game to move, and I wasn't either. Her knee was in my ribs and I could hardly breathe. When I think of that photo shoot, I can't help grinning at the way we used to do things. Just imagine a record executive and his secretary acting as models in today's set-up. Look at the fun and variety of work they're missing out on!

I enjoyed working in the studio with a band of musicians, although I've had difficulty over the years in getting some of them to play the kind of music I wanted. I even had the original Delltones singing on some of my tracks, and out on tour, I missed the more solid band backing. So when Joy was going to Sydney for a week to see Anne and do some business, I told her to get a bass-playing friend to help her select and buy an electric bass, which was all the go in the rock bands.

'And who's going to play that?' she enquired.

'You are, dear,' I replied. That floored her, and she didn't have much to say for quite a while.

She came back with a Hofner 'Beatle' bass, and after a few lessons, Joy became the first electric bass player on the grounds and, no doubt, the first in any country band around. A couple of years later, she had to substitute for rocker Johnny Devlin's bass player for a couple of days, and after blowing three speakers in one day decided that she wasn't cut out for rock'n'roll after all. However, she became a good, solid bass player who followed my every vocal movement onstage just as Bazza did, and it was Joy and Barry who provided the backing for the marathon recording of 'The Man from Snowy River' which ran for nearly eight minutes.

Before we started, I warned them.

'I can't do this over and over again, it's just too long. So concentrate like hell, don't make any blues.'

This was in the days when, if you made a mistake, you had to do the whole song over again from the start. Barry and Joy played that whole song, and I sang it, and we put it down on the first take.

Ron Wills' next project was to cash in on the popularity of the singalong albums which were selling so well. 'Slim,' he said, 'I think you could do a good singalong of Australian songs, don't you?'

I hadn't given it any thought, and I wasn't all that keen. It was a totally new concept for me, and it entailed a lot of work in finding the songs and putting together the brackets so that the songs would suit in key, style and format. So I tried to get out of it, 'Ah, well . . . I suppose it sounds a good idea, but I wonder . . .'

Ron knew when he had me beat, but he also knew he was right. 'Good. I'm glad you'll take it on. I think it'll be a winner for you.'

136

It was a winner, the 'Aussie Singsong'. It also caused heaps of trouble between Joy and myself because she landed the job of contacting and visiting publishers to get copies of old songs we didn't know, and finding some we'd never heard of.

'What's this—"The Bells of St Mary's"?' I was beginning to splutter when this one and 'Bless This House' were being included.

'You can do it, love. Of course you can. You've got a good, clear voice, and it's just a matter of learning it properly.' My wife has always had a rose-coloured view of my capabilities, and a determination that I should take the same rose-coloured view, despite the fact that I'm a pessimist from way back. I beat her on this one, though. I asked Jimmy Parkinson to stand in and do the solos. I was somewhat bewildered a few years later when a choir master congratulated me on my excellent tenor voice. Indeed, I was quite flattered, until I realised he was referring to Jimmy's rendition of 'The Bells of St Mary's'. On this album, the group of backing singers consisted of Jimmy, Neil Williams, and Ross Higgins. Every one of them was a top soloist in his own right, but they hopped in and filled my request that the recording sound like a team of blokes in the pub having a bit of a singalong.

I didn't like 'Another Aussie Singsong' half as much, mainly because this time we couldn't get the singers we wanted, so the musical director hired a quartet. One of the blokes had a voice like a bull and he loved hearing it, so he hung on every finish longer than anyone else, hogged the mike and generally wrecked the sound so far as I was concerned. EMI's new musical director was Englishman Geoff Harvey, whose very first job was to deal with me. Poor Geoff didn't know what was in store for him.

Joy and I had collected a group of songs we liked, and put them into the brackets we thought would suit. So far, so good. Geoff organised the band, and was going to direct the musicians and supervise the arrangements, hoping everything would go faster and more smoothly than previously.

'Slim, what key do you sing this in?' Geoff queried.

'Well, I don't know what key it is, but I put the capo on *here*, and play in E shapes [shape of fingers in an E chord] and when I get to the chorus . . .'

Geoff threw his hands in the air and walked away in despair. 'Do it your own bloody way, then,' he said. 'It sounds like F sharp to me.' Geoff's a great bloke, and he's such an Aussie now that I think we can forgive him for having been born in England (only joking, Geoff).

It was just after recording the first singalong album that I recorded 'Return of the Stockman', one of Stan Coster's songs. I met Stan in a pub at Longreach. Dot Coster had insisted Stan see me and tell me about the songs he was writing. I said, 'Yes, great. Come on down after the show and let's hear a couple.' It was two years later at Rockhampton before I saw Stan again. He apologised for not keeping the appointment with me. 'You know how these things happen, mate. Things sort of got going in the pub, and I just didn't make it in time.'

I knew quite well 'how these things happen'. I wasn't a mate of Gordon's and Tim's for nothing. 'Never mind. Send me some on tape, and I'll see how I go with them,' I said.

Just the same, it was another two years before the tape turned up. It was worth the wait. On it was one of the best collections of bush songs that had been sent to me up to that time. I have recorded nearly all of them over the years, but by the time I recorded the first one of Stan's, I had left the showgrounds.

We played each year at all of the Royal Shows; Sydney, Melbourne and Adelaide were regular events for us, and in 1961 we went to Perth and also up to Darwin. Each February, we played the Hobart Regatta, taking the show across Bass Strait on the *Princess of Tasmania* and night showing Tasmanian towns while waiting for the Regatta in February. It was in Hobart in 1961 that Pauline joined the show as usherette. She also took on the cooking of meals for the blokes in the show, Barry being one of them. Baz was most impressed by Pauline, and as I tell him, he was even more impressed by her cooking, which is top rate. They had a great wedding in Hobart during the 1962 Regatta, and when we returned to the mainland, Barry had a new caravan waiting for his bride. No Lotus Pink in sight, either.

My dream of having a band onstage with me would go up one minute and down the next. When Johnny Devlin was on tour with us, his band would play for me as well. Warren Smith, saxophonist, led his band and was the perfect example of the entrepreneur he turned out to be when he eventually opened his successful booking agency in Sydney. John's drummer at one time was Gary, a jeweller by profession and a rock drummer by inclination. Gary's misfortune was that he had the face of a rock star, and Warren was determined to make one out of him. Gary didn't want to be a rock star, he wanted to play drums. Warren insisted Gary could sing; Gary was sure he couldn't. Of course, Warren won, to a certain extent. Gary stood up and sang Rick Nelson's hit 'Mary Lou', all the girls in the audience sighed, and Warren reckoned he had a money-making star on his hands. He began to enlarge Gary's repertoire, Gary began to mutiny, and John nearly lost his drummer on the spot. Finally, John called Warren off, and Gary went back to his drums and happy obscurity.

Even with John's line-up onstage, Barry played lead guitar, and after one bass player grumbled about my complaints that he was two frets out of tune, Joy played bass. When we went back to the country runs where we didn't use the extra rock acts, I hired a drummer to fill in behind Baz and Joy. Stuart Heinz was one of the first drummers we used on the show-grounds, and his dry wit got him in and out of trouble constantly. Stuart was useless where physical or manual jobs were concerned, and we generally kept him out of the way. However, we'd had to sack Bluey, one of the current warbs. Bluey had been doctoring the petrol dockets, and then he helped himself to money from one of the other warbs' wallet without asking. The girls in the show were finding him a nuisance as well.

'Well, Stuart,' I said. 'We've got to put the tent up and there's just you and Barry. Great responsibilities rest upon you. Lot of work to be done, you know.'

'Oh, sure,' Stuart replied. 'You might as well give Barry the day off, too. He'll only get in my way.'

We had booked a new act. Marlene Oakley was a rope spinner and sharpshooter, who shot out candle flames, balloons, and best of all, shot chalks from between the knuckles of whoever would hold them for her. She even shot balloons while she was blindfolded—shooting from between her knees. Now Marlene was a very good shot, and demonstrated her ability before asking who was going to stand there and hold the chalks for her?

No one volunteered, and everyone in sight fell over their feet stepping backwards. Stuart was the slowest to move, as usual, so he got the job amidst much protest. The first day he was literally prepared to die, but when he didn't, and when his workmates eyed him with admiration, he fronted up the second day dressed to the nines and proud as a peacock. Just the same, he worked out that compensation would be £100 per knuckle.

Part of the assistant's job was to tie on Marlene's blindfold for her. In his early days as Marlene's assistant, Stuart was so clumsy that first of all, he couldn't put on the blindfold without dropping it on the floor. Then he couldn't get it tied properly and when it *was* done up, he couldn't get it off. He ended up reefing it over her head, nearly pulling out her hair by the roots. After her opening act, his next job was to pick up her ropes. To fill in time while Stuart cleared away the ropes, Barry, who was compering, made a few cracks about Stuart's 'experienced handling of the ropes. Takes real talent to do that, folks. Take a bow, Stuart.'

So Stuart flourished the ropes, bowed, turned to go out,

somersaulted over a loose rope, flew through the air with the greatest of ease, and landed flat on his seat in the sawdust while Barry and the audience roared with appreciation.

Frank and I had invested in a Ghost Train, which Frank's cousin managed for us. We had also set up Samson the Strong Man in his own show, and both these ventures were going well. Samson was a Greek who was immensely strong in his chest, neck, teeth and arms. He was also a classic good looker in the Greek fashion, and when some hefty roadworker took up the challenge to smash huge rocks laid on Samson's chest, the girls oohed and aahed in anxiety. There was always a queue of ladies waiting for Samson's autograph, and at each town, he had his pick of a date for the evening.

The maddest thing Samson ever did, I think, was to start eating razor blades as part of his show. He simply believed that he was invincible, and whereas any other act didn't actually chew and swallow the blades, Samson most certainly did just that. We tried to stop him, but couldn't. The best we could do when he started bleeding was cart him off to a doctor who told him to eat something after each razor blade went down. From then on, we took a pie or bread roll around to him after each show and someone stood there to make sure he ate it. The other thing that caused a bit of a panic was the time he was doing a publicity stunt for the papers before the Mildura Show.

Samson lay down on the ground with a piece of hessian across his chest (to protect his leopard skin outfit, of course), and the local council truck manoeuvred into position. The idea was that the truck would drive straight across Samson's chest, and he would be unharmed. That was fine except that the driver, in his nervousness, stalled the truck when it got up onto Samson's chest, and for some nerve-racking seconds couldn't start it again. We thought Samson would be crushed, but not Samson the Strongman! He bragged about his strength for weeks, and although he was a bit sore, he did his usual stint of shows that weekend and enjoyed the fuss caused when the picture of him underneath the truck wheel was published in the district newspaper. He was a genuine strongman, and he never used any sort of trick when doing his feats of strength.

I stayed on the showgrounds for six years, doing the country runs and all the capital city Royal Shows. Frank and I incorporated young rock singers in the capital city shows, and there I met people such as John Devlin and Lucky Starr. I appeared on TV shows like Brian Henderson's *Bandstand* and the *Johnny O'Keefe Show*. I had my photo taken with showbiz celebrities (including the busty Sabrina) and they had their photos taken with my Gold Record. Life rolled on, and on.

That was the trouble. Life just rolled on, and I was being more and more absorbed in the showground community. That was great in so many ways, and it gave me time to meet and make friends with a variety of people all over the place. On the downside, it was separating me from my country roots and making it hard to write my songs. I had achieved much of my dream but not all of it, and I was becoming restless again. What was the use of being a household name, as everyone said I was, if I didn't know and understand just what those households were like? I was beginning to wonder if I was becoming isolated from the people I was singing for.

It was also becoming harder to keep my marriage and family together. Joy and I were a different kettle of fish from many showpeople in that we came from country backgrounds, and our outlook on life, family and marriage was stricter than some we came across. I'm not saying our outlook was necessarily the right one, I'm just saying that we were stuck with what we were . . . morally and emotionally.

There were influences at work all the time to split us up. Without each other, we would not be as strong. I was a fairly good money-making proposition at that time—I'd be a hypocrite to pretend otherwise. My name got our business into places and to people that would have been out of reach otherwise, but to work with me meant working with Joy as well. Joy saw a lot more than she was supposed to at times, and that made her a bit of a nuisance to some. The general opinion was that with her out of the way, I would be a lot easier to handle. I don't think I would have been as easy as some thought, because I have a fair amount of back country suspicion in my make-up. Nevertheless, we could see that the best way to stay together, and to go ahead with my dream, was to eventually go back on the road by ourselves.

We split with Frank in 1963, at Grafton. There were reasons for the final quarrel, but the separation was amicable, as they say in the divorce papers. We loaded our shares of the equipment into separate trucks, and prepared to move out; us to Brisbane to regroup and Frank to the show run with the other two shows.

Chapter Eleven

ON THE OUTBACK TRACK

Hey! Let me sing where the rafters ring,
in an old-time country hall . . .
'OLD-TIME COUNTRY HALLS' SLIM DUSTY

In Brisbane, we took stock of our position. We had with us Barry and Pauline, Teddy Trevor, plus Kid and Kitty Young. If we were going nightshowing again, Barry would resurrect old Mulga Dan, and Teddy would go out as advance agent. Kid Young was a whip cracker and rope spinner, and even without his 45 Colts (which had been confiscated by the police in Brisbane after one particularly brash publicity stunt) he was a good act. We advertised for a dancer, and contacted a lady juggler we knew. What we didn't know was that she had incorporated a strip into her act of juggling firesticks and clubs.

We booked three weeks out through south-west Queensland to run ourselves in, and nearly got ourselves run over. The roads were dry and dusty, and when the road trains hurtled along, the dust clouds rose into the sky. In the Territory in 1961, we had seen Kurt Johannsen's road train, the first to successfully negotiate bush roads with anything up to three trailers on, all tracking perfectly behind the prime mover. We had become used to seeing the road trains in Queensland, thundering along the dirt roads.

This particular day, we saw a road train coming and as we had reached a cattle grid across the road, I pulled off to the side to wait until the truck and its load had passed. I began to pull on to the road again after the truck had bashed its way past my wagon, which was towing the girls' caravan. To my horror, out of the cloud of thick dust came thundering the next road train, following too closely behind the first. I yanked the steering wheel over, throwing the station wagon back to the side of the road and saving it from a head-on smash. Just the same, that movement threw the body of the caravan into the line of the truck, which simply smashed its way through the frail timber. We sat there petrified as the big wheels passed within inches of us, each one as high as the station wagon. The timber of the caravan gave way to the onslaught, which was just as well for us. If it had been a metal van, we would have been dragged under the wheels of the semi and its trailers.

There was a funny side to it. The driver of the truck couldn't see where he was going because there were dancing girls' frilly costumes draped over his windscreen, and there was an array of girls' underwear and belongings all over the bonnet, so he ended up rolling over the embankment without coming to any harm. The girls flew out of the wagon bewailing the loss of their belongings, and picking up jewellery and underwear from the dirt road. They abused the driver for breaking the cardinal rule—he should never have travelled in his mate's dust cloud.

We still showed that night, after towing in the chassis and wheels which were all that remained of the hired van. We stayed an extra day, waiting for another caravan to arrive from Brisbane, and Kid Young took the opportunity of shopping for a new shirt. He was mates with the saddler and western gear stockist in Goondiwindi, but being Kid he didn't get to the shop until after closing time as his mate was tidying up. Never daunted, Kid hammered on the door and shop window until he was let in.

'Need some new shirts, mate. What size is that one there? Here, let's try it on.'

So far quite normal, wouldn't you say? However, as Kid stripped off his shirt to try on the new one, two women walked by the glass shopfront and stopped to admire the saddle on display there. What they saw, or thought they saw, was the back of a well-built lady with long, wavy brown hair, stripping off for the saddler's enjoyment 'right in front of their very eyes'! Kid Young wore his hair down to his shoulders as part of his 'Buffalo Bill' type of act, being one of the first Australian entertainers to do so, and therefore managed to scandalise the good ladies of Goondiwindi who were used to short back'n'-sides for men.

Millie had been ill for some years with kidney disease that caused ever-increasing weakness and hospital treatment, and in August 1962 at the Brisbane Exhibition, the police came to Joy in the ticket box to tell her that her mother was desperately ill and that she should go home to her immediately. It was the last night of the Ekka, and after doing her usual spot in the show and doing the books, the wages and getting the banking ready, she took the first plane next morning for Sydney. David and I travelled by car and caravan, arriving some days later to find Millie near death and the family distraught. She died eighteen months before the first kidney transplant, a much-loved lady and core of the family.

After the loss of her grandmother, Anne had travelled with us for a while, but in 1963 had to start boarding school. Our efforts to teach her by correspondence failed because the school and the post office couldn't get their act together. A travelling showman's daughter was not the usual pupil, and her constantly changing address had the post office baffled as well. Boarding school was the only answer if Anne was to be educated, and we had our hearts set on that.

There was no family Christmas in 1962, so I took my own little family to Metung and spent time with Mack and the Gilsenans. As a result, we bought a small block of land at the head of Chinamans Creek, and Mack and his brother-in-law began building us a modest house. We didn't plan on living there full-time, but it was nice to have somewhere to come back to for Christmas and for a bit of a break. We had become close to Lorna and Mack, and also to Cora and the rest of the family.

By the time we came back for our first Christmas at 'Homewood', the small house at Metung, we had toured Queensland and New South Wales; had hired and fired everyone from babysitters, rock singers, comperes, drummers, strippers, and dancers; and ended up with Kid Young on whips and ropes, Dante the magician, Barry Thornton and his mate Mulga Dan, and Allan Swanson the fiddle player and singer. Teddy Trevor was still doing the advance work, and every now and then would return to the show and sing a couple of songs on stage. Versatility was the name of the game, especially in those days when everyone had to pitch in and help.

Everyone helped set up the stage, not that it took much doing. But often we had to unload and set out our extra seats, and clean up the hall before we could use it. The girls worked the ticket box, took tickets, kept order during the show, packed up the seats afterwards, and helped sweep up the hall when necessary. All these jobs had to be done as well as the stage work, doing your act, working in skits, switching lights for blackouts and pulling the curtains. Offstage, I operated a turntable for the backing music for the variety acts and as a 'chaser' after skits and between acts. I also played bass for Joy's singing spot. Barry had switched from his singing spot to guitarist, solo and backing, plus dashing on and off in his role of Mulga Dan. During the hot weather in some of the sweatboxes of halls, you could just about see the trail of per-spiration following his footsteps.

It was a full-time job to keep the show on the road, quite literally, because moving every day taxed the vehicles to the limit. The roads were bad, and although a corrugated gravel road was not so bad for a car, it was murder when you were towing a caravan, especially a big one behind a truck. We had to travel together when we were out in more isolated areas. The rule was that each driver kept the following one in sight. If the following vehicle disappeared, you had to stop and wait for twenty minutes, which allowed for the changing of a tyre. After that time, you had to turn and go back looking for the missing vehicle. With that system, no one should be left without help.

We showed through the Gulf country of North Queensland, and I was driving Thunder, the big Inter with our big caravan behind it. Leaving Camooweal on the Territory border, we headed for Burketown, our first stop in the Gulf in blistering heat. David was in the truck with me, Joy was driving a car and van, Barry and Pauline were in their outfit and the others were following behind. When we came to the river the road petered out. We drove across slabs of rock beside the river until we found a crossing as there was no bridge, of course.

'Hey, Dad. Now we're across, can I have a drink?'

There was not much water in the so-called river, and the holes looked stagnant, so David and I shared a warm can of beer that was under the truck seat. He was about five, I think. Nothing like training them young, but his mother wasn't too pleased. We reached Burketown about six o'clock, everyone rushed out of the pub and cheered as we drove in, and rolled up for the show. They said we could have charged twice as much, and if we'd come again, we'd have the hall rent-free. I'm sorry I haven't been back, although I've been several times to Normanton, Croydon and Georgetown.

Television was spreading its net all over the east coast, and we were feeling its effect. No longer was the live show the only entertainment except for the picture theatre, and patrons stayed home in droves. In 1964, Kid Young urged me to take the show to Western Australia where television was not widespread, and where (he assured me) my records were popular. In NSW, the Snowy Mountains Hydro-Electric Scheme was in full swing and we showed the camps at Island Bend, Cabramurra and Khancoban; rough as guts, some of them were! We used to worry a bit about our pretty singer and dancer getting too close to the edge of the stage. We mightn't have been able to pull her back if those workers had got their hands on her!

We used to show for ten months of the year, and one of the biggest jobs was to keep peace in the camp. The other job was to look after any young lass in the show. The girl's mother would hand her precious daughter to Joy, and issue parting instructions on how Joy was to be responsible for her welfare— not that there would be any problem with the dear girl, of course. The lass would look as though butter would not melt in her mouth; however, once she got away from Mum, it was a different story. There was the seventeen-year-old from Brisbane, for instance, who was to help look after David during the show at night and to help with the housework during the day. David was, by this time, having correspondence lessons. When Joy found the lass spending her day off in the local pub with the much older rock singer, the responsibility became too much, and the lass was sent home to Mum to explain why she was no longer suited to her job.

This left us, once again, with the problem of looking after David and teaching him his correspondence lessons, as well as working and travelling, organising the itineraries and keeping Teddy supplied with publicity and lists of towns.

'What I need is someone like my Aunty Una,' Joy wailed despairingly.

Aunty Una was the youngest of her father's family, and had never married. In between looking after her aged parents for years, and becoming the family's finest and most famous cook,

Aunty Una had worked at all sorts of jobs without ever losing her sense of humour.

'Why don't you ring her?' said ever-practical me.

'*What!* You don't think she'd ever come out here, do you? She's looking after everyone at home, anyway.'

I insisted, however, and forced Joy to the telephone. I think we were in Walgett or Bourke. Sure enough, Aunty Una thought that, yes, she would be able to come and help out for a few weeks.

Joy had a slightly dazed look as she hung up the phone. 'I said I didn't think she'd be able to come, of course, but just thought I'd ask anyway and I nearly fell over when Aunty said straightaway that she'd come. Then I told her we had to go out through Cobar and Wilcannia as soon as she came and you know what she said?'

'Well, what did she say?' I demanded.

'She said—she's always wanted to go to Wilcannia!'

'Why bloody Wilcannia?' I wanted to know.

So Aunty Una came by train to help out for three weeks, and ended up travelling with us for over eight years. She started as David's teacher, and finished up as our front of house lady, selling tickets, throwing out drunks, chastising kids, and keeping us in order. As well as all that, she drove a car and caravan and turned her hand to any job that needed doing. I think Aunty Una is the only lady to tick me off without my answering back.

In February 1965, I took the show to Western Australia. At that time, the Nullarbor Plain stretched for 700 miles of dirt and dust road from South Australia to the west. It was a lonely trip with few roadhouses and those that were there were as rough as bags, and basic in every way. Just the same, they were like oases in the desert . . . quite literally. Some were petrol stops only, like the Gurney family's station, and others, like Cocklebiddy, had grown up out of necessity and chance. For instance, show-people called Macdonald used to cross the Nullarbor from the east to the Perth Royal Show. They were broken down one time and waiting for spare parts and they found travellers begging a cup of tea from Mrs Mac. She and Bill ended up building a shanty on the spot, supplying tea and food for travellers, and eventually taking up a property around Cocklebiddy and building the present-day roadhouse and motel.

There were signs up saying 'Beware of the bulldust', and we thought they were joking. After hitting one hidden hole, we learned our lesson. Bulldust is like talcum powder and it covers the holes in the road. No matter how carefully we drove, the bulldust rose in the air and cascaded down over our vehicle to the extent that we sometimes used the wipers to clear the windscreen. If we tried to wash the dust from our hair with normal soap, it would stand straight up like porcupine quills because the Nullarbor bore water is salty. There were three murders along the track one year and after hearing about them, we had no trouble in having all our drivers keep each other in sight. No one wanted to tear off ahead in case he had to camp on his own overnight.

We had no air-conditioning in the vehicles and as we approached Norseman, the first town, the sun sank lower in the afternoon and the only relief from the heat was to drape wet cloths over the open quarter windows and around our necks and legs. The corrugations hammered the caravan undercarriages, and we used many of the spare parts and tyres we'd loaded on in South Australia.

I used to take a fair number of people on the road, and because we planned to tour for at least ten months of the year, I followed the showground principle of having the whole family travelling with the show. This meant that a programme featuring Joy, Barry, Dante, a singer, perhaps a fiddle player and another variety act required at least six caravans as well as the bachelors' quarters built onto the back of Thunder, the larger International truck. It also meant that we had wives and children in the camp, and while this made us a little travelling community, it didn't make for the most peaceful of times. Long travelling days under bad conditions created grizzly, tired, fighting kids and cranky, touchy young mothers, which in turn kept the tension in the air thick enough to cut with a knife at times.

Dante had joined me for a tour, and ended up staying for three years. The old gentleman enjoyed the touring, but deplored our methods. Some of the towns we played were not worthy of his presence, and he certainly let us know. As for some of the hotels he had to put up with before he brought his caravan . . . well! As I once said, when John Dante gets to heaven, he'll put in a complaint that the place is a dump and the Pearly Gates are squeaking!

When Dante did bring his caravan and his wife, Elizabeth, he also brought Kim, a savage cocker spaniel, and Jo-Jo the budgie.

There was constant warfare over who got the shadiest spots to park their caravan, and who had to park next to the noisiest and earliest risers in the camp—Dante complained constantly. I used to set him off by saying, 'Nice cool spot you've got there, John.'

Elizabeth, exasperated, would sigh. 'You would have to come along, wouldn't you! I've only just got him quietened down.'

Off would go John again with his grizzles, I'd have a shot back, and John and I would be stiff-backed and stiff-necked for the better part of the day. About three, I'd start to feel a bit stupid about it and I'd slip down to John and suggest that perhaps we should indulge in a visit to the local?

'Well now, I think that would be quite nice, my boy. Just a half brandy will do me, thank you,' and John and I would yarn away for an hour or so. He always said that moderation in all things was the secret to a long life and he was probably right. He was ninety when he died, but was still travelling with me when he had his eighty-first birthday, with champagne, cake and birthday gifts from everyone in the team. Except, of course, for Delando.

While Dante had grumbled and complained his way across the Nullarbor and everywhere else, Delando had occupied himself sewing sequins on a new costume. Hired unseen from a Sydney agent, he had been described to us as a balancing and juggling act, and as we needed someone extra we had grabbed him. However, he was never satisfied with his present act and was intent on trying out every act he could think of, while on tour with us. When he began incorporating some little magic tricks, complete with swishes and waves of his sequinned cape, Dante began smouldering. Chips began to fly and John's white whiskers and goatee waved up and down with temper. Delando complained bitterly to the world that he was being persecuted and he was not, absolutely not, going to contribute anything towards that horrible old man's birthday present.

While Barry and I kept the wheels of the wagons rolling, Joy and I endeavoured to keep our show together and to stop our two variety stars sabotaging each other's stage acts. Delando added some hip-wobbling dance steps to the act, and after being gently advised about the possible reaction of the station hands up north, regretfully dropped that part of the act. Things came to a head when the male singer began referring to him as Rosie, and Dante began making loud remarks about amateur would-be magicians who had no stagecraft, no manners, and weren't a stage artist's bootlace anyway. Delando packed his belongings and stood outside the hall under the stars declaring that he had been thrown out in the middle of nowhere with no place to lay his brilliantined head, and that he was going back to his friends in Sydney where he was appreciated. The gentle smile on Dante's face was not completely hidden in his whiskers.

Dante was with us again in 1966 when I decided to take the show right around Australia. But this time there was no opposition variety act. He had seen to that. The old devil was as shrewd as they make them where showbusiness was concerned, but rather unworldly in other kinds of business. Nevertheless,

I was very attached to him and he taught me nearly all I know of stage work. I have to say, too, that I've not seen anyone with his stage presence. A small man, immaculate in white tie and tails, he worked without a microphone and after the first minute held the attention of a sometimes rowdy audience. He knew how to 'milk' an audience, and how to win applause. John used to say one of the most important things to know is how to get onstage, and then how to get off it. Another of his sayings was, 'You have to be on some sort of stage, even if it is only a six-inch-high dais . . . that bit of height puts you above them in their minds. You have to let them know you are in command.' I do miss John.

Mack: 'It's like paying for something with crocodile skins and taking your change in dingo scalps.'

This was the year that decimal currency was introduced. Mack Cormack from Metung had decided to come along for the round Australia trip as a change from boat hiring and SP book-making, and he was lecturing me on the ease of making the changeover to dollars and cents.

'You just put an "0" in front of it, see? Easy, m'lad.'

We fronted up to the post office to send some money to Teddy, the advance agent, and got into bother immediately because our money was in pounds, shillings and pence. I called on Mack for assistance, and Mack got flustered. We both got nowhere and I happily said, 'Just put an "0" in front of it, eh, Mack?'

Mack swore at me.

This was also the year when we had to send David to boarding school. He was only seven years old, but was in the process of becoming an isolated child as I had been. He raced through the correspondence lessons when we could get them, and as we moved six days of every week he had no chance to go to a local school or to make friends of his own age. 'Why don't you go and play with those other little boys, Davy?' Joy would suggest.

Sometimes he would go, but mostly he began to reply, 'What's the use? I'll be gone tomorrow.'

So he went by plane from Whyalla, through Adelaide and thence to Sydney to start school. Joy began crying at the slightest provocation, and when Anne left to go back to school as well, the waterworks flowed in and out of the caravan for three weeks. I was ready to give up travelling and go back to the kids. If I had, though, they wouldn't have had the education and chances they've had, and, thank God, to date neither of them seems to hold it against me. I'm not too sure about my wife, though!

When we showed the southern part of Western Australia in 1965, we revelled in shorter distances, magnificent jarrah and karri forests, beautiful coastlines, and then wide wheatfields and mining towns. Our audiences included large percentages of Aborigines, and we found that the gulf between black and white was more pronounced than we were used to. In one town the audience was comprised mostly of Aborigines, and we wondered where all the whites had got to. We were told next day that the whites didn't come to the show because the Aborigines had all come to it. So in 1966 we thought, 'Okay. We'll show two nights, and we'll have reserved seats and that will sort it out.'

It didn't, of course, because the Aborigines came both nights, bless them. Without the support of the Aboriginal people through all the years, we couldn't have survived. However, I have to say that in that particular town we began to see why the whites stayed away. I don't believe in colour bars of any kind, and we were appalled to see toilets marked 'Ladies' on one door and 'Natives' on the other in the women's section of the hall facilities. But the state of those same facilities after the show was shocking.

For years, the 'Dog Act' had been in force, namely that Aborigines were not allowed alcohol. If an Aborigine were an exceptionally good citizen, then drinking rights, among others, were extended to that person. But about 1966, total voting and drinking rights for all came into being and we noticed the impact immediately. Being allowed to drink was such a novelty that just about everyone had a go. The kids camped on the steps of the hall, waiting for Mum and Dad to come out of the pub, which they didn't do. Aunty Una would see the shivering kids who had no money for tickets, and as soon as the show started the back rows would mysteriously fill up with these kids, courtesy of Aunty.

The crack Aboriginal shearing teams disintegrated. They worked a few days to get a cheque, downed shears, demanded to be paid and went back to town to blow it. By that time, another team had taken the place of the original team and there was no work for them. We saw the colourful new shirts on the men who came to the shows change to the old and grubby. The well-dressed, happy-looking family groups were fewer and fewer. It might sound silly, but we worried and talked endlessly, trying to work out what was happening, and what would happen.

It had its lighter side, too.

We were heading north, and Aunty Una was selling tickets and patrolling the front as usual when five or six Aboriginal ladies with their dogs, and newspaper packets of fish and chips, arrived late, wanting tickets to the show. They had obviously spent hours in the pub and were quite loud and argumentative amongst themselves. One was being held upright by two mates, language was flying and Aunty Una decided that she already had enough to cope with inside the hall without this little lot as well, so she refused them admission.

There were loud protests and lots of promises, but Aunty had heard it all before and stood firm. When it finally sank in that she meant it, and they couldn't see the show, the largest lady turned to the loudest, smashed her packet of greasy fish and chips over the loudmouth's head and screamed at her,

'You silly black bastard, now look what you've done! It's all your fault!'

Fish and chips went everywhere, and dogs flew in to get their share, as five swaying ladies tried to reclaim the wreckage, and Aunty hid in the ticket box with a fit of the giggles.

We were fascinated by the goldmining town, Kalgoorlie, and the old town of Coolgardie. In Kalgoorlie, we showed in the town hall which had red velvet seats and curtains and reeked with the atmosphere of theatre from the goldrush days. Kalgoorlie was about to boom again with new gold, and then nickel, strikes. When the nickel hysteria did hit the city, it filled once again with prospectors, mining engineers and brokers. You could almost taste the fever and feel it revving you up.

To get to the caravan park we were booked into by our advance agent, we took a backstreet route and I tried to distract my wife's attention from the unusual-looking houses which lined this particular street. I had no luck at all.

'For goodness sake, look at that one. All those coloured lights strung up, and look, no front yard at all. Why have they got those corrugated iron walls up, and those funny looking alleyways to the front door?'

'How should I know? Just concentrate on finding the park, will you?'

'But . . . but . . . *ooh!*'

The penny dropped when she came abreast one house that did business in the daytime and she saw a couple of ladies sitting in the doorway dressed in their best undies, and from there to the park her head swivelled non-stop.

It was more picturesque when we drove past at night after the shows. All the coloured lights were lit and strung along the fences and light flooded out the doorways over the ladies sitting there, maybe chatting to prospective customers. Kalgoorlie's famous street has survived to this day, one way and another, though there have been various petitions and indignation meetings. Old traditions die hard, like the equally famous two-up school on the outskirts of town. I think they tried to knock that on the head as well, but howls of protest from the tourist authorities as well as the two-up players saved the game.

Our first round Australia trip aimed to reach Darwin in time for their show week, and to go on to Mt Isa for the famous Isa Rodeo in August. So we headed up the north-west coast of Western Australia through Geraldton towards the Pilbara region, booming with the iron ore mines. Heading there was one thing, but getting there was another. We'd had absolutely no idea that the roads were as bad as they turned out to be, and, naturally, no warning of an exceptional weather pattern which led to cyclonic-type rains during a period when the rains had no business to be falling.

Enough said when I tell you that we were marooned in one small place, Roebourne, for a week. So we showed for a week, changing the sketches and songs each night. At least that paid the caravan park and put something towards the wages. All this responsibility made me touchy, and I was likely to blow a fuse the minute some problem, big or little, occurred. The problems just seemed to keep coming those days.

When we moved, we were the first vehicles out of Roebourne, but we had to go in a big circle out through the asbestos mining town of Wittenoom and back to the coast to get to Port Hedland. Port Hedland was booming. Iron ore was the black gold of the day, not oil. Workers and their families by the hundreds, and then almost thousands, swarmed into the town and wanted accommodation. Port Hedland was over-whelmed with the demand for supplies of food, water and beds; the caravan park was filled to bursting, and when we got to town, was filled with dysentery sufferers.

We camped behind the hall, despite the town clerk's efforts to shift us. We had enough problems without the whole show being exposed to dysentery down at the park, so we stayed put. By the following year, the town clerk had managed to get a by-law passed that prohibited any camping in the hall yard, but the town facilities had improved by then anyway. The whole situation provided us with material for a song which wasn't flattering . . . just truthful.

By this time, I realised that we had not allowed ourselves enough time to get from one isolated town to another. The truck with all the chairs, sidewalls and the lighting plant was pulling the big caravan and it slowed us down. I calculated that we needed three hours to do one hundred miles, with all the vehicles and caravans and allowing for short stops, but we couldn't even do that under the present conditions. So I tried moving the team for a couple of hours after the show at Port Hedland. I was watching the sky for more rain, and I panicked if I spotted one small cloud. The road ahead ran through the Pardoo Sands, and then over the Mardie Plain. Our current Happy Jack who drove the truck and helped on the front was smiling all over his mournful face as he informed me how bad it was going to be.

It was bad enough. The Pardoo Sands were miles of one-lane road through the sand dunes, north of Port Hedland. Over the years, the road had been graded until it was so low that walls of white sand towered each side of us. It was like driving through a white tunnel, with every now and then a wider space dug out so that two vehicles could pass. We just beat a road train to one of the bypasses, and within the day began to cross the Plain. It had rained, of course, and we sat there like ducks for a couple of days, along with stranded truck drivers and brave tourists. Luckily, we always kept the bunk cupboards loaded with tinned and dried food, juices and extra water. If we hadn't, there'd have been a few hungry drivers sitting it out on the Mardie.

Broome, when we reached it, was heaven. A camp near a beach, plenty of water and our lighting plant to run lights and refrigerators. A night off was indicated and we left the cleaning up of vans and vehicles till tomorrow. We'd even eat out! But we couldn't see where . . . until someone told us to go down to Chinatown, and look for a certain corrugated iron house. It stood among other similar houses lining the street on both sides, it was painted green and had small bushes growing in the tiny front yard. And yes, it was a Chinese eating house with basic tables and chairs in each small room.

'Pass the sauce, please,' I asked. 'No, don't worry, I can reach.'

I swear that grinning Chinaman knew what I was going to do, but it was too late to stop me. I tipped the sauce over my meal, took a big mouthful and choked. My face went purple, and the steam came out my ears as I felt the full effect of the homemade chilli sauce. We were all a bit silly that night, with the relief of actually getting this far and knowing there was a sealed road to the next town.

It was at Derby, the next town, that I first sang 'Trumby' onstage and had such a reaction that I had to sing it again. The only other time I've had to do that was in Camooweal, Queensland, when I first sang 'Camooweal', and in Dimbulah when I sang Stan Coster's 'New Australian Bushman' to an audience of Italian tobacco farmers.

The words of 'Trumby' were given to me in Longreach, Queensland, by Joe Daly. It was originally titled 'Our Jacky', a name I didn't like, so I changed it. The story of an outstanding ringer (or stockman), who died because he couldn't read the warning notice at a poisoned waterhole, made a huge impression on the Aborigines. I was told at one time that it was responsible for a great rise in literacy class enrolments throughout the north-west and the Territory, as it told the story of the good man who couldn't read or write.

By this time, 1966, I had been getting reports from record company reps and retail stores about my good record sales which were not only consistent but climbing steadily. The 'Pub' had made my name known, and I had followed it up by recording regularly and touring constantly to publicise the records.

One thing went hand in hand with the other. It was no use my recording and sitting at home waiting for sales; I had to get out there and tell the world all about it. By the same token, it was no use touring and looking for big crowds if they had never heard of me and didn't know my songs or my show.

So while my ads were sent to newspapers and radio, I went to every radio station that would interview me and play my records. I was in contact with radio announcers in every town with a station, and often managed to get stories in district newspapers. Our show was an honest one, and was one of the extremely few to travel the more remote areas so that I got to know people and the conditions they lived and worked under.

I'm sometimes asked why I think I am one of those country people when I'm either on the road or based in a town or city. It's because I lived and worked under their conditions for the first forty-three years of my life, and even now when I don't tour ten months of the year, I keep in close touch. When I began touring full-time, I had to learn when was the right time to show in any district anywhere in Australia. I found out the hard way that when the wheat farmers of Western Australia were sowing at a certain time in a district they kept the tractors going by headlights all night, and, naturally, didn't come to my show. If I expected station people in the Territory or in the Queensland Gulf, for example, to come to the show, then I had to let them know at least six weeks in advance so they could plan their work ahead. Fat chance I had of getting a good crowd out there if they were all in the middle of mustering for the year!

My livelihood depended on theirs . . . if they had a good year, then so did I usually. Our destinies and our pockets were tied together.

'Slim, I think you should have a look at this wheel . . . dear.'

We rolled into Fitzroy Crossing on the way to Halls Creek. Joy went to the caravan door to open it, and stopped in her tracks. She didn't want to be the one to tell me the bad news, but she was stuck with it. The caravan had a double axle with four wheels, and when I looked at the one nearest the door, I could hardly believe it. The tyre had blown, and the road was so bad that I hadn't felt it. Miles and miles of that bloody road had wrapped the metal rim around the hub and I'd been travelling on three wheels and the hub!

I just exploded, and everyone quietly disappeared.

There was no hall at Fitzroy Crossing so we still had to erect the canvas sidewalls, build a makeshift stage, unload and set up all the seats plus the lighting plant, see if we could scrounge any power from the pub or the store, and fix this wheel before we did the show. So while all the kids in the district (and further) checked out which trees they could perch in and see the show for nothing that night, we got stuck into it. We had a great crowd, and next morning, when I discovered that some of the kids from Go Go Station hadn't been able to fit onto the truck coming into the show, I went out there and sang them a few songs. It was worth it to see their faces.

We camped two days at Derby with another showman, who apparently 'forgot' to deliver the message he had been given, namely, that we had to contact a certain official in Perth and get permission to show Halls Creek on the Sunday night. Otherwise, we could sit there while the customers went crook about coming a hundred miles or so and still not seeing the show. Ernie Bridge went into action and by phone located the official, had him dragged off the golf course and got the necessary permission.

Ernie Bridge must be the only country music singing politician in Australia, and is descended from one of the pioneering families of the Kimberley area. Back in the 1960s he ran the family station, the town's butchery and airline agency, and also the open-air picture show. Added to that he was the Halls Creek shire president, and the youngest man to hold that position.

We turned north on the road, winding through spear grass

alongside creek beds where carbines and river gums grew beneath battlements of stone. We drove in silence mostly, just looking. We never did get tired of this scenery, and little did we know how close we were to the fabled Bungle Bungles, those domes of layered sandstone hidden and yet so close to the road and settlements. The Aborigines, of course, had known about them all the time.

On to Wyndham and Kununurra, across the Victoria River (which had no bridge then) and over to the Territory. Through Katherine and up to Darwin, ready for the next leg of our ten-month trip. The Darwin Show is held in July, and we showed in the Cavanagh Theatre, a small venue that was demolished years later by Cyclone Tracy. We then went down through the Territory, over through Camooweal to Mt Isa, hoping that the town had recovered from the drastic seven-month strike the previous year which had caused a state of emergency to be declared. In Mt Isa, we met one of the men whose papers were marked 'Never to be employed again' in the mine offices.

The seven-month strike at the Mt Isa mine had ended at least eighteen months before we arrived for Rodeo Week in August 1966. The town was decked out for the rodeo, but the shopfronts hid the fact that there wasn't as much stock as usual. The miners' families didn't have money to throw around, and some of the ringleaders who wanted to stay in the Isa had to do other jobs. A taxi driver that we met still writes lyrics for me today. He could never get work in the mine again, and I think he was making up his mind what he would turn to next.

We showed the Isa for a week, and did our usual free show in the rodeo arena one night. Mt Isa is a huge mining town, in the north-west of Queensland, and from the first time we showed there in 1960 in the big showground tent, we were treated as honorary residents. Back in 1960, as we were pulling down the big tent, local people kept calling in with gifts of fresh vegetables from their backyard gardens. 'You won't get anything fresh where you're going' was the repeated remark when we tried to thank them. They were quite right; in those times there were very little fresh vegetables or fruit and no cow's milk on the track to Darwin.

Chapter Twelve
ME, A RACIST?

Just a tall, dark man in the saddle,
he's as tough as they come from anywhere . . .
'THE SADDLE IS HIS HOME' SLIM DUSTY

Despite the fact that my recording royalty cheques were steadily increasing in size, I was convinced that I couldn't last in the touring business forever. With this in mind, I had been looking around for some sort of backstop other than plastering. Mack Cormack reckoned passionfruit growing was all the go around the Metung district, and I decided to buy a few acres. I could plant it when I was home at Christmas and Mack would take over looking after the vines. It was a good idea at the time, but on thinking it over, I wondered how much Mack knew about passionfruit growing. It would have to be a lot, because I knew nothing. I ended up buying a small farm where I could run a few cattle; a job I knew I could do, and so could Mack.

We worked on the principle that the touring show had to pay for itself and the royalty cheques went into the bank as insurance against a rainy day; in other words, a bad run. Our kitty was therefore able to buy us a small grazing and/or dairy farm with a small house, fruit and nut trees. I felt better when

I had that behind me because although the touring was still keeping us going, good old pessimist Slim reckoned it couldn't last too much longer. I deliberately ignored the fact that the royalty cheques were getting bigger, and so were the crowds in most places. I figured that even if I couldn't keep travelling I would have a farm to go back to, and I could keep up my writing and recording. But then I decided that the acreage wasn't big enough for grazing and raising vealers for the Melbourne market—which was what I wanted while I was still on the road—and we looked at an adjoining place. After talking the Italian owners into selling to us we had to find the money.

I looked again at those royalty cheques, and decided to give it a go. I'd bite EMI for an advance on my royalties. They apparently had a look at the royalty statements too, and advanced me the money for the other half of the farm. I was glad to have it, but I was going to miss the security of those royalties coming in for the next couple of years. The show would have to keep its end up.

Before we left on the tour, I went into the studios for a marathon recording session. As well as tracks by Joy and Anne, in eight days I recorded thirty-three songs and did cover photo sessions for two albums: 'Essentially Australian' and 'Songs My Father Sang to Me'. There was a last-minute panic later in the year when we were one song short for the second album and had to use one of the spares to fill it. It has been said that I have recorded nothing but Australian songs. To date, I've recorded about 900 songs, I suppose, and there are some non-Australian songs among them. These were mostly recorded in the 1960s when I did some old-time songs and two albums with American songs on them: 'Songs for Rolling Stones' and 'Sing a Happy Song'. The first one, as I mentioned earlier, caught me short of songs because I had already recorded all I had on hand, and the second one I did for fun.

In 1967, we planned on cutting down the size of the show. There were too many vehicles, which upped the expenses, and because I planned to go right around Australia again, I knew the trip was just too hard on the families. It was a difficult decision, but after one go at the north-west and Kimberley through to Darwin, I had to trim the outfit to travel faster over the bad roads.

Barry decided to stick with me, and Pauline with the two children settled into the farmhouse, while Mack Cormack looked after the farm and the cattle. The place was being improved with a new dam and new fences, and before long, was looking good. That is, till the worst drought for years hit the place.

Teddy Trevor and his wife Barbara had new twin girls, so Teddy decided to go back to the showgrounds instead of doing the advance work on his own. This meant that we had to either get a new advance man or work out how to do the booking of halls and advertising the show ourselves. It meant a lot of work, but we reckoned we could do it. Joy and I had already been working out the runs, and knew all the papers and radio stations for each district.

It worked like this. We booked the run, sending deposits where necessary. We mailed our newspaper and radio advertisements ahead, having the photo blocks sent on from one paper to the next. It meant a lot of checking, and our timing had to be right, but most newspapers were very co-operative and we had few disasters. The same idea worked with radio stations.

In the 1960s in country towns, the show posters were one of the main advertising ploys for travelling shows and it was usual to give a complimentary ticket in return for displaying the poster. So how were we going to get the posters up? We turned to labour-intensive advertising, namely, rolling the posters ourselves and sending them out. But where to? We bought the country telephone directories for each district, and mailed the posters to every likely-looking shop in every village in a circle around the town we were going to show.

Mack and Lorna Cormack helped us roll the first lot of posters which were done in the kitchen of Homewood, kids and all getting stuck into it. Then Mack and Lorna offered to take on the poster rolling and mailing for us, which was a godsend. It meant we didn't have to carry the heavy, bulky posters in the truck and caravan, and it was a time-consuming job we wouldn't have to do. Next thing, we discovered that Margaret Mile, who was coming on tour as singer and skit girl, was a typist and would be happy to earn a bit extra bashing out address labels on the old portable. Everything was working out!

It was too easy at first glance, and we had some nervous moments over the next couple of years, but on the whole it worked. We kept up the supply of address labels to Mack back at Homewood where he had the kitchen covered wall-to-wall with posters, labels, paper and paste. That's not to mention the little printing set and its purple ink which was used to print the name of the hall and the date we would be showing. Lorna made sure the local printers kept up the supply of posters to Mack, and all in all, the system went well. It meant that we hadn't a spare moment on the road. What with keeping the show rolling on wheels as well as on stage, booking halls well ahead and checking that the advertising was coming out on time, it's hard to believe that we both found time to write songs as well, but we did.

I told earlier of meeting John Ashe in Townsville, and how I began recording John's songs. The only songs apart from my own that I recorded before John's were 'Rusty, It's Goodbye' (lyrics by Thel Carey), 'Our Wedding Waltz' (Joy), 'Since the Bushland Boogie Came This Way' (Mack Cormack), and 'Rutland Rodeo' (Wave Jackson). Waverley Jackson from Injune got me started on looking for songs of the outback; songs of western Queensland and the Territory. I hadn't travelled that country much when I first met Wave; that was to come. After recording three of John Ashe's songs in 1957 plus one of

Joy's, I put down the 'Pub' as well as a couple more of Wave's, and by the end of the year I had twenty-four tracks recorded.

When the 'Pub' hit, everyone began pushing for an 'Answer', and then for a 'Sequel'. I recorded them both, and ended up with a gold 78 plus a gold 45 for the 'Pub', and a gold 45 for the 'Answer to the Pub with No Beer'. The 'Sequel' didn't get one, but made a good talking point for a television show called *True or False*. It's surprising how many people thought I had a gold record for each of the pub songs. On the B side of the 'Answer' I recorded Shorty Ranger's classic, 'Winter Winds'. It has lasted longer than the 'Answer'. Barry Thornton's guitar solo became his trademark, and still is.

I love recording, and I love writing and finding new songs. I get a rush of adrenalin when I hear a song or read a set of lyrics that I know will record well and will say something I want to say, or will tell a story, whether it's humour or even tragedy. Over the years, I've built up quite a circle of writer friends and a mixed lot we all are.

There was John Ashe, the accountant from Townsville, who was at heart a composer of country, island and comedy songs. Then Wave Jackson, a cattle grazier from central Queensland, who loved rodeo riding and composed songs without the benefit of a musical instrument to guide him; Mack Cormack, who wrote with both the humour and the sadness of a Lawson; and then old Dan Sheahan, the Irishman with his ironic humour. Shorty Ranger still sent me songs from the Nulla Creek and Kempsey, and his songs rang true of the coast and the hills. My wife, Joy, wrote in differing styles from bush ballads, old time and then to rockabilly in the sixties. Gordon Parsons, who wrote the 'Pub' as it is known today, kept turning up every now and then.

I knew Gordon was unreliable so far as shows go, but I couldn't resist taking him on tour again one year, and he actually went up to Darwin and back as far as Mt Isa before he disgraced himself. We always showed Mt Isa at rodeo time, and of course, Gordon knew heaps of the rodeo riders and every last one of them knew him. I used to reckon the whole world knew Gordon, and he was too goodhearted to tell anyone to clear off. Besides, they might have a cold beer. The caravans were parked behind the hall, and I made sure Gordon was carted into the van for a cup of tea or coffee at interval time to keep him out of mischief, until one night when he was nowhere to be found at the interval.

He was due onstage in the second half, but he didn't turn up. We threw in extra songs and worked double parts in skits, and did that for the next three nights. Gordon turned up eventually, telling us what a rotter he was and how he had let us down, and so on and so on. Having heard most of this repertoire on previous occasions, we waited for the punch line.

'Well, then, I think a man ought to get out of the road.'

'Here it comes,' we thought. Yes, sure enough, he reckoned he'd head back to Sydney; so with much heartburning we put him on the plane. We didn't give in to the request for the cash for his airfare; we bought the ticket and put him on the plane. Once my mate was on the tear, there'd be no holding him for the rest of the tour, but we missed him very much. Even though I was pretty wild at the time, I had to laugh about it and used to tell the tale to other showpeople who knew Gordon and his ways. When I told Rick Carey, he laughed.

'What are you talking about! He shot through on you for three days; when he left me, I didn't see him for three weeks!'

The most prolific of songwriters I've met would be Stan Coster, who finally got around to sending me that tape of his songs. I think I've recorded nearly everything he ever sent to me, the first being 'Return of the Stockman' in 1962. Stan was working either on stations or on the construction of the big beef roads that were being built through western Queensland, and later still, on the Greenvale line from the nickel mine to the coast near Cairns. His writing was raw, rough and ready in some songs, but full of humour in others, such as 'Cunnamulla

Feller' and 'The New Australian Bushman'. His lyrics told it the way it was out there and 'By Fire of Gidgee Coal' has become a classic bush ballad. After a few years of my recording Coster songs and Stan beginning to sing them around the camps himself, he became a professional singer too.

I didn't run into Joe Daly until about 1964. There's an old photo somewhere of me and Joe outside the caravan at Longreach (again!) when he was showing me the words of the song he called 'Our Jacky'. He had another one, 'Road Trains', and after setting them to music and changing the name of the first one to 'Trumby', I recorded them both. Joe's words caused some protests in later years as the word 'racist' sprang up and was used to run down anyone and anything. It was a bit strange, really, when you realise that, as Joe wrote to me once, 'I've got a bit of Murri in me' (or words to that effect) and here he was being branded as racist. This only occurred in cities or big towns, never in the bush.

Aboriginal station manager (laughing): 'They call me a racist—me! Just because I tell them to get off their arses and do a bit. Racist! I'm as black as they are.'

The song 'Paddy Gramp', words by Joe Daly, caused much enjoyment among outback cattlemen, white and black. It told of the white boss ripping off his Aboriginal stockman as he took dollars out of the stockman's pay for supposed supplies from the station store. The stockman takes it very calmly, in the end telling the boss that he's been duffing (stealing) 'clean skin mickeys' (unbranded cattle) for a year or more, so they're quits anyway.

The point I'm trying to make, I suppose, is that the real bushman and the outback stockman, black or white, is well enough adjusted to laugh at himself and is not looking for offence where none is intended. Take 'A Word to Texas Jack', for instance. Henry Lawson wrote this about an American buck-jump rider who arrived in Sydney bragging about his record 'back home', and challenging all and sundry. Lawson slung off

171

at the American saddle and style of riding, saying that he'd seen bush girls ride better. When I showed Injune one time, I wondered if I should sing it as there were quite a few American property owners in the district and they had come to the show. I decided to go ahead and see what happened, and 'Texas Jack' was the success of the night with the Yanks laughing the loudest and sending messages backstage for it to be sung again.

The same happened with 'The New Australian Bushman' which has a line saying 'I do not like Australian men to call me greasy wog' . . . the whole song giving the New Australian's point of view. Well, the Italian tobacco farmers at Dimbulah on the Atherton Tablelands just about rolled on the floor laughing, pointing their fingers at each other and calling each other wog. They knew their neighbours were good mates, and they took no offence any more than I would if my mate swore at me with affection. It's not what you say, but how you say it, I reckon.

From the early sixties, writers began sending me songs and verse. The trickle then has turned to a flood now, and my policy of having one of us check every song or set of lyrics that arrives is now time-consuming and results in a waiting list which often takes me weeks to get through. I try to look at everything because you just never know when that good one will turn up.

As I travelled, I began to actively search out songs and verse which accurately described the life and outlook of the people I was singing to each night. There were some funny or unusual ways of receiving songs, I can tell you.

Backstage at Surat, Queensland, there was a thump on the outside door and this bloke fell through it as it opened. The last thing we want backstage during a show is a drunk, so we threw him out. He barged back in, and though amiable, he was a nuisance, so he was thrown out once again and the door barricaded. The piece of paper that he dropped as he was forcibly assisted to the outside had a poem called 'The Crow' written on it. A lady called Margaret White was the writer of the tall story which

I later recorded, and she lived on a station where her husband worked. She couldn't get in to the show and Bill, the cook, had volunteered to deliver her verse to me. Bill had stopped at the pub for a while before he wandered over to the hall.

Up on the wall of the roadhouse at Dunmarra in the Territory was a poem cut out of the *North Queensland Register*. It was called 'The Wave Hill Track' and the writer wrote under the name of 'Rumbottle'. Obviously, if I wanted to record it I had to find the writer, and it took quite some detective work to find George Crowley in Charters Towers.

I had to go through the same process to find Tom Oliver after I saw his 'From the Gulf to Adelaide' in the *North Queensland Register*. Once I was in contact with a writer, it was amazing to see the wealth of material just sitting around in a drawer or an old exercise book. I like to think that I might have been responsible in some small way for bringing out the talent in these bush writers by recognising how important it was to record their factual or humorous outlook on events in their daily life. Over the years, the songs I've found have built up a picture of a changing country. I didn't set out to be any sort of historian, I just wanted to sing about Australia; but the more I travelled and the more time I spent in the outback, the more my life became tied to the land and the people out there.

Overall, until the beginning of the seventies, most of the songs I recorded were my own with increasing input from others in the sixties. After the gold records for the 'Pub' and the 'Answer', I struck gold again for the 'Aussie Sing Song'. In 1968, I received three more for the 'Pub', and two for the 'Aussie Sing Song'.

After three round Australia trips, we had a go at the east coast again and to our surprise, did very well indeed. In 1968, in a pile of mail that caught up with us, was a letter from the theatre chain Kerridge Odeon in New Zealand, offering us three weeks' work over there. We were doubtful, as we'd never worked for anyone else, and we had no idea either how much we were worth. Seeing that we didn't mind one way or the other, we sent off a figure which we thought was a bit much and next thing, we were engaged for a New Zealand tour to take place in May 1969. We must have sold ourselves cheap, I thought later.

We were all pretty tired by this time. It was constant work, showing six nights a week and travelling every day on roads that varied from potholed bitumen to potholed gravel. We'd been night showing for six years straight, with six to eight weeks' break in between. In this 'holiday', we'd go to Sydney and record anything up to twenty-four songs, go to Kempsey to see my mother, and spend time with Anne and David. Then we would also book the next itinerary, send out the posters and advertising, and off we'd go again.

A break from the never-ending diplomacy required to keep the show together, to soothe council caretakers' dignity, and simply to put on a good show under sometimes primitive conditions was needed badly. I justified the break by recording twenty-four tracks in March and April, mostly for the 'Cattle Camp Crooner' album. Barry used to come over to Homewood in the evening, and we'd work out the guitar arrangements and practise together (after catching the occasional fish). Then we'd send tapes of our finished product up to Sydney to the arranger who was putting the band together. We still had deadlines so far as recording time was concerned, and it was hard to get good takes of every song in the time allowed. If I did a good one, you could be sure one of the musicians would be just about cutting his throat because he had accidentally messed it up . . . everyone can't be perfect all at the one time. No, I shouldn't say that. The musos were amazing the way they could turn out a good live performance so many times in a day.

The touring band mostly consisted of Barry Thornton on lead guitar and Joy on electric bass or keyboard. I called the three of us 'The Bushlanders', and it was great to have someone like, say, Allan Swanson the fiddler join the show for a while.

I invited Allan, who toured for eighteen months with us in 1963 and 1964, to come to New Zealand with us. I thought that the country fiddle would be a novelty there, just the same as it was here in Australia. It had always been a struggle to get musicians who could play country music, and who could play country instruments like pedal steel and dobro, banjo, mandolin and particularly fiddle. It was even difficult to find guitarists who could play country at all, because they had been trained on cabaret-style jazz and dance music only. Some couldn't understand how a hick like me had the hide to say that they were unsuited to the recording session, and I found it hard to understand how I had the hide to do it, too. There were some good musicians among them, but I just couldn't get the message across.

Kerridge Odeon told us that our support act would be the Hamilton County Bluegrass Band (HCBB).

'What do they do?' we replied.

Boy, did we find out.

We had expected the weather to be cold in New Zealand in contrast to Australia, but we didn't expect it to be as frosty as the reception we got from the HCBB. I'm a shy sort of person, I know, but Joy is very outgoing and friendly and even she got nowhere. The HCBB had become stars overnight courtesy of a New Zealand television show called *The Country Touch*, hosted by Tex Morton. Tex was born in Nelson, New Zealand, but as a young man came to Australia and almost single-handedly kicked off country music here. He later went to the United States for nearly twelve years, and on his return called in to his homeland for a while.

Allan Swanson was no novelty because the star of the HCBB, whether she liked it or not, was Colleen Bain. She was a classically trained violinist who naively wandered along to the Hamilton Folk Club one night with her violin in tow. Paul Trenwith and Alan Rhodes spotted her, and when they heard her, they couldn't believe their luck. Paul played banjo, Alan picked guitar and a bit of pedal steel and sang lead tenor. With Colleen's training and their guidance, she swung into bluegrass as if she'd been born in Kentucky, instead of windy Wellington. Later, they added mandolin, slap bass and dobro to the group. They were an instant hit in their home town, and when they appeared on *The Country Touch* they became stars as they sang their harmonies and played like tornadoes.

It was just unfortunate that they had heard a lot of hype about 'big stars' from across the Tasman and that they had included us in that category. After all, how could they know we were just family people who made our living touring the outback of Australia? By the time they realised this, we were looking for a copy of Dale Carnegie's *How to Win Friends and Influence People* to put in the mandolin player's instrument case (autographed, in case he didn't know where it came from). When it sank home that we just wanted to play music and act comedy sketches and we didn't greatly care who had the best lighting or stage set-up, they took us to their hearts and we took them to ours. Alan and Colleen played duets, they all wanted to take part in the skits, and we all talked about how good it would be if only they could come to Australia.

I had always wanted to have a full country band onstage for our tours, but country musos were few and far between ... good ones, especially. Here was a group of young, enthusiastic people dying to come over and work and I didn't think I could afford to bring them. The Hamilton County Bluegrass Band was the first homegrown bluegrass band I ever saw in action 'live' and when they did come to Australia in 1971, they galvanised the local musicians into action. Since their visit, bluegrass musicians and bands have mushroomed to an amazing extent and I give the HCBB credit for raising the standard of recorded country music, as well as the live appearances here. Paul and Colleen, who are now Mr and Mrs Trenwith with a family of four boys, are excited and amazed at the number of bluegrass musos in Australia, and their imaginative playing.

Chapter Thirteen

AT THE CROSSROADS

And they still talk about the way the travelling show
came to Top Springs . . .
'TOP SPRINGS' JOY McKEAN

Anne and David travelled with us on all school holidays. David was with the show until he was seven-and-a-half years old, Anne travelled with us for two or three years before school began for her, and again for a year when Millie was ill. They were both used to show life from the showgrounds to the out-back night showing, and they loved it. Both grew up with music, and Anne in particular took to the stage like a duck to water. Every holiday, she would have new songs to sing and she was very popular with other kids, especially the Aboriginal girls. We four looked forward to the holidays, and spent every minute together whether it was working the show or having a week off.

After the New Zealand tour, we headed north with a show which included Gordon Parsons and a dog act. Armstrong landed on the moon at the same time as I was covered in grease underneath the caravan. I heard the news and wished him luck as I slapped a bit more grease into the undercarriage. It was also the year we showed at Wave Hill in the Territory, finally arriving at nine o'clock at night to find people camped in the dry river bed by their campfires, waiting for us. We didn't have time to set up the sidewalls or the stage, and certainly had no ticket box. In its place we stood two forty-four gallon drums, and everyone filed through the drums to pay their way. I believe that not even one person tried to join the circle without paying for a ticket.

This was also the year we showed Top Springs. I've told this story before, and Joy eventually wrote it into a song which some people probably take for a tall story. However, it is true . . . every word of it. In fact, it was a wilder night than even the song makes out. There was a beef road going through the district and the road gangs included some big, tough Islanders who didn't get on with the local ringers from VRD (Victoria River Downs), the huge cattle station.

Top Springs was on the back road from Elliott in the Territory to Halls Creek in the Kimberley. We thought that if we cut across through Wave Hill and Top Springs to Halls Creek, we could circle back through Wyndham and Kununurra to the Northern Territory, ready for the Darwin Show and the run south.

We also thought Top Springs was a station, and we'd be able to stop off and just play a night there as a stopover and for petrol money. Joy wrote to them, and their reply reinforced all this, but when we got there it was a grog shanty, run by a sister of the one-time famous strongman and bodybuilder Don Athaldo, *and* it was close to the new beef road under construction.

The district stock inspector offered us the use of his home paddock when we realised that it would be fatal to try and set up anywhere near the licensed building, which had a verandah running along the front, a yard full of forty-four gallon petrol drums and a bar doing good business already. So out came the sidewalls, seating, stage and lighting plant. We started the show, and the opening singer copped a full beer can in his chest. He recovered, and went on singing while a couple of blokes from the beer can area got into a tangle. When the fight began to spread, I grabbed the microphone and bellowed into it: 'If you bastards up the back want to see a show, you better behave yourselves. Or you can get out, please yourselves. Just shut up, and give us a bit of a go!' I don't quite know what I'd have done if they'd started heaving full beer cans at me as well, but to my relief and slight surprise, they simmered down. I cut out interval, and pushed that programme through at a gallop.

No sooner had we finished than the blue erupted. We hadn't even got off the stage when a big Islander and a whacking great ringer from the VRD got stuck into it. The women and kids scattered and the families headed for home while bodies swayed back and forth, fists thumped into heads and jaws, and brawlers fell over our seats. At first I thought that they'd wreck the joint, and I had visions of a smashed stage and amplifiers, not to mention singers who couldn't sing for broken jaws. When one Islander the size of Ayers Rock headed for me I made sure I stuck my hat on, but he only said, 'Eh, Slim! No hard feelings, eh? They been asking for this for weeks . . . no hard feelings now?'

What could I say? Who's going to disagree with someone who has just flattened two tough ringers and is looking for a couple more to thump?

The bloke with the dog act was getting dramatic with a shotgun in his hands, getting ready to defend home and country (that is, his caravan, tipsy wife and beloved kelpies). I had to put a stop to that before he shot one of us by mistake. Gordon Parsons was standing by the sidewalls with a grin on his face. 'By Christ, Ned, she's a good one. Look at that bloke go . . . whoa! He's downed another one!'

Aunty Una and Joy had decided that the men were harmless after all, and began folding and stacking our wooden chairs. Whenever a fighter stumbled towards them, they simply poked him in the chest with the leg of a chair and he wandered off looking for someone else to hit. Every couple of minutes, either a ringer or a road worker would come up and apologise to them: 'Sorry, missus, but we can't have that sort of behaviour going on in Slim's show. Have to teach 'em a lesson.' Who was teaching who a lesson, I'll never know.

There were very few left standing in half an hour, and those that were simply loaded the bodies into the back of utilities and lorries and headed off into the night. The silence was deafening and the stars were bright as Gordon unveiled a carton of cold beer he'd found planted under our truck.

'Well, Ned,' he declared 'I don't know when I've had a better night out. Here, have a cold one!'

I originally set out to make records on the coveted Regal Zonophone label. That achieved, I went on to try to make a living out of singing by working in concerts and then by taking my own touring show out on the road. When the 'Pub' hit, I was on the showgrounds in partnership with Frank Foster and received my first, unique gold record. After leaving the show-grounds, not for a moment did I think of settling down.

If I wanted to continue recording, I had to continue appearing live before the public. There were no longer any organised country music concerts in or around Sydney as there used to be, so the only alternative was to tour. As the recordings sold more and more and the gold records began arriving, I was living a fairly isolated life out on the road. I had no inkling of just how unusual my career appeared to the record company, which was beginning to want more and more releases.

In the process of touring, I formed a bond with the people who listened to my songs and who inspired more songs and stories. As time went on, I found my attachment to them meant that I went back time and time again to places where hall conditions were pretty bad, where crowds were small, and where vehicles and people were bashed to pieces on the roads. So why did I go? Apart from being a stubborn person who will endure to achieve a purpose, I felt the greatest satisfaction in performing to the ones who inspired me. I took, and still take, pride in the friendliness shown to me by ordinary people like myself. Some councils and officials took the chance to throw their weight around and make life very difficult for us at times, but they were not the people who mattered.

As well as my touring work, I began accepting requests to visit people who couldn't get to my shows. The leprosaria outside Darwin and Derby, the nursing homes for the old and ill, small schools, big schools . . . every place had something to show me, and I learned a lot from the people I met. I showed in such small places that I was often asked, why bother? Well, it was a financial necessity; if I couldn't show six nights a week, I couldn't make a go of it. So if two paying towns were too far apart to travel from one to the next on consecutive nights, a small place in between would at least pay for the petrol for all the vehicles to get from one to the other. Those small towns paid me in another way, by forging close links with their life and mine.

The Aborigines all over Australia stuck by me through those early years. I appreciated them and their contribution to the cattle industry, as well as their friendship. Their sense of humour always appeals to me, and we get on well together. I've got lots of Aboriginal mates and we respect each other. They've taught me a lot.

My first contact with the people of the Daly River was through Miriam Rose Unganmerr. As a young girl, she wrote to me when I was in Darwin one year, early in the piece. None of her people, especially the children, could get to Darwin to see me. She and the children of the Daly River mission had saved up five dollars and were willing to pay me this amount to bring the show to the Daly and perform for them. Well, five dollars wouldn't even pay the petrol of course, but five dollars was a lot of money for those kids to raise and to me, it was as good as a million.

We had one spare night on our way south to catch the
Mt Isa Rodeo, so we turned off the highway and headed for
the Daly River. We weren't expected when we arrived, but we
were invited by the nuns and brothers to share what dinner
they had. The convent was a very basic building with cement
floors, the nuns' habits were patched and mended, and the
meal was meat of some kind (we didn't ask what it was, but
gathered that it was provided by the men hunters) and fruit
that they grew themselves, pawpaws and bananas. The excitement of all the people was infectious, and we almost thought of
ourselves as stars that night.

Miriam presented me with the performance fee, which I
accepted. It was the most valuable performance fee I have ever
been paid and I only made one stipulation. When we returned
next year, I would not expect to be paid in money. If we performed for the people of the Daly, then I would ask them to
perform for us in return. That would be a most satisfactory
repayment for me, and the bargain we struck that year was
kept for a long, long time.

Nevertheless, it has been my love of songs and recording
them which has driven me to do what I've done, and by 1970
I realised that I now had the opportunity to record a lot more
frequently. How was I to do that?

My family was growing up, and my daughter Anne would
be finishing high school at the end of the year. A decision had
to be made about Anne, coming straight from a girls' boarding
school to . . . what?

Barry Thornton, who had been with me from the beginning, had a small store near Metung which he was thinking of
selling, but would Baz want to settle down a bit more?

Were Joy and I to continue travelling ten months every
year?

Were we to stay based in Metung?

How could I manage to update my recording and touring,
and cope with my family responsibilities?

Over and over, the questions kept coming. I knew that once again, I was at some sort of crossroads in my life and I didn't want to make the final decision. I'm a great believer in looking for the sign which will turn me into one channel or another. The bottom line this time was that recording was my first love, and I would have to spend more time in Sydney to fulfil the demand for records. The next big thing was that Anne would go to university next year, and as we knew no one in Melbourne, we wanted her to be in Sydney where we had relations and friends. But we would have to leave Metung and Homewood, we would have to leave Mack and all the friends we had made there. I was torn in two.

The channel was chosen; we would get a home in Sydney, Anne would go to university there and we would spend more time based in the city while I recorded and we arranged a home-base for Anne. David was still at boarding school, and he had the choice between remaining at his Gippsland school or coming to Sydney. He chose to remain for a year before moving to Sydney.

After our tour of Western Australia in 1970, we managed to find a house in Sydney. We planned to move into it after Christmas, and in the meantime began getting ready for another big adventure . . . a tour of Papua New Guinea. By this time, I was getting quite a lot of offers to do shows and tours, and had even done a few Sydney clubs. I was talked into doing my first club by an agent, an ex-singer/compere, who used to work on all the old country shows in Sydney in Tim McNamara's day. By the time Barry, Joy and I fronted up to the club, I was physically ill with nervousness. So were they, I might add. It was an anti-climax to find that the audience was enthusiastic when I had expected catcalls. You have to realise that when rock'n'roll came into fashion, it also became the fashion to belittle anything or anyone vaguely approaching country. We were used to having to defend our ballads for the genuine grass-roots reflection of our society that they are. I used to work up a heap of aggression in readiness for any confrontation in those days. *These* days, I take Joy's suggestion and laugh at their ignorance (sometimes).

Our PNG promoters, far from being professionals, were two very nice blokes who had won Tatts, the big lottery. They were Ted and Raphael. Ted was an ex-patrol officer, and Raphael was his Sepik River man offsider. Ted decided he should run for the PNG parliament, and one of the best ways of getting the attention and respect of a majority of the local people was to bring Slim Dusty to PNG. One thing I didn't know was that my records were played non-stop in PNG and right throughout the Pacific Islands. The other thing was that every record sold was a pirated record. Not one penny ever came my way out of the many thousands sold up there, and the situation hasn't altered.

However, I grabbed a couple of offsiders to complement the old team of Joy and Barry, added Anne, who was singing well, and took David along as critic and gofer—go for this, and go for that . . . know what I mean? The first thing I had to establish was that we weren't morning drinkers. It wasn't that we didn't want to, but in that heat we wouldn't have been able to work that night if we'd happily taken part in all the welcome parties. Ted was sad, but said: 'You've made your point.'

We showed Port Moresby, where the crowd increased by about 500 per cent when the lights went out and they swarmed over the low fences around the oval where we were showing. We showed Lae, in a hall made of cement blocks with air spaces in between each two blocks, so that the hundreds outside took turns at the best spots to see the show for free. It poured with rain, but that was no worry to them. We showed Mount Hagen in the highlands, flying there over mist-shrouded mountains in an old DC3 aircraft. We went to the markets, and were mobbed. We tried to walk down the streets, and were followed by crowds of hundreds. We had a look at the hotel swimming pool only to find that the trees all around the grounds were bending under the weight of the people perched upon the branches, getting a closer look at me and the family. Our heads should have been like pumpkins.

Police Officer: 'There are more people here to greet you than there were for the Pope or for the Queen!'

At the close of the tour, Ted wanted to take me over to the Solomon Islands for a few informal appearances, so Barry and I went over there while Joy and the rest of the team returned to Australia. I will never forget my welcome to the Solomon Islands when people swarmed over the airport surrounds to greet me, and thousands crowded the wharf area the night I sang there. We also went to some of the surrounding islands, and the welcomes were just as overwhelming.

We were in Tennant Creek, Northern Territory, about to head over to Queensland for the Mt Isa Rodeo in August when I received a telegram from my half-brother Victor. I had to ring him, and when I spoke to him he told me that my mother had died half an hour before. She had not been ill, just tired after a long life, and died peacefully. I grieved for my loss, and for my isolation which meant that I saw her only once or twice a year. When she was in hospital the last year or so, we had only our letters as contact. Living in a caravan, there was no direct tele-phone contact, and usually moving every day brought the same old problems of mail missing us and never catching up. Joy and I went by plane to Adelaide, through Melbourne to Sydney, and then on by plane to Kempsey; arriving thirty minutes before Mum's funeral. My distance from her in these last years was driven home to me; as was the distance from my children in miles, but not in love. I knew then that I was doing the right thing in going to Sydney after all.

I wished, though, that I had shared my big secret with Mum. I wanted to surprise her and everybody else just as much as Government House had surprised me. We were at Homewood in between tours when the announcement arrived in the post that I was to be made a Member of the Order of the British Empire, and would I please ring to indicate whether or not I would accept the award of MBE?

I was amazed. Never had such an achievement entered my mind; I had never even thought about it. I'd just gone on my way; out on the road, and collecting my songs to record. If I *had* given the possibility any thought at all, I would have dismissed it immediately. I certainly didn't hesitate in accepting the award, especially as it meant, to me, recognition of Australian country music at long last. We were used to having to defend our ballads for the genuine grassroots reflection of our society that they are. For many years, country music was bottom of the ladder in trends, and even keen country listeners kept their records out of sight. Many country singers dropped country from their repertoire in favour of rock or calypso when they became all the go.

So in October, I fronted up to Sir Rohan Delacombe in Melbourne to have my MBE pinned on the lapel of my brand new suit, bought in honour of the occasion. Mack Cormack and Joy came to the investiture with me. Only two guests were permitted, and as I thought Joy was the most important person to accompany me, I couldn't choose between Anne and David as the second person. So Mack came, all dressed up, and on his best behaviour.

'Strewth, never thought I'd see the day! I take back what I said about bringing up a pig, m'boy.' He didn't, though, because he said it again quite a few times.

My MBE is on display with other memorabilia in the Australian Country Music Foundation in Tamworth, New South Wales. The funny thing, when I come to think about it, was that I was a Member of the Order of the British Empire and yet not a Member of the Order of Australia.

We were getting worried about Barry. He'd been rather withdrawn, but we blamed that on being tired and perhaps thinking about the home business and its attendant problems. Then he began having some queer turns, changing colour to pasty white and having to lean against anything handy rather than falling over. He didn't want to go to a doctor on tour.

'I'll go when I get back home' was his regular reply.

When we did get home in November, the local GP suggested a specialist's opinion. The specialists in Melbourne couldn't see him for three months. We were very upset by now, so we called everyone we knew in the medical profession. The result was an appointment in Sydney, early in January.

'Right!' I said. 'Start packing, *now*. We'll move into the Carlingford house before Christmas, and Barry and Pauline will come with us so that he can see the specialist in January.'

That's how we moved to Sydney, helped to pack by a sad Mack Cormack who knew better than I did that it would never be the same again. Homewood would never again be our permanent home. 'You'll never come back again,' he said.

I didn't believe him.

My family and I had developed a special relationship with Mack Cormack. He adopted us, and he became a second dad to me. I had someone I had to report to, as it were. At the end of each long year's touring, we'd have a break-up party at Homewood and Mack would lean against a door jamb and recite one of his latest works. Since his first efforts with 'Since the Bushland Boogie Came This Way', Mack had written quite a number of lyrics for me. Bush yarns like 'The Frog', 'How Will I Go With Him, Mate?', 'Camooweal' and 'The Last Thing to Learn'. He was someone I could relate to, someone who read Lawson and Paterson and other old bush poets as I did, someone who understood the restlessness of a traveller and who could see the good and bad in me but still liked me, and stood by me.

Mack: 'I should have killed you at birth, and raised
a pig instead.'

I laughed at the time, but there were occasions when I'm inclined to believe that he meant it. He was on tour around Australia with us one year, and when the going got tough and the tough were supposed to get going, I got going alright and the air turned bright blue. Mack decided that my behaviour was unbefitting any sort of gentleman, especially as my temper was upsetting my wife, so he pulled me into gear the best way he knew how. He ignored me for two days. No jokes, no yarns, and worst of all, no sympathy. Then he gave me a piece of his mind for good measure.

So you see, it was indeed a wrench for me to make Sydney my home base in place of Homewood, and to have neighbours either side of me rather than Mack and Lorna across on the ridge by Chinamans Creek, and the waters of the Gippsland Lake in front of me. I missed my fishing mates, and the friendly gatherings in the local pub. I missed the evenings at Homewood over Christmas, playing cards with Anne and David and Joy's dad, another Mac.

Barry insisted he was alright and was still insisting when they put him into hospital for tests, and he was correct to a certain extent. His problem was not a tumour, as was the early suspicion, but some other vague diagnosis no one understood, plus an imbalance of the middle ear.

'Told yer so,' he said. 'Nothing wrong with me. When's the recording session?'

Just the same, everyone was glad he wasn't going to keep on keeling over now and then, and we could all stop being polite and concerned. Now we could go back to our old casual selves. I was so glad to get into the studio; at least the surroundings there were familiar, unlike the solid brick house with lawns and pool and fences that I grudgingly looked after now and then.

Anne came in and did some backing vocals for me in the January sessions, and in March, when I was putting down the tracks for 'Songs from the Land I Love', I walked out of the studio one day and nearly fell over Paul and Colleen Trenwith from the HCBB.

'What on earth are you doing here?' It wasn't the warmest of greetings, but they were the last people I expected to see wandering around Studio 301 when I thought they were hammering out bluegrass breakdowns in New Zealand.

Colleen had her fiddle with her, and after explaining that they had come over to do some work with Tex Morton who was now back in Australia, she was hoisted into the studio to put down fiddle tracks on the spot. Paul's banjo got a workout on some of the following sessions, and it went on from there. There were two new members of their band, and we all got on like a house on fire. Many were the barbecues and jam sessions, and many were the earplugs our neighbours probably used over the next few years as music poured out of the suburban home. Country and bluegrass music roared out the front door, the side windows and over the paddocks outside our back fence; the horses in the paddock were curious and came to listen before they took off, pounding across the grass.

I had always wanted to have a full country band on tour with me and here was this great band looking for work, but unable to come to Western Australia with us because they had committed themselves to waiting for club dates, which never eventuated.

There were many changes in the air. Radio station 2TM Tamworth had originated a nightly country music session called 'Hoedown', and at the time, the genial and sincere host was John Minson. John was a harmonica wizard, a builder of musical instruments when he had the time and the inclination, and a great encouragement to all country music artists whether they were established, were getting there or just wanting to be. When we first heard of 'Hoedown', we were in

Queensland on tour, but we quickly woke up to the fact that it would be an ideal vehicle for advertising our touring show. The manager of 2TM and BAL Marketing, which was the corporate arm of the radio station, was a man called Max Ellis, and although Max wasn't really a country music follower, he could see the potential of the music for 2TM. He began staging country music shows in the old town hall, and the profits were put aside for another project he had in mind, an awards night in the style of the American Country Music Awards. We did a few of these shows, and were happy to have the proceeds go towards another dream—a headquarters for country music in Australia, and the revival of our music at long last.

We were rather sceptical when EMI told us that one of their Melbourne retailers, who was a show promoter on the side, wanted to talk to us about appearances in Melbourne. We still smarted from our early Melbourne experiences, and we considered that the bloke must have given EMI the wrong name. He couldn't have meant me when he said he was booking the Melbourne Town Hall and other places such as a theatre at Monash University. But he did mean me, and no one was more astonished than I was when we actually did the deal for the HCBB, Barry, Joy, Anne and me to appear in Melbourne. I thought he'd do his dough, but the man had done his homework. Looking through the record catalogue one day, he came across my listing.

'This Slim Dusty's got more albums listed than the Beatles! He's got to be good for concerts!'

No sooner said than done, and when Melbourne Town Hall filled and the reception was good, I felt a bit better as we headed for Monash University the next day.

'Just stick close by me. Those uni students are going to be real smart asses with their "country hicks" shots, you can back it in.' Pessimist Slim was in good form.

I walked onto the stage, getting ready to give as good as I got, with the aggro building up like mad. I stopped in my tracks. I just couldn't believe my eyes and ears as the entire audience of young uni students came to their feet and gave me a standing ovation. I finished the long walk to the microphone and sang my old bush songs with all the confidence in the world. They seemed to know them all.

'Didn't you know that you have a cult following in the universities?' the promoter asked me after the show.

No, I didn't. I thought they must have got me mixed up with someone else.

It was the same thing later that year when EMI, again, asked me to do a concert in Newcastle City Hall for a prominent record retailer and promoter there. It was the first time country music had been presented in the City Hall for years and years. In fact, it might have been the first time, but the place was packed to the rafters and it was such a success that we were booked for a repeat performance.

'Crikey,' I said to Joy. 'Looks like we can work anywhere we like in between the tours and the recording. Hard to believe, isn't it!'

She pulled out a list of requests for appearances and club bookings which we had rejected in favour of our Queensland and Territory tour. 'They'll still be there next year,' she said hopefully. They were, too.

My wife can do a lot of different things, so I expect her to do them. If she didn't want me to know just how many jobs she can handle, she should have played dumber than she did. What I'm getting at is that Joy used to manage to turn out some good songs now and then, as well as being a tour manager, stage performer and backing muso, wife and mother, diplomat and peacekeeping mission, all in one. She could blow her top at times, and when it happened we all ran for cover, as the peacekeeping mission shifted on to a war footing.

In June 1971, we were to open the northern tour at

Kingaroy in Queensland. Joy, Barry and I had to meet the rest of the team at Warwick, just over the border. We each drove a vehicle and caravan, aiming to get from Sydney to Warwick in the one day. Baz and I each drove a truck and van, while Joy piloted a station wagon and caravan. It was a long drive up the New England Highway, through the Hunter Valley, through Tamworth and up over the Moonbi hills through the Great Dividing Range to the north.

I was ahead of Joy, and had the big van parked by the time she arrived about nine o'clock at night.

'I wrote a song while I was driving,' she announced.

I was busy with the mechanics of getting the van set up. 'Did you? Better put it on tape then, before you forget it.' Not exactly excited, you see. She dragged out the little tape recorder and set it up, got a guitar out of its case, and sang her new song. I don't remember listening to it, and when I wanted to rehearse something a week later, I wiped most of the song off.

Joy found out about that at Christmas time when Colleen and Paul Trenwith were staying with us at Homewood, and she wanted to play it to Colleen.

'You wiped it off! What for?' This was when the peacekeeping mission began to fall apart. 'You're always grabbing tapes and not caring what's on them!'

'Well, can't you remember it?' I wanted to go fishing.

I took the others with me, and when we came home, Joy had finished the song 'Lights on the Hill'. When she started up through the Moonbi hills that evening in June, headlights from the vehicles heading south hit her eyes at every turn. Because of her polio-affected left leg, she had the use of only one foot to operate accelerator, brake and also the headlights dimmer which was situated on the floor. This meant that every time a car or truck came towards her, she had to take her foot off the controls to hit the dimmer switch and for that second or two, she felt out of control. The story came naturally, and she fitted the rhythm of the engine to the words.

'What do you think?' she wanted to know. 'It might suit you to record.'

I listened to it again. 'No, you've got too many words in each line. Maybe if you changed it a bit, perhaps.'

'But that's the idea of it.' She protested, but I was quite certain that first, it was not my style, secondly, it had too many words, and thirdly, I wasn't going to use it.

That is, until Colleen pulled out her fiddle that evening and backed Joy's singing of her new song. The cajun-style double stopping fiddle drove the rhythm along, and by the time Colleen, Paul and then the rest of the HCBB had raved about 'Lights' I was convinced. I had to work out where to fit in a breath before I passed out blue in the face, and on principle I was not enthusiastic to begin with, but I recorded it in February 1972 and it has become my biggest and most consistent seller since the 'Pub'.

It was the first successful Australian-written truck song (took a while for our truckies to realise that Joy had written it, not me); it won the first ARIA (Australian Record Industry Awards) award for a country song or album; the album went gold many times over; it has been recorded by numerous artists here and a couple in America; it won Joy the APRA song of the year award at Tamworth's first Australasian Country Music Awards, and for me, the best single or extended play the same year. In 1972, my recording of 'Lights' won Best Country Single at the Federation of Australian Broadcasters' Awards in Canberra.

I remember only too well how we plugged that single. In Busselton, Western Australia, I bought some brown paper, cardboard and string. Between us, we wrapped and posted copies of 'Lights on the Hill' to every radio announcer we thought would play it, and they certainly did play it. It was a new development in country writing here in Australia.

Just after I recorded 'Lights', EMI celebrated my twenty-five years' recording with them by presenting me with gold records number nine and ten, a couple of sculptured game cocks (I wonder if they meant anything by that?) and even gave me a twenty-five year service company lapel pin. It made me stop and think, that did. The farm boy who walked into the makeshift Homebush studio in November 1946 was still there beneath the tailored suit I wore at the reception twenty-five years later in the carpeted foyers of the big Studio 301; but this time the managing director was making a presentation to me, and my daughter and son were there to see it. I allowed myself to feel very proud, and very grateful to life.

Anne was at university and about to record her first single; David was at school in Sydney and doing well in lessons and in sport; Barry and his family were settled in Sydney; the HCBB were livening things up both musically and socially; my records were selling better than ever and I was in demand for personal appearances and concerts. The telephone seemed to be constantly ringing, and for the first time in more than twenty years we felt part of a new, exciting live music scene. More way out groups were emerging, especially in Melbourne, and after years of isolated touring in the outback, we were stimulated by all this action.

But it was back on the road for us, and the HCBB set out for the northern tour with us.

Chapter Fourteen

I DON'T THINK I'LL MAKE IT

But you meet a friend or two along the highway . . .
'WALK A COUNTRY MILE' JOY McKEAN

As the HCBB remarked, 'If we'd driven as far as this in one day back home in New Zealand, we'd have driven straight off the edge on the other side.'

We'd left Sydney in June and our first overnight stop was in Orange, on the way to Bourke in western New South Wales. Joy and I froze, but the HCBB loved the heavy frost. They felt right at home. Up through Cunnamulla and Charleville, Barry had Mulga Dan going full bore and everyone took turns working in the comedy skits with him. On our nights off, we camped off the road with the caravans pulled into a circle so that the big campfire was in the centre. Sometimes, we had an entertainment night where everyone had to 'do a turn', but it had to be different from the person's usual onstage act. The band acted a play, Barry yodelled, I had to make Tich the performing dog do his tricks, and Joy did a memory act that a friend had taught her years before.

It was on one of these camps, between Winton and Boulia, that we saw a small plane circling in the distance. The caravans

195

were on a flat spot in the red earth, ringed by the spiky spinifex that slashed your ankles as you walked up to the ridge nearby. We began yelling and waving our arms but the plane landed some distance away. Next thing, it came taxiing along the road and over to the camp. The pilot and his wife were people we knew and had been expecting. They'd flown from their camp over near Innamincka in the backblocks of South Australia to visit and perhaps see the show in Boulia. Next morning, they took the plane out onto the stretch of sealed road and began taxiing for take-off. A small campervan was bowling along the road too, and the driver nearly had a heart attack when he was being overtaken by a plane. We all hooted and cooeed as he wobbled off the road, and sat there in disbelief.

It was a happy tour as we introduced the HCBB to some of our friends along the track. At Halls Creek in the Kimberleys, Ernie Bridge took them mustering on the station. We set out across country to Wave Hill and, as usual, things happened. Barry was driving the truck, and with Graham from the HCBB, set out ahead of the rest of the troupe. When he wasn't waiting for us at the arranged spot, we all waited two hours and then headed for Wave Hill, thinking he must have got the instructions mixed. I was driving my new purple Fairlane, pride of my heart, and cursing Baz because I had two flat tyres and had to keep pumping them up every half hour or so. I had two spares, but they were both in the truck.

I had recorded a song that said, 'No more walking bullocks, along the Wave Hill Track'. Well, I found one or it found me. This dirty great bullock charged out from behind some scrub on the very edge of the road and smashed into me. He rolled over the bonnet, looked like coming into the car with us, then tumbled into the dirt and galloped back into the bush. Purple and I limped into Wave Hill looking the worse for wear, but at least roadworthy.

In Wave Hill, we waited and waited for Thunder, the big truck with all the gear, to turn up. We couldn't work out what had happened. Showtime arrived, and everything was in the missing Thunder. The big crowd waiting for us helped us get a single light bulb slung up over the back of a truck, and the store ratted through their largest size and lairiest shirts and pants to outfit Miles, the bass player.

We had no amplifiers, and only acoustic instruments. The crowd listened quietly, and being in the open air, the sound carried and they heard it all. Miles pranced around doing Mulga Dan's act with make-up all over his face. He had a real moustache at that stage, but wouldn't let the girls put black on it to make him look a bit like the real Mulga. We all enjoyed his performance, and so did the crowd. The only one that didn't was Miles.

In the meantime, Barry and Graham were sitting in the truck seventy miles away. The only supplies they had with them was some dried up fruitcake that had been in the cabin of the truck for a month or so. They had been gasbagging, had missed the Wave Hill turn-off and didn't wake up till they reached the aptly named Mistake Creek. Even with the saddle tanks on the truck it was doubtful if they would have enough fuel to get back to the main road and into the settlement. It was even more doubtful if they'd make it for the show; maybe interval, perhaps. Barry decided to cut across country on station roads through the properties, heading for Wave Hill by sketchy maps and by following his nose. The old Inter ploughed along through wire gates and almost non-existent tracks, reaching the main road just after dark. Then the generator, shaken to pieces by the track, gave up the ghost and there they sat in the dark until some of the team came looking for them after the show. If they hadn't made it to the main road, they might still be sitting there. We'd never have looked out in the bush for them.

In Darwin, they met Aunty Billie Pitcheneder. A very big lady, Aunty Billie drove transports up and down the 'track' during the Second World War. When Darwin was bombed by the Japanese, civilians including Aunty Billie were evacuated. She landed back in Darwin the moment she was allowed. Aunty Billie could talk a mile a minute, and she mostly talked with effect when she was raising money for charity. She would have to be the top fundraiser for charities that the Top End has ever had, and she had taken us under her wing from the moment she saw Joy endeavouring to hang out the washing and comfort a crying small son at the same time. From then on, when we came to Darwin, Aunty Billie had iced water backstage for us, supper at the caravans, and tales of her latest doings. In 1972, her latest 'sit-in' raised $2700 for the Blind Appeal. She was always busy.

The old Darwin was a place of character and characters. Aunty Billie was one, Jim the newspaper editor was another, the people who ran the little Cavanaugh Theatre; they all became friends we met up with year after year. We got to know families who came regularly, station owners, station hands, Aboriginal and Islander people. We went to Bathurst Island by plane to perform for the people there, and we flew down to Port Keats to visit and perform. We met up again with Margaret Mile, who had toured with us and shared a caravan with Aunty Una for a couple of years. The Kerrs who ran the camping area at Howard Springs outside Darwin always had a quiet camp for us, so that we could come home from the show and have our 'wind down' time.

Each year, we took up our friendships where we left off. It was not as though we'd been apart for twelve or eighteen months, but as if it were yesterday. When we reached Mt Isa for the rodeo week, there were friends to see. People like old Grannie, bringing up two grandchildren on her own, who remembered the Isa as a tent town. Little Frank who painted the tunnels of the Mt Isa mine, and brought us fresh vegetables from his garden along with all the gossip and doings of the town. The rodeo organisers who would help us get our repairs done quick smart; the radio station staff who made us part of rodeo week events; and the professional man who loved nude sunbaking.

We went over to the Queensland coast at Cairns to introduce the HCBB to Australia's tropical wonders and some
more of my interesting friends and then all the way down to
the south, where we finished the tour at Tamworth and I
recorded another 'live' album. One of the songs I recorded,
Stan Coster's 'Election Day', came in handy when we went
down to Melbourne for more shows and election fever was
heightening. All in all, with Anne finishing her university
degree and planning on a trip overseas; with David doing well
in exams and being in the school's top basketball team, Barry
releasing his second EP record of instrumentals, and Joy and
I planning a holiday in New Zealand after the HCBB went
home, it was a happy year.

I was interviewing guitarists. The old Bazza had decided that
after nineteen years on the road with me, a year at home
sounded rather good to him. His two kids were growing up,
and the boy was proving a bit of a handful for Pauline on her
own, so I was interviewing guitarists. Not that I expected to
find one who would just about read my mind like Barry did.

'Now look, next year I'll be first out of the chute. Just this
year to get the family all settled down, and have a bit of a
break.' Barry was quite definite.

All sorts of guitarists turned up to try out for the job,
including the one who looked as though he'd sit around
studying his navel while the rest of us changed a tyre. There
were professional musos who were a bit offended when asked
to come along for a tryout; and there were keen amateurs. In
the end, I turned to John Minson, 'Mr Hoedown' on 2TM
Tamworth.

'I know just the man for you, Slim,' said John. 'He's toured
with Buddy Williams and with Athol McCoy, and he's a good
bush ballad guitarist looking for work. I'll put him in touch.'

John was quite right, of course. Lindsay Butler turned out

to be just the bloke I was looking for, and he toured and recorded with me off and on for years.

On 28 January 1973, the first Australasian Country Music Awards were held in the Tamworth Town Hall, in front of a capacity crowd of artists, record industry executives, radio industry personalities and country music enthusiasts. It was a history making night, and the beginning of an Awards tradition. On that first occasion there was very little media interest, and indeed, for the first fifteen years or so of the Country Music Awards, they were treated with slight amusement. There was the usual haybales and hicks treatment in any write-up, but the Awards continued to become stronger and stronger.

Today, the Golden Guitar trophy is the most coveted win for any country artist, and for plenty of artists who aren't country but depend on country music's tolerance to allow them a foot in the door of fame via country music. The Awards media coverage is second to none, with journalists from paper, radio and television fighting for stories; and also fighting for accommodation, if the truth be known.

The Tamworth locals were not at all impressed with the initial invasions of their city by the country music enthusiasts who moved into every camping site available, and some sites that weren't; the buskers who set up in every possible spot along the main street and provided music good and bad; the bikies who made the Locomotive Hotel their depot; and the general atmosphere of cheerful, casual holidaymaking. They changed their attitude later.

However, that first Awards night was truly exciting. There were only six categories to have trophies presented, and the results and winners of the Capital Country Music Association's talent quest were also announced and awarded. John Minson's 'Hoedown' programme was being broadcast live from the town hall foyer, incorporating the Awards ceremony and interviews with artists and industry executives.

We have rarely missed attending the Awards. We have seen the weekend's festivities, begun as a jamboree and talent quest weekend held by the Capital Country Music Association, grow into nearly two weeks of country music events, with free shows and entertainment in the streets and parks, as well as concerts by the top stars of our music. There are now museums and exhibitions, with the Roll of Renown and Hands of Fame, plus the Songmakers' plaques all on permanent exhibition. The Golden Guitar is the object of fierce competition; Starmaker and New Talent quests have been springboards for some of our finest young stars' careers, and the city of Tamworth's residents now forgive country music for its intrusion, and make its artists and followers very, very welcome.

We had just returned from three weeks' holiday in New Zealand to find a petrol strike in full swing and us with no petrol in the car to get to Tamworth. 2TM came to the rescue with seats on a charter plane, and through the wildest storms and pouring rain, we arrived in time for the Awards ceremony. I wouldn't have missed it for quids, when I think back. At those first Awards, a history making night, I won Best Album ('Me and My Guitar'), Best Single or EP ('Lights on the Hill'), and Joy and I both received trophies when she won the APRA award for Best Composition ('Lights on the Hill'). To top it off, the HCBB won the Best Instrumental. The Best Selling Track was 'Redback on the Toilet Seat' by Slim Newton, and for more than twenty years I have had to deny that I'm the bloke who had that run-in with a spider in the dunny.

I once received a letter that was addressed to: *Slim Dusty, Travelling Showman, Somewhere in Australia.*

I know that there are complaints about Australia Post, and I know I've been guilty of some of those, but I have to hand it to them sometimes. They must have a special detective branch for letters like the one above, and some of the others I've received. Another was, 'Slim Dusty, Homewood, Australia', and still another, 'Slim Dusty, The Pub, Australia'.

A travelling showman is what I am, and after discovering that all the audiences at the city club shows sang out for exactly the same songs as the audiences in the bush, I used to take the same show around Australia and into the cities. It brought home to me with a bang just how many bush folk have had to move to the city to live.

There were still plenty out there away from the cities, and I headed bush again after EMI presented me with a couple more gold records. I had a new team with me, all trying to fit in to touring with me and Joy and a couple of older hands. One of the older hands was one of the 'been there, done that and this is how you do it' types. Between him and some of the officious hall and park attendants, I sometimes frothed at the mouth and began mapping out chapters of a book that I would call *Bastards I Have Met*. The really bright spot was a tape from Paul and Colleen Trenwith saying that they'd love to come back to Australia in 1974 and work with us for a year.

We arrived home from the northern tour to find that Barry had gone bush. City work was a bit mundane after all the years on the road, and he'd been lured to the Centre by the offer of varied work and a bit of flying here, there and everywhere. In the end it didn't work out so well, but it was an experience and a half apparently. In the meantime, I was branching out musically and trying different styles and songs with different musicians.

I missed my family, and I hope they missed me. When we were separating after holidays one year, I tried to lighten the gloom: 'Well, after all, you'll have a nice easy trip south on the plane while Mum and I have to bump along in the old truck and caravan.'

Anne looked me in the eye and said, 'Dad, don't give me that. You know perfectly well you love every minute of it.'

Yes, I know and so do they. What's more, they understand what drives me better than I understand it myself, I think. They've got the music bug, too, and that helps.

Anne was shaping up as a good musician and singer, as was David. Late in 1973, when we toured Tasmania, Anne came with us. As she had done on uni holidays, she had her own singing spot as well as singing backup for others, and she played some bass and some mandolin. That year, she replaced Joy on our New Zealand trip as my bass player. Then when I did some shows before Christmas up in southern Queensland, my drummer was David. The four of us recorded a song called 'Travelling Country Band', and in 1974, I re-christened my band. No one else could really replace the old Bushlanders— Barry, Joy and me—so the new team was the Travelling Country Band. Members have come and gone, but the Travelling Country Band has survived it all and it is surprising what a melting pot of musical styles it has been over the years.

All in all, I was sailing along having a great time recording, touring, doing club shows and special events as more and more promoters discovered that they could actually find me within a required time frame. Paul and Colleen arrived in February 1974, and with Colin Watson on lead guitar, Anne or Joy on bass, we formed the first Travelling Country Band and hoed into a programme of short tours and club shows, writing and collecting songs, and rehearsing them ready for recording. I wanted to record an album before I went north on tour, and Anne was about to put down her first album as well.

There were so many good songs coming in. As well as Mack Cormack and Stan Coster, Tony Brooks weighed in with 'When the Scrubbers Break' in 1971 and he's been weighing in ever since with songs, advice, opinions and arguments. We tracked down Tom Oliver and his tall story 'From the Gulf to Adelaide', and Joy wrote 'The Biggest Disappointment', a song that has become another favourite in my repertoire. I don't know for sure, but I think I may have been the first singer round this neck of the woods to sing the Lawson and Paterson words. To me, they have the rhythm and movement that makes them easy to set to music; Lawson even more so than Paterson. I've been happy to see so many singers later on delving into the Australian poets' works and reviving them in song as I have done.

All in all, I was having a great time. More success at the Tamworth Awards, more Golden Guitars, and EMI were planning to present me with another ten gold records in April. I took the show down to the south-west to do a club show there, and didn't take my own sound system with me, having been assured that the club had a system. They did, and it was so bad that the audience took up a petition at the close of the night, demanding that the club invest in a decent sound system. We all signed it, I think. I strained and strained all through a long programme that night, trying to be heard above the squawks and squeaks and fading speakers.

I have always found that a virus or similar will hit you where you're working hardest, which in my case is my throat. For a singer, it's absolute hell for a loving fan to come up when you're doing autographs and declare, 'I've been in bed with the 'flu for a week, but I just had to get up to come and see you', as they plant a kiss on your cheek or hug you warmly. You know every little 'flu bug is hitching a ride onto your face and into your system. So, at first, I blamed my bad throat on overstrain plus a virus, and fell back on my old stagecraft to nurse it along till it got better. But it didn't get better, it got worse.

As we headed for Darwin, I lost range, I lost volume, I lost clarity. By the end of each show, I was almost whispering. I was terrified . . . any previous throat trouble hadn't gone on and on like this. By the time I faced the fact that I wasn't improving, I was somewhere in the Northern Territory with a full show on the road—vehicles, caravans and people—halls booked, deposits paid, advertising out. I couldn't just stop, I had to get through until we were within reach of Sydney again. The old showman's tradition of 'the show must go on' is truer than most people realise. You hate letting people down, and it's in your bones that you have to keep going. Besides all that, you've got people to pay.

Aunty Una wasn't on tour this year for family reasons, and we hired a shorthand-typist-cum-front-of-house girl, Carol, to help Joy with the mountains of letters, and to help sell records at the shows. After we had come to an agreement with her, she tentatively asked if she could bring her cat. Joy said it nicely, and I said it loudly, but we both said *no*.

'Oh, well, my girlfriend said she'd look after him if I couldn't take him. I suppose that will have to do,' she wistfully said.

We were one day out on the road, when we found out we had another traveller—Pookie.

Anne copped the worst of it. She was driving a station wagon, pulling a caravan for her and Carol, which she now had to share with darling Pookie. Colin Watson, the guitarist, made up the fourth in the car each day, but Anne was responsible for the car and hooking on the caravan and so on. Pookie destroyed every flyscreen on every window of the caravan as he refused to be cooped up in the caravan at night. Often he came flying back through the window to land on Anne or Carol's face, pursued by the howling local cats. Then he never wanted to move onto the next town in the morning, so he'd take off under the nearest building and wouldn't come out.

Me: 'That bastard of a Pookie has to go!'

It wasn't my fault that Pookie was still alive by the time we reached Cairns, but I'd had it. I made up my mind—that bastard of a cat had to go. When Pookie shot under an old building at the caravan park, I went looking for a lump of four-by-two timber, while everyone else coaxed and wheedled him. When I got it, I went round the other side where Carol couldn't see me and I spotted dear Pookie crouched out of reach under the old house. He was looking the other way at all his faithful followers crawling after him when I let fly with the four-by-two, followed up by a couple of house bricks. The wood hit him in the tail, and I had hopes of knocking him out with a brick, but he flew out screeching. I was after him, on hands and knees to start with, and then flat tack across the park, hurling everything I could lay my hands on as dear Pookie headed for home and glory in the shape of Carol's waiting arms. I don't think Carol ever forgave me, but I smiled all the way to the next town.

Meanwhile, Joy rang a friend in the music business to try and find a specialist who understood the difficulties of a stage artist, and who would be the best bet to check out my throat. In September when we flew from Brisbane to Sydney to do a special charity show, we saw the medical man and then resumed the rest of the tour. He diagnosed a nodule on my vocal cords, and assured us both that it was the simplest thing in the world to remove it. My touring schedule for the rest of the year was set, so he made the hospital and operating arrangements immediately. A fortnight's rest for the throat after the October operation, and bob's your uncle, he said.

Naturally, I was worried, but I didn't have any choice. We rang a friend of a friend who'd had the same operation, and again heard how successful it was. 'A fortnight later, I was singing better than ever' was the report.

Well, I wasn't. After the short hospital stay and the prescribed silence to rest the vocal cords, I could hardly speak, let alone sing. My voice wobbled all over the place, and I absolutely croaked. I knew I'd have to persevere, this might be just a case of practising and working the voice in, I thought. But in the end, I went back to the specialist and told him: 'I can't sing properly. I've got no control, nothing! What's wrong, I can't sing!' He didn't believe me. He put me in theatre and said he checked the vocal cords, and there was no reason at all why I should be having any trouble. I marched into his consulting rooms complete with my guitar to demonstrate what was wrong, and he couldn't hear anything wrong . . . so he said.

'Just take a week longer to settle down,' he suggested. 'Have a beer, do everything you normally do.' He seemed to think I was having a bad case of imaginitis.

We cancelled some Sydney shows and the first four shows in the southern tour, opening at Ballarat. When I came off-stage, I smashed my beloved guitar to the floor in despair. I was embarrassed at my performance, and sick of pretending to myself that I was improving. If I lost my ability to sing, then I lost my reason for being—it was that deep with me.

I had another twelve shows booked before the Christmas break, and I went through hell to keep faith and do them. By the end of each show, Joy was singing in unison with me in the finale songs to help me get through, the band was dropping keys and volume to support me, and the sound man wound up the mikes more and more as the night went on. I could barely force myself to go out and do autographs at the end of the show, where all those great people showed concern for me and my 'dreadful laryngitis'.

At long last, I reached the last show . . . at Tamworth. The country music newspaper reported on the show in glowing terms, but couldn't help remarking on 'the King's gravelly rendition' of some songs. More and more, I was being referred to as the 'King of Country Music'; if I was the King, then I had never been closer to abdicating.

In Sydney, Anne said to me: 'Dad, I'm taking lessons in voice production and breathing. Why don't you see if they could help you, too? It can't do any harm, anyway, can it?'

That's how I came to be what they call a mature age student of voice . . . but it wasn't until another of the students recognised me that the teacher discovered who he was teaching. Then he wanted the whole story, why a natural singer, untrained as I was, suddenly required coaching? He became concerned, and concentrated on teaching me how to conserve my voice under strenuous conditions, and encouraging me to keep on trying and improving. It was a humbling experience for me.

We were at Metung for Christmas when Cyclone Tracy hit Darwin on Christmas Day 1974. I immediately reached for the phone to check on our many friends, and then put it down again, remembering the request that people didn't jam the phone lines to Darwin because they were desperately needed by the emergency services. We thought of the young friend living in a caravan, of the family living in the worst hit area, and of the little theatre and its loyal workers. We thought of Aunty Billie, probably trying to feed the multitudes if we knew Aunty. The theatre was razed to the ground; the caravan was tied down and rocked to and fro frighteningly but survived; the family crouched in the bathroom and prayed.

Darwin was literally flattened. There was no power, no water, no housing. People slept in the local high school at Nightcliff, in community halls, or wherever they could find a roof standing. When the government flew me with Joy, Paul and Colleen to Darwin in March on a morale-boosting exercise, we were shocked to silence as we looked around. There was a car still in the pool of the old Travelodge Motel—which was about the only one left standing. Facilities were basic, and we were lucky to get a meal, same as everyone else. House floors stood shakily on the high-rise foundations, exposed to the elements as the houses themselves had just been swept into the air, to fall back to earth in monstrous heaps of rubbish and rubble.

We sang and played in the Nightcliff High School, and talked to people all the time. There were faces of shock and dullness; just as there were the bright, cheeky dials of the kids and many adults. There was a huge ship anchored at the Darwin Wharf, serving as a floating hostel to hundreds, maybe more than a thousand. I don't remember, I was in a state of shock myself, I think. People we knew kept coming up and talking about their experiences; but the last person I expected to see on the ship when we gave the concert was Big Julie, the ex-stripper-cum-juggler. Most of our friends were safe, despite their injuries and losses, but old Darwin was devastated and would never be the same again. There was nothing left, hardly even debris, where the little theatre had been, and its devoted band of workers would never have the funds to rebuild.

If my being there at that time made any difference to the bleakness that was so foreign to old Darwin, then I'm grateful that I had the chance. Since the rebuilding, the character of the city has, of necessity, changed and many who were evacuated never returned.

I had kept very quiet about my throat operation for professional reasons, especially as I hadn't expected any problems afterwards. After appearing at a festival in March, where we stayed in a hotel overlooking the traffic lights on the highway, Joy wrote a song called 'I Don't Sleep at Night', and I planned to record it. The words rang true, because I wasn't sleeping too well as the prospect of recording loomed ahead of me. My voice lessons were getting me by on stage, but recording was much more particular. Any faults stick out like a sore toe. I can always hear the lack of control on that recording, just as I can hear the vast improvement on the 'Lights on the Hill' album which I recorded in May that year.

The record company felt I should do a national tour, appearing in all the capital cities of Australia. They arranged it, and also a New Zealand tour. The upshot was that I now had the credit of being the first Australian country artist to take his show into all the cities, and the first to play the Sydney Opera House. Looking at those sails by the harbour, and at the plush red velvet seats stretching for what seemed miles from the stage to the back of the theatre, it seemed a long, long way from Top Springs or the Daly River. It was a long, long way from the

Nulla to the Opera House, and I'd got there one step at a time. When I faltered or even slipped back, there was a team behind me to hold me in place. My family, the musos, the singers and variety acts on tour, the songwriters, and the people who came to the shows and let me know that they reckoned I could do it.

The old bush ballad was back in town.

Chapter Fifteen

HOW WILL I GO
WITH IT, MATE?

Tall and as tough as a gumtree,
with humour as dry as the track . . .
'TO A MATE' SLIM DUSTY

John Dante was ninety when he died on 4 June 1975, and for me, a lot of the glamour of showbusiness died with him. I cancelled some recording dates and went to Metung to talk to Mack. That always made me feel better, and I hadn't been to Homewood as much as I would have liked. Life was moving at a much faster pace these days.

In November 1975, we were touring Western Australia when Mack's brother-in-law rang me from Metung.

'Slim, Mack doesn't want you to know but I think you should. He's in hospital with lung cancer, and there's nothing they can do for him. He could last weeks or days, we don't know.'

Tom promised to ring me every day, as I prayed for the tour to end so that I could get back to Metung. The crowd was filling the big hotel function room at Geraldton for that night's show when the phone rang in our hotel room. It was Tommy.

'Slim, he's worse. They don't think he'll last more than a couple of days. Can you come home, mate?'

I called in the tour promoter. 'Get us on a plane home. I'm sorry, but that's it. I'm going home.'

They held the plane at Geraldton airport for us to scramble aboard, still in our stage clothes, and with a few belongings in a small bag each. Anne, Joy and I caught the plane in Perth to Melbourne, hired a car and reached Bairnsdale Hospital at 9.45 the next morning.

Mack was ill and tired, but still did not approve of my leaving the show.

'I knew you'd do this, that's why I said they weren't to tell you,' he roused. I think he was glad to see us all, just the same. I spent every minute with him that I could, only leaving to attend David's speech night in Sydney. We hadn't told David how ill Mack was, because he was doing his Higher School Certificate examinations. He was trying for a really high mark to get him into Veterinary Science at Sydney University. He and Mack had decided that Vet Science would suit David's interests and have Mack's approval.

We were all at Homewood when Mack died on 15 December 1975. Whenever I look at a certain doorjamb in Homewood, I can picture Mack leaning on it reciting 'How Will I Go With It, Mate?'

It was a subdued Christmas at Homewood, before I headed into years of change.

David's exam results put him in the top five per cent in the state, and he started Vet Science at Sydney University. Anne joined a country group playing clubs in Sydney. She might have had a uni degree in Biological Science, but she was intent on music as a career instead. She moved out of the house she was sharing at Lindfield, and came home while she sussed out a suitable house to move into. While we were delighted to have her home for a while, David and I knew the battle for bathroom space was on again.

Then at four o'clock one morning, David woke us.

'Mum, Dad. Ryde hospital is on the phone. She's alright, but Anne's been in an accident.'

Our feet hit the floor and started walking before he'd finished the sentence. Anne was lying on a narrow bed in the emergency department, her big grey eyes blurred. I was never so glad of anything in my life as when the tears began to fall from those eyes, and I knew she was alive and not too badly injured. She was stitched on her face, her wrist and on her knees, but she was lucky to have her legs as it turned out.

She had gone to sleep on the long drive home after a show on the other side of Sydney; she'd been househunting for three weeks as well as rehearsing and working at night. The only accidents we've had in the show have been on the way home from a job, when you wind down and relax. Anne had hit a telegraph pole, and they had to chain the chassis together before they could tow it away. She was alive, that was all that mattered, and the young doctor who attended her took extra care to see that her pretty face was almost unmarked.

As Anne recovered, she and David became part of a conspiracy of silence engineered by their mother. I noticed the kids diligently working on sorting photographs and press cuttings, supervised by Joy. That was unusual, and upon enquiry Joy said, 'Well, it's about time they earned their keep, and this job has been waiting for years.'

It didn't sound like Joy, but the kids worked on. The doorbell rang one day, and through the glass I saw a telegram boy. As I opened the door, Anne pushed past me and snatched the telegram.

'Here! What's the idea!' I was rather offended; bad manners like that were unusual.

'Sorry, Dad. I've been expecting it. It's probably about a job I was checking out for next week,' Anne apologised. I walked off, not really interested in telegrams and business affairs.

I went to Melbourne for EMI to attend the Music Industry

Awards, and returning late in the afternoon, had to rush straight to the studios in Castlereagh Street to record and film a television commercial for EMI. Joy had fresh clothes waiting; she and the band were set up and ready to go.

'Right, what do we do now?' I was a bit hyped up by the rush but happy to plough into it.

'They just want to film you working in the studio to start with,' said Joy.

That was fine. I went through a couple of songs for the cameras, changed angles, and started and stopped as requested. After half an hour of this, I began to get edgy.

'Where's the script?' I wanted to know.

'They don't want you to work to a script, just keep singing for now.' Joy seemed unusually vague.

'How the hell can I do a commercial without a script?' My fuse was burning.

Joy was looking hassled as she tried to keep me calm.

Mike Willesee walked into the studio with his hand extended, a big smile on his face as he said, 'I'm Mike Willesee. Slim Dusty, This Is Your Life!' By that time, I was just about ready to hit him or anyone else handy. He'd had a flat on his car and was twenty minutes late. Joy nearly fainted with relief when he finally arrived.

I sat in the television studio that night as all my old mates and colleagues, and my family, both close and extended, told their stories of my life. The researchers had even managed to find Barry Thornton who flew in from the South Australian desert with some help from the Royal Flying Doctor Service. Barry had been out bush for nearly two years, and was now separated from his family. After seeing the programme, his kids rang me.

'Uncle Slim, can you get Dad to come back and see us?'

I didn't know what I could do, but I tried. I contacted Barry, and told him I wanted to do an album called 'Just Slim . . . with Old Friends', and would like him to do some guitar on it if he could come over in May. By the time he arrived and had the recording done, we had talked him into being driven to Canberra to see the family. They took over from there, and they are all still together today.

At the beginning of 1976, I signed a new contract with EMI. I agreed to deliver two albums a year for five years. This meant that every year, twenty-four new songs had to be written or found, rehearsed and recorded. Then I needed to be around for the mixing of all the tracks until we had the final cut. Recording wasn't the simple job it used to be, and took a heap more time. It was quite a workload, taken in conjunction with my normal touring schedule.

The Trenwiths were booked to return to New Zealand by June, so we recorded track after track. I was using all the techniques the voice teacher had taught me, and provided I didn't push too hard, I was getting down some good tracks. We completed two albums and part of the 'Just Slim' album, so I wouldn't have too much recording to do the next year. I planned to get back on the road again in 1977.

A few weeks later, I woke up feeling lousy. My chest had pained all night, and it still pained. The local doctor sent me straight to a heart specialist, who threw me into the intensive care ward. I was met at the hospital door, put into a wheelchair and rushed down to the ward. When I saw where I was, I could have had a heart attack then and there. Joy sat outside for an agonising four hours before anyone had time to tell her what was going on. I didn't have the threatened heart attack, and to this day, I believe it was a combination of the 'flu and a hefty hangover from a series of dinners that week that nearly flattened me.

One good thing about it was the lecture the heart specialist gave me. 'It's about time you were more sensible about your health. Lose weight, and walk every day for at least half an hour. If you do that regularly, rain or shine, you could add anything up to fifteen years to your life. *And* do something about relaxing a bit more.'

The advice to relax sent David and me up to Mission Beach, near Cairns, for a couple of weeks' reef fishing and laying about with some mates I had.

The day after I got back, I had to fly to Mt Isa to do the cover pictures for a new truck album, 'Give Me the Road'. Flying back, the oxygen masks dropped from the plane's ceiling and we were advised to remain calm. The windscreen of the plane developed a crack, so the pilot had to take emergency measures. We arrived safely in Brisbane and stayed there overnight, but I reckon the fright undid all the relaxation therapy Mission Beach had done. I don't like flying much.

I went to EMI's Homebush factory to press the first copy of my hundredth single on 2 September 1976. It had a special label, and two songs written by Joy: 'Sundown' and 'I've Been There'. The whole year was passing in a bit of a blur for me. I'd had my head down in the studios while all sorts of plans were being made for celebrations to mark mileposts in my career, such as the hundredth single, a 'This Is Your Life' album and thirty years of recording continuously for EMI. I was hurried here and there doing radio specials, cover photos, sitting for a young bloke who was sculpting a bust of yours truly as a gift from EMI to mark the thirty-year anniversary, and even collecting a King of Pops award. I recorded messages on 'how to vote' in the coming National Aboriginal Council elections. The aim was to send cassettes of these messages to all Aboriginal outlying settlements to encourage all Aborigines to have a say in electing their representatives.

There was always something to do, an interview to give, a photo shoot, a recording session. It was hard to realise that my dreams had come true with a vengeance. The record company was quoted as saying I was Australia's biggest record seller bar none, and that I was a holder of the world record for recording for one company for thirty years. The other thing which took us all by surprise was the result of a record survey. I was the bloke from the bush, touring the country and the outback and it was there that they expected my records to be big sellers. They were, but the survey showed that the biggest sales of all were in the belt boundaried by Newcastle in the north, Wollongong to the south and by the western suburbs.

We had said for so long that if I was selling well, how much better would I sell with some promotion? That survey and the sales of the 'Lights' album, in particular, jolted the company into action. I must have been the first country artist they had ever advertised on TV campaigns and in every media. The results were quite astounding, as sales climbed and climbed. With the sales came the publicity, and vice versa. I now held forty-six gold records and three platinums, more than anyone else in the business. I was proud of them, too.

EMI Melbourne were saying it was about time they had a gold record presentation in their home city, and arranged for Bob Hawke to do the honours in June 1976. Hawke was at that time chief of the ACTU, and rumoured to be looking at eventually entering Parliament. He had an outstanding record of achievement as head of the ACTU. He was a great negotiator.

Bob arrived, lit to the eyebrows, with two lady minders. This was in the days before he swore off the grog to achieve his ambition of becoming Prime Minister of Australia. He wouldn't remember presenting me with a gold record. In fact, I'm sure he doesn't, because I mentioned it to him one time when he was at last Prime Minister. It was a long time ago.

The minders had a hard time keeping him in check, as Bob was out for a good time. He told an obscene joke to the circle of listeners with women in the front row, he appropriated cigars from pockets, blew the smoke into a lady's face which didn't impress me because the lady happened to be my wife, and then decided he should try to charm everyone he had done his best to alienate. Anyway, I got my gold record, and everyone there got a good story to tell.

All my friends joined EMI in celebrating my thirty years of recording, and then they joined Joy and me in celebrating our silver wedding anniversary. Thirty years of commercial recording, and twenty-five years of marriage. A lot of water had flowed under the bridge since the rain tumbled down in July, and a lot of miles had rolled away under our wheels since old Betsy first took us out on the road together.

After all this star treatment I needed to get back to reality, which meant going out on the road with a new band. I ended up with some country rock musicians, plus two hard core country musos. Then I got down to the real business of life, which to me was singing my way around Australia again. I hadn't been on tour for more than eighteen months

The new musos certainly got cracking as I hauled them from Sydney, through the Riverina, out to Broken Hill and back again early in 1977. Anne and two musos accepted a small plane flight from Mildura to Broken Hill while the rest of us drove the 160 miles. The plane was forced down when a large bird smashed into the windscreen, breaking it open and tearing some of the control wires. As Anne and the musos held wires in place along the ceiling of the cockpit, the pilot glided the plane to a station airstrip nearby and radioed for assistance. Joy and I arrived in Broken Hill to be greeted with the news that our daughter and the blokes were grounded, but safe. That's one more reason I'm not keen on flying, and I found it difficult to appreciate his wit when one of the musos said, 'And I was goin' to have chicken for tea, too.'

I embarked on an ambitious new album, 'On the Move', with a lot of show and touring style songs. It was a very different album for me. I was stretching my musical limits, and enjoying it. I headed out on a tour of all the capital cities, and celebrated my fiftieth birthday in Newcastle with a party after the show. The affable journalist who had the job of reporting what it was like to spend a day on the road with Slim Dusty ('Australia's biggest selling artist, selling more records here than the Beatles, blah, blah'), had a great time even if he did end up wandering home along the streets of Newcastle early in the morning. I sent him off to the tune of 'Lily of Laguna', much to his befuddled amazement.

I spent 1977 touring, because I had two albums still 'in the can' by the end of 1976. 'Give Me the Road', a truck album, was released in October 1976, but 'Just Slim' and 'On the Move' were to fill my recording commitment for 1977. So I appeared in all the mainland capitals, toured Queensland, Victoria, New South Wales and went down to Tasmania to complete the year.

At the Tamworth Awards in January, a Melbourne band called 'Saltbush' won Best New Talent, and I was very impressed with their raw, driving sound. I liked the songs their guitarist, Bernie O'Brien, wrote for them as well. They stirred up the establishment at Tamworth a bit, and when they turned up again at the 1978 Awards there was so much clucking over their doings that I was not game to say that I'd booked them to do the Queensland tour with me. They got themselves 'high' on goodness knows what, locked themselves into the dressing rooms backstage at the town hall during the Awards presentation and refused to come out, until Phil Emmanuel screamed matching obscenities through the door and threatened to call the cops.

When it finally became known that I was taking them on tour, the industry was confounded. I knew quite well they might be a handful, but I always laid it on the line when employing anyone. I had two rules. I don't put anyone under a contract—an unhappy member of the team will never give his or her best and will upset everyone else—so if they want to go, then go, 'just give me time to get a replacement'. The second rule was that everyone has to be sober for a performance, and there's no drinking backstage either. I like my beer as well as anyone, but if you let one start drinking around the show, you will always get the other who'll take it too far and wreck things.

Saltbush knew how things stood, and they did the right thing by me—astounding all the pundits. There were a couple of incidents and, of course, all that orange juice standing innocently in the dressing rooms wouldn't have been spiked, would it? I thought that I needed some comedy or variety in the show, and contacted old Chad Morgan who had apparently reformed in his later years and was off the grog. This was what his manager assured me, anyway, but it turned out to be Chad, rather than Saltbush, who fell by the wayside.

While I was working in Sydney and Melbourne, I had been absorbing the musical atmosphere and mixing with musicians and singers of a different kind. There were some interesting groups emerging, and the singer-songwriters of the seventies were bringing out albums. I began to feel that there were many influences I could bring into my music. I liked the fresh, enthusiastic feel in the air, and best of all, I could now find young musicians who not only played country instruments, but they played good country music on them. I had the time and the inclination to get out and listen to some of the bands that were coming up; people like the original Bushwackers, for instance. Apparently, my interest was obvious because next thing, the alternative life settlers at Nimbin contacted me.

They asked if I would perform at Nimbin for them, for a special reason. They believed if I went there, the local people would come to see me and would perhaps come to realise that the hippies were not all layabout druggies after all. It was to be an exercise in trying to weld the two communities more closely together, and I hope it worked. I heard later that the publican even let them have some beer on tick when he knew it was for me and the band. We had a great night and Saltbush, of course, were in their element.

All the people we looked for every year were there to greet me and say hello. There were some special ones, like Lew Williams at Bowen. Lew was a cattleman and keen rodeo man who I met when I was doing the Bowen Show. Frank Foster and I used to go shooting and fishing on Lew's property, 'Keela Valley', just north of Bowen. It was a beautiful place with long beaches, swamps where the magpie geese gathered, and where you could camp in peace and quiet.

This year, Lew was having a quiet beer on the back verandah when I lobbed in. He was nursing three broken ribs, a legacy from that year's Bowen Rodeo. He was standing by the gate when a bull got loose behind his back. It charged through the gate and knocked Lew flat. He woke up in hospital with someone stitching his ear.

'Forget me bloody ear!' said Lew. 'It's my ribs that need fixing.'

He was the only man I've ever seen kick sheets of corrugated iron under the wheels of a bogged vehicle . . . with his bare feet.

By the time I arrived back in Sydney, after battling with bad sound all through the tour, I was in trouble with my throat again. After each show, I was husky; my voice was tired; and I was physically exhausted with the effort of projecting my voice through a sound system that seemed to drop at my feet. The system was supposed to be tops, the engineer also supposed to be good, but they never seemed to correspond so that they were good and/or tops at the same time.

I no longer had faith in my tone-deaf ear, nose and throat man, and I took the advice of some friends and rang the man they recommended. He examined me and proposed rest, to begin with. So the only thing I did for a couple of months was sing a song with Anne in a concert on the Opera House steps on New Year's Eve. That was quite a night, too. We were picked up from the opposite side of the harbour in a small ferry boat and dropped at the Opera House wharf, to be collected later that night in the same spot. A whole group of us were waiting on the wharf, chiacking and smoking. I hadn't lit up when I was offered a 'roll your own' fag that tasted like a stale Camel cigarette. After a couple of puffs, I was glad to pass it on; apparently that was my one and only go at marijuana and I didn't even appreciate it.

At the 1979 Country Music Awards in Tamworth, Anne won best Female Vocal, I won Best Male Vocal and was elevated to the Roll of Renown, and Joy and Tom Oliver won Best Composition. It was an amazing night, and an overwhelming one.

I think it's about time I said something about Anne's singing and recording. If ever a girl has had a hard row to hoe, it has been Anne. Because she is my daughter, she would have been accepted as part of the family show as 'Anne Dusty' and would have been expected to sing bush ballads and easy listening songs ad infinitum.

Again because she is my daughter, and Joy's, that was never on Anne's agenda. She set out to prove herself as an artist in her own right, doing her own thing. In the beginning, she recorded a few 'father and daughter' style songs from the time she was about twelve years old. I taught her to play guitar and Joy taught her to play electric bass and to sing harmony. Whenever she was with the show on holiday, she sang a couple of songs and the audiences loved her.

We always had lots of different types of music playing in our household and in the caravan, and particularly in the seventies we played a lot of the singer–songwriter artists such as Gram Parsons and Paul Siebel. Besides being brought up on the Carter Family, Jimmie Rodgers, Merle Haggard, Hank Williams, Patsy Cline and ME she was listening to Emmy Lou Harris, Kate and Anna McGarrigle and lots of others. The first time I realised how she had moved on musically was when I brought her down to Melbourne to do a spot at a concert in the Dallas Brooks Hall. She unleashed this incredible voice that had developed while I wasn't looking (or listening) and she knocked me right out.

By then, she was at Macquarie University and involved in

the folk and bluegrass club. By the time she had her degree in Biological Science, she was also playing good enough bass to replace her mother in my band and insisted on taking off on tour with us as soon as she graduated. The rest is history as they say, again and again.

Her first album, 'Down Home', was released in 1974 and Anne received the test pressing out at Camooweal while on full-time tour with our show. But it was during 1978 and 1979 that she moved right away from our orbit to form the Anne Kirkpatrick Band and to perform and record her own style of music. Her first big win was the Golden Guitar at Tamworth in 1979. Her marriage in April 1978 and her daughter Kate's arrival slowed her down a bit (but not enough to stop her touring with us again) until she released 'Come Back Again' in 1987.

Her album 'Out of the Blue' for the ABC label was the big breakthrough for Anne. The first woman to win an ARIA for Best Country Album, she went on to win three more Golden Guitars, a People's Choice Award, two MO awards for Best Female Country Artist and two FEIP Southern Hemisphere awards.

Altogether, Anne has released eleven albums plus the recent 'Travelling Still . . . Always Will' album with me. We have a Gold Record award for this album and Anne wrote the title track about Joy and me. It just about broke us up when she played it to us the first time. I suppose I could go on and on about my daughter, I am so proud of her. But perhaps people like Glenn A. Baker and Craig Baguley (English magazine editor) can say it better than I can.

Glenn A. Baker: 'Anne Kirkpatrick is not only one of the most awarded Australian female country performers, she is also one of the most important. Working from within, from the midst of the revered First Family of country, she has diligently chipped away at the perimeters placed upon the music in this country, not with flash and glamour but with an innate understanding of the essential qualities which render truly great country music so emotionally overwhelming.'

Bruce Elder: 'A true revolutionary . . . in a very real sense Anne Kirkpatrick is the godmother of Australian "new country", determined to drag the music into the 1990s.' And re the album 'Out of the Blue': 'There can be little argument that this is the best country album ever released in Australia. She is now, unambiguously, our finest country performer.'

Craig Baguley: 'Anne is a unique stylist, instantly recognisable, aided by one of the sexiest voices around. She has a wonderfully mellow voice and just about the sexiest little vibrato you're ever likely to hear.'

I could go on, I suppose, but I'd better stop. That's enough about my darling daughter.

I was under a perpetual shadow as I worked and recorded; a shadow of doubt that I would be able to continue singing. The slightest strain, and I was husky or gravelly. The specialist did not want to operate without strong reason, and mostly he kept finding that the vocal cords had a watery swelling on them. When this came up, it interfered with my singing; but with rest, it usually went down and I sang as well as ever. Naturally enough, when this happened I thought I was over the trouble and went off on tour or into the recording studio. We tried allergy testing and treatment; we tried weeks of silence. I don't remember the number of times I was told not to speak for three weeks, and Joy learned to interpret my 'shorthand' written notes.

All this time, I was trying not to let the public know that I had any problems. It would not be good for my career to let on that I was having continued trouble, so I hid it for as long as possible. During this time, I reckon I must have earned a reputation as a dummy; someone who wouldn't hold a conversation with anyone. The fact of the matter was, I didn't dare disobey the specialist's orders, and on the other hand, I wouldn't tell anyone the truth of the situation. Even when there were reports in the media that I had cancer of the throat, they were hood-winked in the end by my coming out on tour and recording again, instead of conking out.

We needed a break by now, and my voice needed rest, so we took off for Peppimenarti in the Northern Territory for a few weeks' holiday. Peppi is Aboriginal country, owned by the Moil River tribe who had often invited me to visit them.

We were at Mission Beach in North Queensland, with the friends who were coming to Peppimenarti with us. Don and Margaret had actually toured with us a couple of years before; Don helping with driving and sound and Margaret in the ticket box. They had a house at Mission Beach and we stopped there before heading through western Queensland to the Territory.

Margaret found a bush rat and six babies ensconced in a dressing table drawer, and Don refused to do anything about it on the grounds that they weren't hurting anything of his. The mother rat hid in the back of the car refrigerator and was nearly incinerated. So the fridge and the drawer were put out on the verandah, hoping that the rats would leave or Sambo, the black cat, would do his duty. When Marg found another nest in the back of the freezer, she bought Ratsak without telling Don. In the meantime, nests of stinging green ants were being built on both the front and back verandahs, angry ants were policing them with vigour, and we had to stay inside or sit on the grass outside. Don says he's a conservationist.

There are two spots in Queensland that always make me feel that I'm in the north. One is when I drop down the range to Sarina, from dry cattle country to paddocks of cane. The second spot is where we top the Cardwell Range and look out over the Hinchinbrook Passage—blue water and dark-green mangroves. Then again, I know I'm in the Territory when I hit the Five Ways above Tennant Creek, where you head either south to the Alice or north to Darwin. We headed north, and turned off the 'track' as they call the good highway, to the Daly River mission and settlement.

There we had to wait for Harry Wilson, the station manager, to arrive back from Darwin with our permits to visit Peppi, and to guide us out. The night before, the men on the stock camp were on the radio to Daly River mission wondering where I was, and whether they should come out looking in case I was on the road and lost! I think they were disappointed to hear I was safe and sound in the Daly, 'waiting for Harry'. It would have been a break from the mustering camp to come out looking for me.

Harry turned up with six blokes in the back of the Toyota, and two in the cabin with him. They were all still wearing their ochre from the previous night's corroboree in Darwin. We crossed the Daly River with the water coming into the floor of the trailer, and turning to mud the dust from the dry road. Five hours later, we reached Peppimenarti settlement to be greeted with news that a cattle buyer was there to inspect cattle which hadn't yet been mustered and yarded. Portable yards were quickly set up and cattle mustered.

In those days, back in 1979, the Daly River mission and Peppimenarti were, by the people's own decision, 'restricted areas'. This meant that liquor was allowed only in one area, which on Peppi was called the 'club area'. This was a shady, grassed area where everyone sat together, having a real 'happy hour'. Some played cards, some worked on baskets, children played together and the men drank the four cans of beer they were allowed, while any women that wanted them could buy three cans of beer. Why were women allowed only three cans to the men's four? Because, and I quote, 'the women go under more easily'.

Peppi had fencing gangs, road gangs, mustering gangs, and they had cattle to work. I went out to the mustering camp for dinner one day, and shared their black tea and bully beef sandwiches.

'Hey, Harry! How about a 'roo for the camp, eh? You better get one for us today, eh?'

226

They reckoned they'd still rather have kangaroo than any other meat.

There were plenty of barramundi in the river, lots of 'roos, and in the mud swamps where the wild pigs had rooted up the mud and left it to dry, the women and children showed us how to look for 'minnamindi'. The dark brown nodules on the roots taste like macadamia nuts. I was more interested in their fish cookery. No one thinks of bringing anything out for the day except a billy with tea and sugar, matches, bread and a knife. They seem to be confident of catching a fish, and when they do, they throw it on the coals of the fire just as is. They didn't even bother wrapping it in mud, and certainly didn't waste time cleaning it. When cooked, the scales fall off and the insides are in one small ball, easily thrown away. Talk about labour saving!

The whole tribe packed some mosquito nets and escorted us to the 'Wild Life', about forty miles away on the coast. It was a hairy trip for us because we were several vehicles behind in the convoy of Landcruisers and trucks, and those in the first vehicle were burning off. They threw lighted matches out of both sides of their truck, and by the time we passed that spot, the spear grass either side of the narrow track was burning fiercely. Our utility and trailer bumped over burnt ground and picked up speed like you wouldn't believe when the flames were too high and much too close.

The 'Wild Life' had swamps leading out to the sea, and the tribe waded in, looking for long neck turtles, as they call them. We had cooking lessons again, when kids brought a plate full of honey-bag from the wild bees. We repaid the courtesy with auto-harp lessons. We went fishing, we went shooting, we sang and visited each other's camps, and we were almost sorry to go back to the settlement. We spent quite some time at Peppimenarti, got to know so many of the people, attended the corroboree and learned how to make the ochre paint stick to our skin. The basket makers of Peppimenarti are acknowledged experts at the game, and one of the best is Regina Wilson.

The night before we left, they held a corroboree. I sang for them, and the favourite, of course, was 'The Plains of Peppimenarti' which I had written during my stay. I tried to tell in the song how the feeling of Peppi affected me, and apparently the old men told Harry that I must be a wise man to know how Peppimenarti hill was the spirit of their country.

When the men, all painted up, danced to the throb of the didgeridoos I could have stayed all night, but I didn't know the necessary etiquette involved. It was tactfully pointed out to me that, as guest of honour, the men would dance until I left . . . and since they 'were just about buggered', it would be a good idea for me to say goodnight and leave. Which I did. One more thing learned.

Back in Sydney, the sense of space and quiet evaporated immediately with the launch of 'Walk a Country Mile' and the national tour. At Tamworth in January 1978, a journalist had been sent to cover the Awards, and he ended up being totally intrigued by my record. He wandered around the camps each night, sitting by the campfires and listening to the ordinary fans' opinions and enthusiastic renditions of their favourite country songs.

After the Awards presentations, he found himself peering through the open door of my motel room where a full-scale, roaring party was going on. He stepped over the legs of those sitting in the doorway, accepted a beer and battled his way through the crowd to buttonhole me and then Joy. We were happy and relaxed and talked freely to him until in the end he said: 'Hasn't anyone written down any of this? Can I come and see you when you get back to Sydney?'

So John Lapsley began writing down the story of my life, so far as it had been lived up to that time. It was released at the end of 1979, with an album to go with it, and it sold well with the album achieving a platinum. But it took eighteen months, really, of interviews and writing to get it finished and we knew the publicity machine for the album and book would swing into action the minute we came back from Peppi.

The phone rang at all hours of the day and night, right up to the minute we walked out of the door to begin our national tour with Anne and David. It was the first time the four of us had appeared on such a tour, and it generated requests for a family album. Anne had always been keen on showbusiness and music, singing and playing instruments. David was quieter in that regard, although he was a good drummer and singer. I was interested to find out that in holiday times at home, he had studied my entire recording output very carefully. He knew just what I was on about, and as the years went on, he was more forthcoming with some very astute comments and opinions on my songs and recordings. So I was pleased to hear him on guitar and a bit of keyboards as well as drums, and when he began singing it was just a natural progression, I guess. Both the kids had grown up with music all around them. I didn't mind particularly what kind of music they played or listened to, but I was tickled to find that both of them approved of what their dad was doing. They both have the 'feel', thank heaven, because if you can't 'feel' country then you haven't 'got it'.

Anne was moving house again. David and I were the removalists as usual, and were fed up with her choice of a flat when we had to hump all her furniture and belongings up numerous flights of outside stairs. We'd just finished when a man in a three-piece suit arrived, looking cool and confident. David and I glowered as Anne introduced Greg Arneman. We knew we were both thinking the same thing: why hadn't he arrived when all the work was in progress? Greg knew what we were thinking and felt embarrassed, although—to be fair—he hadn't known the timing of the big move.

Greg Arneman was managing the health spa that Anne

joined when she decided to get fit, and he mentally decided that she was either a physical education teacher or a nurse. By the time he discovered she was an entertainer, working those ridiculous hours in places all over Australia, it was too late. They were in love, and we held a family wedding on 30 April 1978. It was some consolation to Greg to find that Anne was a very good cook. He had been sure that a professional entertainer wouldn't be able to boil water!

Chapter Sixteen

HE DID WHAT HE COULD

I heard the call for duty so I donned a khaki suit,
And I marched 'way from the gumtrees and the willows by
the creek . . .
'GUMTREES BY THE ROADWAY' SLIM DUSTY

While the going was good, I recorded 'The Man Who Steadies the Lead', and the original painting featured on the cover now hangs on my wall at home. I still had to watch how much stage work I did, and because David and also Anne and Greg were going to have a trip overseas, I let myself be talked into going as well. There was a motive behind my saying 'yes', because I'm not that wrapped in leaving Australia at all, even just for a couple of weeks.

I recorded a song called 'No Man's Land'. This song, about the grave of a young soldier from the First World War, inspired me with the need to find and visit the grave of my uncle, George Kirkpatrick, killed in Flanders. We contacted official-dom to get the exact location of his grave, and I took with me the tape of my recording of 'No Man's Land'.

I have no French at all, and Joy had only smatterings of schoolgirl French. She could read and even write it a bit, but her accent was atrocious and no self-respecting Frenchman or woman would even pretend to understand what she was saying. She wrote it down instead. Her other method was to struggle with the language, then, watching for any glimmer of a smile, would suddenly say: 'I'll bet you speak English better than I speak French, don't you?'

On nearly every occasion, they would laugh and say, 'Well, yes, a little bit!' That's how we managed. We hired a car in Paris to drive ourselves north to Amsterdam in Holland, with the intention of finding Uncle George's grave. First of all, we had to get out of Paris in peak hour with a Mercedes we'd been given to drive back to Amsterdam, instead of the modest little car we'd requested. We got ourselves onto an expressway with a million other cars all hell-bent on getting home before they'd even left there.

They were blowing horns and jamming the lanes and we ended up heading in the opposite direction from where we wanted to go. We tried using blinkers, we tried hand signals, but nothing helped. By dint of slowing down until we were being abused in violent French, and abusing them back in fluent Australian, we got into the correct lane and out of Paris. Just the same, I didn't know my wife had absorbed so much of my language ability.

We found the little town, and we found the war cemetery. When I used to hear about the red poppies of Flanders, I could not picture them. Here they were in the paddocks, all around the white fence that surrounded rows and rows of white crosses, each with the name and number of the soldier who lay there, far away from Australia. It was peaceful there, it was even beautiful. The crosses were white against the green grass, and the red poppies waved gently as they surrounded the white fence and drew the eye to the soft red brick of old, old farm buildings nearby.

George's cross bore his name, number and M.M. for Military Medal. I sat there alone for a while, just understanding that

I was the first, and most likely the last, of George's family to visit his grave. Then I got out the little tape recorder, and there in that cemetery in Flanders, a very Australian voice sang a lament for all those young men lying there.

Excerpt from 'No Man's Land' by Eric Bogle

Did you leave a wife or a sweetheart behind
In some faithful heart is your memory enshrined
And though you died back in 1916
To that loyal heart are you always 19?
Or are you a stranger without even a name
Forever enshrined behind some glass pane
In an old photograph torn and tattered and stained
And fading to yellow in a brown leather frame

Did they beat the drum slowly, did they sound the fife lowly
Did the rifles fire o'er ye as they lowered you down
Did the bugles sing the Last Post and chorus
Did the pipes play The Flowers of the Forest?

And the sun's shining now on these green fields of France
The warm wind blows gently and the red poppies dance
The trenches have vanished long under the plough
No gas and no barbed wire, no guns firing now
But here in this graveyard it's still no man's land
The countless white crosses in mute witness stand
To man's blind indifference to his fellow man
And a whole generation who were butchered and damned.

I remember having a beer with my son-in-law in Paris that year. I couldn't order a decent beer and it was driving me crazy. Number one, the beer was never cold enough and two, they served it in thimbles, I reckoned.

'I'll see what I can do,' Greg said and he beckoned the

waiter. With his French and much waving of arms, '*Grande!*
Grande!', and the waiter grumbled off. Back he came with two
beers in glasses that must have been eighteen inches tall. We
collapsed with laughter, and barely managed to down that lot,
even with a bit of help.

As I said, I like a beer and once I got back home I gave it a
bit of a punishing. I came home from the studios where I was
putting down some tracks for the 'Family Album' in September
1980, and was just enjoying a cold one when Joy came in with
a 45 rpm disc in her hand.

'This is a bit different,' she said. 'Put it on and have a listen.'

It was a very good demo of a song called 'Duncan'. I liked it
so much, and saw so many possibilities in it, that I did the
unusual and recorded it in the middle of an album. The rest is
history.

'Duncan' just went berserk. John Laws plugged it, and we
helped it along, of course, by my recording special verses for
special announcers who were featuring it. Pat Alexander, the
writer, came along when we were making a video clip of it and
brought the real Duncan with him. Duncan Urquhart was a
happy soul who ran a metalwork shop near the Town and
Country Hotel in Petersham, an inner-city suburb of Sydney.
Pat was selling insurance a few years previously, and called
numerous times trying to make a sale to Duncan. Every time,
Duncan would say, 'Well, let's have a beer and we'll talk it over'.
Finally, Pat realised that Duncan had no intention whatsoever
of buying any insurance from him or anyone else, so he gave
up and just enjoyed the beer. Being an amateur songwriter and
band member, he eventually wrote the song and made a demo
disc of it which landed on Joy's desk at just the right time, when
I was in just the right situation and mood to put it down.

There were all sorts of verses for all sorts of christian
names, and there were also some parodies. One going the
rounds was lampooning American singer Willie Nelson, due for
an Australian tour, and in bother over being caught with some

marijuana. The words of 'Duncan' go: 'Oh, I love to have a beer with Duncan', and the parody was 'Oh, I love to have a joint with Willie'. No wonder Willie wasn't happy when he ran smack bang into me in the foyer of the big hotel in Adelaide where we were both staying early in 1981. He wouldn't be rude enough to say he didn't want to meet me, but he was definitely uneasy when we were offered a beer. I believe he said he didn't want anything to do with drugs of any kind, even alcohol. Just the same, he downed the beer as I did.

My other brush with America in 1981 came when the space shuttle *Columbia* passed over Australia on 13 April. The astronauts Bob Crippen and John Young said, 'Here's a bit of Slim Dusty', and my version of 'Waltzing Matilda' was beamed to earth. That must have been the biggest audience I've ever had. I don't know how many billion people heard that all over the world, and I became the first singer to have his voice played in space. An eerie feeling, that was! I sent a thank you message back to the astronauts via the space tracking station in Canberra. When they visited Australia, but on land this time, I was in Charleville in Queensland and couldn't get down to meet them, but they left me a framed, autographed colour photo of *Columbia* blasting off from earth, and an invitation to come over and enjoy their annual chilli cookout at Cape Canaveral in the States.

There was so much happening and I couldn't put a foot wrong, which should have been enough to warn me. EMI, the record company, released the 'Golden Anniversary' album and it went double gold in three weeks, 'Duncan' was still riding the airwaves and providing a great backstop song for every club act in town, my first grandchild Kate was born in March and Anne was bringing her on tour.

'If you can do it, so can I,' Anne said to Joy.

Anne was referring to the fact that she went on the road at the age of two, and David was born 'on the road' and travelled from the day he turned ten days old. However, in those days, instruments and sound systems were decibels lower in volume, and we didn't travel such long distances each day. We managed, but it was difficult. Kate woke regularly at 9.25 each night, just at interval time and refused to go back to sleep backstage.

'I still remember poor Mum, dressed up in all her stage gear, wheeling a howling Kate up and down the lane outside the Bundaberg theatre,' Anne told me.

One way and another, we got through to the final show in Tamworth before a fortnight's break. My voice was gravelly, but I blamed it on a bit of a cold. During the break, I recorded messages to be used to encourage Aboriginal voting in the elections, and then set out on the round Australia tour.

By the time I reached Darwin, it was on again—the weakness, the gravel, the lack of control. This time I was frantic. I was in Darwin, I had to get right around the top and down to Perth. The specialist in Darwin couldn't help me except to tell me to stop singing. Easier said than done at this stage of the game. I decided to cancel every second town on the tour, to give myself a chance to survive the tour. Otherwise, I realised that my voice would completely give out and I didn't know what permanent damage I might do to it. It might not be the greatest voice in the world, but it was the only one I had and I'd been doing alright with it.

As luck would have it, one of the towns to be cancelled was Halls Creek, and because I couldn't tell the whole truth about my voice, the Halls Creek people were disgusted with me. Further along, when another town had to be cancelled at short notice, I received a very hard letter accusing me of deliberately and thoughtlessly disappointing a truckload of children from a station. They weren't any more disappointed than I was, that's for sure.

I battled through the rest of the tour, getting worse and worse. Back in Sydney, at last, the specialist told me to cancel all future bookings. I had a Victorian tour teed up, a concert at the Tamworth Awards, a festival in February and a concert at the Adelaide Festival booked. I also had a five piece band on regular pay with the promise of at least a year's regular work.

What should I do? Tex Morton, that unflappable boyhood hero of mine, rang me up.

'You're not Robinson Crusoe, y'know. When I was on my way over to the States and stopped in Honolulu I just woke up with this lump in my throat. Had to have it taken out, and I was fine after that.'

He must have been trying to cheer me up, because it's the first I've heard of being able to feel the lump on your vocal cords.

'Anyway, when you feel a bit better, come on over and we'll walk along the beach and have a yarn.'

I never got around to it, much to my lifetime regret.

The next thing he asked me was, 'I'm doing that concert in Tamworth in your place, Slim. How much do you reckon I should charge them?' Tex was quite open in some things, and unpredictable in others. In these later years, he was a bit contemptuous of some of the recording companies springing up, but to me, he seemed much more approachable than he used to be.

I was in Charters Towers one time, and a group of us showmen were yarning in a pub with Tex. Tex was a great storyteller, and used to embellish some yarns, so when he talked about knocking around the Towers' goldfields the showies weren't impressed.

'Oh, sure, Tex. Been here digging up nuggets, y'reckon, eh?'

Tex said to me, 'Come along with me. Want you to meet someone.'

We went down the street, and around a corner to a gold assayer's office. We walked in, and the old man sitting at the counter with the scales in view looked up.

'Tex Morton! Haven't seen you for years! How're you going?' He'd been around the goldfields alright.

He also left a trail of guitars around Australia. There are

numerous guitars popping up all the time, with the proud owners relating how they bought Tex's second guitar from him one night after a show. When he was asked what was going on, Tex told the truth.

'I always had a spare guitar with me, not the white mail order ones, just whatever the nearest pawn shop had for next to nothing. Then if I was asked to sell my guitar, or if I've got one for sale at all, I sell the spare one. Made a bit out of it here and there, and they're happy.' So was Tex.

When I had to cancel a whole tour, and big concerts like the Tamworth and Adelaide Festival ones, there was no keeping it quiet any more. We played it down, saying that I had a soft polyp removed and that rest had been ordered. I kept quiet, writing cryptic notes when sign language wasn't sufficient. It was a blow when I went to see the specialist one April morning, and he put me into hospital for another operation that very afternoon. More silence, and more notepads in my pocket. This time I seemed to be on the mend and July saw me recording again. It was getting harder and harder to start again—to pick up my guitar and begin to sing, fearing the worst, dreading the sound of my own voice.

Still, I had been off the road for nine months altogether, and I was excited to head off to Mt Isa in time for rodeo week. I felt I was right on top of it again when I fronted up in Brisbane for a Royal Command Performance for Queen Elizabeth and the Duke of Edinburgh. I was still featuring 'Duncan' in my act, and I couldn't resist singing a verse about Phillip. The establishment gasped in horror, but as one television shot showed, the Queen burst into laughter and turned to her husband, but that particular shot was never seen again.

After the show, we were all lined up on the stage behind the curtain to be presented to the Queen. I had my trusty old Akubra Sundowner on the back of my head. Now, was I to take my hat off for the Queen or not? Blowed if I knew what I should do. I'm not me without my old hat, so I kept it on and

My usual gear on
the outback tours,
taken in the
1960s.

The Hamilton Country Bluegrass Band in 1972. *Left to right:*
Paul Trenwith, Colleen Trenwith (Bain), Alan Rhodes,
Miles Reay and Graham Lovejoy.

One of our camps between Winton and Boulia (in western Queensland), 1972.

Crossing the Victoria River in the Kimberleys before the bridge was built.

Taken by David Parker during the making of the *Slim Dusty Movie*, 1982.

Joy and me at Australiana Village for a photo shoot in the seventies.

The first Australian Country Music Awards in 1973. I received my first Golden Guitar from composer George Dasey for Album of the Year 'Me and My Old Guitar'.

Joy receiving the very first Golden Guitar ever awarded at Tamworth in 1973. It was presented as the APRA Song of the Year for her song 'Lights on the Hill'.

The very first Travelling Country Band, 1974. *Left to right:* (back) Colin Watson and Paul Trenwith; (front) SD, Joy, Anne and Colleen Trenwith.

Tex Morton (left) was really pleased about being the first name on the Australasian Roll of Renown in 1976. He deserved the honour and everyone cheered when it was announced.

A very special awards night. I was overwhelmed by my elevation to the Australasian Country Music Roll of Renown in 1979.

Another TCB line-up from the early 1980s. Behind Anne, me and Joy are (left to right) Stuart Watson, Graham Wardrop, Mike Tyne, Charley Bayter, Jimmy Duke-Yonge, Bill Graham.

I told you I had a photo to prove it—here's Ned in a bow tie and dinner suit, November 1986. He still wore his old hat though!

Papua New Guinea, 1990. The Premier of the Southern Highlands Province officially welcoming me and making the traditional presentation of a fine pig—the most valuable currency of the province.

Joy wearing her medal at her investiture.

January 1989. At the 'Australian of the Year' ceremony, Prime Minister Bob Hawke presented the Australian Achievers medals.

Me and my mates, the TCB, ready to start touring with Yothu Yindi in May, 1994. *Left to right:* Ian Simpson, Rob Souter, Rod Coe, SD ('the singer in the band'), Alistair Jones and Mike Kerin (the Fettler).

Joy and Mandawuy Yunupingu.

ACMF Exhibition, Tamworth. The guitar in the foreground was used when 'A Pub with No Beer' was recorded and the other guitar was used in my first commercial recording—'When the Rain Tumbles Down in July'.

ACMF Exhibition, Tamworth.

Kempsey reunion finale. *Left to right:* Rocky Page, Heather McKean, David, Joy, Shorty Ranger, SD, Anne and Kate, Lawrie Minson, Donal Baylor, Charley Boyter (in background) and Geoff Mack.

Doing the 'waterbag' skit with Mulga Dan at the Kempsey reunion show.

Presentation by Max Ellis, in January 1996, to commemorate my fifty years of recording Australian country music.

On 22 January 1996, at the Slim Dusty Family Concert in Tamworth, I presented a plaque to Joy which contained the original manuscript of 'Lights on the Hill'. This plaque now has pride of place in her office.

Getting the words down on the road.

With John Williamson and Mike Munro during *This is Your Life* in 2000.

Onstage for a get-together with the artists who honoured Slim by performing at the celebrations for his fifty years' recording with EMI at the Regent Hotel, Sydney, in 1996. *Left to right:* John Williamson (obscured), Troy Cassar-Daly, Clint Beattie, Felicity, Mandawuy Yunupingu, Ted Egan, Slim, Judy Stone, Joy, David and Anne, Jimmy Little.

Snapped by John Elliott on tour somewhere, in the nineties.

With the Prime Minister, the Hon. John Howard and
Senator Bronwyn Bishop, receiving the very first Commonwealth
Government's 'Senior Australian of the Year' award, 1999.

Celebrating my birthday with the family in 2000. *Left to right:*
(back row) David, Anne, Danny, Jane, James and Greg,
(front row) Kate and Hannah.

Me and my travelling mate. Many memories shared over our countless miles together.

became known as that man who didn't take his hat off for the Queen. I didn't mean anything by it, certainly no disrespect to the lady.

The curtain wouldn't go up, no matter how they tugged and tugged. Queen Elizabeth came onstage via the backstage entrance which is just a bit different from the red carpet front entrance, and spoke to each person in turn. The Duke was coming along after her, and said to me, 'Is it true you've been all over Australia, but you've never been to Birdsville?'

'Yes, that's right,' I replied. 'Never got there yet.'

He walked on, then turned and came back. 'Are you *sure* you've never been to Birdsville?'

I can't work that one out at all. I didn't get there until 1988.

Many times in previous years, film makers had approached me with the idea that my life story would make good viewing in a movie. I was generally too busy, and not overanxious to get involved with the concept proposed at the time so the idea had died a natural death each time it came up. Then in 1981, up in Cairns, Kent Chadwick caught me in a weak moment. He had been filming and travelling about a week ahead of me through Queensland, and in every town he got the buzz about the Slim Dusty Show coming. It intrigued Kent apparently, and he put forward a good case for trying to get all that excitement and road show onto film. He even travelled with us for a while, and by the time we reached the Territory, I'd said, 'Yes, let's have a go.' I was restless again, and here was a new challenge.

Kent also put forward a rough draft of the form the movie-to-be would take, and it seemed alright to me, so we set about making plans to form a production company and get things under way. Kent was originally from Queensland, and had actually filmed me one year for a documentary he was making up on the Queensland coast. He had worked on television in the UK, and won Australian awards for two of his documentaries. Now he wanted to try his hand at making the *Slim Dusty Movie*, in a sort of flashback-cum-documentary-cum-show-on-the-road style. I had no idea of all the paraphernalia that went towards producing a movie, and left all that to Kent's team, and to Joy.

We worked out an itinerary of the tour we usually did up north and to the Territory, choosing venues and towns which would add colour and depth to the vision and the storyline, and left Kent to it. I went off on my usual tack with recording, going to New Zealand for a television show, getting the Nulla record label started (one of the first recorded was my old mate, Stan Coster), and trying to help Joy cope with her father's illness and death. Anyway, after all sorts of dramas in the battle to get funding to make the movie, a huge convoy of buses, trucks, 4WDs, Coasters and other vehicles left Melbourne and headed for the Isa.

I was astonished at the team involved: wardrobe mistress and designer, make-up and hair artist, a lighting team, sound technicians, huge Panavision cameras with a specialist cameraman and assistants, smaller cameras . . . each single piece of equipment appeared to need at least two people to operate it. There were gophers, best boys, continuity ladies, and two beaut caterers with their own little kitchen van that trundled from place to place feeding all this hungry mob. There was the bloke whose job it was to get all the vehicles supplied for the film and get them for free, or for next to nothing, because the budget wouldn't stretch to buying everything we had to have.

When this mob got on the road, the convoy stretched out for nearly quarter of a mile. I looked in amazement, feeling a bit queer that it was all in aid of telling my story. I said as much to either Kent or someone else.

'But you're a legend in this country, mate. You must know that?'

'I'm no legend,' I replied, 'I'm just one of the mob who made it.'

One especially good part about making the movie was that I could do shows in some of the familiar towns we travelled each year. The Mt Isa rodeo people made us welcome, and we filmed some great rodeo footage while I prepared to do my spot on the back of a truck just as I always used to do each year. Charters Towers, the old goldfields town with the canvas seats in the theatre, really turned it on for us. Down in Bowen, the tropical Summergarden Theatre, again with canvas seats, played host to the show with Lew Williams and his family in the audience. Lew didn't have much time left to live, but he organised a barbecue on his property where we sang some of the old songs and we filmed him speaking some of his verse as he always used to do. He hauled his hefty sons into gear with threats of what he'd do if anyone got out of line before the filming was completed, and they saw to it that Lew had a great night. He died three weeks later; a bushman, a bit of an individual, and a good man.

We went into the Territory, and up to Peppimenarti and my Aboriginal friends, who gave us the run of their homeland. Again, they turned on a corroboree and put up with the invasion of all these people and cameras. The invasion was complicated by the fact that Michael Parkinson, an English television show host, came in filming at the same time. Then we headed south to Alice Springs.

We were to film a concert staged in the dry bed of the Todd River, up near the old Telegraph Station and the site of the original Alice Springs. The crew worked from early morning setting up the stage and sound, and positioning the cameras. Joy, Anne and I were at the motel having make-up done, and doing the everlasting waiting around which seems to be part and parcel of film making. A station wagon whirled into the motel yard, and Kent came in, trying to be calm.

'There's been an accident, Slim. We can't shoot.'

The main cameraman and his focus puller were in a cherry-picker, a tall council crane used for working at heights, getting the big Panavision camera set for some spectacular shots of the Territory scenery below, along and around the river bed with its white gums and red rocks. A bolt apparently sheared off, and the cabin of the crane plummeted to earth thirty or forty feet below with the two men slammed around in the metal cab. The cameraman was badly injured, and his offsider only slightly less so.

We had so many people out there, streaming in all day, that there was no alternative. We had to do the show, and do it well. There are some times in your life when you work on automatic pilot—like the day I heard of my mother's death—and that's how I did the show. When you're part of a team, working and travelling together, you know every person in that team and when one of the team is in as dangerous a condition as that cameraman was, then you have to hope your experience and training will take over.

Later, an upset member of the crew came to me.

'Slim, we just want you to know. We would have worked, we would have filmed for you but it was an executive decision to pull out. You worked, and we want you to know that we would have.'

I thanked him, and I felt for him. Everyone has pride in their job. No one likes to feel that they've dropped their bundle without reason; but by the same token, I think the reason was there.

By this time, I was thanking my lucky stars that I had kept the band together. When I couldn't work because of all the throat trouble, the band had done some clubs with Anne and Joy, together with Gordon Parsons or Tim McNamara now and then. Also, I'd had them recording an album of their own, and doing all the musical backing and arrangements for the artists who recorded on the Nulla label. By keeping them with me and working together, they knew all my songs and those they didn't know took no time at all to rehearse and throw into the film. The band leader was a difficult bloke sometimes, but he kept that band on its toes.

The whole entourage packed up and headed for Melbourne

to do the drama shoot. There I met the two blokes who were to play the parts of 'young' Slim and 'middle' Slim. The feller playing young Slim had dressed up like me when he applied for the part, and he looked right. But he couldn't play the guitar, although he'd not admitted it at the time, and I had to try to show him how to place his fingers. We got over that one alright, and he was a good little actor until we got to the part where he had to ride a horse. He had a pathological fear of horses. He didn't let on at first, saying that he had hurt his leg, but he just about went into hysterics when he was led up to a quiet brown mare, with the helpful crew saying they'd leg him up and once he was in the saddle, his leg would be okay. So much for young Slim, the real bush boy.

Middle Slim was to be played by Jon Blake, a talented young actor. He studied the way I walked, the way I spoke, and my style of handling the guitar. But he, too, had sore fingers by the time he'd done all the guitar practise he needed.

'Here, Jon, keep on dipping the tips of your fingers into this metho. They'll harden up in no time.'

He thought I was joking, but that's an old one that all guitar players know. If you knock off playing for a while, your fingertips soften up and the quickest remedy is to get into the metho. Externally, I mean.

Jon and Sandy Paul, who played young Joy, were good and I mean really good. When they played the wedding scene with Sandy wearing Joy's original wedding dress, I felt a lump in my throat and looked down to see Joy trying not to make a show of herself either. That re-enactment brought back to us our wedding day. It was such an eerie feeling, as though we were both spectators in the crowd watching two strangers being married, and yet those two strangers were us.

The real fun was the showground scene. Blow me down if they hadn't copied the old show banners and built a replica of the tent and show front. Down Sideshow Alley was Sharman's Boxing Tent, with Jimmy Sharman himself supervising and doing a bit of spruiking, and on the line-up board of the Slim Dusty Show was Frank Foster with his daughter Tracey dressed in her mother's Indian outfit and headdress. Further along, who did I see but Vi Skuthorpe and John Brady lining up like in the old days, and I tell you, I got shivers down my spine. Had a bit of a job not to race up onto the line-up board myself instead of Jon when Frank began to call 'Line up! Line up!'

After completing the drama shots, we had an Opera House concert and one more outdoor concert to film and then I got back to real life again . . . on tour in South Australia. I hadn't toured there for quite a while, and the Travelling Country Band had the time of their little lives. I swear that lot were invited out to a party after the show every single night of the three-week tour. They absolutely staggered back to town and hibernated until after Christmas.

The *Slim Dusty Movie* was released in 1984, and although it was no blockbuster in the theatres, it became a best-seller on video and is still selling. Australians are always making movies about dead legends like Phar Lap and Harry Morant; I just got in early.

Chapter Seventeen

HOPE KEEPS YOU GOING

From the silver of the Broken Hill,
to old Kalgoorlie's gold . . .
'INDIAN PACIFIC' JOY McKEAN

That's true, you know. It is hope that keeps you going from one town to the next, hoping that the next town will be better than the last, or maybe, that it will at least be no worse. It is hope that keeps you searching for a song, or for the right words to say what needs to be said. It's hope that stops you giving up when you feel you can't cop much more.

The making of the movie had been a great experience, the adventure of a lifetime. It had also been quite a strain; the raising of the finance, the knowledge that I had to keep going and keep my voice going or all this great lot would fall in a heap, being under the camera lens whenever I sang or moved, and the endless waiting around. I can be very patient in some circumstances, but I do hate waiting around. I like to get into it. I am just not a film star type of person, and I find it hard to live up to other people's wild expectations of me. Like I said before, I'm just one of the mob who made it.

There had been lots of publicity and interviews to do, and

I had been working pretty solidly for years. I'm a fairly quiet sort of person normally, and although I love my work I can get uptight when pressure mounts up. I'd bottled this up inside me and gone on with my recording, which I love.

This all exploded when I went out on tour in 1984, starting in Tasmania. We flew to Launceston, and I was doubled up with pain in my stomach. I couldn't face the waiting media, and had to go to the VIP room to recover out of public sight. We drove towards Burnie, and I drank some milk, thinking it would help me. Instead, I was in agony. I've never had such excruciating pain before, though I certainly had a lot more coming to me. That night, for the first time in my life, I couldn't go on in the first half of the show and sent for a doctor backstage. All he could do under the circumstances was give me some antacid which didn't help much. I did my spot in the second half, and collapsed in a heap back at the motel.

I blamed the episode on 'too much to eat and drink the night before', and we began cooking for ourselves in the motel rooms. Yes, I know it's against all the rules but when you're on the road as much as we are, you get sick of eating out all the time. In this case, we were trying to cook light meals that wouldn't bring on the terrible attacks of pain. As soon as I had a day off in a big town, I had tests done, but nothing much showed up. I consulted a gastroenterologist when I got back to Sydney, but by the time David was married in May, I had lost a stone and a half in weight. Admittedly, it did wonders for my figure, but nothing for my peace of mind.

David had switched from Vet Science to Medicine, and juggled his studies and his rock band. As he was the drummer in the band, later becoming the lead singer and rhythm guitarist, drum practice added to the constant music in our home. After feeling her head bouncing off the end of the bath in time with David's drumbeats, Joy begged me to send for a set of practise pads to ease the volume. After completing his degree, David took up a position at Gosford Hospital, north of Sydney, and there he met fair-haired Jane Bryan, who was doing her Midwifery certificate.

David and Jane were married at our home in Sydney, and the day afterwards set out for Perth, where David had a new job. It was hard to see them go, and I knew just how the children must have felt all those times when we drove off and they watched us out of sight.

All that year, through the rounds of publicity for the movie and a new songbook, I held myself together between attacks of pain. Test after test, x-ray after x-ray, tentative diagnosis one after the other. I couldn't manage to go for my usual walk every morning. The pain came on and left me gasping on the footpath. We went to Perth on the Indian Pacific, and for two days of the trip I was trying not to let the other passengers hear me groaning when the knives bore into my insides. These episodes went on for over twelve months, never knowing when the pain would hit, until a mate gave me a garlic sandwich and then convinced me of garlic's healing properties. I ate fresh garlic every day and after a month, the pains began to ease. After three months, they weren't troublesome so long as I took sensible precautions. When I told the specialist, he burst into peals of laughter.

Today, I run on garlic and honey, plus tea. Those are just the basics, of course. A few other things like a good beer, and another good beer and no smoking, help brighten the horizon no end.

The movie premiered, there was a Civic Reception by the Lord Mayor of Sydney, and then the Victorian Football League Grand Final. I needed to pinch myself to believe it was really me in the middle of all this. I was running from daylight to dark. The VFL, now AFL, Grand Final is *the* big event in football, and the opening and then the game are televised not only nationally, but internationally.

I was invited to sing 'Waltzing Matilda' and the national anthem at the opening, accompanied by the Royal Airforce Band and my guitar. I recruited Joy for some vocal backup and the organisers recruited another three singers. When the announcer's voice boomed out over the oval, 'The man who is Australia . . . Slim Dusty!', I strode out towards the stage. The applause from the packed stands rose into the air, and tens of thousands of voices sang with me. I almost choked up that time. It was awe-inspiring.

To stop my head from swelling too much, I went fishing up north and took Kent with me. We joined the Whop (Don) and picked up Tom Oliver. Kent and I took turns riding in the back of Whop's rattling old truck, while old Blue, the cattle dog, rode in the front. On board my mate's fishing trawler, I took my turn in the galley and got the world back into its proper perspective.

My truck album, 'Trucks on the Track', won Best Album and Best Selling Album at Tamworth in January 1985, and I was looking around for the direction of my next couple of albums. I was more and more disturbed by the situation in the rural sector, and followed the problems with increasing unrest. That's why I recorded 'The Bush Has Had Enough', after country people demonstrated outside Parliament House in Canberra about the high fuel and freight costs. I am not a political sort of person, I have friends both sides of the fence, but some things make me cranky. A song can sometimes make a point much more clearly and more forcefully than all the talking in the world.

I didn't know how much more singing I was going to do. After recording 'Singer from Down Under' for release in May 1985, my specialist friend who was a concerned and considerate man operated once more to try and fix my ever-recurring voice problem. This time, nothing went right. He told Joy that I might be in hospital for three or four days, instead of the usual two. As she left the room that evening, Anne arrived. Shortly after, my temperature rose and rose. A nurse packed ice around me, and worked all night to keep the temperature down. My chest seemed to block up, and the doctor recommended some inhalations to free it but there seemed no facilities to do this in the hospital. I know it sounds a bit strange, but no one seemed to know how to organise old-fashioned inhaling. Joy rang the specialist and got his assent to take me home and nurse me there.

After the usual three or four weeks of silence and pussy-footing around, I'd had it. I felt I just couldn't cop any more. It was now more than ten years since my first attempt to fix whatever was wrong with my vocal cords, and I'd lived with the threat of no singing for all that time. I knew that I had to go up to my den, get my guitar, and start to sing. I just couldn't do it, and I kept making excuses. Until Anne arrived one day.

'Dad, come on. I'll come up and sing with you. Let's try.'

I'll never forget what it was like, and I'll never forget my daughter's understanding.

Just the same, when I had to cancel all my bookings and do no stage work in the foreseeable future, I decided to cut loose and go bush myself for a while. After eighteen months in Perth, and passing his Primaries—the first exams towards becoming a specialist in Emergency Medicine—David and Jane were heading for home. Their method of heading home was to pack a 4WD with every necessity, and turn their faces north towards the Top End. They planned to travel right around the top, and be home in Metung for a family Christmas. We met them at Katherine in the Territory, and together we went to Peppimenarti for the making of men ceremony and then to Kakadu. It was November by that time, and the heat was oppressive.

We left Kakadu and headed for the Atherton Tablelands, where it was cooler, to see Tony and Rita Brooks. Over the years, old stirrer Tony has written some good lyrics for me. My old mate, Gordon Parsons, was flying to Cairns to meet me and we were going out on the trawler again. Joy went home by the same plane, while Gordon and I headed south in the truck and trailer.

249

My specialist asked me if he could get a second opinion. I trusted this man, I knew his competence and his reputation. When he wanted me to see someone else, I felt it was serious.

'Slim, the man I want you to see is very good. When he operates, he uses laser, instead of the scalpel. I think you should get his advice, then come and see me.'

The specialist he recommended was everything he said, and I felt confidence in him even when he said that, yes, there was something there that needed removing and he would use laser beam surgery.

'I'm sure I can get it,' he said. Later, he reckoned he wouldn't have said that, but I'm sure he did!

After the operation, apparently he told Joy that he had removed a tumour which appeared to be malignant, and that he had got it all. Her shock seemed to wipe it from her memory, because we did not fully realise how serious this was until years later when a locum said, 'My word. You were lucky that Dr . . . got that tumour.'

The doctor's main concern was that he'd had to take a minute piece of one vocal cord, and he didn't know whether it would grow back again as straight as it had to be. I had no trouble after the operation, and my voice has gone back to normal. I have regular checkups, and I follow medical advice by having non-smoking shows and keeping out of smoky rooms or clubs.

That non-smoking bit has made me unpopular in some clubs. They seem to think I'm a wowser or something. Standing on a stage in a smoky club, the warm air drifts up to the singer who is inhaling deep breaths as he or she sings. The cigarette smoke is thick in every one of those breaths and in fact, I have been told that to spend three hours doing a show in those conditions means that you inhale the equivalent of forty smokes. Apart from that, the smoke dries out the throat and when the singer puts any force into the song, he or she runs the risk of possibly damaging the voice. I use warm tea backstage, to keep the blood flowing around my throat. There are definitely no ice-cold drinks until I've finished for the night.

As it gradually dawned on me that I had my voice back and there were no restrictions on my activities beyond sensible care, I sailed back into plans for the year. I had two albums released; one of mostly Lawson and Lawson-style relaxed songs, the other was 'Slim Dusty's Beer Drinking Songs of Australia'. I hadn't taken much notice, but the number of songs I've sung about beer and pubs is enough to make anyone take me for a full-time boozer. It's just an Aussie outlook, I suppose, and as the album went gold in three weeks there must be a lot of Aussies looking in that direction.

It was suggested to me that I should try to set up a festival at Kempsey, my home town. I liked the idea of a reunion of some of the singers and musicians who had worked with me over the years. Some of the festivals we'd seen or appeared at were a bit rough around the edges by mid-afternoon as the drunks roared around the foot of the stage, so we hoped to make ours more of a family event, with no alcohol allowed onto the grounds. The families had a great time, but the bikies and the blokes with their Eskies didn't want to know about it, and after a couple of goes I gave that one up. It gave me a great thrill, though, to be invited to unveil a plaque in town that marked the site of the old Mayfair Theatre, where Shorty and I had made our first stage appearances, during interval at the pictures.

I knew from my earlier trip to Papua New Guinea and the Solomon Islands that I was very popular there. I was approached to take the show to the Solomons in the wake of Cyclone Namu, which had destroyed the copra industry there and left the Islanders depressed and with no heart for rebuilding.

Perhaps a Slim Dusty concert or two would raise some funds to rebuild the community centre in Honiara, the capital. It might even raise morale to the point that everyone would cheer up and get cracking again. It seemed a mammoth project to undertake, but the people from Brisbane knew what they were about. They enlisted the help of the government, and a RAAF Hercules aircraft and crew were seconded to fly us with all our gear and sound system to Honiara.

'I've got better things to do with my aircraft than ferry bloody country singers around!' said one of the officers.

He might have had, but for the moment he had no choice. I think that if he had seen the results of that 'frivolous' use of his aircraft, he would have thought again. A television crew from Channel Nine in Sydney accompanied us. The airport tarmac was lined with hundreds of people, and a bamboo band met us and escorted us to the vehicles, after a ceremonious welcome of threatening spears and dances.

In the following vehicles, all the band members were wearing Akubra Slim Dusty hats, much to the bewilderment of the audience. They knew me by my hat, but when they saw all the others, they began to wonder what was going on. In the middle of all the devastation of plantations and villages, they clapped and sang, and I hope they rebuilt with lighter hearts.

On 19 November 1986, I marked my fortieth year of recording with EMI. To celebrate they booked the Sebel Town House in Sydney for a night and laid it on. Absolutely everyone came; my friends from all over Australia, my family, my colleagues in the music industry, radio and newspaper people I'd known for years, lots of my musician mates and all the special people in my world. I was the only one who didn't wear formal black tie; even old Gordon was dressed to the nines, but he still sported his soft stockman hat above his bow tie and black jacket. I've got a photo to prove it.

Bill Robertson, who worked closely with me in the company for years, presented me with a gold record and stepped away as the wall behind him slowly descended to show a display of all my gold and platinum records and awards. There was a collective gasp from the crowd as they all came into sight. That night I received two replicas of the dog and the phonograph, the famous logo of His Master's Voice. One was made here by Australian craftsmen, and the other by the Queen's jewellers in London, Garrards. I treasure them both as I treasure the memory of that night.

The federal treasurer, John Dawkins, came from Canberra to speak that evening and brought with him a citation from the members of federal cabinet. So many people who wished me well . . . it was a very special occasion.

It was time for me to move on. Where to next? What direction was I going? It wasn't the getting there that was driving me now. I had to realise that I was 'there' where I wanted to be, and the frustration of being unable to get out on the road touring was to be a thing of the past.

I coasted along a bit for the next year or so, experimenting with this show and that, doing special appearances and going to industry 'do's' like the ARIA awards. Those turnouts are always crowded to the hilt, and I was fighting my way to the gentlemen's club room when I bumped into young Brian Dennis from Western Australia. I greeted him with pleasure, and quite some surprise. Brian turned up in a different place every time I saw him, from touring with another country show, to being an announcer in Kalgoorlie, and a magazine and radio bod in Perth where I saw him last.

'G'day, mate! Good to see you,' I said. Brian seemed just as pleased to see me. I continued, 'What are you doing here in among all this?'

Brian looked surprised. 'What do you mean, what am I doing here? Don't you know who I am?'

My turn to look surprised. Young Brian was getting a bit up himself, wasn't he?

'Of course I bloody well know who you are. You're Brian Dennis, so what?' I was a bit put off.

'No, I'm not,' Brian replied. 'I'm Kevin *Bloody* Wilson!'

Kevin B. Wilson was the singer of the funniest, dirtiest ditties around, and was there to collect his ARIA Award for the Best Comedy Record of the Year. It's a wonder he didn't get the award for the top-selling record as well. I keep his albums out of my wife's sight and hearing, so that she will continue to speak to Brian.

I went down to Melbourne to appear on *Hey, Hey It's Saturday*—a zany television variety show—where everyone sang along with me. I swapped hats with 'Molly' Meldrum, and then a lady in the audience had her baby boy on the spot. All that laughter must have been a bit much for her.

All Australia seemed to be gearing up for next year, the nation's bicentennial, and I was no exception. Two albums were recorded, plus a Christmas song with my six-year-old granddaughter Kate singing with me, and a great song for the next year, 'We've Done Us Proud'. It became my signature tune for 1988 and beyond.

We no longer handled all the work of setting up tours and advertising, but had a management company owned by a friend of ours do it for us. He suggested that I should mount a nationwide tour for 1988, carrying stage sets from previous theatre shows, and doing three-week stints out from our Sydney base. It was an incredible exercise and took a huge amount of organisation. I think that rumours of my retirement had been floating around for a while and finally surfaced in 1988, a year which would seem to be a flamboyant finale to my career. There was just one hitch . . . me.

What the hell was I going to do with myself in retirement?

For one thing, why retire when my records were selling well, at long last I was free of the voice worry and ready to get back on the road, and my office was being inundated with requests for performances? For the other thing, I was having too much fun.

Chapter Eighteen
WE'VE DONE US PROUD

Right or wrong, he took life as a song
and he sang it his own damn way . . .
'MY MATE NED' SLIM DUSTY

As the Tall Ships moved under sail up Sydney Harbour on Australia Day, 1988, with flotillas of small craft escorting them, I stood in front of cameras from the English BBC singing 'We've Done Us Proud' for the overseas audiences. It must have been a wonderful sight on camera, but I didn't see a thing as I stood with my back to the Harbour, singing away.

The idea of the Celebration Tour, as we named it, was to appear in every state while featuring guest artists from that state where possible. After the Victorian leg of the tour, I appeared at the Sydney Opera House as one of the 'National Living Treasures' series of concerts. When I am honoured with an award or an event like this, which is totally outside my arena of music, I take it as a recognition of Australian country music; an honour not only to me but to the songs and the writers, to the musicians who give their best to the music and to the people who keep it going—the listeners. Without the listeners, there wouldn't be any singers.

When I was one of the first six inductees to the ARIA Hall of Fame at the second ARIA awards night, I reckoned I was in good company. We were a mixed bag, ranging from Dame Joan Sutherland to the heavy rock band AC/DC, with blokes like me and Col Joye somewhere in the middle.

The new Parliament House opened on 9 May 1988, and we were invited to attend along with all the other hundreds who gazed in awe at the marble, at the wall hangings, at the timber work by Australian craftsmen. There were television cameras everywhere, there was make-up plastered on faces in preparation for exposure to international television, and there was also an air of 'well, we've done it, and about time, too'. I'm glad I was there to see such an historic event, but I was also glad to get out of my suit and head down to the Henry Lawson Festival which was more in my line.

A bit later in the year, the television programme *60 Minutes* did a segment on me which included a day's fishing with Gordon Parsons and at long last, a visit to Birdsville out in Heartbreak Corner country. The little hospital out there had been rebuilt, and I was invited to perform the opening ceremony. So it worked in well to have the television crew fly us there and film my visit. The whole town had turned out to celebrate the opening of the hospital; there was a dress-up parade and competition for the best costume, and after the formal opening, I sang a few songs in the hall. Kids had made 'welcome' signs to hold up for me, and the whole community moved over to the pub garden for a barbecue afterwards.

There was a bloke there with camels, and we were offered a ride. I've got it on film to prove it—Joy and I have ridden a camel around the bar of the pub in Birdsville! Pity the Duke of Edinburgh wasn't there to see the fun and to know that, yes, I had been to Birdsville at long last. I'd like to go back too. The barman gave me a bottle of local bore water and a bottle of Bundy rum. He reckons the only way to drink the rum is with that water, and whenever he goes to Brisbane he takes his own supply with him. It's a long way to go though, any time I want to have a Bundy and water.

A little red plane landed at the airstrip opposite the pub while all this was going on. Dick Smith and Pip, his wife, wandered over. Dick was getting in some practise before going off on his Antarctica flight, and trust him to turn up somewhere like Birdsville which would be about as opposite to Antarctica as it's possible to be. I had a helicopter flight with Dick a couple of years later. He wanted to take a birthday cake and a surprise to an old mate of his up in the Megalong Valley, in the Blue Mountains of New South Wales. He asked this mate of his was there anyone he'd like to have call in on his birthday. The reply was: 'Well, I've always thought I wouldn't mind meeting Slim Dusty.' So I was loaded into the helicopter along with the birthday cake, Pip and Dick and we headed for the mountains. The Blue Mountains, when they're not blue, are foggy. This day, it was thick as soup and Dick couldn't see where he was going. After a while, he turned back to Bankstown aerodrome and refuelled. We had another go, and I must have been shifting around in my seat a bit because Pip leant over and said, 'Dick never takes any chances, you know.'

Well, I was glad to hear it, and as we just had to give up the trip and take the birthday cake back home, I didn't meet his mate until Dick's birthday bash in the Megalong the next year. Just the same, I like rubbing it in that here's this adventurer bloke who can fly around the world and all over Antarctica and still couldn't fly me over the Blue Mountains!

We showed in every state of Australia on the Celebration Tour; we were in Longreach when the Queen opened the Stockman's Hall of Fame, we were in the Alice on the coldest night of the year (so we helped christen Ted Egan's cellar and bar which were built before his house was), and we finished the year at the Riverside Theatre in Parramatta. With the little pub stage setting, with all the team around me in that beautiful theatre, I could also see in my mind's eye the old town hall up the other end of town where I did so many shows all those years ago.

The 1989 Australian of the Year Awards were staged in a marquee on the forecourt of the Sydney Opera House. I was named as one of the Achievers of the Year along with people such as Peter Carey (the author), and Laurie Lawrence (the volatile swimming coach). Kay Cottee, that brilliant solo sailor, was named as Australian of the Year to everyone's satisfaction. Looking around me, I saw a gathering of Australian achievers alright. People like Dawn Fraser, the Olympic swimmer, as just one example.

We couldn't stay long, as we had to get the plane to Tamworth. Bob Hawke was Prime Minister and he was due in Tamworth to attend the naturalisation and official Australia Day ceremonies. I was the singer designated to sing 'G'day Blue' which was being used for a few months in government PR work. I sang 'G'day Blue' and turned to get off the stage but the crowd wouldn't let me. I had two musos with me, that's all, and in my confusion and slight embarrassment at holding up the proceedings, decided that 'Done Us Proud' would be too difficult to perform under the circumstances and threw in 'Leave Him in the Longyard' as being easier and one that two musos alone could handle. I didn't stop to think about whether any of the politicians on the stage might take it personally—Hawke did have a grin on his face when he back announced me.

For I don't know how long, I'd been going to make a duo album with Anne. This was the year we finally got around to it. Anne and I get on very well, but it was battle lines now and then during rehearsal and recording. Our solos were fine, no problem, but when it came to working out who was doing what lines in which song, and who got to open the song or close it, and what key would be the main one . . . well, you name it, we argued over it. But it was a good album when we got it finished.

This was supposed to be a 'year off', and Joy was reminding me about it so we asked her sister Heather to come overseas with us. We stopped over in Athens and Crete, where I distinguished myself before we went on to the UK and Ireland. In Crete, we booked to go to a mountain village for an evening dinner with local entertainment. Arriving early (all arranged so that us tourists would have time to spend money in the antique and souvenir shops), Joy went wandering one way while Heather and I sat down for a beer. A little while later, two women came over to the table. One said, 'You *are* Australians, aren't you? We've been dying to hear an Australian voice ever since we left home!'

We invited them to sit down, and about five minutes later, the other one said, 'Er, it isn't you, is it? I mean, of course not, you wouldn't be here but . . . is it you?' I owned up, and the ladies became part of our little group for the evening. Before we left home, my son-in-law Greg had warned me, 'Be careful of the Domestica wine', but when there was nothing else to be had on the tables at dinner I thought I'd try it. The inevitable happened, of course. I treated it with contempt, and on the way home in the bus, the Gloucester ladies and I sat in the back of the bus singing 'Duncan', 'Waltzing Matilda' and the 'Pub' till my two minders poured me out of the bus and into bed. They hauled me out at about five the next morning to catch the plane back to Athens. Queuing up at the airport was a young man from Perth. 'Hey, Slim! What you doin' here? I'm back to show the young feller here to Mum and Dad, they've never seen him.' It's hard to be enthusiastic under those circumstances, but never let it be said that I didn't try.

Ireland captivated me. From the minute I started driving through the country, I began dreaming of one day singing in an Irish pub.

In the States, Texas was the attraction. An ex-US Navy man who was stationed at Exmouth, Western Australia, and married an Australian girl, breeds Texas Longhorns just out of Amarillo on the Panhandle in Texas. We had got to know each other when he visited back to Australia, and he showed us around all his area. We went to New Orleans for the jazz, and hoped even to find some Cajun bands (no luck), we went to visit the Jimmie Rodgers Memorial, and finally went to Nashville.

It wasn't my cup of tea, it wasn't even my glass of beer. But it was interesting to see where all that music came from. It always puzzles me why some Australians have to copy the American style of speech, dress and song. Americans sure as hell won't try to talk or sing like us, so why do we try to imitate them? Beats me. Maybe it's got something to do with hearing nothing much else on our radio?

The American style of living and music that appealed to me was that of Bill Clifton, living in Poor Valley, Virginia. Bill knew old A.P. Carter, that almost fanatical collector and writer of old songs; he knew all the Carter family and took us down to the Carter Fold, a small hall where old-time and bluegrass music was featured every month. There was a cement square in front of the stage, where everyone from eight to eighty 'clogged'. It was like tap dancing, and everyone had a ball including us. That valley was just like home, except that it was a lot more 'way back' than us, and the people in general were a lot more insulated in their outlook.

In reply, you have to hear what the Old Storyteller, Tom T. Hall, has to say about Australians after touring here a few times.

'Australians don't like to make heroes. They have a reluctance to idol worship, I guess. In Australia [referring to entertaining in our clubs], you want something, you buy it. Entertainers come and go by the back, among the dishwashers and the cook. But I couldn't get mad, because that's the way it's done. The people were nice.'

So there you are.

Tom T. promised me champagne if I reach 100 albums and I set out to make him pay.

At the Country Music Awards in January 1990, I received an award as Artist of the Decade. It stands almost as high as I do, and there are replicas in gold of each different mode of recording I have used. The only one they missed was the eight track cartridge which didn't last very long, and they probably didn't have one. It must have inspired me, because instead of having a quiet year, I fairly flew into action.

I went to Charleville in Queensland for the Flying Doctors' Ball; I went to Cooma to launch the Salvation Army's Red Shield Appeal; appeared on flood relief concerts; appeared at the Inter-Dominion Trotting Carnival in front of 26,000 people; and appeared at a charity concert at Lakes. I recorded the 'Coming Home' album. I was here, there and everywhere so I grabbed a few days down at Homewood in August.

I'd had some good fishing in the lakes so I thought I'd ring Gordon and rub it in. He hadn't been to Homewood for a while, and anyway, I just wanted to have a yarn. We always rang each other at least every few days. He rubbished me right and left over the fishing, called me a bloody liar and left me laughing.

Joy rang me very early the next morning, 17 August.

She tried to be gentle, but she had to come straight out with it. 'Slim, Jeannette has just rung me. Darling, Gordon's dead. I'm so sorry, so sorry. It was very sudden, it didn't hurt.'

Jeannette, Gordon's wife, rang Joy from the hospital shortly after she knew that Gordon was dead. She knew how close Ned and I always were. I miss him still as everyone in country music misses him. While he was a fairly 'straight' performer on stage, he had us in stitches round the back, and as he matured stagewise, he began to take that humour and dry wit on to the stage as well. He was the typical Aussie character with a thousand jokes to his name. He was a great bloke, and a good mate.

I went back to work.

I went to Papua New Guinea at the request of the government and people of the Southern Highland Province, who invited me to join their celebrations of fifteen years of independence. Captain Don Hughes of the Australian Army Engineering Unit stationed at Mendi, their main town, organised it for them. Mendi, towards the Indonesian border area, is more than 5000 feet above sea level and surrounded by sharp, high mountain peaks which makes flying hazardous at times. I believe that my voice was one of the first European voices heard by the people of this province, and so they were really keen on seeing me in person as a representative of Australia at this special time. The clouds stopped us flying into Mendi itself, which was a disappointment to the dancers, the children, the people, the Premier and officials, and Army personnel who were gathered at the airstrip to welcome me and the team.

We had to fly on to Mt Hagen, about eighty miles away, and wait for some Army vehicles to arrive to pick us up. It's a three-hour drive over very rough road and when Mendi said they'd send a convoy to collect us, we were rather surprised. We were even more surprised when four Army 4WDs and six police 4WDs arrived, loaded with armed police. We arrived in Mendi about dark in real style with lights flashing, sirens blasting and putting on one big show, after having our own little drama.

Apparently, a few tribes were still having their private wars up there, and having wrecked each other's village gardens, were taking to the old game of highway robbery to keep the home fires burning. Sure enough, as we bumped along, out of the tall spear grass beside the road raced this character brandishing a shotgun and yelling his head off as he aimed the gun. Our vehicle screeched to a stop, and the poor would-be highwayman deflated with shock as the vehicle ahead also stopped and began spewing out policeman after policeman, each armed to the teeth. He'd certainly picked the wrong victims this time.

I'll never forget that visit to Mendi. Some of the people had walked for three days to get there for the 'sing-sing'. They all wore their best headdresses, some colourful and some sombre, like the Mud Men. The women had their own circles of dancers, with feathered headgear and painted faces just as the men had. I stood on the dais out in the oval, and took the salute of the Engineering Unit of the Australian Army. They reckoned they'd been drilling like mad, and I reckon it showed. They were impressive. The army had flown the military band up there as well and they marched and played in outfits to rival the locals.

There were welcome ceremonies where, for instance, I was presented with a live pig which is valuable currency up there. Normally, I would be expected to take the pig back to my home, but because we were flying I was allowed to offer it back to be barbecued that night. I had brought three musicians to do the concert with me: Rod Coe on bass, Ian Simpson on banjo and Charley Boyter on guitar. They had a great time, just as Joy and I did. I've been to some great places, and met some great people, but the welcome there and the extraordinary hospitality overwhelmed me.

The 'Two Singers, One Song' duo album was going well, and I set out with the family on a flying tour around Australia. When I say 'family', I mean it. Anne and Greg now had a son James, born in 1985, as well as Kate. David and Jane had Danny, born in 1987, and our Bicentennial babe, Hannah, born on Aunty Una's birthday. We had the fun of Cork flying and driving; David bringing his family to Western Australia to join us.

It was a lighthearted tour. I dug out a 1960s suit in burgundy with silver boomerangs embroidered on the sleeves and some Edna Everage-style sunglasses, and rock'n'rolled onto the stage in the middle of Anne's uptempo version of one of the songs.

The next year, Joy upstaged me. I had all our touring dates locked in when we got a phone call from Anne to tell us that Joy was to receive the OAM, the Medal of the Order of Australia, in the Queen's Birthday Honours List of 1991. I was very proud of her, while she couldn't quite understand that it was her, and not me, who was on the receiving end this time. Joy has done a lot for Australian country music; not only as a writer and stage performer, but as a strong influence at industry level and a role model for other women in music. I haven't mentioned anything much of her achievements in this book, because that's the way she wants it, but I refuse to miss out on this bit.

Her investiture was to be in September at Government House in Sydney, so Anne took her place on tour for the time being. David and Greg were to escort her on her big day, but as the date drew nearer I began to fidget. We'd always done everything together, and I realised that I wanted more than anything to see her rewarded for her work. Her big day arrived. David picked her up from home, and they headed for the office where Greg was to wait for them.

'Mum, I'll go and see if Greg's ready. Won't be a minute.'

He reappeared. 'Can you come in for a minute? Greg's got two corsages of flowers and he wants you to choose which one you might like to wear.'

Joy walked around a corner to see Greg still in his work clothes. Alongside him, in full city finery, I stood.

She didn't have a heart attack, just shed a few tears of excitement and bewilderment all over my shoulder. Being Joy, she probably wanted to know what was going to happen to the show tonight! I had chartered a plane from Charleville to Brisbane to catch the 8 am flight to Sydney, and I had to be back in Brisbane for the charter plane to reach Roma, also in western Queensland, before dark. I made it, and I even made it onstage for the opening. Next morning (it would have to be early), the ABC picked me up to film a report on the drought conditions in the district.

So far, in 1991, Anne and I had Golden Guitars for Top Selling Album, and I had another for Best Album, 'Coming Home'. Anne, David, Heather and Joy all joined with me to record a live album and video, 'Live into the Nineties'. Joy received the OAM for her services to entertainment, and I was heading for the forty-fifth anniversary of my first commercial recording, 'When the Rain Tumbles Down in July'. Australian country music was being revitalised and recognised for what it was: an exciting facet of Australian music which was expressing our national character. The Australasian Country Music Awards and the Golden Guitars at the Tamworth Festival in January every year had grown in stature and prestige, due to the efforts of the team at 2TM. From being the bastard child of music, country was finally legitimate and being welcomed into the family. And then, the bombshell dropped.

There would be no Awards night in January 1992—the Golden Guitars would be handed out at different concerts throughout the Festival.

The phone began ringing, and the fax began pouring reams of paper onto the floor; this went on day and night for over three months. Our first phone call was from John Williamson's manager, Phil Matthews. With John and Phil we fielded the calls from artists and musicians, and we ran up colossal bills with Telstra contacting artists and country music industry people all over Australia.

Country music was coming into its own again; the Awards were a source of pride for the artists and musicians in the business, and a focal point for the gathering of industry people every year. Whereas the opposition claimed that the Awards were not essential to the success of the festival, we did not agree. If some of us had been consulted or even warned of the decision, we could have talked about it and perhaps reached a compromise. That didn't happen, and I'm afraid that BAL Marketing, the business arm of Radio 2TM, was astounded at the tidal wave of protest and even anger.

Let me say that BAL Marketing owned the Golden Guitars, they and 2TM had stuck their necks out for country music when no one else wanted to know about it, and they had put a lot of money into promoting the festival and the Awards. When they had no major sponsor to help with the costs of the Awards night, and when the same huge problem of where to stage them arose, someone came up with the idea that there need be no Awards night as such. At the various events, such as the New Talent Showcase Concert, the Golden Guitar trophy would be presented, the Heritage Golden Guitar at an outdoor concert one morning, and so on. They simply had no idea of the outrage this would arouse in artists and musicians, people who usually went along with anything so long as they could get on with their music. Their pride in winning an Award, and having it presented in front of their peers, the media and all the record industry executives, made them band together in protest.

Australian country music artists had never had a successful industry body to represent them. This is partly because the artists themselves were not overly interested in an association comprised of record and publishing company executives, no matter how well intended they were. The artists just didn't feel involved. Again, by the nature of our landscape and the nature of our music, artists are seldom in the same place together. They are out on the road, moving from one town to another; or they are showing in a club here, a pub there; and in the days before festivals became the 'in' thing, Tamworth was the only place where they really got a chance to catch up with each other. The Awards night was important to them, and they were not prepared to let it go without a fight.

The four of us, resigned to being later dubbed 'The Gang of Four', recruited Max Ellis, now resigned from 2TM management and with his own marketing company in Tamworth. As Max had been instrumental in originating the Golden Guitars and the Awards, he was a strong adviser and colleague for us.

January 1992 saw the Golden Guitars being presented willy-nilly at events, big and small, all over Tamworth. It also saw a Gala Concert presented by the newly formed Country Music Association of Australia, to show the fans that artists and musicians were banding together. We crammed about 4000 fans into the Showground Indoor Rodeo Arena to stage this concert, and we had so many artists and musos donating their time and their talent to the night that each artist sang only two songs. I doubt if the likes of that show will ever be seen again, even in Tamworth.

The proceeds of the Gala Concert, plus a grant from APRA, formed a fund which would enable us to carry on the fight to retain the Awards. I became the inaugural chairman of the Association, John Williamson the vice-chairman, Phil Matthews was public officer, Max Ellis the secretary, and Joy the treasurer. From that start, with the support and encouragement of country music performers and their fans, the CMAA has gone on to take over the presentation of the Australian Country Music Awards and the awarding of the Golden Guitar trophies. We have been successful in gaining a major sponsor, and we have willing and competent committee members.

It was bitter, sometimes, and I regret that. But after all the years of battling for recognition of our music, and all the years of trying to support those who were promoting it, a kick in the backside was mild to what we felt when the Awards were fragmented.

I remained as chairman of the CMAA until the end of 2000, when Joy took over for the following two years. The Association is strong, and moving forward. The beginnings were slow and difficult, but it will survive now.

Chapter Nineteen

FETTLER!

It's the gettin' up and knowin' that you're on the road again
that keeps you going . . .
'GETTIN' UP AND GOIN'' SLIM DUSTY

The year 1993 marked the fiftieth anniversary of my first recording, and we worked out a new opening for the stage show. With the stage dimly lit and a spotlight on the backdrop with the hat and guitar logo, a tape played the opening few lines of my first process recording, 'Song for the Aussies', made in 1943. After the first four lines, I was to walk out onstage, all the lights would blaze up and I would begin singing the same song with the Travelling Country Band then joining in behind me.

On opening night of the new show, I waited offstage. The TCB was onstage in the dim lighting. The compere on the offstage mike intoned, 'Ladies and Gentlemen! Slim Dusty, fifty years ago!'

Up went the music, and the old Slim Dusty boy's voice sang out over the still audience.

Then: 'Ladies and Gentlemen! Slim Dusty TODAY!'

I strode out onto the stage into a blaze of spotlights, playing my amplified guitar, as the applause broke out. I had almost reached the microphone when my guitar went dead. I knew immediately what had happened, twisted my head around and yelled, '*Fett*, get off my bloody lead!'

End of dramatic new opening.

The Fettler had planted his big, flat feet fair across my guitar lead and pulled it out. He lurked around dressing room corners out of my sight for the rest of the show, and for three weeks I refused to have him on my side of the stage at all.

'He's nothing but a menace. He does it all the time, look what he did only last week . . .' On and on. I was fairly frothing at the mouth, and not for the first time.

Mike, despite his mishaps, has been a member of the TCB for about fourteen years. That says a lot for my forgiving nature, or for his engaging one. Also, he's a very good fiddle player. He is commonly called 'Fett', short for Fettler, because he says he used to work on the Queensland railways for a while. I was always a bit sceptical, until a man came up to me one time and said, 'You've got a feller called Mike Kerin playing for you, haven't you?'

When I had to admit it, he said, 'I thought it was him. I used to work on the railway with him.'

Well, maybe he did, but I always reckoned that if they let Mike loose with railway spikes, the only one he'd drive would be through his own foot.

The Fettler is just one of the musos who have passed through the annals of the Travelling Country Band, formed over twenty years ago now. He left for a while to join the Flying Emus when I wasn't working much, but came back to the fold eventually. He was given a welcome, because after all, who would we have to talk about and go crook on if he wasn't there?

I have a routine when I'm on tour. While the rest of the team are all snoring, I go for a walk all around the back streets and corners of the town. It is amazing what you see early in the morning; amazing what thoughts go through your mind and what songs you can dream up. Of course, you forget the songs when one of the local mongs snaps around your heels because you dare to walk on the same side of the street as his house. Normal people are still in bed or off to work, and therefore I must be up to no good.

I go back to the motel room, do a workout, and boil up— make a pot of tea in the little battered red teapot that has travelled with me for years. Its lid is fastened on, so I haven't managed to lose it . . . yet. If breakfast has arrived, I face up to whatever has survived the trip from the kitchen to the room. If it hasn't, I start looking at my kitchen port to see if I can scrounge a decent breakfast out of it, and I usually can. The kitchen port has a toaster, an electric skillet and sometimes a Birko, plus the usual cutlery, plates and bits and pieces. The little cooler or maybe a small Esky carries perishables from town to town.

After living in motels for the years that I have, you get to know the good ones and the bad ones. You also learn which towns can give you a decent hot meal at lunchtime without having to go to counter meals day after day, month after month. I can't eat a meal of meat and three vegetables, for instance, just before I go on stage. It cuts off my wind, so I have my main meal in the middle of the day. I have a light snack before the show, and another afterwards. Besides, they tend to serve the same menu in every cafe or pub, in every town, and unless it's a large town, you don't get much choice. Of course, there's no problem if you're doing a tour of cities or large towns where there are lots of good eat-up joints open at lunchtime.

I'm generally packed and ready to go any time from nine o'clock, although the accepted time to roll is 10 am. It will depend on whether I want to call and see someone or some place; there may be a keen fan who is very ill and can no longer get to the show, so I call at the hospital; there may be a special school, so I drop in. It just depends.

On most days, I get rolling and if it's a long trip, I keep rolling most of the time. About 11 am, sometimes earlier, Anne used to insist on finding a cappuccino coffee, and after a while, she got me trained too. If we're anywhere near a likely town, or near one of the group's known coffee shops, it's cappuccino time. After years of travelling and poking around country towns, the TCB has a long list of the best coffee shops and eat-up joints in the nation and they keep me up to date.

By the time I reach the next town, there may be telephone interviews to do, there may be radio or newspaper, and the office back home to contact. Sometimes there's a pile of faxes waiting, or copies of the artwork for the next album to be checked over and sent back ASAP. Everybody wants everything done yesterday.

But if all is quiet on the western front, I like opening the door to my room and seeing whether I like it or not. It's a pleasant routine, if the TCB and road crew have arrived, to walk along and see where everyone is. There's always a fair bit of chiacking goes on from room to room, and after the show, a fair bit of visiting and laughing as we wind down. If it's been a lousy show, we can look forward to getting out of the place in the morning; and if it's been a good one, then we can talk about it for hours.

We do our sound check at the hall at 6 pm. and the TCB charges out the stage door at about seven, to invade the local Chinese or pub or cafe or restaurant to eat in time for them to be back onstage, all dressed up, at 8 pm. I like to start the show on time, and dislike the times when the crowd are late coming in or slow in getting to their seats and we have to wait ten minutes or so. We are all hyped up and ready to go and we begin to deflate if we're just hanging around.

While the band are out for dinner, I'm making tea back-stage in the same little red teapot that has been around the world with me, and walking, walking, walking. I walk all night; from dressing room to dressing room (if we've got two); around the sides and watch from the wings; I stand beside the sound engineer working on the stage monitors; rock from one foot to the other; pick up the guitar and put it down; pick it up again. 'Where's my capo? Did you take it?'

'No, dear,' Joy replies. 'I've got my own.'

'Well, who has? It was here before the show. I'll bet—'

'What's that in your pocket? Did you look there?'

'Oh, well, yes. It wasn't there before, though.'

[Five minutes later.]

'Those fellers ought to be back by now. They'll be running like hell to make it in time. One of these nights someone's going to break their neck racing onstage . . .'

'Your watch is fast, dear. They've got plenty of time.'

When I'm on the stage at last, and the show is running, I settle down a bit . . . just a bit.

I always wear my hat when I'm performing, and a lot of the time when I'm not. Back in the mid-sixties, when I thought I was pretty hip, I started going onstage without it. It was alright for a while, then I got the message that I wasn't quite the real Slim Dusty without my Akubra, so I put the old Sundowner back where it belonged. But every now and then, I have to lift it to prove that I've still got plenty of hair left. My hair is so fine that I have to plaster it down to keep it out of my eyes, but at least I've still got it.

I wear an Akubra Sundowner, and Akubra make them by the dozen for me when I need them. The Sundowner isn't generally available now, I believe, but it's the only one that belts into the shape I want. It has a very deep crown, which you need if you're going to get the particular bash that I like. As for the dip in front to keep the sun out of your eyes, well, just curl it down in your hands every time you pick it up to slam onto your head.

Akubra marketed a style of hat they called the 'Slim Dusty', but they didn't have the crown deep enough to make it a replica of the real thing.

At the end of the show, I do autographs and talk to everyone that I can. The only times I skip this is if I'm sick, if the crowd is unmanageable, or if I've come 400 miles today and face another 500 tomorrow. Then I need to get home as soon as possible, because I've got another show to do the next night, and the one after that. If a performer doesn't pace himself, it begins to show in his stage performance, and if you're a professional, then you give the best performance possible every night. Just the same, I don't agree with what one overseas artist is supposed to have said: 'All you owe them is the show you give 'em on the stage.'

When we pull into the motel, everyone holds their breath while I search for my room key. I rat through my pockets, the ashtray in the wagon, then through the clothes hanger holding my other set of stage clothes. By this time, I'm likely to remember that I dropped them in the guitar case back at the hall, and I have to unzip a cover, open the case and grope around in the dark. 'Bugger it! Man can never find anybloodything, why the hell is it never where it's bloody well supposed to be . . .'

'Isn't this your room key?' And there it is, on the seat of the car where it dropped out of my pocket. When I get back in my room, I break out the beer and something to eat. Sometimes I wander along to see what's going on in the other rooms, or I find another beer for whoever happens to land in mine.

Room keys are a problem. So are room doors which slam behind you and lock you out at the most awkward hours. One muso, who will remain nameless, walked out in the wee small hours in the briefest of attire. The door slammed, the office was closed and he was in no position to appear before the female receptionists anyway. He went around to the back window, which faced the street, but would be the most likely spot for him to get in. He was poking and pulling and prising when a car pulled into the kerb behind him.

'Now then, just what do you think you're doing?'

Two large policemen wanted answers.

'Well, I got locked out of my room.' The muso was under-standably embarrassed.

'Yes? How do we know it's your room? Mm?'

'Look, I work for Slim Dusty, we did a show here tonight.' The muso was beginning to babble and I believe the coppers were trying not to laugh. In the end, they helped him do a break and enter.

There was one tour where room keys were no problem.

This was the tour we did as guests of Yothu Yindi, the Aboriginal rock band. Yothu Yindi were to mount a tour of the Northern Territory, going to all the Aboriginal settlements with a message of moderation and commonsense regarding the use of alcohol and drugs.

Everyone knows the problems alcohol has caused the Aboriginal people, and many other people if you want to get down to it.

Yothu Yindi was the first Aboriginal band to make the 'big-time' with chart hits, ARIA Awards, their leader Mandawuy Yunupingu as Australian of the Year, and they were respected by their people. That's why they were asked to undertake this tour, which would draw big crowds to listen to what Mandawuy had to say. When they invited me to tour with them as their guest, I appreciated the compliment. Apparently they believe that I am respected too, and would help enforce the message Yothu Yindi were trying to get across to their people.

I recruited the TCB. 'Look, fellers. This is an important thing to do, and it's something different. We'll be going to Aboriginal settlements, these concerts aren't for the general public. That means no motels or hotels, we'll be sleeping out in tents and swags. How about it?'

Ian Simpson's grin became wider, if possible. As usual, Ian was looking forward to a good time to be had by all. 'Should be great fun!' Ian had his guitars and banjo packed almost on the spot.

Al, the keyboard player, looked a bit taken back. 'Er, no

motels at all? I mean, what about showers and all that?' Alistair prepared himself for the worst.

The Fettler shuffled his feet, and stood around leaning on things. He nodded. 'Should be alright. When do we leave?'

Rod, band leader and bass player, as well as my record producer for twenty years, was enthusiastic as always. 'It'll be great! What a combination! You and Yothu Yindi!'

Robbie, the drummer, checked on the availability of Coca-Cola at the settlements. If it ever runs out, I'll have no drummer 'cause Rob runs on Coke.

That left Joy to talk to.

'I think we might just stretch to a small campervan, don't you? I mean, swags are alright or they used to be, but I think I'd rather have a camper if that's alright?'

I realised that I wasn't being asked, I was being told. So when we arrived at Alice Springs airport, we picked up a campervan. The TCB would travel in the big touring bus with the band.

Arriving at the open area where the bus and the travelling kitchen were parked, we found a spot for the van and looked around for the tents. There were no tents—not set up, anyway. Someone pointed to a pile of canvas and said, 'Plenty of tents if you'd like to put them up, but the ground's like iron for driving in the pegs. Why not sleep out in a swag like the rest of us?'

The TCB grabbed swags and found spots to put their belongings. 'After one night in the swag, your blokes won't want to bother with a tent . . . you wait and see.'

He was right. The musos tried sleeping under the stars in the Territory nights, and I wouldn't have got them into tents if I'd tried. *Except* for out near Oenpelli, where the ground was stony, and abounded with snakes.

Naturally, Mike piped up: 'So I did feel something wriggling under my swag last night.'

'Oh shut up, Fett,' snapped the rest of the TCB.

The big stage was set up outside the Aboriginal settlement near Uluru, and the rock itself was the backdrop. Magnificent in the near distance, its colours lit by the lowering sun, it dwarfed the semitrailers and sound vans. When standing or sitting in front of the stage, it filled the back view. The lights and sound were set up, we all did sound checks, and away we went. I've shown outdoors and in tin sheds out in the Territory plenty of times, but this is the first time I've worked with rock band sound and lighting laid on as well.

It was a good tour, travelling out to Hermannsburg and then out to Yuendemu on the edge of the Tanami desert.

Two men met me when I drove into Yuendemu: 'G'day, Slim! How're y'goin'?' They leaned against the driver's window. 'S'pose you think the old place's changed a bit?'

'Yeah, it has a bit. Where's the old canteen where we did the show . . . that it over there?'

They waved gently towards a corrugated iron building which was rusted and much the worse for wear. I said as much.

'Yairs, she's not used now o'course. You know how long since you been here, Slim? It's twenty-eight years.'

I was embarrassed. Surely not that long ago?

'Twenty-eight years alright, mate. We were only little fellers then, that's how we know. Got a smoke on ya?'

'Sorry, mate. Don't smoke any more these days, can't help you,' I replied.

'That's alright, Slim. Good to see ya, anyway. Be down to the show tonight, see you there.'

I thanked them and went to the camp. There were kids racing around everywhere, getting into everything and mad with excitement. It was different alright. Lots of the younger people had left and gone into the Alice, much to the concern of the old people. Families preferred to sleep in the open rather than the trashed houses standing around. That night, we saw a 4WD full of Aboriginal women driving around the settlement. They were the night patrol, checking on kids running around when they shouldn't be, and giving any drunks the heave-ho and the odd whack if they gave trouble.

Next morning, at the Community Centre, we could hear a young band in full rehearsal with some of the Yothu Yindi musicians conducting a sort of music workshop for them. Over on another side of the quadrangle was a room set up with a viewing screen and microphones. For an hour or so, Mandawuy and I talked in turn to people in a settlement further out. They could see us, and the band members standing behind Mandawuy, just as we could see them while we were talking. Modern technology was bridging the isolation of the Australian Red Centre and the outback.

The desert wind blows unceasingly, dries your skin and spikes your hair. It coats you with red dust, and gets into every crack of your gear. Alistair was cultivating a black stubble, and with the aid of a scarf and black sunglasses, looked just like Yasser Arafat as he smoked his way around the camp. I was remembering the night we showed here twenty-eight years ago. We had to wait till tea was over, and the cement floors and drains hosed out before we could set up gear and put on the show. We changed costumes in the kitchen area, where the European cook had earlier ladled out hot meals and cake that would bounce even on the cement floor.

One of the women had very tactfully remarked on the quality of the cake.

The cook was straight to the point. 'When I first came out here, I used to make nice sponge cakes, and you know what? They fed 'em to the dogs because they weren't solid enough!'

He was a bit indignant at the thought, but I could see the people's point.

'Got no guts,' they'd say.

I had recorded an album called 'Ringer from the Top End' before we went to the Territory. The title track was written about events on Carlton Hill Station in the Kimberley when we camped there the year before. Carlton Hill had its centenary in 1993, and the owners celebrated with a huge 'Tribute to Slim Dusty' concert plus the Centenary pageant, aimed at raising money for the Flying Doctor Service. This took place after the Yothu Yindi tour. There were people from all over the world there, and one of the highlights for me was to see Dame Edna Everage, complete with rhinestone spectacles and glamorous gown, throwing 'gladdies' out to a crowd of stockmen and station hands.

Later in 1993, after a Queensland tour and completing the 'Ringer' album, Joy and I hitched on the caravan and headed up to Keela Valley, above Bowen. We had cousins Terry and Norma travelling with us, and we met up with Tony and Rita Brooks when we got there. After all the rush of Sydney, and the last-minute checking of the cover for the new album, we recharged our batteries by sitting around the fire at night, yarning and telling lies. Lew Williams' sons, Alan and Gary, came out to go fishing with us on the weekend.

I went out in the boat with some of the fellers, and got a good coral trout; a beauty, in fact. The other boatload of blokes caught some big Spanish mackerel. I didn't have any fishing rods with me and was using a handline when one of the mackerel hit.

'Pull 'im in! Pull 'im in!' Alan was yelling. It was alright for him, he's got arms like tree trunks and these mackerel were nearly as long as I was. I lost him, of course.

I went back to do three months' touring, and lived on painkillers the whole time. A big calcium spur in my left shoulder, jerked forward by the mackerel, had slashed into the tendons of my shoulder and my arm. It took the surgeon nearly four hours to repair the damage, and it took eight months of four physio sessions a day to get my arm and shoulder back to normal. I couldn't play guitar, of course. That's why the next album hasn't got my old pick'n'strum guitar sound on it.

The shoulder was painful. Joy learned how to exercise the arm, and four times a day we kept at it. It hurt, and sometimes it was as much as she could do to keep on hurting me, day after day and week after week. At one stage, it looked as though the shoulder was not going to regain its full movement but we kept at it. These days, that arm is the stronger of the two, but it took eight months to get there.

In January 1994, I appeared onstage at the Country Music Awards with my arm in a sling. It's the only time I've sung without playing my guitar, and I do hope it's the last. I had time to look around me at Tamworth that year, and see the remarkable rise in popularity of country music. The CMAA was going well, and the Awards were a bigger event than ever with the Golden Guitar the most coveted trophy in country music. I now held twenty-eight Gold Guitars from sixty-three nominations, and I guess it will take a while for someone else to catch up to me. I received a double platinum award for the 'Live into the Nineties' video, and a single platinum award for the video 'Slim Dusty—Across Australia'.

I was seeing the wheel turn full circle, with country music accepted everywhere again, and I was in the middle of all the action. It was frustrating not to be able to get out on the road— it was as much as I could do to honour one promise made to Charleville, in western Queensland.

Our son, David, was leaving Australia for six months. On sabbatical leave he had arranged to work in Canada for three months at a big hospital. He and his family then planned three months' backpacking: Africa on the way to England, and after the work finished, over as much of Canada as they could manage in the time. We couldn't tour, and I'd finished recording, so we went to Canada (to the Calgary Stampede) and then over the Rockies by train to spend time with David, Jane and the kids.

We stacked ourselves into a seven-seater wagon and drove through Nova Scotia and over to Prince Edward Island, after we'd been up to Quebec and to Montreal. By the time we got out of that wagon, we knew the Canadian national anthem off by heart. Danny and Hannah had attended school in London, Ontario, and every morning, they joined the Canadian children in singing the anthem. It's a very tuneful anthem and for the first two days we quite enjoyed hearing it. After that, we were hoping Hannah would let up, but she sang it every day. I couldn't help wondering how many Aussie kids sing 'Advance Australia Fair' every day.

We parted company then, as the family put on their backpacks and we flew to London to visit Ireland, Scotland and England. Before leaving Australia, I had agreed to become the patron of the Waltzing Matilda Centenary Celebrations that were to be held in Winton, western Queensland, on 6 April 1995. Part of my duties included a London launch of the celebrations, inviting the world to attend an Australian outback event. Before that took place, I went to Belfast, Northern Ireland, to search for my origins.

For years now, I've received mail from Irish and Ulster fans who have managed to collect some of my records. I was in touch with some of them, and they had alerted the BBC in Belfast when I arrived. This resulted in my recording radio programmes with the BBC, and then having a television crew follow me as I looked for the church where Hugh and Mary Kirkpatrick had married, for Hugh's home before he married, and for the spot where my father David was born. I knew then that the vague idea of performing in Ireland would have to become reality. I wanted, more than anything, to sing in Ireland one day.

In London, the little pub selected for the Waltzing Matilda launch was packed with Aussies who thought they might have been hoaxed, but came along just in case it was for real and Slim Dusty *was* there. They sang along with 'Waltzing Matilda' and made wild promises about being home in time to get to the centenary. I wonder how many are home, and how many are still promising themselves. I was talking to one bloke who said he would be coming home to Australia in a year's time. He was quite straightforward in saying that he would not make as much money as in England, where he'd had a flourishing business for the past six years, but he and his wife wanted to start a family, and they wanted to bring them up in Australia.

'They'll have a better life back home, I know that,' he said.

I believe he is right.

Chapter Twenty
ANOTHER DAY, ANOTHER TOWN

And the faces in the front row come from every walk of life
Each one has a story to tell . . .
'THE FRONT ROW' JOY McKEAN

The New South Wales Australia Day Council sends well-known Australians to attend and address Australia Day celebrations all over the state. In 1995, I was appointed as Ambassador to Darling Harbour, a far cry from the small towns I visited in 1993 where I had a marvellous, inspiring time. From there I went to the Tamworth Festival where I staged my own show for the first time in about ten years. It was an emotional night, as Ian, my guitarist and banjo player for nearly eleven years, was returning to his home in Fremantle to have a break from professional music.

Over all the years, in and out of caravans and shifting house, we have managed to salvage quite a lot of things which hold memories for us. They also tell very vividly the story of my life and my career. When the Australian Country Music Foundation building in Tamworth was restored and ready for use, the Foundation board members asked if I would allow them the use of my memorabilia for a Slim Dusty exhibition as their first display. I admit that I was concerned for the safety of the exhibits, so valuable to me and in most cases, irreplaceable.

The Foundation now displays all these articles. There is the battered old cardboard port that carried my worldly goods when I left the Nulla; the little diaries I filled with remarks and information about each hall (and caretaker!); banners from the showground used in the making of the movie; nearly all my gold records and Golden Guitars; various suits and one special hat. Even the guitar I used to record 'Rain Tumbles' and the Gibson I used to record the 'Pub' are on display. There are videos from the *This is Your Life* programme and from the home movies that Rocky Page made when he toured right around Australia with us. There are manuscripts of song words . . . there is my whole life. I have walked through the exhibit a few times, and I never cease to wonder at the amount of memories in that one big room. I remember the people and the places behind each article, and then I wonder how the blazes we fitted all this stuff in our house, and how we're going to fit it in again. It tells not only my history, but a history of Australian country music recording and performing that spans over fifty years.

In recent years, I find I've been increasingly involved with government and community campaigns and events. It's satisfying to take part in some of these things. I have great admiration for the Salvation Army, and have done anything I can to assist them in my small way; there is the Keep Australia Beautiful campaign in Western Australia; industrial campaigns like Clean Up Your Act; Age Adds Value (neither of us mind admitting our age and the fact that we're barrelling on regardless); 'Training doesn't cost . . . it pays', and so on. But my pet project is the residential programme of Noweyung Centre for the Intellectually Handicapped in Bairnsdale.

As well as the proceeds of my Bairnsdale concerts, anything

out of the ordinary that comes my way, such as the fee for the Telstra launch of the Waltzing Matilda phone card, is sent to Noweyung. They get some odd amounts now and then. After one of the concerts I did at Winton, a group of young people at the foot of the stage called out, 'You didn't sing "By A Fire of Gidgee Coal"!'

'Sorry,' I replied, as I was packing up, 'I'll do it next time, eh?'

'Gee, Slim,' said one. 'I'll give you fifty dollars if you'll sing it for us. Go on, how about it?'

I hesitated—it wasn't the money they offered—but then I called Fett to get his fiddle, and there on the front of the stage, with no mike and no amplifiers, we did 'Gidgee Coal'. They held up the fifty dollar note, and I took it . . . for Noweyung. They can use every little bit they get.

As I said earlier, I was patron of the Waltzing Matilda Centenary Celebrations, and I had done quite a lot of PR work here in Australia, as well as the stint in London. I was just as keen to see it a huge success as anyone else. As the big day came closer, the locals at Winton began to feel a bit as though they had a tiger by the tail. The Queensland Events Corporation had taken over the organisation of the event and the refurbishing of the town as well, so that it would look in keeping with the Centenary. Queensland Rail handed over a heritage train for the use of the Centenary to take visitors from Brisbane to Winton, and new lights were erected along the main street, where a billabong and a life-size bronze statue of the poet Banjo Paterson had been placed.

At the sports oval, a huge stage with matching sound and lighting was erected. The middle of the shopping centre was closed to traffic, and marquees, food stalls and buskers appeared. There were poetry recitations, competitions for bush verse, there were races and a big rodeo.

The day before the actual Centenary, I drove the heritage train into Winton. For miles outside town, people stood alongside the track to see her come in from Brisbane and I made full use of her whistle. I'd been wearing a traindriver's cap, but when we pulled into the railway station at the end of the journey, there were about a thousand people waiting. They were all over the track, packed on the station, and murmuring 'Where's Slim?' I lost no time in whacking my hat on my head, and becoming myself again.

The story of 'Waltzing Matilda' is even more confusing than the story of the 'Pub', and it has even more versions to add to the confusion. The main arguments appear to be firstly, whether Paterson really wrote the words or re-wrote an old song which was knocking around the bush for years. Paterson was a decent, honest man and published a book of old bush songs, so would surely have included 'Matilda' with them; besides, he stated in a handwritten letter that he wrote the words, and historians and researchers agree with this.

Secondly, who wrote the tune? There are two versions of 'Matilda' in existence, the Queensland version and the one we mostly sing today.

Paterson wrote the words to fit the tune (his own account) that Christina MacPherson played when they were all visiting at Dagworth Station. Christina said it was a tune she'd heard played by the band at the Warrnambool Races, before she came to Winton. 'The Craigielea March' is supposed to have been based on another old Scottish song, 'O Bonnie Wood of Craigielea', but there doesn't seem to be much resemblance to the present tune used. The more popular version was published by the makers of Billy Tea, and given away with each packet. So in no time it was being sung everywhere. The manager's wife wrote, or arranged, the music which was then said to be based on 'The Bold Fusilier', a Kentish folk song. Until a few years ago, there was no evidence except hearsay that this song actually ever existed. Evidence has now been found, and there you have it.

The words of 'Waltzing Matilda' were written by Banjo Paterson, while the tune is a blend of two folk songs. The story of the swagman was told to Paterson by Robert MacPherson, Christina's brother and manager of Dagworth Station, who witnessed the swaggie's drowning. One day, a jackaroo giving his daily report to MacPherson mentioned having seen two swaggies 'waltzing matilda' down by the waterhole. Those two incidents apparently sparked the idea of the words, and Paterson fitted them to the tune.

On 6 April 1995, I sang 'Waltzing Matilda' in the North Gregory Hotel, where it had first been sung one hundred years ago to the day. The Prime Minister was there, so was the Premier of Queensland, the Mayor of Winton, and more especially, two granddaughters of Banjo. They were two very proud ladies.

Another place I had never been, besides Birdsville, was Chillagoe on the base of Cape York in far North Queensland. That changed in May when the Big Weekend was on, and the organisers flew my whole show to Cairns and on to Chillagoe. The mine there was re-opening, and Chillagoe hopes to expand again. Anyway, it expanded that weekend from a population of about two hundred to a couple of thousand. People were sleeping anywhere they could find a spot, the rodeo was in full swing by day, and our show belting out into the night.

I thought of the contrast when I took the stage at the Palais Theatre in St Kilda, Melbourne, later that year. From beneath the stars of a Queensland night, in front of ringers, rodeo riders, southerners up for the weekend, Aboriginal people from the top of the Cape and Cooktown, I stood in front of a theatre full of VIPs and invited guests, who included the Prime Minister of Australia and the Premier of Victoria. This was the 'Australia Remembers' concert, held to mark the fiftieth anniversary of the end of the Second World War.

The idea was that every artist should sing a song from the war years, and I had chosen 'Don't Get Around Much

Anymore'. A bit different from my usual style, and instead of the TCB, I was backed by the orchestra . . . and my guitar. I enjoyed this change so much, that for fun I put the song into my own shows and it went well, especially when young James brought his saxophone onstage and played with me at a couple of shows. He brought the house down.

Country music changes, and I change too. If I can't have a go at a few different things at this stage of the game, then I ought to give it away. Just the same, I have raised a few eyebrows now and then and I quite enjoy doing that, too. I took a way-out young artist, Keith Urban, on tour with me and recorded 'Lights on the Hill' with him. A very different version, it was Keith's arrangement. Many of the up and coming young ones have been listening to my music for years; Keith, for instance, still has the sheet music of 'Lights' that I autographed for him when he was eleven. He's now in the States, having a go at Nashville in their own backyard.

A phone call that seemed quite ordinary started something very much out of the ordinary. Mark Moffatt had produced two albums for Anne, used to play pedal and produce for Saltbush, and was noted for his production of charting contemporary artists.

'Slim, I've been playing around with your version of "Fiddler Man" on my audio desk. Do you mind if I see what I can do with it? I'd like to do a disco track of it.'

I wasn't quite sure what he meant, actually. I had been to two discos in my life—one in Port Hedland and one in Kalgoorlie, and after being pinned to the wall by the volume, I hadn't been in one since.

'That should be alright, Mark. I'll be interested to hear it.' I certainly was.

'Fiddler Man' in its new version caused a fuss in more ways than one. We made a video and it was getting a fair amount of play. Mark and I were amazed at the reaction . . . was it country? It was a bit hard to say it wasn't when I was singing it. Should Slim Dusty be involved in something as way out as this? Once again, Slim Dusty was doing it the way he wanted, just for the hell of it. The two record companies involved took ages to work out how it was to be released, and we began to think we'd never have it out on the market.

The ten days I spent in Tamworth in January 1996 were the busiest ever. It began when I went up early to introduce and compere the New Talent Showcase Concert, where the five finalists for this award were asked to perform for the public. Their Golden Guitar was judged on the recording submitted to the judges, but the Showcase was an opportunity for them to show a top audience how good they were. For the first time since the CMAA took over the Awards, this Golden Guitar was to be announced and presented on the big Awards night along with all the other Awards winners. It was also supposed to be the first time I've ever been on and off a stage all night without singing a song, and that's the way I intended it. But when the closing act (who was driving from a gig in another town and ran out of fuel, of all things) didn't turn up, someone had to lead the finale song, so there I was back into it and loving every minute of it.

That year, 1996, marked my fifty years of continuous commercial recording for the *one* company, EMI Australia. It's a world record for a singer, I'm told. Ten years earlier, the managing director of EMI worldwide calculated that if they were to record one of my songs from start to finish per day, it would take over three years, working five days a week and fifty weeks per year. It would take them a bit longer now, because I've been pretty busy on the recording front in the last few years.

On the Monday night, 22 January, in the Tamworth town hall, the Slim Dusty Family Concert took the stage. Ten years before, after a show in the town hall, I'd sworn 'never again'. It was so hot that the musos took off their shirts at interval time, and wrung the sweat out of them out the dressing room window. But now the town hall was airconditioned and packed to the ceiling for the night. David and Anne were there with us, and in the second half of the show, Joy joined me onstage to sing backup for her song 'The Biggest Disappointment'.

We were just about to start when David walked onto the stage, carrying a long plaque. He went to the microphone and announced that I wanted to make a presentation, and proceeded to read out the inscription. The presentation was to my wife, Joy, who I believe to be my best and strongest songwriter over the whole of my career. For years she has turned out classics for me to sing: 'Indian Pacific', 'Marty', 'Lights on the Hill', 'The Biggest Disappointment', 'Walk a Country Mile', and many more. I have many great songwriters, and no way could I achieve so much without their work, but if I had to choose one out of all of them, I would choose Joy McKean. I have never publicly acknowledged this before, and Joy was quite emotional. The plaque had the original manuscript of 'Lights on the Hill' framed in glass, and this inscription:

We've walked life's road together
And sometimes it's been rough
But somehow we knew we'd make it
'Cause somehow we've been a bit tough.
A tower of strength you've always been
And your songs are here to stay,
I just say 'thank you' for all you've been
And for our family around us today.
Always
Slim
January 1996

The following night, Tuesday, we staged the Travelling Country Band Reunion Concert. Paul and Colleen Trenwith came from New Zealand, Ian Simpson from Perth; people like Colin

Watson, Michel Rose, Lawrie Minson, Charley Boyter, Lindsay Butler and, of course, old Bazza filled the stage. All these people lent a special buzz to the reunion, with the new TCB onstage all night.

I had realised that February 1996 would mark twenty years of association with Rod Coe, my record producer and band leader. We've worked well together, and we're both full of ideas for the coming year's recordings. I presented him with a plaque to mark the occasion and to show him my appreciation. He's had some rough moments with me, on the road and in the studio, but he seems to cope alright so I won't waste too much sympathy on him! It might make him feel that he's going to get it easy for the next few years . . . which he isn't.

There were about twenty-eight interviews, appearances or signings to be done in five days and I needed a helper. A mate, Paul Donkin, promptly appointed himself to the position of minder. Another mate, Bill Robertson, wanted to know: 'Who bloody well minds you from Paul?'

I did the Tamworth Songwriters' Salute concert, a spot on the Bushwackers' twenty-five year reunion show, a guest appearance with Lee Kernaghan, radio with John Laws (the radio king who made his first ever visit to the Festival), store appearances, television, the annual general meeting of the CMAA, witnessing the signing of EMI's newest country artist . . . it was flat out, and it was terrific. John Laws and I led the street parade on Saturday morning, and presented awards together at the Country Music Awards night.

The Awards night is always exciting. Because there was no venue in Tamworth big enough to hold the crowd, we had the use of the Rodeo Indoor Arena at the Showground. We could fit nearly four thousand fans in there, and it was always a rush to get tickets for the event. Out front, fans queued up from the door down along the road, ready to have the first go at the best of the unreserved seats. Backstage, around the portable buildings, 2TM was doing interviews, television crews were filming the action and doing more interviews, the first acts on were in and out of the dressing rooms and make-up chairs, and all the stars of Australian country music were milling around trying to catch up with all their mates they mightn't have seen for anything up to a year.

When the lights go down in the auditorium and the comperes for the night begin the introductions, the electricity builds and builds. A Golden Guitar is the culmination of the year's work, everyone tries to look calm and unconcerned when they're really as tight as guitar strings. I looked around me and wondered how many of these young hopefuls and young stars would still be around in fifty years' time, or even in twenty? Lots of them, I hope.

I knew that Rod and some of the artists had planned a tribute segment in the show, and I was backstage when it began. Brian Young, a bush balladeer who tours the outback every year, kicked it off with 'A Pub with No Beer'. I heard Anne's voice, unmistakable, as she sang 'By a Fire of Gidgee Coal' and then Lee Kernaghan with 'Leave Him in the Longyard'. Across the stage came the family group, the Dead Ringer Band, to sing 'The Biggest Disappointment', and John Williamson, the 'True Blue' bloke, put such feeling into Mack's words of 'Camooweal'. In each song, the lead guitar was played by the man who had recorded it with me: Barry, Lindsay, Colin or Charley. Then Joy stood at the side mike as I walked on and we sang together 'Walk a Country Mile', which represents our years of travel together, and I finished it off with the song that started it all for me . . . 'When the Rain Tumbles Down in July'.

I lifted my arms to acknowledge the applause, then turned to see Max from CMAA coming across the stage towards me. He spoke of the history my career has made in Australian country music—I was finding it hard to take in after hearing all those singers, all the musicians singing and playing my songs. Every one of them gave their time and talent to pay tribute to me, to whatever I may have achieved, and I was just wiped out. How I have deserved it all, I just don't know.

The inscription on the plaque reads:

Presented to Slim Dusty
IN RECOGNITION OF 50 YEARS OF RECORDING FOR EMI

The CMAA salutes the inspiration, the leadership
and the unique contribution you have made to the
Australian Country Music Industry

Tamworth 26.1.96

I turned to the audience again to thank them. Row after row of people came to their feet until four thousand people stood and applauded. I looked out over the rows of faces, some smiling, some tearful with emotion, but all wishing me well. It was a moment I can never forget, and a moment that could never be surpassed.

What would my father have felt?

'I always said the boy's got talent, you know.'

What would Mack Cormack have said to me?

'Not bad, but you're only as good as the show you do tonight, y'know.'

And Gordon?

'I still say you're a mug fisherman, you bastard.'

Chapter Twenty-One

GOING INTERNATIONAL!

A rolling stone will gather no moss, but who wants moss?
'WHO WANTS MOSS?' JOY McKEAN

With the thoughts of three of the most influential people in my life, I went forward into 1996, my fiftieth year of commercial recording. I wasn't sure of what the future still held, but I felt that I was the most fortunate of men in being able to live my dream.

There was at least one more thing that I wanted to do, regardless of whether it was sensible or even possible. That was, to sing my songs in Ireland, where my father came from as a very young child. These days I had a lot of fan mail from Ireland, Scotland and England and the 'Pub' had been near the top of hit parades in England, and on top in Ireland for ten weeks, but my later releases of albums had been few and far between. Nevertheless, I was determined to make the trip later in the year and to take with me the current Travelling Country Band members (Rod, Robbie, Fettler and Jeff) plus a sound engineer. Joy and Anne were to make up the rest of the team.

My idea gave Arthur (my mate and promoter) a few grey

hairs as he and EMI shook their heads in collective dis-
approval, but I was determined. So Arthur got on with the job
of organising the September UK tour while I blithely carried on
with normal events such as recording and videoing a new
album.

In April 1996, the famous R.M. Williams was to open
another store in Sydney at Chifley Plaza, and to mark the occasion had revived the R.M. Williams Heritage Award. He had
decided that I would be the first recipient of the new award. As
R.M. Williams is one of the most respected figures in Australia,
to have him present me with his Heritage Award made the night
a very special one for me. I admire R.M. immensely; he represents the heritage of Australia, and he also rescued and
published the work of the Scottish poet Will Ogilvie, who wrote
bush ballads of the highest standard during his time in
Australia. Into the bargain, I doubt if there's an item of clothing
in my wardrobe that hasn't got the R.M. Williams tag on it.

Back in 1992, Joy and I had taken our first grandchild Kate
on a trip to Greece and Italy with us. She was eleven years old,
and it was a good bonding experience for all of us. However, we
had established a tradition and it was now time for our grandson James to have his trip with us. James wanted to see a
cricket game at Lord's in London and while the itinerary was
being settled, I had been loudly stating that I was not going
overseas to visit any huge cities such as London or Paris. So I
waved Joy and James off at the airport. Two weeks later, after
visiting Rome, London, Nottingham and Paris, they landed at
Harare Airport in Zimbabwe. I was there to meet them, despite
almost losing myself at Johannesburg airport. I can find my
way on any road or track in Australia, but put me in a big airport and I don't have a clue!

We enjoyed ourselves in the game parks, even when a
cranky elephant began menacing our vehicle. Two Englishmen
in the 4WD spoke admiringly to us later, praising eleven-year-
old James's calm in the touchy situation, but James was quite

matter-of-fact about it. 'I thought I'd better not do anything more because I think it was the click of my camera that upset him in the first place.'

The part I disliked about my ambition to sing in Ireland was the fact that I had to fly there. I have always reckoned that if big planes are meant to fly across the world over all those stretches of ocean, then they should all be equipped with pontoons like the old Sunderland flying boats. I just hate waking on a plane at night to feel air pocket bumps when I know we are over water. It was a relief to land at Heathrow in London.

I won't give a blow by blow account of the trip through the UK, but some places do stand out for me. The very first show was at The Mean Fiddler, a London nightspot where most visiting country artists from the US seem to appear. It was a great welcome, and the crowd was really enthusiastic. Heaps of Australians had turned up.

In England, we played in small theatres, clubs and even in a pavilion on a sportsground. The promoters worked and ran their business from a big touring coach—very US-style. It was clear that American country music was the big influence on English and Irish country music. Australian country is very different in that it is not always easy listening, but has much more spike and power. One European critic is supposed to have remarked on the freshness, energy and drive of Australian country music as opposed to 'the plastic coming out of Nashville'.

At last I got to Ireland. Some of my Irish fans were there to greet me, and I found that the Irish loved a good song and story. I remembered an Irish lady living in Australia saying to me, 'If you offer an Irishman a fiver [a five-pound note] in one hand and a song in the other, he will always take the song', and I do believe that to be true. It was brought home to us that in the midst of all the Troubles, the Irish still wanted to hear a song, and wanted to talk about Australia and their relations who had gone to live there. When Joy began singing her song 'Many Mothers', there were times when the audience stood up in recognition, men even more than women. The song tells of the anguish for mothers all over the world in seeing their sons go off to war and there is no theme closer to home for Irish mothers.

We were to show in Enniskillen, a big town not far from the border between Eire and Northern Ireland. I thought it would be very inconvenient to be accommodated in a small town quite a few miles from the venue in Enniskillen itself. As we drove through Enniskillen on the way to our accommodation, we saw the ruins of one wing of a big hotel. 'Well, yes, that is where you were supposed to be staying, but it was bombed the other night', the tour manager said quite matter of factly. Joy and I exchanged apprehensive glances, hoping that no one would decide to bomb the theatre we were going to play in that night.

Another thing we discovered in Ireland was that football brought out the fanatic in its fans to an even greater extent than the AFL final in Melbourne. County Mayo was a finalist this year, and every house and street in both town and country were decked out in flags of team colours. And I mean every house and street—the bunting and flags must have cost a fortune, plus the cost of putting them up. In Castlebar where we were to show, we arrived to find busloads of footy fans loading up and preparing to travel to the final being held miles away. That night, our audience consisted of music fanatics only— there weren't as many of them as there were of the footy ones.

By the time we got to Cork and Dublin, we'd had a great time and met some great people. The Fettler had made arrangements to come back to County Clare where his father was born and look up some relations he'd never met. Joy had been checking out family ancestors in County Tyrone while Anne and I tried out the Irish cooking, and I cultivated a taste for Guinness. We completed the tour back in England at The Weaver's Arms in London, where we met a group of men who had come all the way from the Shetland Islands in the north to see the show. We caught up with our music friends in the magazine and radio world and headed back to Australia having made little money but having had a wonderful experience.

On September 30, I attended the ARIA awards in Sydney. As always, it was a huge affair, with everyone dressed to the nines either formally or really 'way out'. Every kind of recorded music was represented by artists, record and music publishing executives, musicians and media, and this year a big crowd of young people had been admitted and were up close to the 'catwalk' leading from the audience to the stage.

I don't remember an awful lot about the night; it was such a blur of people and music—loud music! But the Special Achievement Award was announced as going to Slim Dusty, and I tell you, it was a long, long walk through the seats and over the catwalk to the stage. I don't think I realised at the time that the whole audience was giving me a standing ovation, the only one of the night. It was all a wonderful surprise. I do remember thinking for a split second that when I was recording my bush ballads and songs, I would never have dreamed of the recording industry recognising them so wholeheartedly. It was stunning for me.

The first edition of this book was released in October 1996, and the publishers planned a series of book signings in November while EMI planned a celebration of my fifty years of recording for the company. It was held at the Regent Hotel in Sydney, and was a great gathering of friends and music people. I've been a great fan of the old *Star Trek* movies, and of the *Star Trek Next Generation* series so when EMI presented me with a big Star Trek poster signed by all the stars of the show, especially Leonard Nimoy (Spock), I was thrilled. I was also given return tickets for two to the States, with arrangements to meet some of the cast of the show when in Los Angeles.

I was in Victoria in March 1997 when Stan Coster died. He had been ill for a while with cancer, and we knew it was not 'if' but 'when' he would go. When I heard the news, I sat and thought about the many times we met up out in western and central Queensland when Stan was working on building the beef road. I thought about the good time up at the Whop's place at Mission Beach with Stan and Mack Cormack, and Bert, the Whop's mate. And I remembered how, when Stan's mates sent him to Sydney for some specialist treatment on his arm, he and his wife Dot stayed at our home while we were on tour, and he wrote 'Dusty's Den'. Then I couldn't help remembering dusty little Dajarra, that outback town and railhead for trucking cattle.

Stan and his family had been camped just out of Dajarra on one of the road camps. We showed in the little hall, and had had the hide to ask the secretary (by mail) if the hall would be clean when we came, seeing that we had to pay a hefty deposit to guarantee that we would leave it clean. The last time we were there we'd had to clean up the debris from a previous local function before we could use it, and then clean it again afterwards. Because of our cheek, the secretary, a local store-keeper had it in for us. There was no cleaning equipment such as brooms in the hall. We were a wake up to this, and so were Stan and Co. The troops lent us brooms, bins and so on and everyone hopped in and cleaned that hall like it had never been cleaned before. Next morning, the secretary found half a peanut shell and refused to refund our deposit! I saw red and had a flaming row with him in his store (Joy had her eye on a broom to use if it came to fisticuffs). Stan said later, 'My word, you were game, old mate. That bloke can go a bit, y'know.' Well, I didn't know and I probably would not have been that cheeky if I had known. We still didn't get our deposit back.

I chartered a small plane to attend Stan's funeral in Tamworth. Throughout the service I kept thinking that Stan's songs would probably outlive us all. I was walking out of the churchyard afterwards when a man pulled me up. I was feeling pretty upset after seeing Stan's family and sitting through the service. 'Slim,' he said, 'I want to ask you how you do that guitar run in one of your songs. It sounds like a Carter Family style, and I can't think what album it's on.' I just pushed him away saying I couldn't remember. You wouldn't believe it, but he rang the pub where we held the wake and got me on the phone to ask again, and in more detail. I suppose he thinks I am about the rudest person he's ever been unfortunate enough to encounter.

Joy and I are patrons of the Truckies' Memorial at Tarcutta, NSW. Near Wagga, it is a project of Re-Car, a firm that runs a smash rescue and repair service for trucks. When the memorial was first opened and for a long time afterwards, it was the only one in the world. Situated in a park beside the Hume Highway, the curved brick walls set in rose gardens carry plaques engraved with the names of truckies who have lost their lives on the highways of Australia. In October each year, there is a service held at the memorial from the back of a semi-trailer, and each year there are scenes that wrench your heart. I saw a young woman leading a little girl by the hand while a toddler in the other arm rested against her shoulder. Her husband had been a farmer, but when he had to give it up, he had a go at truck driving. One old truckie said to me, 'I hate to hear of farmers going into truck driving. They don't have the experience for the job and the accident rate is just shocking.' Right now, there are 750 names on the wall and more go on every year. Toots Holtzheimer was the first of the women commemorated there.

Men and women of the highways and the byways of this land,
Your lives were spent in one more load to haul,

But while ever we remember you, you'll never really die
Although you now are Names upon the Wall. (Joy McKean)

At the Truckies' Memorial weekend, we were talking to Noel Brown, then national sales manager of Re-Car. The conversation ended up with Noel and his mate, Keith Thompson of Thompson Transport in Castlemaine, Victoria, deciding that they could organise a road train trip for us. No sooner said than done.

I was ready to start work on another truck album, and there could be no better way of getting into the spirit of it than to travel across the Nullarbor Plain in a big road train. Noel drove one Kenworth and Keith drove the other. Wives Bev Brown and Carol Thompson drove a back-up vehicle and photographer friend John Elliott came along to get some cover shots for the album.

It's quite an experience for someone like me who had only driven trucks like our old International with a big caravan on the back. Joy and I took turns to travel either in the T950 or the T900 Kenworth, alternating with the two drivers. So many stories were told, giving a fascinating insight into the life of the long-distance driver. There are so many different angles to the transport industry that are never understood by people like us. Did you know that huge amounts of Christmas mail are ferried across from the east coast to Perth by road trains, and not by air? Neither did I.

We headed out past Port Augusta, stopping at Ceduna overnight, where we were treated to trays of Pacific oysters farmed right there in the bay. It reminded me of the time Eric Watson (later of Selection Records) took me and Gordon Parsons down to the Georges River in Sydney to visit with an oyster farmer friend of his. He said later that he had never seen two blokes wolf down so many fresh oysters so fast. I didn't do too badly at Ceduna either.

Eucla was the next overnight stop and it was a real event

for us and for the locals, too. When we first travelled across the Nullarbor in the 1960s, the road was all dirt and corrugations, potholes and bulldust. I remember one of the acts had glossy, wavy, jet black hair. No-one warned him about the salty Nullarbor water, brought up from underground. So while enjoying a hot shower at the Cocklebiddy roadhouse, he shampooed his hair. 'I'm ruined! I'm ruined!' he wailed afterwards, as we studied his stiff, greyish tresses. I'm not sure whether someone gave him some of our precious drinking water to wash out the salty result or whether his self-esteem had to suffer the rest of the way across to Norseman.

The original Eucla is now buried by the sand dunes, and even then was well on the way to disappearing. The motel, police station, meteorological station and golf links are built up on the escarpment well away from the sand. The water is still not good, so the motel owner set up a plant for desalinating it. He supplies all the locals with drinkable water, and behind the motel is a garden as beautiful as you'd see anywhere. 'You know what?' said the staff member showing it to us. 'The water we use is so clean that it has no nutrients left in it, and if we didn't fertilise this garden all the time, the watering wouldn't have any effect.'

Anyway, we could see that people had been coming into the roadhouse bar all evening as word spread by bush telegraph that our team was at the motel for the night. So I thought it might be best to have an early dinner and get myself off to bed. Somehow, it did not work out like that. I ended up in the bar drinking with this one and that, including a bloke who had come into Eucla on one of his rare occasions. He lived alone many miles to the north, not far from the East–West railway line and was the caretaker of a small airfield at Forrest. We even met up with a young lady who had written a thesis on the history of country music for her degree at a Perth university and wondered if we remembered being interviewed for it and getting a copy. We remembered alright, and still have her thesis.

The other lady I remember from that night is the one all the locals warned me about. 'She could start a fight in Heaven,' they said. This time she was on to me about my friendship with the Aboriginal people. 'You're always sucking up to them', and so on and on. She just would not listen to reason, and in the end I gave up. 'Why don't you just bugger off,' I said. 'Go on, get!' I mean, how often do I have to keep telling people that my career might have died an early death if it hadn't been for the support of the Aboriginal people? And I don't like being rubbished about my choice of friends, anyway.

Apart from her, I had a great time and was really getting into the swing of things. Joy decided that she might as well go to bed so that she would have the strength to nurse me or curse me the next day. We ran out of Bundaberg rum and I don't remember what I was drinking after that, but when the barman chucked all of us out, my mate John piloted me back to my motel room where Joy had left the door open. She knew I'd never remember the number. John reckoned I was the noisiest drunk he'd ever steered home, and as he doesn't drink alcohol he usually gets the job of steering his mates home when necessary. Just the same, I reckon Noel and Keith weren't too quiet either.

Next day, I needed the sleeper cab in one of the Kenworths. So did Keith Thompson, so he gave me a good rundown on driving the semi. I was used to driving a truck years ago, but that *was* years ago. I was glad to feel the rhythm of gear changing coming back, and I didn't have any problems with splitting the gears either. Keith was kind enough to say that I was a natural at it, but that might have been because he wanted some sleep himself. He handed over to me to drive and after checking me out and giving me some very straight advice on what to do when I met another road train, climbed into the sleeper and began snoring. I think he forgot that the Fraser Range was coming up. It's a windy and narrow piece of road and I *would* have to meet another road train on it, of course. I can just imagine the CB radio going:

'Some clown wearing a Slim Dusty hat is driving for Thompsons now.'

Thanks to Noel and Keith, to Bev and Carol and all the folk on the Nullarbor, I got three songs from Joy for the truck album. We called the album 'Makin' a Mile', based on the way some of the truckies say goodbye to another in a roadhouse: 'See you later. Better make a mile.'

The day after my seventieth birthday, my friend Rocky Page died in Adelaide. Rocky (Dean) Page had been in the country music business for many years as a singer, recording artist, music teacher, broadcaster, and also as a stage performer of hypnosis and memory acts. He toured with our show over a two-year period during the around Australia tours, and also worked on the showground in the tent show.

His uncle, a doctor, had interested Rocky in hypnosis and its use. When we were in Darwin where we would show for a couple of weeks, Rocky spent a lot of time helping people with his hypnosis. The treatments were all for free, too. Smokers who couldn't quit were the most frequent patients.

Rocky used to do a very good memory act where he memorised a list of about twenty articles named by members of the audience. He then recalled the list in order, or by what-ever number anyone liked to call out. Another stage act was his being blindfolded and being able to tell what article was in front of him. In our small show, Rocky's performance plus his singing spot took up a big portion of time, so when he had to go home to South Australia from the Pilbara in Western Australia for two or three weeks due to a family problem, it was going to leave a big hole in the programme with no way of get-ting another act at short notice. Knowing that Joy has a very good memory, Rocky and I looked at her with speculative eyes. By the time we'd finished, and Rock had tutored her inten-sively, she did his memory and blindfold act until Rocky got

back to the show. However, after that, she used to get very sus-
picious if I ever began telling her how good she was at anything
because she thought she'd end up with still another job to do. I
conned her into becoming my bass player in the same way.

Ron Adsett from the Country Music Store in Brisbane came up
to me during one of the CMAA meetings. 'I'd like to give you
this, Slim. It's an official invitation to appear on the Grand Ol'
Opry in Nashville in August this year.' That floored me because
the Grand Ol' Opry is an American institution of country
music. To appear on the Opry is *the* stamp of approval from the
country music fraternity worldwide. Held every week, with regular members of the Opry appearing along with guest artists, it
is broadcast to just about every state in the US. He went on to
explain how it had all come about and I think Ron had a lot to
do with it.

I wondered whether to make the trip, and whether the
audience there would understand what I was singing about.
Australian slang and idiom are unusual, to say the least, and
I have always thought that any of my bush ballad albums
would need a full glossary in the booklet for release in the US.
However, I had the two tickets given to me by EMI and they
were burning a hole in my pocket. So yes, I'd love to have the
novel experience of singing on the Opry. Should be fun. *But . . .*
who was going to be my backing band?

I couldn't visualise myself fronting an American band, and
I wasn't about to go and represent Australian country with just
a guitar behind songs like 'Lights on the Hill', for instance.
Young Keith Urban with Peter Clarke and Jerry Flower were in
the States, and having had them playing cricket in my back
paddock when they were in Australia on tour recently, I didn't
mind contacting Keith about the gig. 'Love to', was the immediate response. Keith reckoned that given the style of country
he was playing, this would be the only time he'd ever get to

appear on the stage of the Opry. I don't know about that any more, because at long last, Keith's stickability is paying off and his career is hitting the high spots. Couldn't happen to a nicer young bloke.

Next thing, Lawrie Minson got in touch. 'I'm going to be in Nashville when you're there, Slim,' he said. 'If you need a dobro or harmonica player, I'm your man.' What I decided I needed was a didgeridoo player, and Lawrie was the man there as well.

We flew into Nashville after stopping over in Los Angeles to visit Paramount Studios where the Star Trek 'Next Generation' series was filmed. I enjoyed meeting some of the cast members and being photographed in the original Captain Kirk flight chair.

Tom T. Hall met us with flowers for Joy and whisky for me and himself. Tom and his wife Dixie were very hospitable, and we spent some time with them, including the evening when Tom took us to the old Ryman Auditorium for a bluegrass concert and took us backstage to meet people like the Stanley Brothers. 'Hang on to that backstage pass,' Tom said. 'It's history.' Another night he took us to the Bluebird Café, where all the bands go to play and wind down after a gig. A bluegrass band playing insisted Tom get up on stage and sing a number with them. That's the thing about bluegrass, everyone knows all the songs. They were interested to hear that 'Lights on the Hill' was Joy's song as one of the band members had played on the recording made by Del McCoury, a top bluegrass recording artist in America.

The Opryland Hotel brochures say that the hotel is the second biggest in the world. I don't know where the biggest is, but let me tell you that you have to have a map to find your way around that place. It covers five acres just with its car park, I think. The foyer is big enough to hold a cricket match, and there are restaurants, waterfalls, shops, convention centres and ballrooms laid on. We used to sit on the balcony of our room and watch the 'dancing waters' display each evening. The coloured, floodlit waters rose and fell in time with the music played by a pianist seated at a piano suspended high in the air above the waterfalls. I remembered how years ago, on the showgrounds here, there was a similar show on tour.

As the Opry appearance was coming up fast, I needed to get together with Keith and the boys for some rehearsals. It turned out to be one rehearsal, and I was hoping it would be 'alright on the night'. 'Not to worry,' said Keith. 'Anything goes wrong, I'll just lie on my back and play guitar.' Fortunately, that part of the act was not needed.

There were people milling around backstage at the Opry, they were onstage and in the wings and they were pouring in and out of the dressing rooms. I had two sessions to do, and spent some time talking to two of the artists on the programme. Johnny Russell, writer of 'Act Naturally' and other hits, was there with Charlie Walker and as they both knew a lot about Australian country, we passed the time very easily. Charlie Walker was regretful that his record company had refused to let him record the 'Pub' in its entirety. He thought it would work for him, but the company said no, it was too way out for their market.

James Blundell, another of my young friends, was living in Nashville at the time and was at the Opry that night after having taken us for a bit of a tour around in his beaut old 'Yank Tank'. Little Jimmy Dickens introduced me onstage and that was it, we were on and about to give a sample of real Australian bush ballads and country music to about four thousand traditional American country fans. I was glad to think that every Australian living in Nashville and able to get a ticket was there, as I had been told was the case.

Once I hit the stage, I was fine. The boys were plugged in, and Lawrie had his didgeridoo ready and waiting to lead me in to the first song. I'll say this for the American audience at the Opry, they are enthusiastic alright. Some of the words in 'Ringer from the Top End' and 'Lights on the Hill' and 'A Pub with No Beer' might have been strange to them but they certainly got the idea and let me know they were having a whale of a time.

I thought I'd better tell them what a ringer was—cowboy in their idiom—and I also explained a bit about the size of our cattle stations and so on. Perhaps I should say here and now that the word 'ringer' causes a bit of confusion here in Australia, too. In the shearing shed, a 'ringer' is the man who 'rings the shed'; this means that he has sheared the highest number of sheep. In the cattle industry, a 'ringer' is the stockman doing the mustering and general cattle work on the property. The word seems to be used more in Queensland and the Top End than down south in New South Wales and Victoria. A cowboy here in Australia is usually the bloke who is around the homestead attending to the odd jobs, milking the cow and so on.

When I came off the stage, Ricky Skaggs was the first on hand to speak to me and to say some pretty nice things. I still felt like a fish out of water but people were mostly very warm and friendly. Some of the young Australian country artists have appeared on the Opry in recent years, but I don't think any of them were singing words that could puzzle the audiences the way mine did.

By the time we had spent a couple of weeks looking around Arizona and making friends with some of our co-travellers, we were ready to come home and attend the ARIAs, Anne's record launch of 'Cry Like a Man', do some touring and then go out past Broken Hill for a festival. This particular festival was to raise money to help the locals keep their small town running. Cockburn is basically in no man's land, between New South Wales and South Australia, and no one seems to want to take responsibility for its school, post office, amenities and so on. Well, after the Grand Ol' Opry, Cockburn sounded like it would be getting back to the nitty gritty, and I can tell you it certainly was. They had expected about three hundred, but about three thousand turned up. The temperature was up at the top of the thermometer, and the crowd had been drinking solidly for two days before we arrived. They were full of enthusiasm and alcohol, and ready to tear the place apart.

I was back home.

Chapter Twenty-Two
DRAMAS

Had it easy, done it hard, seen a lot of life's backyard . . .
'I'VE BEEN THERE, AND BACK AGAIN' JOY McKEAN

I had been keeping a secret that came out on Australia Day, 26 January 1998. I was announced as an Officer of the Order of Australia with the investiture to be made in May. As I had been made a Member of the British Empire (MBE) way back in 1970, I was very, very honoured to be able to put the letters AO after my name. There had never been any chance that I would have a university degree to add to it, but this was from my country and I think that's just the best honour or degree I could have. I wondered what my dad would have said if he had known that his faith in me was not misplaced.

It seemed that this year was to provide one surprise after another. The National Trust of Australia asked the public to vote for their 100 National Living Treasures, and I was voted one of them. I was beginning to feel a bit overwhelmed by all this attention, and also worried that my friends would think I was getting a bit above myself.

Sydney Town Hall is a grand old building, and the main room was beautifully decorated, crowded with tables full of people. Hundreds of people were honouring the ones chosen as National Living Treasures and in the process raising funds to carry on the work of the National Trust in preserving our heritage. Some of the honoured that I met were friends such as R.M. Williams and Dick Smith; others I enjoyed meeting included that lovely lady Hazel Hawke. I sat on the stage alongside all those distinguished people and looked out over the audience. I could see in my mind another very different audience of almost fifty years previously.

One of the earliest shows I did in Sydney was right here in Sydney Town Hall. Via his 2SM radio show, Tim McNamara had organised a huge talent quest and the final was held here. The Town Hall was packed with country music fans from all walks of life, and it was on this night that Reg Lindsay, George Payne and Shorty Ranger won their places in the finals with the reward being to record for the Rodeo label. Backstage were featured artists such as the McKean Sisters and Gordon Parsons, and hordes of hopefuls. Life was exciting, something new was happening every day, and scenes of future stages and crowded audiences had me dazzled. Stage performing was still a new experience for me, and I watched the other performers for tips, while pretending that I was an old hand at it all. Now I guess I am an old hand at last.

As always, when I was getting too big for my boots, I went back to touring. There's nothing like being out there on stage, connecting with the folk who come to hear my songs and tell me about what's going on in the real world. And, of course, there are always the minor dramas of everyday touring. Including the constant chasing of my hat. I don't like carrying a spare because I think it might jinx me. However, there have been times when I should have had a spare in the car. Like the time we went up to Kerry Packer's complex outside Scone. We were booked to show at his place in the little club that the locals used, and we were almost there when Joy asked me, 'Where is your hat?'

'Hat? Hat? On the back seat.' I thought that was the case.

'No, it's not.'

'Look over the back with the guitar.'

'It's not there. You *told* me you put it in.'

'I did. I know I did.' I knew I was in trouble, firstly for not putting it in when I told her that I had and secondly for refusing to carry a spare, something Joy was always nagging me to do.

You might think a hat is a minor thing to worry about when you have a full show to do, but that old hat is a part of me and I'm not the person people come to see if I haven't got it on. It was too late to go back home for it, and when I tried to borrow one on arrival they were all too big or too wide in the brim. So Joy's straw western-style hat was grabbed and pummelled into some sort of shape and made its debut on the show. I should have kept a photo of myself in that hat to remind me of what happens if I'm careless.

Another hat drama was at Twin Towns Services Club on the far north coast of New South Wales.

I thought I had left my hat at the motel when I discovered it missing. Someone went back and searched, but no hat. I couldn't believe it at first, but at five minutes to go to starting time there was still no hat. Paul Kelliners, stage manager and calm person backstage, went out into the audience. There he spotted two young ringer-style blokes wearing their battered Akubras.

'Hey, mate. Can I possibly borrow your hat?' he asked the first one. The owner bristled. You don't just walk up and want to borrow a bloke's treasured hat; you have to have a thumping good reason. Paul thought he was going to get clobbered so he started talking a lot faster. 'No, no, not for me. Slim's lost his hat and we've got to start the show, can I borrow one of your hats for him? We'll return it . . .' and so on. Before he had finished, he had two hats pushed onto him with loud good wishes from the owners. I met them both after the show and signed the hats into the bargain. I hope their hats went back into their original shape after I had punched them into my bash.

I can't just walk into a shop and buy myself a new hat when I need one because the Sundowner isn't available in Australia anymore, although I believe it still sells in the States. So the blokes at the Akubra factory in Kempsey make me a dozen at a time when I'm running out of supply.

Anyway, after that there was no more argument. A spare was carried until I managed to start 'forgetting' to pack it.

For the second time in my life, I drove up to Government House in Sydney. This time it was for my own investiture and Joy, Anne and David were with me. It's a bit nerve-racking at first when you are taken aside into a separate room and given the drum on how to behave and what to do. But after actually having the medal on its ribbon placed over my head, and shaking hands with the Governor, getting official photographs taken (which didn't come out), and joining the family outside in the sunlight, I began to feel quite pleased with myself. I hadn't fallen over anything and I'd remembered all the right things to do, and the family was taking me to lunch. To top it off, I met Eric Joliffe and that made my day. Apparently Eric wanted to meet me too, and someone introduced us.

Eric Joliffe is famous for his Saltbush Bill cartoons and his cartoons based on Aboriginal life. I can always get a laugh from looking through the booklets of Eric's work that I keep by my desk.

As I've said, we had begun the tradition of a trip overseas with each grandchild when he or she was eleven years old. It's a great way of becoming good mates with them because the three of you are out there on your own. This time it was Danny's turn and he wanted to go to hotspots like Egypt where tourists were being shot at, so he was talked out of that one. He settled for South America and that suited us fine. It also suited

Danny, who has been a climber since he was born. There were plenty of walls, ruins and mountains for him to conquer and there was a lot of bargaining to be done as he shopped for gifts to take home.

We spent time in Cuzsco, Peru, a fantastic town where buildings have bases of old Inca stone, still standing solid without mortar of any kind, and we went to Macchu Picchu, the mountainside city of the past. We were in Oaxaco (pronounced Waharco) walking along a street when we heard a shout from across the street: 'Slim! Slim! How ya going? What're you doing here?' It was a young couple from Broken Hill on holidays!

A lot of things had been happening over the previous few months. EMI had decided that in view of my constant recording schedule and the remarkable length of time we had been working together, and also because they had sold their Studio 301 where I always worked, they would build me my own studio above the garage at my home. I was excited at this idea, and very appreciative, as you can imagine. For a while, I had been recording at different studios and had not settled into one, although I found Phil Punch's Electric Avenue Studio very congenial as well as getting a top sound.

So there had been architects, builders and studio designers swarming over the place for months. Apart from one bloke who thought he was going to lift the roof off the building to lower in a pre-built drum booth, we all got along fine. We've got our drum booth, but without touching the roof, thank you very much.

Over the years, I have recorded mostly at EMI's own studios. First of all, the fibro lean-to out at the Homebush factory was where I made my first recording. To get there, you had to walk down Columbia Lane from Parramatta Road to the back of the buildings. Gladys Moncrieff and Peter Dawson, both famous Australian singers, were among the hordes of musicians, singers and actors who walked down that narrow thoroughfare.

I was talking about all this to a mate of mine who will remain anonymous, when he said, 'Have a look on your verandah one day this week, will you?' I kept an eye out and blow me down, one morning I found the old yellow and black wooden street sign from Columbia Lane sitting there. Another mate said to me afterwards, 'Yes, that so-and-so beat me to it. I took my ladder and everything, but it was gone and the new sign in its place.' The council was about to change the old wooden sign for a new metal one, and my mates had decided that the historic old sign had to be retrieved. The successful retriever was good enough to give it to me and it now hangs above the stairs to my little studio. There's also another souvenir: I usually recorded in Studio A at EMI's 301 studios, so one of the musos climbed up and took down the big 'A' and nailed it above the door to my studio. Memories, eh?

Another bit of building was going on, too. But this time it was in the city of Tamworth. For years, the Golden Guitar Awards organisers had struggled to find a venue suitable for housing the big night. They tried the Town Hall (too small and too stifling in the January heat), the high school hall (ditto), the big tin shed out at the airport (a thunderstorm on the tin roof drowned out the singers and ruined the recording), and even the Big Top. That had tremendous atmosphere and seated a big crowd but the wind began to lift the tent poles and scared the life out of the organisers so that was never mentioned again. Old showies like me and Tex Morton loved being in the tent, but we couldn't get them to repeat the exercise.

As the city had to turn away conventions and the like for lack of a suitable venue, there had been considerable agitation about it until a group of businessmen got together and guaranteed an amount of finance if the council would do the same and build a venue worthy of the city. The country music festival brought huge amounts of money into the place, but the Awards night, the centre of the festival, had nowhere to house the big crowds it drew. At long last, the council bit the bullet and 1998 saw the completion of the Tamworth Recreation and Entertainment Centre, known to all as the TREC.

The CMAA was madly excited at the prospect of holding the Awards there the following January, and set about organising a super opening concert in September. Everyone was there, I think, and the TREC got off to a flying start.

It was a year of big events for me. The Kempsey country music fraternity honoured me with their Living Legend Award, the Gympie Muster was a roaring success, and then the touring team and I took off for the Solomon Islands once again. The Gold Ridge Mine near Honiara was due to open in September, and a week of celebrations was planned, including performances by our band. This time, the Fettler was off seeing the world by way of playing fiddle with an Irish Riverdance-style company, so Peter Denahy took his place in the Travelling Country Band.

The mining company had moved a whole village from the mine site to a completely different location and provided every amenity they could think of in the way of piped water, a meeting hall and good cottages. However, there was still a feeling of discontent rumbling around the village, we felt. The first day in Honiara, we were to perform at the hotel for a big gathering of corporate and company executives and their wives from Australia, together with the Solomon Islands Government officials and ministers.

As we prepared to start the performance, a member of the hotel staff made moves to eject a small boy who was standing in the midst of the instruments and amplifiers. Robbie, the drummer, hastened to his rescue: 'No, no! That's Rex . . . he's with us!' Young Rex had attached himself to our group by offering to assist Robbie, who was wearing a plaster on one forearm. Robbie was a keen tennis player and on tour, was the main organiser of band games whenever there was an opportunity.

One day, he tripped and fell back onto his wrist and bingo! It was Robbie, the one-armed drummer for a while. Although he was plastered up, he was still playing well, and Rex became his offsider for the visit. Rex travelled around in the minibus with us, ate with us and generally 'made hay while the sun shone' in that he took every opportunity to be a new member of the TCB.

We went out to the new village the next day to play a concert in the new meeting hall, and that evening, set up for the big event in Honiara. The mining company had built a big stage, and the dressing rooms were styled like an island hut. The company had also flown in a full sound system and sound engineer, Harry, and the football ground was packed with about twenty thousand islanders. They were the nicest and best-behaved open-air crowd I've ever played to, as they clapped and cheered and sang out for favourites. They listened to everything, and at the end went happily on their way talking and laughing and giving no problems at all to the traffic organisers.

A visit to the hospital next day was the chance for a bit of a short-notice concert, though unfortunately I had to take off my frangipani leis so that I could play the guitar. These garlands of fragrant flowers were hung around our necks at every opportunity and Joy even brought a couple home to show to the family. We left on a 2 am flight to Brisbane, with dancers there to farewell us as they had greeted us when we arrived.

Touring in New South Wales was a bit of an anti-climax, I suppose, but in a way it was comfortable getting back to the old runs. I had been feeling tired, and getting a little uptight at times, but Joy and I put it down to my heavy workload. Besides the touring and all the exciting events of the year, I had been recording and out promoting records and the book release. On top of that, I had the thrill of seeing a CD release of 'Not So Dusty', a collection of my recorded songs reworked by people such as Midnight Oil, The Screaming Jets, Ross Wilson, and even Tom T. Hall, and quite a few others. It was an eye-opener to hear the different versions, and I was complimented by the fact that so many artists from different styles of music were willing to take part in the project.

I went down to a city pub for a media release of that album, and got to know Dave Gleason and the Screaming Jets. Apparently they didn't know if they should invite me to have a beer or not; perhaps the old boy wouldn't be up to it? Several beers later, we were all the best of mates, swapping yarns and I was rocked in my seat by their version of 'Cunnamulla Feller'. I bet old Stan Coster would have been rocked, too. It's amazing what a different treatment can do to a song. I like to listen to all kinds.

Early January 1999 and it was about 31 degrees in the shade. But I was bent on cleaning up the back paddock and raking out the chook house and doing all the odd things that had needed doing for ages, so I kept at it for hours. I went to bed early, but couldn't settle down. I had the same old tight feeling that I had noticed off and on over the past few months, but it mostly went away after a while. Tonight, it was taking longer than usual to stop, so I propped myself up on the pillows and prepared to sit it out.

David was staying overnight with us for some reason or other, and after dinner was doing something on his computer, enjoying a glass of red, when Joy said, 'David, Dad is still awake and it's eleven o'clock. He's tired but he says he feels a bit tight in the chest and he can't settle down. You know he usually crashes early.' David closed the lid of his laptop, carefully put aside his glass of good red, and said, 'I just might take a look at him'.

I was still sitting up in bed feeling grizzly when my son came in, made a short examination, told his mother to pack an overnight bag for me 'just in case' and said he was taking me up to Emergency for a check-up. Everything seemed to go into over-drive from then on. They kept me in overnight, sent me for a stress test, and the cardiologist booked me in for an angiogram immediately.

After the angiogram, Joy was sitting by my side waiting to be told when I could get dressed and come home, and giving me a hard time about being a drama queen or some sort of rot, when the doctor came around the corner of the room still in his theatre gear. He didn't mince his words: 'This is a life threatening situation. You have a 95 per cent blockage at the junction of the two main arteries of your heart. You will have to have a bypass operation as soon as possible.'

I looked at him quite blankly. Joy's mouth dropped, and she gave a nervous giggle. We looked at each other, and back to the doctor. He proceeded to lay down the law about how I was not to move out of that bed, and to tell us arrangements had to be made immediately for surgery. Well, I was wired up from head to toe for the next few hours until I was trundled into an ambulance for the trip to the hospital, where I was to have the bypass done. The most I remember about all of that was the way the air-conditioner in the back of the ambulance dripped water onto my forehead all the way there.

All I can say is that I had the best of surgeons, the best after-care in the intensive care ward, and the best of everything else possible. When I left the hospital after nearly a fortnight we sent chocolates and flowers to the telephonists and receptionists to thank them for coping so well with the flood of calls from friends and the public. There had been a wave of concern that I knew nothing about for a number of days, and when I did know, I was only sorry I couldn't thank each and every one of the callers personally. I was also glad that this took place before I went to Tamworth for the Awards, as apparently I was a fatal heart attack just waiting to happen. No wonder I felt so breathless and tired in the heights of Bolivia and in Macchu Picchu in South America.

For nearly twenty years, I have walked every day for about an hour, no matter what the weather. I gave up smoking around the same time that I began the walking routine, and although I admit I like my drinks, I don't think I overdid it and we have

318

always eaten fairly sensibly. So it was quite a shock and I don't know what to blame! Of course, I have to say that the main reason I have done all the above is so that I can continue the singing and touring that is my lifeline, and unless I keep myself fairly fit I wouldn't be able to do a good job of it.

I've always been a person who looks forward, and when I headed into the bypass operation my concentration was on getting it over and getting back into harness as quickly as possible. At no time did I consider changing my lifestyle or slowing down; at no time did I think that I might lose my life, my family, my career. It didn't seem to even occur to me that I might not be able to continue my singing and touring. That would have been to think the unthinkable.

It was a dramatic beginning to 1999 but it did get better. The tours were going so well, and I was honoured as Father of the Year by the NSW Father's Day Council. Later in the year, I was also honoured as the inaugural Senior Australian of the Year. I went to Canberra in September for the presentation by the Prime Minister, John Howard, and Minister Bronwyn Bishop. That was a great night, and I guess I can always say I was the first.

Chapter Twenty-Three

LINKS IN THE CHAIN

From now on you will find me where the air is fresh and sweet,
Where forever there'll be gumtrees and willows by the creek.
'GUMTREES BY THE ROADWAY' SLIM DUSTY

The world finally made it—a new millennium. What was this great year going to bring? First of all, it brought the news that Australia Post had chosen me as their 'Australian Legend of the Year'. This news became public on 26 January, when it was announced at the Australia Day official luncheon in Sydney. We had known about it for some time as journalist Peter Bowers had been commissioned to write a booklet for publication on Australia Day. This had involved Peter and photographer John Elliott joining up with our West Australian tour in November the previous year and giving Peter a crash course on touring with the Slim Dusty Show. He survived, so did we, and he did us proud with the story he turned out.

It was a terrific feeling to stand on the stage in front of all the Australia Day guests and be presented with a solid gold copy of the official Australia Post stamps that were being issued to mark my special year. It was also a strange feeling to later see my face on the stamps of letters arriving and going out of the office. Our assistant, Lesley, had a shot to make: 'Don't tell me I'm going to have to lick the back of the boss's head all this year?'

I am never very far away from the microphone, either on stage or in the studio, and this time I was concentrating on recording four sides with my boyhood friend Shorty Ranger. Since we set out together all those years ago, we thought it was about time that we had something down on an album. We had to make arrangements by long distance as he was still living in Kempsey and I was mostly in Sydney. It worked after all, with Shorty coming to Sydney to record in my studio with me. We finished up with 'The Men from the Nulla Nulla'.

Now, I had known I was getting towards the one hundred album mark but didn't realise how close until some collectors and then some record executives did some serious tallying up. After arguing the toss about what should be included and what should not, they finally agreed that in 1999, I would be releasing my ninety-ninth album. Naturally, that was what the album was called but the big deal was that in this year of 2000, I could be releasing my hundredth album. (Look out, Tom T., it's getting closer to your payout.)

EMI was a hive of activity as it prepared for the launch of the hundredth album. It was an historic mark for them as well as for me. I was the only artist in the world to have recorded 100 albums for the one company, and they planned to celebrate in style. One department seemed to be spending every minute on the arrangements, and while I was recording and touring, I was vaguely hoping that the album was going to live up to expectations. The invitations for the launch were specially made from Australian timber, the invitee's name carved on it. There was a box set, 'The Man Who is Australia', carrying more than seventy recordings, some never before released, plus interviews and a booklet of quotes, career highlights and a reproduction of the portrait painted by Judy Cassab. The cover photo was taken while I was on tour. The tempo of the whole project just speeded up and up to the final night in June.

EMI hired the Theatre Royal in Sydney for the evening and we were able to invite many of our friends. Some of our writers lived so far away that they couldn't make it but sent their good wishes. Kerri-Anne Kennerley and Richard Wilkins from Channel 9 compered the proceedings, introducing the speakers and the artists. Paul Kelly and 'Uncle Bill' sang 'The Sunlander', John Williamson sang 'I Must Have Good Terbaccy When I Smoke' and Graeme Connors sang 'When the Rain Tumbles Down in July'. The Screaming Jets whaled into 'Cunnamulla Feller' and shocked the fan club members in the gallery.

Dobe Newton from the Bushwackers spoke on behalf of the country music fraternity, and Dick Smith told the true story of that helicopter trip over the Blue Mountains. 'Slim, there you were, thinking how this bloke who had been to the South Pole and all of that, would be OK to get you to the Blue Mountains and all the time I was in trouble. What you didn't know was that I was well and truly lost in that fog, we were only fifty feet above some of the ridges and I was trying to get Pip to pass me the maps without panicking you.' Typical of Dick. I wonder if he will take me on his next round the world trip or if he thinks I might jinx him?

Tony Harlow, the young English managing director of EMI, spoke glowingly of my career and of events that had occurred even during his short sojourn with us.

'I think that building Slim's studio was the best investment we ever made,' he said. Then he went on to present me with the Silver Disc Award from England. When the 'Pub' was at its height in England, the record industry there refused to award me the very first Silver Disc because, they claimed, the bulk of my sales had occurred before it was inaugurated. Tony, being English, had gone to bat for me and forty-odd years after the event, I received it from his hands. I was tickled pink and proud to hang it on my wall at home. So far as I'm concerned, Tony's an honorary Australian.

By this time, I was beginning to think that the evening was

a pretty dry argument and that if all the speeches and songs were over, I could get together with the musos and my other friends and down a beer or two. Then while I was trying to thank Tony for the Silver Disc Award and the whole shebang, Tony was gently pushing me around to acknowledge someone else on the stage. It was Mike Munro from Channel 9 saying, 'Slim Dusty, This Is Your Life.' Well, you could have knocked me down with a feather. You see, twenty-five years ago the TIYL team had done a programme on my life and it never occurred to me that they would do a second one. But like they said, there were not too many artists who'd had as long and varied a career as I'd had and there was more than enough material for a second and special programme.

Among the guests that night were the Wiggles, those amazing four blokes who have every kid in the world singing along with them. I had made a video and recording with them of their version of 'Duncan'—that is, 'I'd Like to Have a Dance with Dorothy'—and thanks to that, I'm getting fan mail from all the littlies, including one little girl who told me what a good dancer I was. I didn't have the heart to tell her that the legs and boots doing the dancing did not belong to old draught horse me.

Besides my family there were old friends from the showground days: Teddy Trevor and Johnny Devlin, John Williamson, Graeme Connors, Adam Brand and Beccy Cole. On video and tape there were messages from Johnny Cash and Tom T. Hall, videos from Keith Urban in America, Kasey Chambers in London, Gina Jeffries and Troy Cassar-Daley. Then onto the stage walked Paul and Colleen Trenwith from the old Hamilton County Bluegrass Band of New Zealand, who had travelled for so many years with us here. My sister Kathleen had made the trip to be with me; also Joy's sister Heather, who had been so wary of me all those years ago and was now my good mate.

The programme finished with everyone onstage and a tremendous version of 'Lights on the Hill'. The night went on and on, as the crowd poured out into the foyer and I tried to catch up with everyone. Smoky and Dot Dawson, Ron and Psyche Wills, Col Joye, Judy Stone, Aunty Una and Tony Ray, Kathleen and her family, Teddy Trevor and friend after friend were wishing me well. I'm a lucky man.

By the way, Tom T. paid up like the gentleman he is.

Three days later, I left for overseas with Hannah and Joy. We travelled in Spain with a tour group of mostly Americans. Didn't we get some surprised letters later in the year from Hannah's contacts who hadn't taken much notice of her grandfather!

You'd think nothing could top the hundredth for me, but there was more to come. John Spence, producer of musical events, rang me very quietly. It was to be top secret, but David Atkins and John, who were producing the closing ceremony for the Sydney 2000 Olympics, were inviting me to be the closing artist for the whole ceremony. I couldn't say 'yes' fast enough, and then went out on tour to keep myself in trim for the big turnout.

There was a huge rehearsal out at what used to be an airfield in the west of Sydney, so Joy and I had a preview of the scale of the presentation, and I began to think I might have bitten off more than I could chew. However, with John handling my end of it, he left me in no doubt that he'd have everything under control, including the sound. As I had to walk out from the dark across the arena, climb up the steps to the huge stage where everyone else was standing, and sing 'Waltzing Matilda' as I went, I had to be wired up for sound. I also had to make sure I didn't trip and fall flat on my face as I went up the steps. There was a cool wind blowing as it was September, and I put on my three-quarter length coat. 'Great!' said John and the sound man. 'That's perfect to cover up all the sound equipment we've got to wire onto you.'

That's why I was wearing a coat on the night of 1 October 2000, when I strode out across the arena with just my guitar strumming behind my voice as I sang what is really our national song, 'Waltzing Matilda'. John was right with me until the moment I had to step out. He said, 'If the kids are in your way, keep going. They will move for you . . . now GO!' The children in the pageant were smart enough to keep out of my path, I kept going and mounted the steps going higher and higher with the voices of about 100,000 people singing with me. I was just so high myself that I think I was hugging little Kylie Minogue to death because she was unlucky enough to be standing alongside me!

All the Australian artists performing during the Olympics were very proud to be a part of it all and I think they showed the world a wealth of talent and creative power as they did so. 'The best Olympics ever!' I like to think so, anyway.

The day after the Olympics, I flew to Perth to begin two and a half months' touring and get ready for the next year's events. At the Golden Guitar Awards in January, 'Looking Forward, Looking Back' did not win Best Album but did get Best Selling Album, and at the ARIAs later in the year it did take out the Best Country Album award. That's one award that Anne beat me to, as she won Best Country Album with 'Out of the Blue' in 1991.

Another National Trust concert in Sydney Town Hall was a fundraiser for the National Trust, and organiser Michael Ball had requested that the entertainment be by the great pianist Roger Woodward, violinist Richard Tognetti, the young leader of the Sydney Chamber Orchestra, and Slim Dusty. There was certainly going to be a bit of a contrast between the artists I reckoned. Then Richard and I were asked if we could possibly combine with a performance of some song together. That was a curly one indeed.

Richard took it in his stride, and decided he should have a run through with our fiddle player, the Fettler. They got on like a house on fire and decided that they would play the twin fiddle part for 'Lights on the Hill'. On the night, I sat in the body of the hall to watch Richard playing with his quartet and was worried to see Mike Kerin hovering on the side of the open stage, fiddle and bow at the ready. I nearly fell over when Richard and Mike played a short classical piece together. Trust Mike to give me heart failure.

The setting of the stage in front of the organ pipes was something to see as different coloured lights played across the ceiling-high pipes. Then we swung into 'Claypan Boogie', with Richard and Mike having a ball. Two players from opposite ends of the violin style of playing—a highly accomplished classical violinist and concert conductor, and a country and Irish fiddle player. A very different evening, indeed, as some of the guests in evening dress gave in to the impulse to stand up and dance among the tables.

There was one thing after another: the Yeperenye Festival in Alice Springs, a Federation Year celebration and gathering of every Aboriginal tribe in the Centre and the Northern Territory; a dinner with the Queensland Government to meet Ted Turner, organiser of the Goodwill Games, and a chance to catch up with the Premier Peter Beattie; a concert in Sydney; the release of two more albums, 'West of Winton' and 'Men from the Nulla Nulla'; the ARIA awards where I presented Keith Urban with a Special Achievement Award and in turn received Best Country Album.

But as the year went on, I grew more and more tired to the point of exhaustion, and more and more uptight. I knew there was something wrong besides a heavy though enjoyable workload plus my age, and after seeing me having to lie down and rest before I could get on stage in Brisbane, Joy determined to get some answers. She had been trying to find out what was wrong with me for some time. Apparently she reckoned that I was such a resilient and strong person physically that I should have been bouncing back as usual, and I certainly was not.

In November, a CT scan showed a tumour on my left kidney.

That was Wednesday, and on the Monday I was in surgery to have the kidney and tumour removed. My spleen was removed at the same time. It took a few days to recover from the surgery, of course, and it meant that I had to forego an appearance in Canberra on the Peoplescape concert. But Anne, Kate and Hannah performed instead and I was filled with pride as I watched the telecast of the performance. Those girls, with Mike and Jeff backing them, did a great job in my place.

We had planned a party to celebrate our golden wedding anniversary in December, but settled for a quiet family dinner instead. The family was what counted, and it was the family that always stuck to both of us when we needed support. I just concentrated on getting myself back into trim for the Family Concert in Tamworth Town Hall (now air-conditioned!) the following month of January.

After the rumours about my surgery, the whole industry and many of my fans were convinced that this concert would be my final appearance on stage. It was sold out as soon as tickets were available, and standing room only was the go. We had no inkling of this at the time, but when we were made aware of it, Joy went onstage to say quite definitely: 'Rumours of Slim's demise are greatly exaggerated! The only way you'll get him off the stage is to drag him off kicking and screaming.' Actually, I always said that when I have to go I'd like to fall head first into the footlights or the sound wedges at the front of the stage.

I performed at the Golden Guitar Awards again, but it was a sad time for us. Aunty Una's husband, Tony Ray, died in Guyra on 24 January. He had fought a courageous battle against cancer, and was witty and in control up to the last minute of his life. We were concerned for our beloved Aunty Una, who had just as much courage as Tony but would be lost without him.

I had albums 101 and 102 under my belt, number 103 had been released (a collection of Australiana) and I began working on number 104 with Anne. It was to be a duet album that didn't quite end up as a conventional duet album but more of a collaboration effort. The title track, 'Travelling Still . . . Always Will', was written by Anne and I have to confess that Joy dissolved when she first heard it and I had to swallow hard and look for the box of tissues. Anne wrote it about us, and it is a beautiful and insightful song (and I am *not* biased).

She also wrote the music for 'I Wonder If the Creeks Are Flowing Still', and recorded it with her daughter Kate and our other granddaughter Hannah just before Kate left for a year at university in Germany. One of the songs on the album, 'Bonner', was a tribute to Senator Neville Bonner, who became the first Aboriginal Member of Parliament. I sang it the first time at a dinner in Canberra organised by Dr Brendan Nelson to launch the Bonner Foundation, aimed at providing scholarship funds for further study by young Aboriginal achievers. The album was launched in April.

Most of the knowledge I have of my family's early history comes from research done by my niece, Noeline Kyle. Noeline launched her book, *Memories and Dreams: A Memoir of Nurse Mary Kirkpatrick*, in Kempsey where we dedicated headstones to Nurse Kirkpatrick and to my parents Dave and Mary. Standing there in the quiet graveyard, I wondered why my life had been so different from theirs and why I had been so blessed in so many ways.

In June 2001, we all went over to South Australia and flew into Maree up in the north of the state. I was to take my show there for the closing concert of the Great Cattle Drive. This drive was part of the Year of the Outback celebrations, and began in Birdsville in the corner of New South Wales, travelled down the Birdsville Track through Mungeranie, collecting donated cattle all the way and ending at Maree where the cattle would be auctioned for charity. John Williamson did the Birdsville concert to kick off the drive, Lee Kernaghan did the Mungeranie show and I was to wind it up at Maree.

What a turnout! In the dry dust of Maree, nearly six thousand people arrived to take over the caravan park, or throw their swags in the red dirt along the old railway line or on the verandah of the pub. There were tents and swags everywhere you looked. That was besides a tent city where Anne and the boys were billeted, while Joy and Heather and I were billeted in the home of Bev and Eric Oldfield. Eric was boss drover of the Great Cattle Drive, and although he hadn't been droving for some years but had settled in Maree at his caravan park, he took to the old job as though he had never been away. His family was obviously proud of Dad.

There was a constant stream of friends and relations in and out of the house, moving Bev to remark that they had thought it might be quieter for me and Joy than being over at the tent city, but somehow she reckoned she just might have been wrong! There were roll-your-owns, rum and cups of tea in never-ending supply around the kitchen table, and mountains of tucker. I've never been made more welcome anywhere in my life. The show went like clockwork and finished off with a presentation being made to Eric of a book of photos of the events in his life to mark his successful boss droving of a huge cattle drive.

This was a year of events, some good and some very sad. We had lost Tony, and in late July Barry Thornton, my old guitarist and comic on the road for nineteen years, died suddenly in Launceston while in town to do a performance on the 22nd. Bazza knew quite well that he could go at any time, as he had spent months in hospital the previous year. He had a narrow escape from dying then, and knew that the fragile arteries could not take surgery but would give way at some unknown moment. In January he told me, 'I'm not going to sit around and wait for it to happen, mate. I'm going out there to do what I always do and I'll keep on playing until I can't do it anymore.'

That's exactly what he did. He was in Tasmania to do a job when it happened. Pauline, his wife, and Meryl, his daughter, brought him home to Maroochydore, Queensland, and it must have been one of the biggest funerals ever seen in the district. There was a link to my past gone forever.

In October, Ron Wills, my old producer and the man who fought the radio stations to get the 'Pub' played on air, died in Sydney. We were good friends throughout all the years. Yet another link gone.

One bright spot around that time was the invitation from Edith Cowan University in Perth for me to be awarded an honorary doctorate in music. I have the cap and gown at home now, and the certificate hangs on the wall. Life has some surprises; indeed, especially as I did not dream of ever having a university recognise my work in this way.

The other bright spot was the success of our album, and being presented with a gold record for 'Travelling Still . . . Always Will'. It was Anne's first gold record, and she swore she would hang it on her front door! I've a good mind to keep her to that.

There were lots of other important things shaping up as well. Back in 2001, we were having dinner with our friend Doug Thompson when we mentioned to him that my old home (originally called Melody Ranch) and acreage around it was being advertised for sale. Noeline had told Joy about it. I did not want to think about it because I felt I could not handle running a sizeable property up there when I was flat out with recording and performing. Doug was absolutely shocked at the prospect of someone apart from the family owning Homewood. There was the worry that a new owner could get very tired of tourists visiting and looking at the place, and might put a bulldozer through it.

'Aren't you going to buy it back?' he asked anxiously.

'Well, no, I can't handle the running of it and looking after it,' I replied.

'I believe that your children and your grandchildren would want to have the place back,' Doug said. 'They'd never forgive you if something happened to it.'

Joy smiled. 'Alright, Doug. Go you halves!' she said.

'Right! You're on!' replied Doug.

And that is how we came to buy back the family farm plus the one next door at Basin Flat, the old Kyle property. Since then, we have bought 'Arrowdell', the farm adjoining it, and settled a farm manager and his family there to run the farm. Altogether, we now have about 2200 acres and quite a few head of good cattle.

I like to remember going down to Kyle's to play with the other kids now and then, as Basin Flat was a cheerful and bright place to be. The old house is gone, but there is the shell of a cottage built by a film crew making *The Chant of Jimmy Blacksmith*. Most of the film was shot there at Basin Flat. Up the other end of our property is the Nurse Kirkpatrick Bridge, originally dedicated back in the 1930s but without a name sign for years until recently. And now the old Armidale road from Kempsey to Bellbrook, the village near the Nulla, is to be tagged 'The Slim Dusty Way'.

A lot of these historical events have come about through the progress of plans for the establishment of the Slim Dusty Heritage Centre in Kempsey. Originally, Kempsey Shire Council approached us about building a museum to house all our memorabilia and documenting the history of my career and of country music on the north coast, 'the cradle of country music'. That was in the very late 1980s and since then, plans have gone ahead to the extent that the design and concept of the Centre is now a concrete fact. The site has finally been set-tled upon as the old showground in West Kempsey, the design team of Tony Sattler and Craig Pattison has presented the architectural design and the concept of the interior displays. A model of the building will be on display at various times in different venues as fundraising begins. It is a very ambitious project, costing in the vicinity of ten million dollars. People have been buying pavers engraved with their names to be fitted into a memorial walk, and a huge red cedar tree from the Nulla Nulla Creek farm has been milled into slabs of precious timber, ready for crafting into objects for sale and auction to raise funds for the building to begin.

The Centre will be a point of community activity with the outdoor amphitheatre for concerts, space for conventions or an art gallery, restaurant and café, and a story of my life and career through reconstructions of the various places and themes of my music. The Prime Minister and the Premier of NSW are both taking an interest in the project as it will be a great boost to tourism in the Kempsey district, as well as doing what we hope it will do: provide jobs, and provide scholarships for young performers to assist them in their careers. This will not be a museum of glass cases; it will be a real journey through my life and my experiences. I am very excited about the whole thing, as my beginnings were in the Macleay and I want to see my life giving something of value back to that beautiful valley.

So what next? A bit of a shock, that's what.

Medical check-ups have been the order of the day since the kidney removal, but it was still disappointing to have the doctor tell me that the cancer has spread. The problem is that renal carcinoma does not respond to chemotherapy, and is not very responsive to radiotherapy either. However, the family and I decided to have a go and I underwent some pretty severe treatment during December. It knocked me around quite a lot, but it has improved the situation a little and I am still around giving Joy and the family a hard time when they need it.

Just the same, I was in no shape to front up to a concert at the Tamworth Country Music Festival in January, and it caused all sorts of rumours when I had to cancel. One journalist even published an article based on an interview done before the cancer was discovered, quoting me as saying I'd had chemotherapy and so on. I was a bit disgusted with that effort.

Anne went to the Golden Guitar Awards, and stood in for me to accept my thirty-sixth Golden Guitar. She held it high, and said how proud she was for me.

And in the back of my mind, I could hear John Williamson as he said to me, 'You old bastard, we'll never catch you now.' Maybe no, maybe yes, but I want to see all those country artists get their act together and aim for thirty-seven. Otherwise, I might just beat them to it. Wish me luck!

My final song shall be just for you . . .
SLIM DUSTY, WRITTEN AND RECORDED IN 1943

REPRISE

What is there for me to say?

I have not retired, but I am taking it a bit easier from now on. I don't want the rust to set in, and I would like to think that I would still be singing from now till doomsday. But I do realise that there comes a time when I have to stand back and take a long, hard look at my life.

Do I have regrets? No, not really. Perhaps I should have spent more time with my friends and family instead of being in the studio and out on the road so much. Perhaps . . . perhaps what? I am a restless soul and there is always so much more to do and to look forward to. Though I do regret that I probably won't be onstage at the age of eighty. I'm sorry, too, that I didn't get to take up Tex Morton's invitation to come over and have a yarn and a walk along the beach with him when I was crook with the recurring throat problem.

I think of my son David and my daughter Anne, brought up to understand the life of a travelling showman. They have always cared about me, have always believed in me and understood me. I notice that they and their life partners have made sure that they are there for their children at all times, whereas Joy and I were often on the other side of Australia when a special time came around for ours. Despite all the distance and the hard miles, they are still our best friends. I can't say more than that, except that I love them.

My doctor son is a specialist in emergency care, and was instrumental in saving my life by his prompt action over the heart scare. (Thanks, David.) He is also a darn good singer and musician. My daughter is a recording artist in her own right and was the one who got me singing again after all my throat problems. (Thanks, Anne.) My wife has been there always to steady me and support me in my ambitions and dreams, and sometimes to bring me down to earth when I needed it. (Thanks, Mother!) Like I said before, I am a lucky man.

I have four wonderful grandchildren: Kate is the eldest at twenty-two, completing a five-year degree at the University of Technology, Sydney, and enjoying a bit of singing as well; James is eighteen and just beginning his degree course at Macquarie Uni. He's a good cricketer and plays electric bass. These are Anne and Greg's children. David and Jane have two children as well: Danny is sixteen, a good athlete and footie player, while Hannah at fourteen is a good athlete as well as a singer and flautist. They are a real mixed bag, and I hope they continue developing into good people who live long and happy lives.

Over the long years, I've covered many miles and seen many changes. From the days of the travelling shows through to the beginning of television, from the style of the old variety show to the present-day concert-style gig, the entertainment scene is different. The bush is changing, the small towns are no longer as vibrant; the cities grow bigger and bigger. I wonder, too, why everything is taken so seriously? How about having a laugh at yourself sometimes? I remember the Italian tobacco farmers at Dimbulah, on the Atherton Tablelands in North Queensland, just about rolling on the floor at a new song, 'The New Australian Bushman', and sending requests backstage for me to sing it again. They could really take a joke. I reckon if you look for offence, you'll find it. Some people should stop looking.

I love Australia. This country holds everything a man needs or could want. Australians will give you a fair go if you deserve it. They gave me one and I am thankful. If this land is to be a haven and shelter for oppressed people, I hope that they in their turn will keep it as a haven and not a copy of the hard place they left behind. If anyone wants to sling off at Australia, I reckon they need to spend a couple of months somewhere else in the world and they might be very glad to change their tune. Nowhere is perfect, but to me, this land comes pretty close to it.

It seems I've done most things I wanted to do, but of all things, I think I most enjoy finding good songs and recording them. There are so many songs I want to record that I will be kept busy for as long as I can keep it up.

I've said it before and I'll say it again: I will not forget the people who stuck with me over the years. The writers, the musicians, the road crews, the singers, the circus performers and rodeo riders, the showies, the Aboriginal people, and the audiences filled with people of all age, colour and creed. They were all my mates. It is the people you meet along the road of life who make the travelling easier.

No wonder I loved it all.

ALBUM
DISCOGRAPHY

Catalogue No.	Title	Track Listings	First Released

8141882 CD	AUSSIE SING SONG	ROAD TO GUNDAGAI, THE
		I'M GOING BACK AGAIN TO
		    YARRAWONGA
		MAN FROM THE NEVER NEVER, THE
		THAT OLD BUSH SHANTY OF MINE
		CLICK GO THE SHEARS
		OVERLANDER TRAIL, THE
		WALTZING MATILDA
		PUB WITH NO BEER, A
		GOODBYE MELBOURNE TOWN
		BOTANY BAY
		ROVER NO MORE
		OH, SYDNEY I LOVE YOU
		BACK TO CROAJINGALONG
		BEER BARREL POLKA
		BELLS OF ST MARY'S, THE
		BOOMERANG
		TIE ME KANGAROO DOWN SPORT
		WHERE THE DOG SITS ON THE
		    TUCKER BOX
		KEEP THE HOMEFIRES BURNING
		PACK UP YOUR TROUBLES
		BROWN SLOUCH HAT, A
		IT'S A LONG WAY TO TIPPERARY
		ANSWER TO A PUB WITH NO BEER, THE
		WHISPERING BUSH, THE
		LITTLE BOY LOST
		SUVLA BAY
		BLESS THIS HOUSE
		OLD SUNDOWNER, THE
		SILVER IN MY MOTHER'S HAIR, THE
		NOW IS THE HOUR
			July 1962

8147342 CD
 	
7800524 TC
	SONGS IN THE SADDLE	MAN FROM THE NEVER
		    NEVER, THE
		WHEN THEY MUSTER ON THE
		    GOLDEN PLAIN
		RODEO DANCE, THE
		SAT'DAY IN THE SADDLE
		SPRINGTIME ON THE RANGE
		ONCE WHEN I WAS MUSTERING
		SADDLE IS HIS HOME, THE
		MY PONY WHIPSTICK
		SADDLE BOY
		JUST SADDLE OLD DARKY
		MAREEBA'S ROEDO SONG
			July 1963

8141882 CD
7801624 TC
	ANOTHER AUSSIE SING SONG	MURRUMBIDGEE ROSE
		WODONGA
		WHERE'S THAT OLD COBBER OF MINE
		I'M LONESOME FOR SYDNEY TONIGHT
		MURRAY MOON
		BEAUTIFUL QUEENSLAND
		OUR WEDDING WALTZ
		OLD BULLOCK DRAY, THE
		SNAKE GULLY SWAGGER, THE
		GAME AS NED KELLY
		WOOLLOOMOOLOO
		MY HOME ON THE SUNBURNT PLAINS
		DYING STOCKMAN, THE
		I'M GONNA HUMP MY BLUEY
		BOLD TOMMY PAYNE
		SWINGIN' ALONG THAT ROAD THAT
		    LEADS TO HENTY
		SNOWY RIVER
		ON THE ROAD TO ANYWHERE
		WHEN A BOY FROM ALABAMA MEETS
		    A GIRL FROM GUNDAGAI
		LITTLE BOY CALLED SMILEY, A
			September 1963

TOWN LIKE ALICE, A
SEQUEL TO THE PUB WITH NO BEER, A
WHERE THE BLUE GUMS TURN RED IN
    THE SUNSET
BUSHWACKER
GIVE MY LOVE TO SYDNEY TOWN
NEVER NEVER
EUMERELLA SHORE
WILD COLONIAL BOY
I'VE GOT A POSSIE WAY BACK IN AUSSIE
OUT OF THE BLUE GUMS
A-N-Z-A-C

Catalogue No.	Title	Track Listings	First Released
7801522 CD 7801524 TC	PEOPLE AND PLACES	SONG OF THE MACLEAY DOWN AT CHARLEY GRAY'S KEELA VALLEY OLD WOOLSHED DO, THE MIDDLETON'S ROUSEABOUT GAME AS NED KELLY LAND OF LOTS OF TIME, THE OLD BUSH MATES OF MINE MAD JACK'S COCKATOO SWEENEY COSY INN CHARLEY GRAY'S BARN DANCE	October 1964
7801542 CD 7801544 TC	THE NATURE OF MAN	HIGH WIDE AND HANDSOME WHEN YOU'RE SHORT OF A SMOKE KEEP THE LOVELIGHT SHINING HOW WILL I GO WITH HIM, MATE? LOVE'S GAME OF LET'S PRETEND TO A MATE I LOVE YOU BEST OF ALL WHEN YOU'RE SHORT OF A QUID OLD LOVE LETTERS NATURE OF MAN, THE OUR WEDDING WALTZ I MUST HAVE GOOD TERBACCY WHEN I SMOKE	March 1966

7801632 CD
 	
7801634 TC
	AN EVENING WITH SLIM
	    AND JOY
		WILD LIFE YOU LEAD, THE
		WHEN IT'S LAMPLIGHTING TIME IN
		    THE VALLEY
		SPINNING WHEEL, THE
		ROAD OF LONELINESS
		OLD PAINT
		DOWN THE DUSTY ROAD TO HOME
		ROAD TRAIN BLUES
		BARB'RY ALLEN
		MY LOVE'S A STRANGER NOW
		IF JESUS CALLED ON YOU
		BURY ME BENEATH THE WILLOW
		MORNING MAIL
			May 1966

7801642 CD 7801644 TC	ESSENTIALLY AUSTRALIAN	CAMPFIRE YARN OLD MEN'S HOME AS GOOD AS NEW SINCE THEN ANSWER TO THE OLD RUSTY BELL FROG, THE LEAD ME DOWN TO THE STOCKYARD SHEARING SHED BLUES OLD LADDIE SCRAP WITH A BUCK KANGAROO PICTURE OF HOME, A OVER THE HILL	May 1967

Catalogue No.	Title	Track Listings	First Released
7801652 CD 7801654 TC	SONGS MY FATHER SANG TO ME	GRANNY'S HIELAND HAME OLD LOVE LETTERS JANE O'HARA OLD LANTERN WALTZ, THE SHIP THAT NEVER RETURNED, THE AN OLD FASHIONED LOCKET IT TAKES AN IRISH HEART WHEN THE HARVEST DAYS ARE OVER, JESSIE DEAR MY OLD KENTUCKY HOME MY OLD PAL TWO LITTLE GIRLS IN BLUE GIRL I LEFT BEHIND ME	October 1967
8147342 CD 7486564 TC	SONGS FROM THE CATTLE CAMPS	FAIR ENOUGH DREAM TIME VOICES CROW, THE GHOSTS OF THE GOLDEN MILE BACK IN THE SADDLE I MUST HAVE GOOD TERBACCY WHEN I SMOKE HARD HARD COUNTRY ST. PETER OLD MAN DROUGHT BACK WHERE I BELONG OLD BEAU OLD MATES	May 1968
7801662 CD 7801664 TC	SING ALONG WITH DAD	SING ALONG WITH DAD SAD CIGARETTE YOU CAN'T TELL ME A THING BEEN A FOOL TOO LONG FRANKIE AND JOHNNY STEPPIN' ROUND AUSTRALIA DEAR OLD SUNNY SOUTH BY THE SEA ANGELS IN DISGUISE MISSOURI WALTZ DARK DEPTHS OF THE BLUES SIDE BY SIDE OLD RUGGED CROSS, THE	September 1968
7801672 CD 7801674 TC	CATTLE CAMP CROONER	ARCADIA VALLEY DRY WEATHER WIND GETTING AWAY FROM IT ALL CASEY'S LUCK OLD TIBOOB'RA SOMEWHERE UP IN QUEENSLAND CATTLE CAMP CROONER RIBS COOKED ON THE COALS RELICS OF THE PAST PADDY GRAMP HORSE AND HOBBLE DAYS WAVE HILL TRACK, THE	August 1969
7800362 CD 7800364 TC	SLIM DUSTY ENCORES	MY OLD AUSSIE HOMESTEAD YOU STEPPED OUT OF LINE PAPER BOY, THE OLD HOME WEEK YOU'VE GOT THE CLEANEST MIND FAIR DINKUM PASTURES OF HOME DREAMIN' ON THE SLIPRAIL THAT'S A SAD AFFAIR LONELY LONESOME BLUES WHISPERING BUSH, THE WHERE THE WESTERN CLOUDS AT SUNSET TURN TO GOLD	November 1969

Catalogue No.	Title	Track Listings	First Released
7801682 CD 7801684 TC	SING A HAPPY SONG	SING A HAPPY SONG IF YOU FALL OUT OF LOVE WITH ME BIG BEGGIN' FOOL SET'EM UP STEP DOWN FROM THIS MOUNTAIN I'M LAYIN' IT ON THE LINE PARALYSE MY MIND HE DON'T DESERVE YOU ANYMORE I AIN'T A-GONNA BE TREATED THIS-A-WAY CINDERELLA SUGAR SHED LANE HELLO TROUBLE	April 1970
7801692 CD 7801694 TC	SONGS FROM THE LAND I LOVE	WHEN THE SCRUBBERS BREAK ROAD IS STILL MY HOME, THE DROVER'S COOK, THE LAND OF NO SECOND CHANCE RETIRED DROVER, THE AUSTRALIAN BUSHMEN WHEN SNOWY SINGS OF HOME BIG JOHN MEN WHO COME BEHIND DUST FROM THE LAND I LOVE CAMOOWEAL WILLY WILLY	June 1971
7801702 CD 7801704 TC	GLORY BOUND TRAIN	GLORY BOUND TRAIN TEN GOLDEN RULES BYE AND BYE CALVARY HILL WINGIN' MY WAY BACK HOME THAT'S THE KIND OF RELIGION FOR ME PRECIOUS LORD WHAT THE MAN SAID JOYBELLS IN YOUR HEART IT'S WORTH IT SOFTEST TOUCH IN TOWN, THE HEAVEN COUNTRY STYLE	September 1971
8142952 CD 8142954 TC	LIVE AT WAGGA WAGGA	GOOD OLD COUNTRY STYLE SWEENEY DROVER'S COOK, THE GUM TREES BY THE ROADWAY WHEN THE RAIN TUMBLES DOWN IN JULY SOMEWHERE BETWEEN PUB WITH NO BEER, A L.A. INTERNATIONAL AIRPORT HOW WILL I GO WITH HIM, MATE? NED KELLY WAS A GENTLEMAN IF I ONLY HAD A HOME SWEET HOME BYE AND BYE HE'S JUST THE ONE OLD TIME MUSIC	April 1972
7801712 CD 7801714 TC	ME AND MY GUITAR	RAMBLIN' SHOES MAN FROM SNOWY RIVER, THE SECOND CLASS, WAIT HERE THAT WAS YEARS AGO SHE WASN'T THERE TO MEET ME MACKENZIE COUNTRY BOOTS OF MANY COLOUR ANTHILL STYLE PETER ANDERSON AND CO DO YOU THINK THAT I DO NOT KNOW ROUGHRIDERS BIRDSVILLE TRACK, THE DROUGHT	September 1972

Catalogue No.	Title	Track Listings	First Released
7801722 CD 7801724 TC	FOOLIN' AROUND	FOOLIN' AROUND CAUSE I HAVE YOU TOP OF THE WORLD PROUDER MAN THAN YOU, A THIS SONG IS JUST FOR YOU ETERNAL LOVE GOD'S OWN SINGER OF SONGS MANY MOTHERS KINGDOM I CALL HOME, THE HAPPY ANNIVERSARY DAY I MARRIED YOU, THE LONG ROAD, THE	February 1973
8377232 CD 8377234 TC	LIVE AT TAMWORTH	PICKIN' & SINGIN' OLDTIME DROVER'S LAMENT OLD GIDGEE TREE ELECTION DAY IF I WERE FREE COUNTRY LIVIN' LOUISIANA MAN CUNNAMULLA FELLER END OF THE PUB PICTURE OF HOME, A BANKS OF THE OHIO MIDDLETONS ROUSEABOUT KELLY'S OFFSIDER LIGHTS ON THE HILL MY CLINCH MOUNTAIN HOME GLORY BOUND TRAIN	August 1973

8323662 CD
8323664 TC
	DUSTY TRACKS	LEANING POST
		ARAJOEL WALTZ
		SWEET TALKING GIRL
		DON'T LAUGH IN THE FACE OF
		  FATHER TIME
		WHEN THE MOON ACROSS THE BUSHLAND
		  BEAMS
		I DON'T WANT NO WOMAN AROUND
		WAGON TRAINS NORTH
		WEDDING BELL BLUES
		A FRIEND INDEED
		HAPPIEST DAYS OF ALL, THE
		SLOW DOWN
		BOYS WHO NEVER RETURNED, THE
			August 1973

7801732 CD 7801734 TC	TALL STORIES AND SAD SONGS	BELIEVE IT OR NOT JIMBERELLA KID, THE DOG WHO STOLE MY HAT, THE FROM THE GULF TO ADELAIDE ONLY THE TWO OF US HERE HAPPY JACK MAN FROM IRON BARK, THE HANGOVER SONG, THE GIVE IT A GO I HOPE THEY FIGHT AGAIN BALLAD OF THE DROVER HOLYDAN CANETOAD'S PLAIN CODE	December 1973
7801592 CD 7801594 TC	AUSTRALIANA	GRANDFATHER JOHNSON CLANCY OF THE OVERFLOW LAME FIDDLER, THE SQUATTER'S PRAYER, A HENRY LAWSON DROUGHT TIME STICK TO HIM BLUEY WRITTEN AFTERWARDS BEQUEST, THE PUBS STILL MAKE A QUID, THE	August 1974

DROVERS LIFE, A
LAST OF THE BREED

8142982 CD
8142984 TC

DINKI DI AUSSIES

DESERT LAIR, THE   October 1974
RETURN OF THE STOCKMAN
NEW AUSTRALIAN BUSHMAN, THE
ROSE OF RED, A
MAN FROM THE NEVER NEVER, THE
LITTLE OLD ONE HORSE PUB
ROAD TRAINS
BRIGALOW BILL
DINKI DI AUSSIE
SADDLE IS HIS HOME, THE
THIS CHAP WHO KNOWS A LOT
SO LONG, OLD MATES

7462592 CD
7462594 TC

LIGHTS ON THE HILL

PUSHIN' TIME   July 1975
HOME RUN, THE
WORST IN THE WORLD
FOGGY MIRRORS
RIDIN' THIS ROAD
INTERSTATER
LIGHTS ON THE HILL
BENT-AXLE BOB
THERE LIES A WORKHORSE
TRUCKIN'S IN MY BLOOD
TRUCKIE'S LAST WILL AND TESTAMENT, A
HEAR 'EM GO

7800512 CD
7800514 TC

WAY OUT THERE

WAY OUT THERE   December 1975
PAY DAY AT THE PUB
SUNNY SOUTHERN SUE
FADED COAT OF BLUE
SILVER SPURS
BIG MOON
MY HOME ON THE SUNBURNT PLAINS
HIGHWAY BLUES
MY JOURNEY HOME (IT'S NEVER THE SAME)
MOTHER'S WEDDING BAND
DECIMAL CURRENCY PUB, THE
SHOWERS OF BLESSINGS

8147352 CD
7801604 TC

THINGS I SEE AROUND ME

THINGS I SEE AROUND ME   June 1976
BLACKENED QUARTS ARE BOILING
COPPED THE LOT
NOT MUCH TO SHOW
COMMERCIAL D.T.'S
HARRY BOWDEN . . . DERELICT
SMILES
THREE RIVERS HOTEL
END OF THE CANNING STOCK ROUTE
GOOD OLD DAYS
LAST OF THE BUSHMEN, THE
BULL STAG, THE

8147332 CD
7801604 TC

GIVE ME THE ROAD

GIVE ME THE ROAD   October 1976
ANGEL OF GOULBURN HILL, THE
YOU TAKE HER FROM NARRANDERA
BOSS MAN, THE
WE'VE BEEN TRUCKING TOO
DANGER ROAD TRAIN
HIGHWAY ONE
ROARING THROUGH THE NIGHT
KELLY'S OFFSIDER
YOU JUST CAN'T MISS IT MATE
GREAT AUSTRALIAN WHINGER, THE
ROAD TRAIN BLUES

Catalogue No.	Title	Track Listings	First Released
8142962 CD 8142964 TC	SONGS FROM DOWN UNDER	OLD RIDERS IN THE GRANDSTAND CERTAIN KIND OF GOLD, A LETTER FROM DOWN UNDER BALLAD OF HENRY LAWSON JUST GOING HOME ROADLINER COBB AND CO. TWITCH SADNESS AND I WANDER HOME WILD RUGGED LAND THAT I LOVE SONG OF THE WEST WALTZING MATILDA RODEO RIDERS	November 1976
7801752 CD 7801754 TC	JUST SLIM WITH OLD FRIENDS	ABOUT THIS HAT I'LL MEET HIM TOMORROW THAT OLD BLUE DOG OF MINE ROUND TABLE, THE GATES OLD GILBERT BUSH POETS OF AUSTRALIA STOCK HORSES JOE PALMER'S GHOST DROVER'S YARN, THE LAWSON'S GHOST CATCHING YELLOWBELLY (IN THE OLD BARCOO)	April 1977
8147352 CD 7801764 TC	ON THE MOVE	ON THE MOVE MY TIME INDIAN PACIFIC FINALLY MADE IT HOME YOU KNOW WHAT I MEAN ANYDAY WOMAN ISA FRONT ROW, THE BILLY MAC HIGHWAY BLUES JOE (DON'T LET YOUR MUSIC KILL YOU) WHAT AM I DOING IN THIS TOWN	August 1977
8326132 CD 8326134 TC	TRAVELLIN' COUNTRY MAN	TRAVELLIN' COUNTRY BAND GOD'S OWN SINGER OF SONGS ALTHEA SADNESS AND I WANDER HOME SPANISH PIPE DREAM IF THOSE LIPS COULD ONLY SPEAK THE ROSE IN HER HAIR STREETS OF SYDNEY JESUS TAKES A HOLD BIG TIME (JUST BECAUSE YOUR'E IN DEEP ELEM) FOOLIN' AROUND I BROKE A PROMISE I HEARD THE BLUEBIRD SING LIFE IS LIKE A RIVER	August 1977
7971832 CD 7971834 TC	TO WHOM IT MAY CONCERN	TO WHOM IT MAY CONCERN BEAT OF THE GOVERNMENT STROKE OLD BUSH BARBEQUE LETTER FROM ARRABURY, A 5 AM BLUES AND THE BAND PLAYED WALTZING MATILDA HIGHWAY FEVER MARTY 42 TYRES SOME THINGS A MAN CAN'T FIGHT	August 1978

| | | IRONBARK JIM | |
| | | MAN IN THE GLASS | |

| 8383492 CD | THE ENTERTAINER | TRAVELLIN' COUNTRY BAND | December 1978 |
| 8383494 TC | | PICKIN' AND SINGIN' | |

ABOUT THIS HAT
PUSHIN' TIME
MOVIN' ON
WHEN IT'S LAMPLIGHTING TIME IN THE
   VALLEY
RED RIVER VALLEY
KELLYS OFFSIDER
WALK RIGHT IN
I MUST HAVE GOOD TERBACCY WHEN
   I SMOKE
WHEN THE RAIN TUMBLES DOWN IN JULY
MIDDLETON'S ROUSEABOUT
TRUMBY
DROVERS' COOK
PUB WITH NO BEER, A
FRONT ROW
THREE RIVERS HOTEL
INDIAN PACIFIC
ROAD TO GUNDAGAI, THE
JAMBALAYA
I FALL TO PIECES
LISTEN TO A COUNTRY SONG
CRAZY
OH LONESOME ME
SUNSET YEARS OF LIFE
CAMOOWEAL
CATCHING YELLOWBELLY (IN THE OLD
   BARCOO)
LEAD ME DOWN TO THE STOCKYARD
COUNTRY LIVIN'
CLOSEST THING TO FREEDOM
ANGEL OF GOULBURN HILL, THE
BIGGEST DISAPPOINTMENT, THE
LIGHTS ON THE HILL
GLORYBOUND TRAIN

| 7801772 CD | SPIRIT OF AUSTRALIA | SPIRIT OF AUSTRALIA | May 1979 |
| 7801774 TC | | NINETEEN EIGHTIES BUSHMAN ON THE | |

   MOVE
OLD IVENHOE
JOE MAGUIRE'S PUB
DROVING BY TRAIN
WHILE THE DAMPER COOKS
GIVE IT A GO, MATE
HARRY THE BREAKER
MOUNTAIN MAN'S GIRL
FAMILY OF MAN
WESTWARD HO!
LOSIN' MY BLUES TONIGHT

| 8525182 CD | RARITIES | SONG FOR THE AUSSIES | May 1979 |
| 8525184 TC | | MY FINAL SONG | |

YOUR BEST PAL IS MOTHER
MY SWEETEST LULLABY
BORN TO BE A YODELLER
HEADING FOR THAT BRUMBY TRAIL
SOLDIER'S WIFE, THE
BABY OF MY DREAMS
LOVER'S LAMENT
HAPPY DROVER

8142712 CD	RODEO RIDERS	ROUGH RIDERS	June 1979
8142714 TC		OLD RIDERS IN THE GRANDSTAND	
		MAREEBA'S RODEO SONG	

ROPE AND SADDLE BLUES
RODEO RIDERS
NOT MUCH TO SHOW
CATTLE CAMP REVERIE
THE BATTLE WITH THE ROAN
STOCK HORSES
ISA RODEO, THE
HOW WILL I GO WITH HIM, MATE?
WHOA BULLOCKS WHOA

Catalogue No.	Title	Track Listings	First Released
7971842 CD 7971844 TC	WALK A COUNTRY MILE	WALK A COUNTRY MILE SON OF NOISY DAN WHEN THE RAIN TUMBLES DOWN IN JULY JOHNNY FOSTER (THE OLD TIME TRAVELLING SHOWMAN) MUSIC MY DAD PLAYED TO ME OLD STOCK RIDIN' DAYS D TOWARDS THE HEAD DAY I WENT BACK HOME, THE SEND 'ER DOWN HUGHIE PUB WITH NO BEER, A MANY YESTERDAYS AGO OLD BUSH MATES OF MINE TERRITORY RINGER IN MY HOUR OF DARKNESS	September 1979
7971852 CD 7971854 TC	THE MAN WHO STEADIES THE LEAD	MAN WHO STEADIES THE LEAD, THE LEAVE HIM IN THE LONG YARD DREAMING FOXLEIGH RODEO, THE NOW I'M EASY AN INDEPENDENT BLOKE BALLAD OF BIG BILL SMITH, THE NO MAN'S LAND PLAINS OF PEPPIMENARTI CLEARING SALE, THE FOOLSCAP TOMBSTONES GIVE MY REGARDS TO EDNA PEARL OF THEM ALL, THE	September 1980
7801872 CD 7801874 TC	THE SLIM DUSTY FAMILY ALBUM	WHAT I AM OLD TIME CHRISTMAS TROUBLE LOCAL MARY MAGDALEN MEMORIES COUNTRY REVIVAL COUNTRY MUSIC'S IN OUR BONES MY OLD CHINA PLATE OLD SUNLANDER VAN FEELING SORRY FOR ME RODEO CLOWN WIND UP GRAMOPHONE NOBODY HEARD	December 1980
7461914 CD 7461912 TC	NO 50 GOLDEN ANNIVERSARY	COUNTRY REVIVAL LEAVE HIM IN THE LONG YARD PUB WITH NO BEER, A WALK A COUNTRY MILE CAMOOWEAL INDIAN PACIFIC HIGHWAY FEVER MAN FROM SNOWY RIVER, THE LIGHTS ON THE HILL THREE RIVERS HOTEL BEAT OF THE GOVERNMENT STROKE I DONT SLEEP AT NIGHT WHEN THE RAIN TUMBLES DOWN IN JULY ANGEL OF GOULBURN HILL, THE	March 1981

KELLYS OFFSIDER
THINGS I SEE AROUND ME
BIGGEST DISAPPOINTMENT, THE
DUNCAN

Catalogue No.	Title	Track Listings	First Released
8323622 CD 8323624 TC	WHERE COUNTRY IS	G'DAY BLUE DINKUM BUSHMAN'S HANDS WHERE COUNTRY IS BIG WET IS OVER, THE MACK — A FINAL TRIBUTE NO PLACE ON EARTH LIKE AUSTRALIA ONE TRUCKIE'S EPITAPH BOGONG, THE OCKER, THE INIGO JONES — INDIGO JONES REDFORD BIG YABBIES FROM THE CREEK	September 1981
7971862 CD 7971864 TC	WHO'S RIDING OLD HARLEQUIN NOW	WHO'S RIDING OLD HARLEQUIN NOW NULLA CREEK EVERY LITTLE BIT OF AUSTRALIA OLD DAN BRASS WELL, THE YOUR COUNTRY'S BEEN SOLD BANJO'S MAN OLD KING COAL LAST THING TO LEARN I GUESS YOU HAVE CAPTAIN THUNDERBOLT IT TAKES A DROUGHT	October 1982
8323632 CD 8323634 TC	ON THE WALLABY	AUSTRALIA'S ON THE WALLABY ANOTHER DAY, ANOTHER TOWN ROCKY'S RUN WATER — IF IT TOOK FIFTY YEARS OLD FELLER ARE THE GOOD OLD DAYS GONE FOREVER OLD TIME COUNTRY HALLS TWO RATS AT TOBRUK SO MANY BALLADS TO PLAY DUST AND SADDLE GREASE GETTIN' UP AND GOIN' SONNY	June 1983
8326152 CD 8326154 TC	I HAVEN'T CHANGED A BIT	AUSTRALIA IS HIS NAME COMING DOWN THE BARKLY CALLAGHAN'S HOTEL PUB ROCK, THE DROWNIN' MY BLUES LIFE IS LIKE A RIVER DON'T FOOL AROUND ANYMORE BALLAD OF PORT MACQUARIE, THE AUSSIE DOGHOUSE BLUES MELBOURNE CUP, THE I HAVEN'T CHANGED A BIT THIS COUNTRY OF MINE GOLDRUSH COUNTRY NEVER MIND	October 1983
8147332 CD 7971874 TC	TRUCKS ON THE TRACK	THREE HUNDRED HORSES LONG BLACK ROAD I'M MARRIED TO MY BULLDOG MACK TRUCKS ON THE TRACK FROM HERE TO THERE AND BACK DRIBBLER BILL DIESELINE DREAMS FILL 'ER UP HOME COOKIN'	May 1984

TRUCKS, TARPS AND TRAILERS
DOGS, DUST AND DIESEL
THAT'S NOT ME

7801952 CD

7801954 TC

THE SLIM DUSTY MOVIE

MAN WITH THE HAT — September 1984
TURNED DOWN IN FRONT, THE
COUNTRY REVIVAL
ISA RODEO, THE
ROUGH RIDERS
CUNNAMULLA FELLER
ISA
JUST ROLLIN'
CORROBOREE SEQUENCE
PLAINS OF PEPPIMENARTI
HOW WILL I GO WITH HIM, MATE?
PUSHIN' TIME
PUB WITH NO BEER, A
CAMOOWEAL
INDIAN PACIFIC
ARE THE GOOD DAYS GONE FOREVER
GUMTREES BY THE ROADWAY
WHERE COUNTRY IS
SONG FOR THE AUSSIES
OLD SUNLANDER VAN
WALK A COUNTRY MILE
WIND UP GRAMOPHONE
TROUBLE
LOSIN' MY BLUES TONIGHT
ONLY THE TWO OF US HERE
OLD FELLER
MY FINAL SONG
WHEN THE RAIN TUMBLES DOWN IN JULY
BACK TO MY OLD NORTHERN HOME
OLD TIME COUNTRY HALLS
BIGGEST DISAPPOINTMENT, THE
LIGHTS ON THE HILL
GYMKHANA YODEL
STAY AWAY FROM ME
KEEP THE LOVELIGHT SHINING

8319402 CD

8319404 TC

I'LL TAKE MINE COUNTRY
STYLE

CUNNAMULLA FELLER — April 1985
DADDY'S GIRL
CHRISTMAS ON THE STATION
YOU'D BETTER BE WAITING
I'LL TAKE MINE COUNTRY STYLE
DRUNKARD, THE
MY PAL ALCOHOL
ROAD TO GUNDAGAI, THE
ACE OF HEARTS, THE
IF YOU WALK OUT THAT GATE
MAPLE SUGAR SWEETHEART
WHERE THE DESERT FLOWERS BLOOM
ROSE OF RED RIVER VALLEY
SOMEBODY'S MOTHER

8323612 CD
8323614 TC

SINGER FROM DOWN UNDER

SINGER FROM DOWN UNDER — July 1985
BORN WITH AN ENDLESS THIRST
YOU'VE GOTTA DRINK THE FROTH TO
    GET THE BEER
MY SON'S GUITAR
BALLAD OF HENRY HOLLOWAY, THE
TONIGHT THE WOOLSHED SWINGS
STRINGYBARK AND GREENHIDE
HENRY LAWSON'S PEN
THEY DRANK AND DRANK AND DRANK
I'M DUSTY ALL OVER
LIFE'S RIDE
TRAVELLERS' PRAYER

Catalogue No.	Title	Track Listings	First Released
7016792 CD 7016794 TC	TO A MATE—SLIM DUSTY REMEMBERS 'MACK' CORMACK	TO A MATE PICTURE OF HOME, A HAPPY JACK FROG, THE WHEN THE MOON ACROSS THE BUSHLAND BEAMS HOW WILL I GO WITH HIM, MATE? THAT WAS YEARS AGO CATTLE CAMP REVERIE CAMOOWEAL SO LONG, OLD MATES GIVE IT A GO OLD MATES IN MY HOUR OF DARKNESS	October 1985
7971882 CD 7971884 TC	BEER DRINKING SONGS OF AUSTRALIA	HE'S A GOOD BLOKE WHEN HE'S SOBER YOU'VE GOT TO DRINK THE FROTH TO GET THE BEER PUB WITH NO BEER, A HANGOVER SONG, THE MAD JACK'S COCKATOO MY PAL ALCOHOL WHISKY BLUES PAY DAY AT THE PUB OLD BUSH BARBECUE THREE RIVERS HOTEL BOXING KANGAROO, THE BORN WITH AN ENDLESS THIRST JOE MAGUIRE'S PUB PUB ROCK, THE PUBS STILL MAKE A QUID, THE PUB THAT DOESN'T SELL BEER, THE ANSWER TO THE PUB WITH NO BEER, THE CALLAGHAN'S HOTEL DUNCAN END OF THE PUB	October 1985
7946552 CD 7946554 TC	AUSTRALIA IS HIS NAME	TRAVELLIN' COUNTRY BAND WHEN THE RAIN TUMBLES DOWN IN JULY ROAD TO GUNDAGAI, THE I'M GOING BACK AGAIN TO YARRAWONGA MAN FROM THE NEVER NEVER, THE THAT OLD BUSH SHANTY OF MINE IRONBARK JIM OLD BUSH BARBECUE SPIRIT OF AUSTRALIA SEND 'ER DOWN HUGHIE LIGHTS ON THE HILL ALONG THE ROAD OF SONG AUSTRALIA IS HIS NAME LETTER FROM DOWN UNDER OLD WOOLSHED DO ISA RODEO COBB AND CO TWITCH ANSWER TO THE PUB WITH NO BEER, THE SUNDOWN ANGEL OF GOULBURN HILL, THE WALTZING MATILDA CATTLE CAMP REVERIE DARWIN (BIG HEART OF THE NORTH) HORSE AND HOBBLE DAYS LEAVE HIM IN THE LONG YARD BANJO'S MAN OLD TIME COUNTRY HALLS PUB WITH NO BEER, A WILLY WILLY OLD MAN DROUGHT MELBOURNE CUP, THE	November 1985

BOX		GOOD OLD COUNTRY STYLE WHEN THE RAIN TUMBLES DOWN IN JULY INDIAN PACIFIC BOOMERANG TIE ME KANGAROO DOWN SPORT WHERE THE DOG SITS ON THE TUCKER AUSTRALIAN BUSHMEN CLANCY OF THE OVERFLOW BUSH POETS OF AUSTRALIA THINGS I SEE AROUND ME DYING STOCKMAN, THE WALK A COUNTRY MILE BIG FROGS IN LITTLE PUDDLES SEQUEL TO THE PUB WITH NO BEER, A TRUMBY JOE MAGUIRE'S PUB EVERY LITTLE BIT OF AUSTRALIA BIRDSVILLE TRACK, THE G'DAY BLUE OLD BULLOCK DRAY, THE SNAKE GULLY SWAGGER, THE GAME AS NED KELLY WOOLLOOMOOLOO FROM THE GULF TO ADELAIDE BRASS WELL, THE HARRY THE BREAKER WHERE COUNTRY IS WHEN A BOY FROM ALABAMA MEETS A GIRL FROM GUNDAGAI LITTLE BOY CALLED SMILEY, A TOWN LIKE ALICE, A LAST THING TO LEARN CHARLEY GRAY'S BARNDANCE HENRY LAWSON DIESELINE DREAMS PUB WITH NO BEER, A	
8377192 CD 8377194 TC	THE SLIM DUSTY FAMILY 'LIVE' ACROSS AUSTRALIA	KELLY'S OFFSIDER MIDDLETON'S ROUSEABOUT FRONT ROW, THE GIVE MY REGARDS TO EDNA FOOL SUCH AS I, A CRYING TIME I'M THINKING TONIGHT OF MY BLUE EYES ORANGE BLOSSOM SPECIAL GOOD HEARTED WOMAN LAST TRAIN TO NOWHERE LUXURY LINER GYMKHANA YODEL I NEED SOMEBODY TO HOLD ME WHEN I CRY YODEL DOWN THE VALLEY LEAVE HIM IN THE LONG YARD ONE TRUCKIE'S EPITAPH GLORY BOUND TRAIN	January 1986
7463002 CD	STORIES I WANTED TO TELL	MOUNT BUKAROO OLD JIMMY WOODSER, THE BREAK O' DAY WHEN THE CURRAWONGS COME DOWN I'VE SEEN HIS FACE BEFORE SHEARING SONG, THE BIBLE OF THE BUSH TO AN OLD MATE TWO OLD GENTLEMEN WHY DON'T YOU JUST GO FISHING ANDY'S RETURN ON THE NIGHT TRAIN	June 1986

Catalogue No.	Title	Track Listings	First Released
8142742 CD 8142744 TC	COUNTRY LIVIN'	CITY BROTHER AH, FORGET IT TEENAGE COUNTRY STYLE BOOMERANG THERE'S A RAINBOW ROUND MY MEMORIES NIGHT WATCH BLUES REDWING COUNTRY LIVIN' MY PEOPLE MOVIN' AWAY CUNNIN' ROO SHOOTER, THE WE'LL HAVE TO STICK TOGETHER TINY BLUE SHOE GOD WILL PREVAIL	January 1988
7486562 CD 7486564 TC	CATTLEMEN FROM THE HIGH PLAINS	CATTLEMEN FROM THE HIGH PLAINS INNAMINCKA MUSTER AXE MARK ON A GIDGEE BIG GULF RIVERS LAND HE CALLS HIS OWN, A MAD COOK,THE BUSH HAS HAD ENOUGH, THE THAT'S MY KIND OF BRAND ANNUAL RODEO SHOW, THE KEEROONGOOLOO STATION WHEN THE BITUMEN REACHES POONCARIE BULLOCK DUNG NARRATION KING ALLIGATOR BAKING A BROWNIE	March 1988
7901402 CD 7901404 TC	HERITAGE ALBUM	WE'VE DONE US PROUD GHOSTS OF THE GOLDEN MILE GRANDFATHER JOHNSON TONIGHT THE WOOLSHED SWINGS NAMATJIRA CLANCY OF THE OVERFLOW GAME AS NED KELLY BRASS WELL, THE KING BUNDAWAAL MAN FROM SNOWY RIVER, THE MAN FROM IRON BARK, THE MIDDLETON'S ROUSEABOUT OLD TIME COUNTRY HALLS ISA RODEO, THE EVERY LITTLE BIT OF AUSTRALIA WAGON TRAINS NORTH BANJO'S MAN WALTZING MATILDA	May 1988
7971892 CD 7971894 TC	NEON CITY	GOTTA KEEP MOVING MY OLD MIDNIGHT SPECIAL (AND ME) NEON CITY SALLY — THE GIRL ON CHANNEL 8 I'M THANKFUL WHITE LINE BILLINUDGEL OLD KENTUCKY RIG WORLD'S LAST TRUCK DRIVIN' MAN, THE OLD DINGO BLUE PACIFIC RIG I KNEW YOUR FATHER REAL WELL	August 1988
7016802 CD 7016804 TC	SLIM DUSTY SINGS STAN COSTER	THREE RIVERS HOTEL BIRDSVILLE TRACK, THE WHOA BULLOCKS WHOA THE BATTLE WITH THE ROAN ITCHING FEET	October 1988

COBB AND CO TWITCH
OLD RIDERS IN THE GRANDSTAND
CLAYPAN BOOGIE
CATCHING YELLOWBELLY (IN THE OLD
   BARCOO)
SOME THINGS A MAN CAN'T FIGHT
BY A FIRE OF GIDGEE COAL
AUSTRALIAN BUSHMEN

7801872 CD
7801874 TC

G'DAY G'DAY

G'DAY G'DAY   November 1988
GOOD OLD FEED OF FLATHEAD
CHRISTMAS, WHEN I WAS BIG AS YOU
GIRL FROM THE LAND, A
I CAN STILL HEAR DAD SWEARING
BREAKAWAY
HOW'S YOUR MEMORY?
SITTIN' ON THE OLD FRONT VERANDA
JOHNSONVILLE DANCE, THE
BLOODY BONZER MATE
BOSS, THE
UP THE OLD NULLA ROAD

8147322 CD
7924554 TC

KING OF KALGOORLIE

ON MY ROAD   July 1989
LIKE A FAMILY TO ME
KING OF KALGOORLIE
STILL THE WAY I FEEL
STRAIGHT AHEAD
LAST RIDE, THE
BALLADEERS OF AUSTRALIA
CITY OF MOUNT ISA
LADY LUCK
SANDS OF TANAMI
THOUSAND YEARS AGO, A
JIM

8326102 CD

8326104 TC

**HENRY LAWSON AND
BANJO PATERSON**

SWEENEY   October 1989
MIDDLETON'S ROUSEABOUT
BILL
WORD TO TEXAS JACK, A
AS GOOD AS NEW
SINCE THEN
ST. PETER
CALLAGHAN'S HOTEL
MATE CAN DO NO WRONG, A
MEN WHO COME BEHIND
SECOND CLASS, WAIT HERE
PETER ANDERSON & CO
DO YOU THINK THAT I DO NOT KNOW
PROUDER MAN THAN YOU, A
ONLY THE TWO OF US HERE
BALLAD OF THE DROVER
WRITTEN AFTERWARDS
BRASS WELL, THE
MOUNT BUKAROO
OLD JIMMY WOODSER, THE
BREAK O'DAY
TO AN OLD MATE
ANDY'S RETURN
ON THE NIGHT TRAIN
MAN FROM SNOWY RIVER, THE
MAN FROM IRON BARK, THE
CLANCY OF THE OVERFLOW
WALTZING MATILDA

7931902 CD

7931904 TC

TWO SINGERS, ONE SONG

CRYING ON EACH OTHERS' December 1989
   SHOULDER
THERE AT THE SIDE OF THE ROAD
TWO SINGERS, ONE SONG
MY OLD PAL
LIKE A BOOMERANG

MURRAY MOON
DROVIN'
IN MY GRANDMOTHER'S ARMS
MY FAVOURITE PEOPLE
ROCK THIS JOINT
I LOVE MY TRUCK
WE CAN CHANGE THE WORLD

7952822 CD   COMING HOME
7952824 TC

ONLY WAY, THE   October 1990
FURTHER OUT
FLYING DOCTOR'S BALL, THE
GOOD HARD DOG
OLD BUSH PUB
LOGAN *
SALE DAY AT ST LAWRENCE
CLARA WATERS
NARDOO BURNS
ROY
HUMPTY DOO WALTZ
DINOSAUR

* NOT AVAILABLE ON CD VERSION

WHERE I'D SOONER BE *
LACE-UP SHOES
YELLOW GULLY
TEX MORTON
REGAL ZONOPHONE
WORLD'S BIGGEST CEDAR TREE, THE
ONLY TIME A FISHERMAN TELLS THE
    TRUTH, THE
OUTBACK'S NOT SO WAYBACK
    ANYMORE, THE
NEBO PUB
CAMP COOKS
MY OLD COOLOOLAH HOME
FOOTSTEPS COMING HOME

8525212 CD   A LAND HE CALLS HIS OWN
8525214 TC

CATTLEMEN FROM THE   September 1991
    HIGH PLAINS
AUSTRALIA'S ON THE WALLABY
SITTIN' ON THE OLD FRONT VERANDAH
OLD KENTUCKY RIG
WHEN THE CURRAWONGS COME DOWN
HENRY LAWSON'S PEN
NULLA CREEK
SHEARING SONG, THE
GRANDFATHER JOHNSON
MY SON'S GUITAR
CROW, THE
MOUNT BUKAROO
BIRDSVILLE TRACK, THE
HARRY THE BREAKER
DOG WHO STOLE MY HAT, THE
G'DAY G'DAY
DINKUM BUSHMAN'S HANDS
SON OF NOISY DAN
HIGHWAY FEVER
SINGER FROM DOWN UNDER
CATCHING YELLOWBELLY (IN THE OLD
    BARCOO)
STOCK HORSES
IT TAKES A DROUGHT
HARD HARD COUNTRY
KEEROONGOOLOO STATION
DROVIN'
CAMPFIRE YARN
WHEN SNOWY SINGS OF HOME
CAMOOWEAL
MY TIME
FRONT ROW, THE
SOME THINGS A MAN CAN'T FIGHT

NO PLACE ON EARTH LIKE AUSTRALIA
PLAINS OF PEPPIMENARTI
FOXLEIGH RODEO, THE
MORNING MAIL
END OF THE CANNING STOCK ROUTE
KING OF KALGOORLIE
PUBS STILL MAKE A QUID, THE
PUSHIN' TIME
STEPPIN' ROUND AUSTRALIA
SCRAP WITH A BUCK KANGAROO
BALLAD OF THE DROVER
DROVING BY TRAIN
LAWSON'S GHOST
LAND HE CALLS HIS OWN, A
ANOTHER DAY, ANOTHER TOWN
UP THE OLD NULLA ROAD
SECOND CLASS, WAIT HERE
PROUDER MAN THAN YOU, A
BALLADEERS OF AUSTRALIA
ABOUT THIS HAT
CRYING ON EACH OTHER'S SHOULDERS
HOW'S YOUR MEMORY?
DROUGHT TIME
ROUND TABLE, THE
LAST OF THE BUSHMEN
PEARL OF THEM ALL, THE
WHAT I AM
TRAVELLER'S PRAYER

Catalogue No.	Title	Track Listings	First Released
8377222 CD 8377224 TC	SLIM DUSTY SINGS JOY MCKEAN	LIGHTS ON THE HILL FRONT ROW, THE GRANDFATHER JOHNSON WALK A COUNTRY MILE MARTY GHOSTS OF THE GOLDEN MILE D TOWARDS THE HEAD INDIAN PACIFIC CATTLEMEN FROM THE HIGH PLAINS KELLY'S OFFSIDER NULLA CREEK ANGEL OF GOULBURN HILL, THE BIGGEST DISAPPOINTMENT, THE OUR WEDDING WALTZ	October 1991
8334194 CD 8334194 TC	TRAVELLIN' GUITAR	ROVIN' GAMBLER BUMMING AROUND WHISKY BLUES CAN I SLEEP IN YOUR BARN TONIGHT THREE TIMES SEVEN LITTLE BLOSSOM TRAVELLIN' GUITAR DOWN THE TRACK I'LL BE A BACHELOR TILL I DIE SOMEBODY'S MOTHER TONIGHT SPENDING MY LIFE IN THE SUN WINTER WINDS WHIPLASH	October 1991
7990252 CD 7990254 TC	LIVE INTO THE 90'S	G'DAY G'DAY I'M GOING BACK AGAIN TO YARRAWONGA FLYING DOCTORS BALL, THE THINGS ARE NOT THE SAME ON THE LAND AUCTIONEER LACE UP SHOES CATCHING YELLOWBELLY (IN THE OLD BARCOO) WHEN THE CURRAWONGS COME DOWN AUSSIE DOGHOUSE BLUES TO WHOM IT MAY CONCERN	February 1992

		BEEN A FOOL TOO LONG	
		THAT'LL DO ME	
		THREE HUNDRED HORSES	
		HIGH DRY AND HOMELESS	
		I'M STILL HERE TO GIVE IT MY BEST	
		YODEL MEDLEY: 1) PRAIRIE LOVEKNOT	
		MEDLEY 2) THE VALLEY WHERE THE	
		FRANGIPANIS GROW	
		MEDLEY 3) MY SUNSET HOME	
		MEDLEY 4) YODEL DOWN THE VALLEY	
		LIGHTS ON THE HILL	
		LOSIN' MY BLUES TONIGHT	
7806432 CD	THAT'S THE SONG WE'RE SINGING	THAT'S THE SONG WE'RE SINGING	October 1992
7806434 TC		JACK O'HAGAN	
		SHE'LL BE RIGHT, MATE	
		TIBROGARGAN	
		THAT'S THE WAY I AM	
		DAY WE SOLD THE FARM, THE	
		BUCKING HORSE CALLED TIME	
		MANGROVE BOOGIE KINGS	
		MY DAD WAS A ROADTRAIN MAN	
		HARD AND CALLOUSED HANDS	
		MEMORY HOTEL	
		ALL MY MATES ARE GONE	
		LIFE BEHIND THE WINDSCREEN	
		LAST OF HER LINE, THE	
		OLD BUSH ROAD	
8271942 CD	RINGER FROM THE TOP END	RINGER FROM THE TOP END	October 1992
8271944 TC		WHEN THE COUNTRY'S WET	
		I'VE BEEN, SEEN AND DONE THAT	
		WHERE I WANT TO BE	
		LIFE'S GETTING BETTER ALL THE TIME	
		DOWN AT THE WOOLSHED	
		GEORGINA'S SON	
		CHARLEVILLE	
		OLD RIVER GUM	
		YOU CAN'T TAKE AUSTRALIA FROM ME	
		POONCARIE	
		SHANTY ON THE RISE	
		FIDDLE MAN	
		BUNDA WATERHOLE	
		AFTER ALL	
7896102 CD	THE ANNIVERSARY ALBUM NO. 2	SONG FOR THE AUSSIES	October 1993
7896104 TC		SPIRIT OF AUSTRALIA	
		PLAINS OF PEPPIMENARTI	
		WHERE COUNTRY IS	
		G'DAY BLUE	
		NO PLACE ON EARTH LIKE AUSTRALIA	
		BRASS WELL, THE	
		BANJO'S MAN	
		AUSTRALIA'S ON THE WALLABY	
		YOU'VE GOT TO DRINK THE FROTH TO GET THE BEER	
		TRAVELLER'S PRAYER	
		CATTLEMEN FROM THE HIGH PLAINS	
		WE'VE DONE US PROUD	
		G'DAY G'DAY	
		KING OF KALGOORLIE	
		FLYING DOCTOR'S BALL, THE	
		LACE-UP SHOES	
		THINGS ARE NOT THE SAME ON THE LAND	
		SHE'LL BE RIGHT, MATE	
		DROVERS ARE BACK, THE	

Catalogue No.	Title	Track Listings	First Released
8308472 CD 8303474 TC	NATURAL HIGH	UNDER THE SPELL OF HIGHWAY ONE NATURAL HIGH CALLING, THE KOKODA TRACK DON'T YOU WORRY ABOUT THAT WHEN YOUR PANTS BEGIN TO GO YELLOW OLD BULLCATCHER TAKING HIS CHANCE SOME THINGS NEVER CHANGE OUT HERE ANNIE JOHNSON RED ROO ROADHOUSE DICK DRUMDUFF AND ME BLUE GUMTREE BALL, THE AS LEICHHARDT SAW IT THEN	October 1994

8142472 CD
8142474 TC
	REGAL ZONOPHONE
	COLLECTION
		WHEN THE RAIN TUMBLES
		  DOWN IN JULY
		MY FADED DREAM
		HOW CAN I SMILE WHEN I'M LONELY
		BEEN A FOOL TOO LONG
		YOU DON'T KNOW HOW SAD I FEEL
		MODERN YODELLING SONG
		MY MOONLIGHT TRAIL TO YOU
		MY AUSSIE HOME
		GIVE ME ONE MORE CHANCE
		SAT'DAY IN THE SADDLE
		MY PONY WHIPSTICK
		MY HAPPY VALLEY HOME
		STAY AWAY FROM ME
		SONG OF GRANNY, A
		SPRINGTIME ON THE RANGE
		WHY WORRY NOW
		ANSWER TO THE SILVERY MOONLIGHT
		  TRAIL
		I BET YOU FEEL THE SAME
		SUN VALLEY ROSE
		GOOD OLD SANTA CLAUS
		WHISKY BLUES
		YOU MADE ME LIVE LOVE AND DIE
		GRANDEST HOMESTEAD OF ALL, THE
		DOLLY DIMPLE DANCE
		WHEN THE SUN GOES DOWN OUTBACK
		WHEN THE HARVEST DAYS ARE OVER,
		  JESSIE DEAR
		RUSTY IT'S GOODBYE
		LOSIN' MY BLUES TONIGHT
		ROSE OF REMEMBERANCE
		RAIN STILL TUMBLES DOWN, THE
		WHEN I FIRST SAW THE LOVELIGHT IN
		  YOUR EYES
		I MUST HAVE GOOD TERBACCY WHEN
		  I SMOKE
		BABY OF MY DREAMS
		GOLDY GIRL
		SUNLANDER, THE
		SHOWMAN'S SONG, THE
		BUSHLAND BOOGIE, THE
		ANY OLD TIME
		LOVER'S LAMENT
		FRANKIE AND JOHNNY
		IF I ONLY HAD A HOME SWEET HOME
		BROKEN HOME, THE
		TAKE MY WORRIES AWAY
		SWAGMAN'S STORY, THE
		MOTHER
		OUR WEDDING WALTZ
		LITTLE GIRL DRESSED IN BLUE, A
		OLD LOVE LETTERS
			August 1995

LOMESOME ROAD OF TEARS
KING BUNDAWAAL
RANGE OF GLORY
RUNAWAY HEART
INTRO: OH! JOHNNY OH!
GOING TO THE BARNDANCE TONIGHT
SINCE THE BUSHLAND BOOGIE CAME
    THIS WAY
JUST SADDLE OLD DARKIE
RODEO DANCE, THE
SUNNY NORTHERN ROSE
RUTLAND RODEO
HARRY THE BREAKER
QUEENSLAND STATE SO FAIR
WALKIN' ON MY WAY
GUMTREES BY THE ROADWAY
PASTURES OF HOME
DREAMIN' ON THE SLIP RAIL
ROARING WHEELS
NATURE OF MAN, THE
SADDLE BOY
PUB WITH NO BEER, A

8145722 CD

8145724 TC

COUNTRY WAY OF LIFE

ROCK 'N' ROLL IN A
    COWBOY HAT
ROUGH RIDIN' RODEO
WHO WANTS MOSS?
AS THE BUSH BECOMES THE TOWN
MY HEART'S IN AUSTRALIA NOW
I WON'T BELIEVE IT'S NEVER GONNA RAIN
OLD ROCK 'N' ROLLER
JOE DALY
OLD WOOLSHED BALL
TOP SPRINGS
FIFTEEN HUNDRED HEAD
ME AND MATILDA
BROWN BOTTLE BLUES
COUNTRY WAY OF LIFE

September 1995

D 1150

C 1150

FIDDLER MAN
    (AUDIO MURPHY)

FIDDLER MAN
    (AUDIO MURPHY)

November 1995

8324072 CD

324074 TC

THE SLIM DUSTY SHOW —
    LIVE IN
TOWNSVILLE 1956

RUTLAND RODEO, THE
HEY GOOD LOOKIN'
BUSHLAND BOOGIE, THE
HONKY TONK BLUES
NO GOOD BABY
GOIN' TO THE BARN DANCE TONIGHT
FOOL SUCH AS I, A
RANGE OF GLORY
I'LL GO STEPPIN' TOO
PUB WITH NO BEER, A
BLACK COTTON STRAND

January 1996

300701300 CD
300701500 TC

COUNTRY CLASSICS — SLIM DUSTY
(3 CD/3 CASS. SET) AVAILABLE ONLY
DIRECT FROM READER'S DIGEST

September 1996

DISC 1 1947 -1969

WHEN THE RAIN TUMBLES DOWN IN JULY
    (ORIGINAL VERSION)
MY AUSSIE HOME
SAT'DAY IN THE SADDLE
SPRINGTIME ON THE RANGE
GRANDEST HOMESTEAD OF ALL, THE
WHEN THE SUN GOES DOWN OUTBACK
RAIN STILL TUMBLES DOWN, THE
OUR WEDDING WALTZ
KING BUNDAWAAL

A PUB WITH NO BEER (ORIGINAL VERSION)
SADDLE BOY
ALONG THE ROAD TO GUNDAGAI
BY A FIRE OF GIDGEE COAL
SONG OF AUSTRALIA
MIDDLETON'S ROUSEABOUT
DOWN THE DUSTY ROAD TO HOME
CAMPFIRE YARN
OLD LANTERN WALTZ, THE
GHOSTS OF THE GOLDEN MILE
STEPPIN' ROUND AUSTRALIA
CATTLE CAMP CROONER

DISC 2 1971 — 1979

CAMOOWEAL
AUSTRALIAN BUSHMEN
GLORY BOUND TRAIN
MAN FROM SNOWY RIVER, THE
BIRDSVILLE TRACK, THE
MAN FROM IRONBARK
CLANCY OF THE OVERFLOW
HENRY LAWSON
LIGHTS ON THE HILL
THINGS I SEE AROUND ME, THE
THREE RIVERS HOTEL
KELLY'S OFFSIDER
BUSH POETS OF AUSTRALIA
INDIAN PACIFIC
ISA
SPIRIT OF AUSTRALIA
LOSIN' MY BLUES TONIGHT
WALK A COUNTRY MILE
WHEN THE RAIN TUMBLES DOWN IN JULY
PUB WITH NO BEER, A

DISC 3 1980 — 1995

DUNCAN
LEAVE HIM IN THE LONGYARD
PLAINS OF PEPPIMENARTI
COUNTRY REVIVAL
G'DAY BLUE
NULLA CREEK
LAST THING TO LEARN
OLD TIME COUNTRY HALLS
SINGER FROM DOWNUNDER
BIBLE OF THE BUSH
REGAL ZONOPHONE
DROVIN'
CRYING ON EACH OTHER'S SHOULDER
THAT'S THE SONG WE'RE SINGING
JACK O'HAGAN
CHARLEVILLE
RINGER FROM THE TOP END
WHEN YOUR PANTS BEGIN TO GO
ME AND MATILDA
WHO WANTS MOSS?

8147122 CD 8147124 TC	91 OVER 50	BORN A TRAVELLING MAN	October 1996

I HOPE THEY FIGHT AGAIN
WORD TO TEXAS JACK, A
HOW WILL YOU GO WITH HIM, MATE?
MUST'VE BEEN A HELL OF A PARTY
GUMTREES BY THE ROADWAY
DO YOU THINK THAT I DO NOT KNOW
NED KELLY WAS A GENTLEMAN
CATTLECAMP CROONER
KELLY'S OFFSIDER
RINGER'S STOMP
DUNCAN
WHEN THE RAIN TUMBLES DOWN IN JULY
OLD TIME COUNTRY HALLS

Catalogue No.	Title	Track Listings	First Released
300701300-1/2/3 CD	READER'S DIGEST COUNTRY CLASSICS	WHEN THE RAIN TUMBLES DOWN IN JULY	September 1996
300701500-1/2/3 TC		MY AUSSIE HOME	
		SAT'DAY IN THE SADDLE	
		SPRINGTIME ON THE RANGE	
		THE GRANDEST HOMESTEAD OF ALL	
		WHEN THE SUN GOES DOWN OUTBACK	
		THE RAIN STILL TUMBLES DOWN	
		OUR WEDDING WALTZ	
		KING BUNDAWAAL	
		A PUB WITH NO BEER	
		SADDLE BOY	
		THE ROAD TO GUNDAGAI	
		BY A FIRE OF GIDGEE COAL	
		SONG OF AUSTRALIA	
		MIDDLETON'S ROUSEABOUT	
		DOWN THE DUSTY ROAD TO HOME	
		CAMPFIRE YARN	
		THE OLD LANTERN WALTZ	
		GHOSTS OF THE GOLDEN MILE	
		STEPPIN' ROUND AUSTRALIA	
		CATTLE CAMP CROONER	
		CAMOOWEAL	
		AUSTRALIAN BUSHMEN	
		GLORY BOUND TRAIN	
		THE MAN FROM SNOWY RIVER	
		THE BIRDSVILLE TRACK	
		THE MAN FROM IRON BARK	
		CLANCY OF THE OVERFLOW	
		HENRY LAWSON	
		THE LIGHTS ON THE HILL	
		THINGS I SEE AROUND ME	
		THREE RIVERS HOTEL	
		KELLY'S OFFSIDER	
		BUSH POETS OF AUSTRALIA	
		INDIAN PACIFIC	
		ISA	
		SPIRIT OF AUSTRALIA	
		LOSIN' MY BLUES TONIGHT	
		WALK A COUNTRY MILE	
		WHEN THE RAIN TUMBLES DOWN IN JULY	
		A PUB WITH NO BEER	
		DUNCAN	
		LEAVE HIM IN THE LONGYARD	
		PLAINS OF PEPPIMENARTI	
		COUNTRY REVIVAL	
		G'DAY BLUE	
		NULLA CREEK	
		LAST THING TO LEARN	
		OLD TIME COUNTRY HALLS	
		SINGER FROM DOWN UNDER	
		BIBLE OF THE BUSH	
		REGAL ZONOPHONE	
		DROVIN'	
		CRYING ON EACH OTHER'S SHOULDER	
		THAT'S THE SONG WE'RE SINGING	
		JACK O'HAGAN	
		CHARLEVILLE	
		RINGER FROM THE TOP END	
		WHEN YOUR PANTS BEGIN TO GO	
		ME AND MATILDA	
		WHO WANTS MOSS?	
814314-2 CD	LAND OF LOTS OF TIME	EASY GOIN' DRIFTER	March 1997
814314-4 TC		THE WESTERWAY WALTZ	June 1998
814874-2 2CD-SET	& SONG OF AUSTRALIA	THE LAST OF THE VALLEY MAIL	
		SONG OF THE MACLEAY	
		KEELA VALLEY	

THE OLD WOOLSHED DO
LAND OF LOTS OF TIME
OLD BUSH MATES OF MINE
MAD JACK'S COCKATOO
COSY INN
CHARLEY GRAY'S BARN DANCE
THE OLD ROCKING HORSE
THE DYING STOCKMAN
BILL
THE BLACK VELVET BAND
HIGH, WIDE AND HANDSOME

856732-2 CD	A TIME TO REMEMBER	DON'T GET AROUND MUCH ANYMORE	April 1997
856732-4 TC		HAVE YOU EVER BEEN LONELY?	

AS TIME GOES BY
AIN'T MISBEHAVIN'
TRY A LITTLE TENDERNESS
WHAT A WONDERFUL WORLD
INTO EACH LIFE SOME RAIN MUST FALL
RED SAILS IN THE SUNSET
UP THE LAZY RIVER
MOOD INDIGO
TO EACH HIS OWN
WHEN I GROW TOO OLD TO DREAM

814315-2 CD	OLD TIME DROVER'S LAMENT	WHEN YOU'RE SHORT OF A SMOKE	June 1997
814315-4 TC		KEEP THE LOVELIGHT SHINING	
814873-2 2CD-SET	& DOWN THE DUSTY ROAD	LOVE'S GAME OF LET'S PRETEND	August 1998

I LOVE YOU BEST OF ALL
WHEN YOU'RE SHORT OF A QUID
WHERE THE GOLDEN SLIPRAILS ARE DOWN
MIDDLETON'S ROUSEABOUT
OLD TIME DROVER'S LAMENT
TRUMBY
GRASSHOPPER LOOSE IN QUEENSLAND
IF WE ONLY HAD OLD IRELAND OVER HERE
SNIFF, THE DIGGER'S DOG
NAMATJIRA
DARWIN (BIG HEART OF THE NORTH)
THE FROG
THE MIN MIN LIGHT

823304-2 CD	MAKIN' A MILE	MY HEAVEN ON EARTH	October 1997
823304-4 TC		RECYCLED RINGER	

BOOMAROO FLYER
STAR TRUCKER
NAMES UPON THE WALL
THE LADY IS A TRUCKIE
MECHANISED SWAGGIES
NO GOOD TRUCKIN' MAN
THE FLOOD OF '95
RINGERS, RIGS & DRIVERS
BIG OLD MACK
DEAD ON TIME
HAULIN' FOR THE DOUBLE 'T'
SOMETHING IN THE PILLIGA

814046-2 CD	TALK ABOUT THE GOOD TIMES	TALK ABOUT THE GOOD TIMES	January 1998
814046-4 TC		CARRY MY OWN GUITAR	

ANYWHERE I AM
CLOSEST THING TO FREEDOM
TRAIN WHISTLE BLUES
A MATE CAN DO NO WRONG
MISSISSIPPI DELTA BLUES
I'VE GOT THAT LONESOME FEELING

GUESS WHO FELT SILLY
THE LIGHTS ON THE HILL
NO GOOD BABY
I'LL COME AROUND
CAMOOWEAL
YOU'RE STILL ON MY MIND

Catalogue No.	Title	Track Listings	First Released
814316-2 CD 814316-4 TC 814873-2 2CD-SET	DOWN THE DUSTY ROAD & OLD TIME DROVER'S LAMENT	YOU CAN NEVER DO WRONG IN A MOTHER'S EYES PADDY GRAMP BIG FROGS IN LITTLE PUDDLES THE OLD RUSTY BELL ANSWER TO THE OLD RUSTY BELL LAST TRAIN TO NOWHERE THE WILD LIFE YOU LEAD ROAD OF LONELINESS WHEN IT'S LAMPLIGHTING TIME IN THE VALLEY DOWN THE DUSTY ROAD TO HOME ROAD TRAIN BLUES IF JESUS CALLED ON YOU MY LOVE'S A STRANGER NOW MORNING MAIL CAMPFIRE YARN OLD MEN'S HOME	March 1998
814874-2 2CD-SET	LAND OF LOTS OF TIME	EASY GOIN' DRIFTER THE WESTERWAY WALTZ THE LAST OF THE VALLEY MAIL SONG OF THE MACLEAY KEELA VALLEY THE OLD WOOLSHED DO LAND OF LOTS OF TIME OLD BUSH MATES OF MINE MAD JACK'S COCKATOO COSY INN CHARLEY GRAY'S BARN DANCE THE OLD ROCKING HORSE THE DYING STOCKMAN BILL THE BLACK VELVET BAND HIGH, WIDE & HANDSOME BORN TO BE A ROLLING STONE ALONG THE ROAD OF SONG SWEENEY DOWN AT CHARLIE GRAY'S WHEN THEY MUSTER ON THE GOLDEN PLAIN ONCE WHEN I WAS MUSTERING THE MAN FROM NEVER NEVER JUMPIN' THE RATTLER SONG OF AUSTRALIA BACK TO THE SALTBUSH PLAINS LAUGHTER IN THE HILLS CONDAMINE HORSE BELL THE BUSHMAN'S SONG A PUB WITH NO BEER THE ANSWER TO A PUB WITH NO BEER SEQUEL TO THE PUB WITH NO BEER	June 1998
495728-2 CD 495728-4 TC	THE VERY BEST OF SLIM DUSTY	A PUB WITH NO BEER THE LIGHTS ON THE HILL THE BIGGEST DISAPPOINTMENT THREE RIVERS HOTEL RINGER FROM THE TOP END WHERE COUNTRY IS LEAVE HIM IN THE LONG YARD PLAINS OF PEPPIMENARTI DUNCAN	November 1998

CHARLEVILLE
INDIAN PACIFIC
SWEENEY
G'DAY G'DAY
WALK A COUNTRY MILE
WHEN THE RAIN TUMBLES DOWN IN JULY
I'M GOING BACK AGAIN TO YARRAWONGA
OLD TIME COUNTRY HALL
CAMOOWEAL
WE'VE DONE US PROUD
COUNTRY REVIVAL
CUNNAMULLA FELLA
BY A FIRE OF GIDGEE COAL
LOSIN' MY BLUES TONIGHT
WOBBLY BOOT

495739-2 CD
495739-4 TC

WEST OF WINTON

WALTZING MATILDA   September 1999
WEST OF WINTON   (LIMITED RELEASE)
SADDLE UP AND RIDE   October 2001
THE VANISHING BREED(GENERAL RELEASE)
THE OLD SADDLE
TRUTHFUL FELLA
OLD SCOBIE
BACK WITH THE SHOW AGAIN
FINNEY'S HOME BREW
THE SHEARER'S STORY
OLD DINGO (VERSION TWO)
HAPPY ANNIVERSARY
HAM AND EGGS
SASSAFRAS GAP
DAN THE WRECK

520594-2 5CD-SET

THE TRUCKIN' SONG
COLLECTION

INCLUDING: September 1999
LIGHTS ON THE HILL
GIVE ME THE ROAD
TRUCKS ON THE TRACK
NEON CITY
MAKIN' A MILE

523488-2 CD
523488-4 TC

NINETY-NINE

BINDI-EYE BALL   October 1999
THE SWAGLESS SWAGGIE
ABALINGA MAIL
BANJO
DIGGIN' A HOLE
IT'S GOOD TO SEE YOU MATE
THE GHOST OF BEN HALL
KELLY'S COUNTRY KITCHEN
OUTBACK
NO BIDS FOR THE BAY
WHEN MUSTERING'S IN FULL SWING
BUSHMAN'S PRAYER
ALONG THE ROAD TO NULLA NULLA

527160-2 CD

527160-4 TC

LOOKING FORWARD
LOOKING BACK

LOOKING FORWARD   July 2000
  LOOKING BACK
NEVER WAS AT ALL
THERE'S A RAINBOW OVER THE ROCK
MATILDA NO MORE
THE BLOKE WHO SERVES THE BEER
PADDY WILLIAM
OUR OWN BACKYARD
OLD TIME COUNTRY SONGS
A BAD DAY'S FISHING
PORT AUGUSTA
GOOD HEAVENS ABOVE
HOOKS & RIDE
KEELA VALLEY COALS
MEMORIES AND DREAMS
LOOKING FORWARD LOOKING BACK
  (REPRISE)

527649-2 5CD-SET
527649-4 4TC-SET

THE MAN WHO IS AUSTRALIA

THE RAIN STILL TUMBLES DOWN   July 2000
HELLO AND GOODBYE
TRAVELLIN' THROUGH
I WANT A PARDON FOR DADDY
MOTHER, THE QUEEN OF MY HEART
EUMERELLA SHORE
MUSIC MY DAD PLAYED TO ME
HAPPY JACK
YOU TOOK THE JOY OUT OF LIVIN'
IF I ONLY HAD A HOME SWEET HOME
I'VE BEEN TALKING TO GRANNIE
MANY MOTHERS
MY SON
SWEET THING
THE SUNSET YEARS OF LIFE
DEATH ROW
CAMOOWEAL
RAMBLIN' SHOES
JUST LOVIN' YOU
RIDING THIS ROAD
I'VE BEEN THERE (AND BACK AGAIN)
DUNCAN
KILOMETRES ARE STILL MILES TO ME
WHERE I'D SOONER BE
LOGAN
TO WHOM IT MAY CONCERN
WHEN THE RAIN TUMBLES DOWN IN JULY
LARRIKIN'S LANDING
THE LIGHTS ON THE HILL
CHARLEVILLE
MAD JOE THE FISHERMAN
ANOTHER NIGHT IN BROOME
MORNING COMES EARLY
I NEED TO FIND A PLACE
MITCHELL GRASS
LEAVING ONLY DUST
A PUB WITH NO BEER
RINGER FROM THE TOP END
THE LIGHTS ON THE HILL
NATURAL HIGH
CHARLEVILLE
QUICKSILVER
WHY WORRY
TRUTHFUL FELLA
MY PAL ALCOHOL
BEEN A FOOL TOO LONG
WALTZING MATILDA
WHEN THE RAIN TUMBLES DOWN IN JULY
I'M GOING BACK AGAIN TO YARRAWONGA
NATURAL HIGH
SANTA'S GONNA COME IN A MAIL COACH
CHRISTMAS ON THE STATION
SANTA LOOKED A LOT LIKE DADDY
SEND BACK MY DADDY FOR CHRISTMAS
A PUB WITH NO BEER
INTRODUCTION
WALK A COUNTRY MILE
MIDDLETON'S ROUSEABOUT
DINKI-DI AUSSIE
INDIAN PACIFIC
I MUST HAVE GOOD TERBACCY WHEN
  I SMOKE
SWEENEY
TRUMBY
THE BIGGEST DISAPPOINTMENT
SHE'LL BE RIGHT, MATE
HE'S A GOOD BLOKE WHEN HE'S SOBER,
  BUT . . .
DUNCAN

		CATTLEMEN FROM THE HIGH PLAINS	
		GLORY BOUND TRAIN	
		A PUB WITH NO BEER	
		MY DAD WAS A ROADTRAIN MAN	
		CHARLEVILLE	
		THE LIGHTS ON THE HILL	
		WALK A COUNTRY MILE	
		ABALINGA MAIL	
		THE WAY I SEE IT (CONVERSATION WITH NICK ERBY)	
531072-2 CD EXCLUSIVE TO AUSTRALIA POST	A PIECE OF AUSTRALIA	WALTZING MATILDA A PUB WITH NO BEER HE'S A GOOD BLOKE WHEN HE'S SOBER, BUT . . . DUNCAN WOBBLY BOOT BOOMERANG TIE ME KANGAROO DOWN, SPORT WHERE THE DOG SITS ON THE TUCKER BOX RINGER FROM THE TOP END G'DAY G'DAY INDIAN PACIFIC ABALINGA MAIL CLICK GO THE SHEARS THE OVERLANDER TRAIL WALTZING MATILDA G'DAY BLUE CHRISTMAS ON THE STATION THE ROAD TO GUNDAGAI I'M GOING BACK AGAIN TO YARRAWONGA THE MAN FROM NEVER NEVER THAT OLD BUSH SHANTY OF MINE CUNNAMULLA FELLA A WORD TO TEXAS JACK AUSTRALIA'S ON THE WALLABY	January 2001
536243-2 CD	THE MEN FROM NULLA NULLA – REUNITED & REVISITED (WITH SHORTY RANGER)	THE MEN FROM NULLA NULLA RIDING THROUGH THE VALLEY IN SPRING FAR GRANDEST HOMESTEAD OF ALL GOOD OLD DAYS DRY WEATHER WIND EASY GOIN' DRIFTER WILLY WILLY TEN GOLDEN RULES OLD KENTUCKY RIG SONG OF THE MACLEAY THE OLD RUSTY BELL ANSWER TO THE OLD RUSTY BELL SOMEWHERE UP IN QUEENSLAND JOYBELLS IN YOUR HEART HEAVEN, COUNTRY STYLE MY OLD AUSSIE HOMESTEAD THE BALLAD OF PORT MACQUARIE SOMEBODY'S MOTHER THE PAPER BOY SOMEBODY'S MOTHER TONIGHT ROSE OF RED RIVER VALLEY WINTER WINDS	October 2001
538034-2 CD 538034-4 TC	TRAVELLIN' STILL . . . ALWAYS WILL (WITH ANNE KIRKPATRICK)	END OF THE BITUMEN TRAVELLIN' STILL . . . ALWAYS WILL TRACKS I LEFT BEHIND MAN ON THE SIDE OF THE ROAD JUST AN OLD CATTLE DOG BELT AND BUCKLED BONNER (THE QUIET ACHIEVER) YOU AND MY OLD GUITAR	March 2002

364

I WONDER IF THE CREEKS ARE FLOWING
    STILL
CLAYPAN BOOGIE
SUNDOWN
TAKING ON WHAT'S NEXT
THE MEN WHO TRY AND TRY

INDEX

hachette
AUSTRALIA

If you would like to find out more about Hachette Australia,
our authors, upcoming events and new releases you can visit
our website, Facebook or follow us on Twitter:

www.hachette.com.au
www.twitter.com/HachetteAus
www.facebook.com/HachetteAustralia